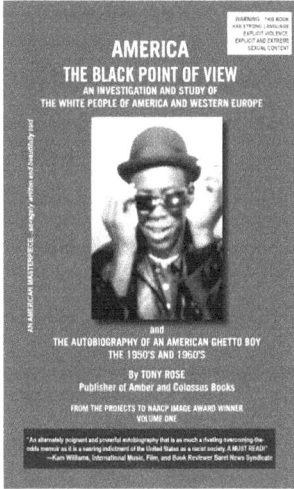

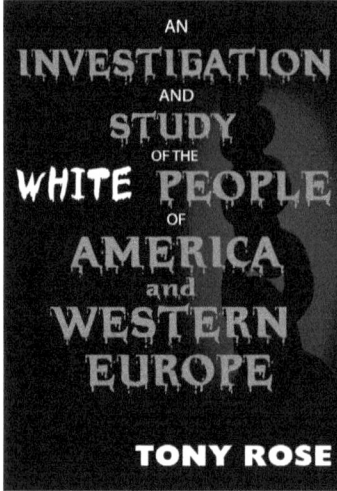

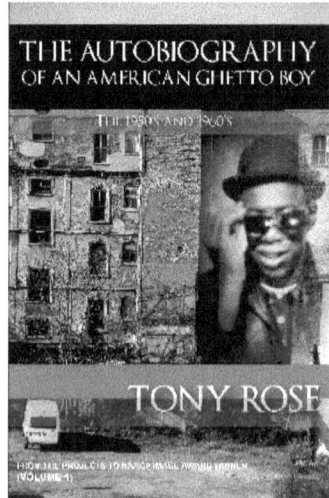

BOOK REVIEWS FOR
THE AUTOBIOGRAPHY OF AN
AMERICAN GHETTO BOY

The Whittier Street Housing Projects in Roxbury, (Boston) Mass. where Tony Rose grew up from 3 to 18 years old.

I can't put it down, the book is written with such passion. *I get so emotional about triumph and this book is a triumph.*
—**Kay Bourne**, *Arts and Entertainment writer and critic, and The Boston Theater Critics Association, "2015 Elliot Norton Award", recipient.*

****

An American Masterpiece....savagely written and beautifully told.

I found out early on that this was not going to be an easy book to write. *I wanted to write an autobiography about my early childhood and teen years and the horrific murderers, pimps, gangsters, drug dealers, drug addicts, rapists, child abusers and thieves, that I grew up with, lived with, called family, and write about in* **The Autobiography of an American Ghetto Boy**. I soon realized that I could not write about me as an African American child and teen living in America, without writing about White America, what it was like when I was a child, how it shaped the people around me and what it is like to now live in America, which for tens of millions of African American children is horrific, terrifying, and not so very different than it was for me as a child.

I also wanted to write about what it was like for a child and young teenager to grow up in the real ghetto, the projects, and come from a dysfunctional and violent family where contrary to what poor Black people are always depicted as; *there was no God, no church on Sunday, no marching with Martin Luther King, Jr., and no singing in the church choir.*

—TONY ROSE

****

Often White reviewers make the same mistake as this reviewer, from the Kirkus Book Review has in thinking that White Western European and White American extermination, slavery, racism, segregation and the brutal colonization of Africans, African Americans, Native Americans, Native South Americans, India, the Middle East, Native Australians and other people of color throughout the world, is as this reviewer states, *"an exaggeration"*, and they tend to dwell more on the evils of the American ghettos and projects and find ways to excuse White Western European and White American capitalism, greed and racism as the prime problems for the destruction of tens of millions of African Americans living in our American cities. Although this reviewer has at least found the balls to say, *"my rambling exposition of the history of slavery and racism, contains **much truth"**. —**Tony Rose**

KIRKUS BOOK REVIEW

*White racism, slavery, and ongoing bigotry are to blame for the problems of black America, as well as the author's violent youth, according to this manifesto memoir, says Rose, a publisher and former record producer. **The Autobiography of an American Ghetto Boy** includes the sins of white people against Africans, surviving the horrors of the Middle Passage; the violation of slave women by white owners in the American South and the brutalization and emasculation of black men;* the drug trade in black communities, which he contends is organized by the U.S. government; police killings; and the ingrained racism of some 70 percent of whites. ***Rose's rambling exposition of the history of slavery and racism, contains much truth.*** *However, it also contains exaggeration and stereotyping of people of European descent,* **whom he characterizes as "primitive, barbaric, vicious white monkeys [who] descended with the horrors of their psychotic desires and thirst for blood, rape and death on so-called uncivilized African and people of color throughout the world."** The book recounts Rose's grim upbringing in the purgatory of Boston's housing projects in the 1950s and '60s. **He writes of being perpetually hungry; abandoned by his father, a career pimp and mob hit man who was often in jail;** regularly beaten by a mentally unstable mother; and preyed upon by merciless gangs—until he joined one and started committing robberies. His story also has its heroes, including his genteel grandmother, sympathetic grocers, the nuns at his parochial school, a caring Boy Scout leader, and finally, the U.S. Air Force, which gave him training and discipline. Overall, the memoir is fragmented and repetitive. *However, his prose is vigorous and vivid, and sometimes pungent, scabrous, and sexually graphic.* It leaves a lasting impression of the chaos, deprivation, and psychic ravages of the ghetto, but also gives readers a more nuanced, three-dimensional view of its social life and its people. *A sometimes-distorted and sometimes-revealing portrait of a nightmarish United States.*

—**David Rapp,** Kirkus Book Review

****

KAM WILLIAMS BOOK REVIEW

...His absentee-dad was rarely around after being caught molesting his daughter, not that the heroin addicted-pimp/Mafia hit man would have made much of a role model. Consequently, Tony's mom was totally dependent on that bi-weekly Welfare check from the government. And up until she lost her mind in 1956, the emotionally-abusive woman was fond of routinely reminding her kids that they were "black and ugly" and that nobody wanted them. Nevertheless, Tony was wise enough not to lay all of the blame for his nightmarish childhood on his parents, since so many of his friends had to deal with similar dysfunction. After all, he describes the Whittier Street Housing Projects in Roxbury, (Boston) Mass., where he grew up as "a red fortress filled with screaming children, cold brutal gangs and women." Rose states that, "70% of White America that remains ostensibly indifferent to the country's shameful legacy of slavery, segregation and institutional racism". *For, their destructive by-products exact a continuing toll as evidenced in the African-American masses' ongoing suffering in squalor due to a seemingly-irreversible cultural collapse. Following that damning digression, Tony proceeds to relate his own heartbreaking life story, warts and all, in a vivid fashion that just jumps off the page.* The jaw-dropping opus covers only his formative through teen years, a period he spent doing everything from killing roaches to subsisting as a child on celery soup to standing up to neighborhood murderers and rapists. *An alternately poignant and powerful autobiography that is as much a riveting overcoming-the-odds memoir as it is a searing indictment of the United States as a racist society. "A MUST READ".*

—**Kam Williams**, International Music, Film, and Book Reviewer - Baret News Syndicate

****

This book answers many questions I have had over the years about black ghettos, the overall black mentality and also the mentality of the white diaspora. I have not read anything as raw and in my face as the delivery of this book. **I was jolted upward the entire time I read this masterful work of truth.** *Sometimes the truth hurts, but it was necessary to read what so many of us have been denying for too long. This book is saying so many poignant things.* **One thing that stood out to me was that a lot of behavior that we see among blacks, especially in ghettos and low income neighborhoods, stems from the evil that was done by white people for hundreds of years, including the years preceding the trans-Atlantic slave trade.** *That is one of the hard truths in this book, among many others. I was impressed with how Mr. Rose laid out his theses on various topics throughout the book. After finishing this book, I was left to re-examine my own thought processes regarding our people and also the white diaspora. I am guilty of prejudging without understanding pathology.* This book has given me a better understanding of history and how history has affected and infected generations of our society at large. **It's truly an eye-opening read.**

—**Teresa Price**, Avid Reader, Amazon.com

****

NAACP Award Winning Author, Tony Rose gives America **the opportunity to remove rose colored glasses and examine the rise of a ghetto boy surviving poverty, abuse, and racism** with his new book. The book graphically describes the young life of Tony Rose and his courageous determination to beat the odds of insanity in ghetto life and death. **The Autobiography of an American Ghetto Boy** speaks to men and women stripped of every dignity they believed they have lost; the book speaks to the abused soul of individuals who think they understand black and white life and death. **Over 300 pages of horrific raw ghetto life balanced with history and the escape out of hell is delivered in Rose's book.** Some may not get through one reading as the book can require a grasp on the brutal reality of a ghetto war zone. America gets to look deep inside the complications of a Black man's life before judging swagger so often misunderstood. *"When a White child commits atrocities in America it must be because he fell through the cracks and didn't get the mental help he so deserved.* **When a Black child commits horrific crimes and murder, it's because he's black and by birth is a brutal animal and gets life and forever in jail, where his or her abuse and life continues to be one long night in hell.** *"* Dysfunction in families across America has never been described the way Tony Rose pens his life and ghetto family's truth in this autobiography. It rings the likeness of many souls recovering from insanity's near death experience. *Author Tony Rose describes a common thread of dysfunction that with understanding may unravel a rope of racism. 'The Autobiography of an American Ghetto Boy'* by Tony Rose offers an understanding to the evils of ghetto life without accepting its destruction to the human soul. *Read the book over and over again if you can take the truth.*

—**Deborah Rene'** is a book critic and entertainment editor.

****

Tony Rose's cautionary tale and analysis of what legacies still remain in urban communities such as the streets of Boston of his youth that he survived. The sheer violence, fathers incarcerated, streets filled with drug and alcohol addicted residents, gangs, brutal police engagement *which is still **a timely discussion and commentary of what is occurring in the lives of youth today trying to survive the ghettos of America with increasingly limited resources,*** jobs and viable opportunities with the ability to make good choices for service, entrepreneurship, or education that can lead one to live a prosperous life and one safe from harm, ruin even death. *This book is a must read for everyone.*

—**Lynette McMillon**, President, The Tushe Group, Public Relations.

****

Tony Rose, one of the nation's leading publishers, literary pioneers and music industry entrepreneurs has penned a poignant and powerful examination of race relations in America *and adeptly weaves it into a brutally frank and revealing look into his own childhood and teenage experiences.* From the streets of Roxbury and true "hood" life to the corporate board room and numerous awards and accolades, Tony's journey proves that one can overcome their challenges to excel and rise to be a role model. *After the incidents in Ferguson, New York, Baltimore, Charleston and the birth of the Black Lives Matter Movement,* **this book is timely and right on point.** *A must read.*

—**Kendall A. Minter, Esq**. Legendary Entertainment Attorney and Author of *Understanding and Negotiating 360 Ancillary Rights Deals—An Artists Guide to Negotiating 360 Record Deals.*

****

Thank you for an informative and compassionate look at life in America. **I highly, highly, recommend this book!**

—**Maggie Linton,** The Maggie Linton Show,
Sirius XM Radio, Channel 126.

****

Took my breathe away!

—**Terrie Williams**, Founder/President of the Terrie Williams Agency, Mental Health Advocate/Author of *Black Pain: It Just Looks Like We're Not Hurting.*

****

Congratulations Tony. ***This is an outstanding literary accomplishment.***

—**Earl Cobb,** CEO and Managing Partner, Richer Life, LLC and co-host of "Living a Richer Life—Life Changing Talk Radio".

****

Why do thugs emerge? The uncensored autobiography of legendary gold and platinum record music producer and book publishing mogul, Tony Rose, NAACP Image Award winner, ***tells you how in an R-rated, due to violence, sexual abuse, language, rape, drugs and rage style. In a riveting,*** makes you wanna holler... searing indictment of America in the "benign neglect" of a dog-eat-dog world, where the alpha dog preys on the weak in *Roxbury/Boston's Whittier Street Housing Projects, where Black males going to the lockup becomes a passé rite-of-passage to manhood.* His one-boy heroic campaign to eradicate child rape in the projects almost cost him his life, if not for the final intervention by a streetwise Mafia father/man, *who teaches his manchild how to hustle on an even grander scale.* ***His careening life-and-death course between the criminal underworld and a caring world for America's underclass, represented by a hustler father, scoutmaster, nuns and priest, military, business leader and a transformation, that leaves you holding on to your pants.*** *Finally, Tony Rose gives us concrete steps to become part of the solution through his newly found foundation for disadvantaged youth in the projects, ghettos and rural reaches before a new generation of thugs emerge.* ***America is indebted to Mr. Rose for writing this biting, brutally-honest, wake-up call masterpiece.***

—**Roland Barksdale-Hall**, Librarian, Black Caucus of the American Library Association (BCALA), Community Activist and Author of *The African American Family's Guide to Tracing Our Roots: Healing, Understanding and Restoring Our Families*

****

Tony Rose has provided a unique look and report on the white people of America and Western Europe. His perspective is real and should be read by everyone who wants to know the "real" history. This historical study, his family genealogy, and his autobiography for the first 20 years of his life, is an amazing story. Tony Rose has shared his personal struggles and the many barriers and obstacles that could have prevented success, but that he overcame to become the success he is today. **Well done!**

　　—**Farrell Chiles,** Activist and Author of *As BIG As It Gets: A Chairman of the Board's Rise and Tenure at the Top—Lessons in Leadership and African American Warrant Officers...In Service To Our Country.*

****

I have personally and repeatedly witnessed the extraordinary genius of Tony Rose; however, his written words in *THE AUTOBIOGRAPHY OF AN AMERICAN GHETTO BOY* have outdone all accountings that I have seen written by anyone in an attempt to outline a true and thorough history of man's evolution and his ancestry as it crossed the color lines and evolved throughout the world. *Rose has not only detailed the foundation of the evolution, but he has brought the reader into a three-dimensional ghetto community—his childhood community—wreaking of havoc, murder, mayhem, poverty, hunger, insanity, rape, drugs and all the dangers associated with growing up loveless and lifeless in an American ghetto—* particularly in his gloomy abode in the Whittier Street Housing Projects, Roxbury, Mass. *In spite of it all, Tony Rose defeated the odds and became one of the world's most notable music producers and an NAACP Image Award Winner for Outstanding Literature.* If you are interested in knowing the Truth about the white man's effect on the Black man's slave mentality and the chains that have not been broken because of centuries *of degradation which began in the slave ships and still exists to this day, READ THIS BOOK!*

　　　　　　　—**Yvonne Rose**, Director of Quality Press, Associate Publisher, Amber Communications Group, Inc.
　　　　　　　—www.qualitypress.info—www.amberbooks.com

****

THE AUTOBIOGRAPHY OF AN AMERICAN GHETTO BOY *proves to be a very timely tome, as it even addresses the epidemic of shootings of unarmed blacks like Trayvon Martin, Jordan Davis and now the nine Charleston churchgoers by cowardly whites.* The author points out that *"the weak white coward is not interested in going up against the real black gangster, they know the difference; but, they use the real black gangster as their excuse"* for killing the innocent and the defenseless.

—**Troy Johnson,** Founder and Webmaster of the
African American Literature Book Club (AALBC.com)

****

*Tony, My thanks to you. I am halfway through your latest book **that I truly believe that everyone of African American and White descent needs to read.***

—**Marc Medley**, Host of the Reading Circle Radio Show
on WPSC 88.7, Wayne New Jersey.

****

*Hey Folks. Please check out the newly released, **provocative, informative and compelling life journey/history lesson** written by my close friend, partner, client and extended family member Tony Rose. **To say it's right on time would be an understatement.***

—**Kendall Minter, Esq.**, Legendary Entertainment Attorney
and Author of: *Understanding and Negotiating 360 Ancillary Rights
Deals—An Artists Guide to Negotiating 360 Record Deals.*

****

*Tony, I got the book last night. Up reading it till 3:00am. **High powered and rapid** machine gun fire!!! **TOTALLY ENGROSSING.** THE AUTOBIOGRAPHY OF AN AMERICAN GHETTO BOY is **a brilliantly written book and will most certainly be a 21st Century Classic.***

—**Rod Ambrose**, Prevention Education Coordinator,
City of Phoenix Parks and Recreation @ South Phoenix Youth Center,
BRAVE Project Office

****

*"The Autobiography of an American Ghetto Boy" by Tony Rose, **is a book that should be required reading in America's public schools and every College and University. A must read book***! *I found this book to be a source of reference regarding the development and tragedy of the journey of Africans to America.* What struck me was the well-documented account of his life. In summary, everyone who thought the world is against them, needs to read

this book. *Tony has done remarkably well in living the American dream of business ownership and leaving a legacy for all of America to read. Congratulations Tony for well written book!!!*

—**Cal Stevens**, President, Tacada Marketing, LLC,
Author of *You Can Sell to Uncle Sam: Getting Government Contracts.*

****

Thank you Tony. *It is a must read for all of us.*

—**Jim Lopes**, Attorney and Law Professor
at the University of Massachusetts—Boston Campus.

****

I admire your sharing your story. It's helpful to the soul and also can possibly save others. I really feel that it should be in school systems and outreach programs nationally.

—**Brandi Butler,** Boston, Mass.

****

I have been waiting for you to write your story. Thank You for writing your powerful story from the voice of Tony Rose (the child). Thank you for honoring the pain. I am recommending the book to everyone working with at risk boys and to every angry African American male I know. Thank you for risking your life to stop the rapes in The Whittier Street Housing Projects.

—**Revola Fontaine**, Atlanta, Georgia

****

I am still reading and have changed some of my long standing beliefs based on your writings. The "Creature" and "Fred" make quite an impression! *Once I started reading the book it was difficult to put down.*

—**Bruce Matthews**, All State Life Insurance Adjuster.

****

I scanned the book and was impressed with the major transition you've made in your life to be and accomplish the things you have done and found the perfect woman to give you balance. I was also surprised when I learned your roots begin in Roxbury, MA. I have close family from there as well.

—**Andrew Jackson,** Executive Director, Langston Hughes, Community
Center Cultural Center-Queens Borough Public Library.

****

Excellent book!
—**Dr. Kimberly Shedrick**, Host of The Entrepreneur Show on Blog Talk
Radio and Author of *Black and White in Stripes: Sherriff Joe's Tents.*

****

Tony, there was nothing better than getting this treasure from you. *The*
work you put in is amazing.
—**Charlotte D. Grant-Cobb**, PhD, Co-Publisher, Richer Press
(an imprint of Richer Life, LLC) and co-host of "Living a Richer Life—
Life Changing Talk Radio"

****

This is an amazing, interesting book that, with everything happening in
America today, is especially important. I recommend it highly and think
it will also be of interest to readers all around the world. I feel certain
we can make sales of it to publishers in many of the countries around the
world that we deal with.
—**Evelyn Lee,** Global Book Rights, Literary Agent

****

Your insight and desire to make a difference through a foundation
empowering public housing residents is commendable. Look forward to
talking with you about prospects for the future.
—**Roland Barksdale Hall,** Librarian, Community Activist and
Author of *The African American Family's Guide to Tracing Our Roots:*
Healing, Understanding and Restoring Our Families

****

You are amazing.
—**Prince Charles Alexander,** Professor, Berklee College of Music,
Boston, Mass

****

Congratulations on writing a great book, Brother Tony.
—**Rev. Willie Wiggins,** Minister Concord Baptist Church,
Boston, Mass.

THE AUTOBIOGRAPHY OF AN
AMERICAN GHETTO BOY
THE 1950'S AND 1960'S

FROM THE PROJECTS TO NAACP IMAGE AWARD WINNER

THE AUTOBIOGRAPHY OF AN AMERICAN GHETTO BOY THE 1950'S AND 1960'S

FROM THE PROJECTS TO NAACP IMAGE AWARD WINNER

BY TONY ROSE

Amber Books

Phoenix

New York   Los Angeles

THE AUTOBIOGRAPHY OF AN
AMERICAN GHETTO BOY
By Tony Rose

Published by
Amber Books
An Imprint of Amber Communications Group, Inc.
1334 East Chandler Boulevard, Suite 5-D67, Phoenix, AZ 85048
Amberbk@aol.com // www.amberbooks.com

Publisher's Note

Copyright 2016 © by Tony Rose
Paperback ISBN #: 978-1-937269-52-4
eBook ISBN #: 978-1-937269-53-1

Library of Congress Cataloging-in-Publication Data:

Names: Rose, Tony, 1953-
Title: The autobiography of an American ghetto boy: the 1950's and 1960's from the projects to NAACP image award winner / by Tony Rose.
Description: Phoenix, AZ: Amber Books, [2016] | Includes bibliographical references and index.
Identifiers: LCCN 2016011067| ISBN 9781937269524 (pbk : alk. paper) | ISBN
9781937269531 (ebook: alk. paper)
Subjects: LCSH: Rose, Tony, 1953- | African
Americans--Massachusetts--Boston--Biography. | Rose family. | Public housing--Massachusetts--Boston--Anecdotes. | African Americans--Social conditions. | African Americans--History--Anecdotes. | Slavery--United States--Influence. | Sexual abuse--United States. | Criminals--Massachusetts--Boston--Biography--Anecdotes. | Boston (Mass)--Social conditions--20th century.
Classification: LCC F73.54.R68 A3 2016 | DDC 974.4/61043092--dc23
LC record available at http://lccn.loc.gov/2016011067

THIS BOOK IS DEDICATED TO:

God for bringing me through and always answering prayers;

The poor, black, hungry and abused children who live in the ghettos and housing projects of America. This book will tell you how you got there. Why your there. Who put you there, and how you must stay alive, survive and learn to be great under the worst possible conditions.

Father Paul Francis; Monsignor George V. Kerr; The Sisters of St. Francis de Sales Church and School and the Blessed Sacrament; The Salvation Army; The Society of St. Vincent De Paul; The Boston Welfare Department; Al's Grocery Store; Frederick B. Rose; Frank "Fuzzy" Hector; Melvin B. Miller; William Harrison; Staff Sargent Jenson; Thomas A. Atkins; Valor Breez; Lizbeth L.; Anua Maulpin; Warren Lanier, Sr.; Brenda Lee; Cuba Gooding, Sr.; Marcia Tappin; Maurice Starr; Prince Charles Alexander; Yvonne Rose; Kay Bourne; Hubert Yorra; Neil Cooper; Kendall Minter; Samuel P. Peabody; All who in one way or another saved my life.

My Grandparents: Burleigh Smith-Rose-Chisholm (Grandmére) and Ralph Chisholm (Papa Ray).

I also dedicate this book to my Great-Great Grandmothers and Great-Great-Great Grandmothers who were slaves in the United States of America.

Contents

BOOK ONE

BOOK TWO

BOOK THREE

About the Author

Tony Rose, Publisher/CEO, Amber Communications Group, Inc.
2013 NAACP Image Award Winner for Outstanding Literature
2014 African American Publisher of the Year

Tony Rose, was born in Roxbury, (Boston) Massachusetts and raised in the Whittier Street Housing Projects. He is an *NAACP Image Award Winner for Outstanding Literature,* the Publisher and CEO of Amber Communications Group, Inc., the nation's largest African American Publisher of Self-Help Books and Music Biographies and the *2013 44th Annual NAACP Image Award Winner for Outstanding Literature* (Youth/Teens) for the title, *Obama Talks Back: Global Lessons – A Dialogue for America's Young Leaders* (Amber Books) by Gregory J. Reed, Esq.

Rose is the editor of numerous books and the co-writer of the national bestseller, *Is Modeling for You? The Handbook and Guide for the Young Aspiring Black Model,* written with Yvonne Rose, and has penned the critically acclaimed, international best-seller, *Before the Legend: The Rise of New Kids On the Block and A Guy Named Maurice Starr, The Early Years*.

He has written, compiled, edited and published, the award winning, international best-seller, *African American History In The United States of America—An Anthology—From Africa To President Barack Obama, Volume One*, a Top Ten Best African American Book and has recently written the critically acclaimed, international best-seller, non-fiction book of the year and a Top Ten Best Black Book of 2015, *America the Black Point of View—An Investigation and Study of the White People of America and Western Europe & The Autobiography of an American Ghetto Boy—The 1950's and 1960's—From the Projects to NAACP Image Award Winner, Volume One.*

And has recently revised into a separate book An Investigation and Study of the White People of America and Western Europe and also re-vised into a separate book The Autobiography of an American Ghetto Boy.

WWW.AMBERBOOKS.COM
WWW.QUALITYPRESS.INFO
WWW.AFRICANAMERICANPAVILION.COM
WWW.THEBLACKPOINTOFVIEW.COM

Author's Note

I have read a few biographies and autobiographies during my decades on earth and one of the things that I have always felt is that a biography and autobiography should be honest in the way it is written. That being politically correct and safe when writing and not using the thoughts and language that one used in the moment of that time period is not being honest. I hope that once you have read *The Autobiography of an American Ghetto Boy,* you will have found it to be an honest piece of literature from a *Ghetto Man.* Thank you.

—Tony Rose

About the Book

The story of an African American child and young teenager growing up in the real ghetto, the housing projects. Coming from a dysfunctional and violent family where contrary to what poor Black people are always depicted as; there is no God, no church on Sunday, no marching with Martin Luther King, Jr., and no singing in the church choir.

This is a children's story. A story of tens of millions of African American children locked away, in the segregated, red lined ghettos and housing projects of America. Living in a bad environment, in horrific conditions, with bad parents, in bad schools, where death rides hard and is known by everybody.

The screams and howls of centuries of terror, violence and brutality transcend time as you, the reader, are taken on a tremendously honest, epic journey from Africa to Western Europe to the Americas in this compelling, violent, and true story of two turbulent and distinct African American families of unbridled good and evil, both born and raised in the brutality and horror of American slavery, segregation and Jim Crow.

The journey takes you all the way to the terrifying, vicious and savagely honest, invisible black ghetto world of a child, and then teenager, growing up in the Whittier Street Housing Projects, where the schools of hard knocks and real fucked up shit are taught, lived, and died in, side by side.

I come from a place that is so invisible you can hardly see me.
Yet, I am despised, hated and feared more than anyone or anything.
I am invisible, I live in the real ghetto, the projects and I am poor and hungry, I live in the underbelly of America and I am poor and have nothing. I am a black man, I am a black woman, I am a black child, and I am invisible, until someone kills me or I kill someone.

—Tony Rose

Prologue

I found out early on that this was not going to be an easy book to write. I wanted to write an autobiography about my early childhood and teen years and the horrific murderers, pimps, gangsters, drug dealers, drug addicts, rapists, child abusers and thieves, that I grew up with, lived with and called family.

I soon realized that I could not write about me as an African American child and teen living in America, without writing about White America, what it was like when I was a child, how it shaped the people around me and what it is like to now live in America, which for tens of millions of African American children is horrific, terrifying, and not so very different than it was for me as a child.

Preface

I began writing this book in my mind while riding across America with my cousin Cornell Landers, now known as *The Illustrious GranddaddyO 'Valor Breeze',* during the summer of 1973. A judge had told me that if I came back to her court again she was going to put me in jail to do some serious time and suggested that I leave town. So I decided to escape and see if I could put my life together. I had already secured my gun and I tell people all the time that if I hadn't taken that Judge's advice I would be serving the second half of my life sentence for killing that bitch.

I hit the road and Cousin Cornell, who was twenty, came along as my side-kick. I had no idea where we were going or what I was going to do, but we must have stopped in every Black ghetto housing project along the way; East Cleveland, Detroit, South Side Chicago, East St. Louis, we felt at home in the projects, and I'm telling you, there's many a home girl today who could tell you stories about two cats from Boston with no shirts on, traveling in a 1969 gas-guzzling VIP Plymouth car, white with a black top, and ropes holding the doors closed, that she bathed, fed and fucked.

I had already received a couple of short story writing awards at UMass Boston and I was thinking about writing a book about me, my mother and father and my life in the projects. So while I and Cousin Cornell were in Amarillo, Texas trying to get some pussy, I saw it, I saw the vision; the book would be about Black people and how we live in American ghettos and why. While I was thinking about that, I realized that even though I was only twenty-two-years-old and had already lived a lifetime, I had a whole lot more living to do before I could write that book. Then life kicked in and the real adventure, that would last forever, well at least for forty-two more years, began.

One other thing I learned on that long summer road trip that would end in Los Angeles, California for me, where I would metamorphosis into a beautiful butterfly; besides the fact that one day I would write this book, happened in the New Mexico desert. We came to some red muddy water along Route 66 and decided to turn off the highway and follow the red water into the desert and find the source. Eventually we came to a big waterfall in the desert that emptied into a big round red muddy water hole. We got out the car and climbed to the top of the waterfall and I said to my cousin let's jump in; he said there could be sharks or alligators in that shit, and I stripped down and said fuck it and just jumped in. From then on I always called life, *'just jump into the water'*, *'just jump into the motherfuckin water.'* It's like trust in God and everything will be alright.

The thing was, you know those things that hang down from caves with pointy edges, well, there were things that came up from the bottom of that red muddy water hole with pointy edges. When I jumped in my right arm scraped against the edges of a pointy thing, I still have the scrape mark, it bled pretty heavy at the time; well, four or five inches to the right and my ass would have been impaled on that thing and I might possibly still be there today, impaled underwater forever, with some pointy thing up my ass. In fact, in some ways I'm still there at that red muddy water hole, it was a near miss, and that means that a part of me, the other part of me, the old part of me, is always still there.

So, ladies and gentlemen, boys and girls, forty-three years after Amarillo, Texas, *'The Autobiography of an American Ghetto Boy.'*

BOOK ONE

PRELUDE

HUNGER IN THE PROJECTS

BY
TONY ROSE

I wrote most of this short story of my life when I was seventeen, and finished it in 2011. It's about my quest to eat as a child.

1
BLACK, UGLY AND CRAZY

It had been two years since my mother had gone crazy, four years since I had started to do time at the Whittier Street Housing Projects, and one year since my sister and I had eaten anything of substance. We were down to eating celery soup, made with celery sticks and boiling water. We were below the ground poor people and lived in a three-room apartment, two bedrooms a kitchen/front room and a bathroom, on the fifth floor, on welfare, in a building with other poor people, all on welfare, all single black women with children, all poor, all hungry, all victimized with poverty and violence, in a housing project with seventeen buildings, seven stories high, containing five-hundred people per building, all poor, all victimized, all black, all hungry.

2
THE CHECK WOULD BE FUCKED UP

It was the Fifties and civil rights, the police, God and the church had not reached us yet. This was old time welfare where you got a check on the 1st and the 15th of the month and God bless you if it was stolen by the big boys or your man or some man or the boogieman, cause that's all you had and that's all there was, there was nothing else. We could eat from the 1st to the 3rd and the 15th to the 18th and then some shit would happen, and the check would be fucked up, my mother fucked up by her man or the boogieman and we would all be hungry again; and my mother would go crazy again and the violence would begin again and shit would happen and we would be back on celery soup again. After the beatings, violence and hunger, my mother would check me at night to see if I was still breathing.

3
BLACK IS BEAUTIFUL

At eight years old, I lived in a strange surreal world of women and children, all who were as my mother always said we were, *"Black and ugly and nobody wants us"*. We were all poor, black, ugly and hungry and nobody wanted us, and Stokely Carmichael's Black Power and Black is Beautiful, hadn't reached us. In that world I began to forage for food. There were three grocery stores that surrounded the projects, all Jewish. Joe's on Tremont Street, Morris' on Cabot Street and Al's on upper Cabot Street.

4
WORN OUT GYPSY WOMAN

Joe was okay, he was an old Jewish guy with a scraggly beard and looked old and tired. I knew that he was from an alien world even then, because his wife sat in back of him all day, smoked black cigarettes and looked like the brown, old worn-out gypsy women, I had seen in the books I was beginning to read and love. They smelled bad like we did and looked poor, so they fit right in except we had to give them money for food.

5
UGLY WHITE GHOSTS

Morris was nasty and treated all of us like shit, he was fat and hated us. He had been there long before us, when it was something else and he probably couldn't get out. There were people who lived across the street from the projects who didn't look like us, they looked like ugly white ghosts and made fun of us. There had probably been more of them at one time, but, now it was down to just all poor people who couldn't get out. Morris and his store smelled bad, but, he did accept the Pepsi-Cola and Coca-Cola bottles I could exchange for money, two cents a bottle, bottles I scrounged from the back alleys and surrounding lots of broken glass, garbage, shit and Cynthia.

6
FUCKIN GUYS ON THE COUCH

Cynthia was Ronald's mother and all she did was sit around all day, drinking Pepsi, fuckin guys on the couch and having babies. The Pepsi-Cola bottles I collected from her house all had roaches in them. The roaches would crawl into the bottles after she drank them and threw them on the floor or something and get stuck. I knew a lot about roaches, in fact, roaches had been my first job.

7
KILL TWO OR THREE HUNDRED ROACHES A NIGHT

When I was four my mother told me that she had a job for me, she said, this is what I want you to do every night. She showed me one night by getting me up at 12:00 midnight, and said this is your job, and I want you to get up every night, and, she walked me to the bathroom and turned on the light and began killing roaches with her slipper. I joined in with her and we killed roaches with our slippers for a while. So every night, and, I'd been holding this job down for four years now, along with my paper route and my going to the store for people job, that I'd been holding down for two years, since I was six. So every night for four years now, I had turned the light on in the bathroom and with my slipper began killing roaches. It was a surprise attack and I loved it. See, the light would stun them for two seconds and I could kill at least a hundred of them in that brief moment or two. I became very fast with my hands and I've always attributed that to the type of violence I could inflict upon my enemies as I got older. I recommend it as a training technique for young fighters as they're coming up. I was fast, and could kill with my slipper two or three hundred roaches a night.

8
PEPSI COLA BOTTLES

Well, once I got the Pepsi-Cola bottles from Cynthia's house and my other friend's house and from scrounging around the project, I had to clean them, wash them out and get them ready for sale at Joe's, Morris's or Al's.

9
HOSTESS CUPCAKES AND TWINKIES

Al's was at the top of the hill on Cabot Street and it was owned by Al the Father, who was a quiet, clean man with an apron and sawdust on the floor, and Al the son, who was my friend. Al the son had been feeding me for a year now; I used to come up to his store with my Pepsi-Cola and Coca-Cola bottles and he would give me two cents for each clean bottle plus a slice of cheese or baloney to eat. Sometimes he'd give me a package of Hostess Cupcakes or Twinkies. Al loved feeding me, he knew I was hungry, and I would save a cupcake or Twinkie for my sister, sometimes.

10

PRIESTS AND NUNS WOULD SAVE MY LIFE

I loved being at Al's, it was clean in there and smelled of fresh meats and pickles. Al the father was a short, hairy man and Al the son was a young, taller, hairier man with a kind heart for a poor, black, ugly, hungry child. We would talk, about what I can't remember, but, what I will always remember is that, that Jewish guy saved my life, too. I was always up at Al's. Al's was on the way to one of my other jobs, where I would shovel snow and run errands for the nuns and priests at the St. Francis de Sales Church Rectory. They would feed me also, with cookies and little cakes and pay me a dollar to shovel the snow. There was a lot of snow in those Boston winters, especially in the Roxbury ghetto I grew up in, where I'm sure I never saw Santa Claus or a snowplow. In six months, those priests and nuns at St. Francis de Sales Church in Roxbury would save my life too, and I would finally find God. But, that's another story.

11

VIOLENTLY BEATEN AND STARVED TO DEATH

One day I'm up at Al's, it's my eighth year, and I'm slowly being violently beaten to death and starved by my mother, and I smell, and I'm poor, and I'm hungry. I know that there is a welfare check and it's supposed to feed me, because this lady, who every time she comes to my project apartment, my mother hides stuff and tells us to shut up, says so. I tried to find her one time after she left to tell her that I was hungry, but, I never could find her. That day, Al's behind the counter waiting on a customer, an ugly white ghost, those people way up the street from us. These are the people that Al regularly serves and a woman from the projects comes in; she is the mother of a kid I know. I'm slowly eating a piece of cheese Al has given me, and watching everything; there is something to do here, something important; I know there is, but, I can never figure it out. But, I'm watching everything very closely, especially that day.

12
TWO BAGS OF GROCERIES

Al's behind the counter, the woman from the projects is now being waited on. Al is pulling items, cans, boxes, wrapping meats, cheese and bagging groceries for this woman. Al says something to the woman and the woman says thank you. Al pulls something from the wall in back of him and writes on it. The woman walks off and I don't see any money being given to Al by that woman, but, I see that woman walk out of the store with two bags of groceries in her arms.

13
GET ALCOHOL, RUN NUMBERS,
GET CIGARETTES AND KOTEX

Now, this is very important, very important to me. I know by now that everything has some monetary value attached to it. That money can buy you stuff, that money can buy you food and that my mother never has any money, so we never have any food. Now, I've been making some money for two years. I've got my shoeshine box for my men customers in the clubs near the projects, who I serve at night, while selling them a dime newspaper for a dollar; and my women newspaper customers in the projects with my running errands hustle, where I get the women's alcohol, run their numbers and get their cigarettes and Kotex.

14
ARE YOU ON WELFARE

I'm known by everyone, and in my eighth year, I own two buildings in the projects and carry a baseball bat in my newspaper sack, 'cause you can't fuck with me and sell shit to my customers in my buildings. I make enough money to buy something to eat for me and my sister, but, my mother takes it from me most of the time and we're always hungry. So anyway, the woman from the projects leaves without giving Al any money and I say to Al, *Al, how come she didn't give you no money!!*

Al looks at me and then looks at me like he just saw me and says, *Are you on welfare?* I say, *Yeah!!!* Because, isn't everybody? I mean, everybody I know is on welfare, I didn't know anyone who isn't on welfare, so, *Yeah, Al, I'm on welfare!* And he says, *Come here.* So I walk up to the counter and look up at him and stand on my tiptoes so I can look over the counter, and he pulls down from in back of him a piece of cardboard with a lot of names on it, and he opens the door to the rest of my life and begins to save me and my little family, and he says, *Do you get the check?*

Well, sometimes if my mother is depressed or sick or angry or upset, or too lazy, well, yes I go down to the basement of my project building and try to protect and get the check. Often I'm not too successful when I have to do that. The check has already been stolen from the mailbox or the big boys will steal it from me or a man will or the boogieman will steal it from me, so my mother will then have to go to the welfare office and get emergency money and I will get beat the fuck up.

15
SOME PANCAKE MIX AND SOME ORANGE JUICE

But, I know that something different is happening here, so I say, *yeah, I get the check.* Al says, *Good, here's what I'm going to do, I'm going to bag you some groceries: some baloney, some cheese, some bread, some milk, some butter, some cereal, some pancake mix and some orange juice.* It was like nothing I had ever heard, I had never heard the sound of words like that, I had never heard all that together. It seems so simple now, a few words, some basic food products, but, to me it was like nothing I'd ever heard before. He said as he bagged the groceries, *I'm going to give you these groceries today and when you need more, you come back and I will bag you more. On the 15th you come back with the check and I will cash the check and take off for the groceries I'm giving you, give you the rest of the money, and bag you another bag of groceries.*

16
FRIED BALONY AND CHEESE SANDWICHES

I took the bag of groceries and went home to my project apartment and told my mother what Al had said. I put the groceries down and told her that I was in charge of the check, that from now on I was going to get the check every 1st and 15th, that I would guard and protect the check, that she was not to get the check. She looked at me like I was crazy and then my sister, my mother and I ate fried baloney and cheese sandwiches. In the morning we ate fried baloney, drank milk and had cereal for breakfast.

17
PROTECTING THE CHECK

On the fifteenth I took a big knife from the drawer, went down to the basement and waited for the Harry the mailman. I told him who I was and what I was doing, and began a six-year odyssey of guarding and protecting the check. I held that deal down with Al until I was fourteen years old; until welfare cheese, welfare meat, welfare powdered milk and a big block of butter replaced my deal. My mother was still crazy, but, not that crazy that she fucked with my deal, because, Al only dealt with me. She still beat on me like a dog, but, the deal stayed intact and we ate. Life got worse and better and worse and once in a while better, but that's another story

THE AUTOBIOGRAPHY OF AN AMERICAN GHETTO BOY

VOLUME ONE

LIFE ON PLANET EARTH – 4,000,000 B.C. - AD 1970

SLAVE ROW AND THE GHETTO

CHAPTER 1

WHERE I WAS BORN

I was born on a very, very small rock in deep Outer Space called Planet Earth in the Milky Way Galaxy and I am a part of at least 100 billion stars, which may have up to 400 billion planets. The Milky Way Galaxy contains at least one planet per star, resulting in up to 100–400 billion planets. There are as many as 40 billion Earth-sized planets orbiting in the habitable zones of sun-like stars and red dwarf stars within the Milky Way Galaxy. 11 billion of these estimated planets may be orbiting sun-like stars and the nearest such planet may be 12 light-years away, and so I am not alone.

In the Milky Way Galaxy where I was born is the Solar System where I live. The Milky Way is a barred spiral galaxy that measures about 100,000 light-years across, and the Solar System, where I grew up at, located in the Orion Arm, is located about 25,000 light-years to the galactic center and 25,000 light-years away from the rim of the Universe. The Solar System where I am writing this book from is only 4.568 billion years old and knew me when I was one second old, and so I am always never alone. The Solar System comprises a Star/Sun and the objects that orbit it, whether they orbit it directly or by orbiting other objects that orbit it directly. Of those objects that orbit the Sun directly, the largest eight are the planets that form the planetary system around it, while the remainder are significantly smaller objects, such as dwarf planets and small Solar System bodies such as comets and asteroids.

The Solar System formed 4.6 billion years ago from the gravitational collapse of a giant molecular cloud. The vast majority of the system's mass a Star/Sun, with most of the remaining mass contained in a planet called Jupiter. The four smaller inner planets, Mercury, Venus, Earth and Mars, also called the terrestrial planets, are primarily composed of rock and metal. The four outer planets, called the gas giants, are substantially more massive than the terrestrials. The two largest, Jupiter and Saturn, are composed mainly of hydrogen and helium; the two outermost planets, Uranus and Neptune, are composed largely of substances with relatively high melting points (compared with hydrogen and helium), called ices, such as water, ammonia and methane, and are often referred to separately as "ice giants". All planets have almost circular orbits that lie within a nearly flat disc called the ecliptic plane and revolve around the Star/Sun

The Solar System also contains regions populated by smaller objects. The asteroid belt, which lies between Mars and Jupiter, mostly contains objects composed, like the terrestrial planets, of rock and metal. Beyond Neptune's orbit lie the Kuiper belt and scattered discs, linked populations of trans-Neptunian objects composed mostly of ices. Within these populations are several dozens to more than ten thousand objects that may be large enough to have been rounded by their own gravity. Such objects are referred to as dwarf planets. Identified dwarf planets include the asteroid Ceres and the trans-Neptunian objects Pluto and Eris. In addition to these two regions, various other small-body populations, including comets, centaurs and interplanetary dust, freely travel between regions. Six of the planets, at least three of the dwarf planets, and many of the smaller bodies are orbited by natural satellites, usually termed "moons" after the planet Earth's Moon.

****

CHAPTER 2
WHO I AM

I was born a human being on the planet Earth, third planet from my Solar Systems Star/Sun. My skin color is light brown and I am a direct descendent of the first human, the original man from the continent of Africa, the cradle of humankind, and at birth I am four million years old. This humanoid is the father of every human being on my planet and his name is *Australopithecus Africanus*.

The closest living relatives of humans are chimpanzees (genus *Pan*) and gorillas (genus *Gorilla*). With the sequencing of both the human and chimpanzee genome, current estimates of similarity between human and chimpanzee DNA sequences range between 95% and 99%. By using the technique called a molecular clock which estimates the time required for the number of divergent mutations to accumulate between two lineages, the approximate date for the split between lineages can be calculated. The gibbons (*Hylobatidae*) and orangutans (genus *Pongo*) were the first groups to split from the line leading to the humans, then gorillas (genus *Gorilla*) followed by the chimpanzees and bonobos (genus *Pan*). The splitting date between human and chimpanzee lineages is placed around 4–8 million years ago during the late Miocene epoch.

The earliest fossils that have been proposed as members of the hominin lineage are *Sahelanthropus tchadensis* dating from 7 million years ago, and *Orrorin tugenensis* dating from 5.7 million years ago and *Ardipithecus kad-abba* dating to 5.6 million years ago. Each of these has been argued to be a bipedal ancestor of later hominins, but, it is possible that either of these species is an ancestor of another branch of African apes, or that they represent a shared ancestor between hominins and other Hominoidea. The question of the relation between these early fossil species and the hominin lineage is still to be resolved. From these early species the australopithecines arose around 4 million years ago diverged into robust (also called *Paranthropus*) and gracile branches, one of which (possibly *A. garhi*) went on to become ancestors of the genus *Homo*.

The earliest members of the genus *Homo* are *Homo habilis* which evolved around 2.3 million years ago. *Homo habilis* is the first species for which we have positive evidence of the use of stone tools. The brains of these early hominins were about the same size as that of a chimpanzee, and their main adaptation was bipedalism as an adaptation to terrestrial living. During the next million years a process of encephalization began, and with the arrival of *Homo erectus* in the fossil record, cranial capacity had doubled. *Homo erectus* were the first of the hominina to leave Africa, and these species spread through Africa, Asia, and Europe between 1.3 to 1.8 million years ago. One population of *H. erectus*, also sometimes classified as a separate species *Homo ergaster*, stayed in Africa and evolved into *Homo sapiens*. It is believed that these species Homo sapiens, were the first to use fire and complex tools.

The earliest transitional fossils between *H. ergaster/erectus* and archaic humans are from Africa such as *Homo rhodesiensis*, but seemingly transitional forms are also found at Dmanisi, Georgia. These descendants of African *H. erectus* spread through Eurasia from ca. 500,000 years ago evolving into *H. antecessor*, *H. heidelbergensis* and *H. neanderthalensis*. The earliest fossils of anatomically modern humans are from the Middle Paleolithic, about 200,000 years ago such as the Omo remains of Ethiopia and the fossils of Herto sometimes classified as *Homo sapiens idaltu*. Later fossils of archaic *Homo sapiens* from Skhul in Israel and Southern Europe begin around 90,000 years ago.

Human evolution is characterized by a number of morphological, developmental, physiological, and behavioral changes that have taken place since the split between the last common ancestor of humans and chimpanzees. The most significant of these adaptations are 1. bipedalism, 2. increased brain size, 3. lengthened ontogeny (gestation and infancy), 4. decreased sexual dimorphism. The relationship between all these changes is the subject of ongoing debate. Other significant morphological changes included the evolution of a power and precision grip, a change first occurring in *H. erectus*.

Bipedalism is the basic adaption of the hominin line, and it is considered the main cause behind a suite of skeletal changes shared by all bipedal hominins. The earliest bipedal hominin is considered to be either *Sahelanthropus* or *Orrionn*, with *Ardipithecus*, a full bipedal, coming somewhat later. The knuckle walkers, the gorilla and chimpanzee, diverged around the same time, and either *Sahelanthropus* or *Orrorin* may be humans' last shared ancestor with those animals. The early bipedals eventually evolved into the australopithecines and later the genus *Homo*. There are several theories of the adaptational value of bipedalism. It is possible that bipedalism was favored because it freed up the hands for reaching and carrying food, because it saved energy during locomotion, because it enabled long distance running and hunting, or as a strategy for avoiding hyperthermia by reducing the surface exposed to direct sun.

We developed a much larger brain than that of other primates – typically 1,330cc in modern humans, over twice the size of that of a chimpanzee or gorilla. The pattern of encephalization started with *Homo habilis* which at approximately 600 cc had a brain slightly larger than chimpanzees, and continued with *Homo erectus* (800–1100 cc), and reached a maximum in Neanderthals with an average size of 1200-1900cc, larger even than *Homo sapiens* (but less encephailzed) The pattern of human postnatal brain growth differs from that of other apes (heterochrony), and allows for extended periods of social learning and language acquisition in juvenile humans. However, the differences between the structure of human brains and those of other apes may be even more significant than differences in size. The increase in volume over time has affected different areas within the brain unequally – the temporal lobes, which contain centers for language processing have increased disproportionately, as has the prefrontal cortex which has been related to complex decision making and moderating social behavior. Encephalization has been tied to an increasing emphasis on meat in the diet, or with the development of cooking, and it has been proposed that intelligence increased as a response to an increased necessity for solving social problems as human society became more complex.

The reduced degree of sexual dimorphism is primarily visible in the reduction of the male canine tooth relative to other ape species (except gibbons). Another important physiological change related to sexuality in humans was the evolution of hidden estrus. Humans are the only ape in which the female is fertile year round, and in which no special signals of fertility are produced by the body (such as genital swelling during estrus). Nonetheless humans retain a degree of sexual dimorphism in the distribution of body hair and subcutaneous fat, and in the overall size, males being around 25% larger than females. These changes taken together have been interpreted as a result of an increased emphasis on pair bonding as a possible solution to the requirement for increased parental investment due to the prolonged infancy of offspring.

By the beginning of the Upper Paleolithic period (50,000 BP), full behavioral modernity, including language, music and other cultural universals had developed. As modern humans spread out from Africa they encountered other hominids such as *Homo Neanderthalensis* and the so-called Denisovans. The nature of interaction between early humans and these sister species has been a long standing source of controversy, the question being whether humans replaced these earlier species or whether they were in fact similar enough to interbreed, in which case these earlier populations may have contributed genetic material to modern humans. Recent studies of the human and Neanderthal genomes suggest gene flow between archaic *Homo sapiens* and Neanderthals and Denisovans, from non-Africans.

In summary this dispersal out of Africa is estimated to have begun about 70,000 - 125,000 years BP from northeast Africa. Current evidence suggests that there was only one such dispersal and that it only involved a few hundred individuals. The vast majority of humans stayed in Africa and adapted to a diverse array of environments. Modern humans subsequently spread globally, replacing earlier hominins (either through competition or hybridization). They inhabited Eurasia and Oceania by 40,000 years BP, and the Americas at least 14,500 years BP.

The genus *Homo* diverged from other hominins in Africa, after the human clade split from the chimpanzee lineage of the hominids (great ape) branch of the primates. Modern humans, defined as the species *Homo sapiens* or specifically to the single extant subspecies *Homo sapiens*, some proceeded to leave Africa and begin to colonize all the other continents and larger islands, arriving in Europe and Asia 125,000–60,000 years ago, Australia around 40,000 years ago, the Americas around 15,000 years ago, and remote islands such as Hawaii, Easter Island, Madagascar, and New Zealand between the years AD 300 and AD 1280.

In greater summary, all human mankind that has ever lived to this very second, on the planet Earth, has come originally from Africa.

****

CHAPTER 3
WHAT I AM

I entered the planet Earth, through the opening of a human woman on October 11, 1950. I weigh 7.8 pounds and 21 inches long, and I am one of 7.125 Billion human beings living on the planet Earth today. There have been countless billions and trillions of life forms on this 4.5-Billion-year old planet before me.

My planet orbits around my Star/Sun from a distance of 93 million miles every three hundred and sixty days. It is called a year, and rotates once in about 24 hours with respect to the sun and once every 23 hours 56 minutes and 4 seconds with respect to the stars. On average it takes 24 hours—a solar day—for Earth to complete a full rotation about its axis relative to the Sun so that the Sun returns to the meridian. The orbital speed of the Earth around the Sun averages about 30 km/s (108,000 km/h, or 67,108 mph), which is fast enough to cover the planet's diameter (about 12,700 km, or 7,900 miles) in seven minutes, and so we have day, which faces our Star/Sun and night which faces away from our Star/Sun.

Most of my human body is made up of water, H_2O, with cells consisting of 65-90% water by weight. Most of my body's mass is oxygen (65%). Carbon (18%), the basic unit for organic molecules, comes in second. 99% of the mass of the human body is made up of just six elements: oxygen, carbon, hydrogen, nitrogen, calcium, and phosphorus. Oxygen (65%), Carbon (18%)Hydrogen (10%), Nitrogen (3%), Calcium (1.5%), Phosphorus (1.0%), Potassium (0.35%), Sulfur (0.25%), Sodium (0.15%), Magnesium (0.05%), Copper, Zinc, Selenium, Molybdenum, Fluorine, Chlorine,

Iodine, Manganese, Cobalt, Iron (0.70%), Lithium, Strontium, Aluminum, Silicon, Lead, Vanadium, Arsenic, Bromine (in trace amounts).

I am made up of a mortal body and an immortal soul, which God joined together at my conception. Death occurs when my body and soul are separated, but my soul never dies or goes out of existence.

This is life as I know it, and all I know of life in the Milky Way Galaxy in Deep Outer Space.

****

CHAPTER 4
WHERE I'M FROM - SLAVERY AND THE GHETTO

I was born on the Planet Earth, a place of great water and oceans, where all life on Earth had come from. I am an air breather, who can no longer breathe underwater or anywhere outside of this planet, in this Solar System, except in this planet's atmosphere, with something called gravity, on a land mass, a continent called North America, in a place called the United States of America, at Boston City Hospital, in a town called, Roxbury, the colored part of Boston, Massachusetts, where violence, liquor stores, crime, heroin, welfare, pimps, gangsters, hustlers, serial killers, drug addicts, rapists, murderers prevailed and lived alongside college educated, bourgeois, middle class lawyers, doctors, school teachers, and good black working people and families.

It looked a lot like a small village, but it was a ghetto full of Black people some doing real good, most doing real bad. Just like in the days of slavery, living in the slave quarters was set up the same as living in the ghetto. Some slaves did real good, but most slaves did and lived real bad. Those that did real good usually had some dealings with the White man, usually the plantation owner and worked in the main or big house, tending to household duties or the owner's children or tended to the white man's other property like his horses and specialized in carpentry and other building, farming or plantation skills and were usually the plantation owner's children of slaves or in-bred lighter skinned slaves.

The ones who did real bad were the slaves that were worked to death, the do or die slave, the menial worker slave, the cotton, tobacco, and farm field hand slave and they were the majority. They were the workers and they made the plantation owner wealthy. They were usually darker skinned slaves and were treated badly by everyone, slave owner and the so called house slaves alike.

But all the slaves had one thing in common, they all had to live in slave row, they all had to live together, in a ghetto of sorts and so they formed a hierarchy of those who did well and those who did not do well, with the lighter skinned slaves lording it over the darker skinned slaves and the darker skinned slaves hating the lighter skinned slaves. In other words, the plantation owner treated the lighter skinned slaves with some leniency and kindness and the darker skinned slaves as mules and so the lighter skinned slaves treated the darker skinned slaves the same as the owner and his family did, and kept the darker skinned slaves in line by telling the owner of any uprisings, or discontent, or any bad talk a field slave might have or feel towards his or her enslavement.

It was a perfect situation for the owner because a slave could not trust another slave with his or her life, none of them had any power, but the lighter skinned slave had power over the darker skinned slave and neither trusted the other. It followed the Willie Lynch letter to the tee and inside that slave ghetto, the white man wasn't the only one doing the raping. There was in-breeding, incest, the strong preying on the weak and the weak finding ways to survive. There were gay slaves, pedophile slaves, crazy slaves, evil slaves and jealous slaves; anytime you have a lot of people thrown together in an uncompromising situation all the vices available are going to happen. The whole plantation, Southern and American way of life was corrupted. The system of slavery was so evil, that everyone Black and White was tainted by the excess of sexual and immoral behavior.

Unlike the films that I mentioned *in America the Black Point of View: The Investigation and Study of the White People of America and Western Europe,* *The Birth of A Nation*, which portrayed Black Americans as sexual deviants and corrupted individuals and *Gone With The Wind* which portrayed slaves as always thinking about and worried about white people's happiness. The truth is somewhere in between, white people had corrupted black people with their own White sense of corruption and deviancy, and black people who had no sense of hope or power, used whatever means they could to survive.

It's really simple, the strong preyed on the weak, the same as White America preys on its weak, uneducated and poor people. We are all children of those slaves, we are all, Black and White, children of those slaves. We are all part of America's horrors, its wars, its poverty, its perversions, its corruption, its hypocrites, its politicians, its slaves. We are all children of the slaves that America made in its image. Its weak, uneducated, poor, corrupted and vile children.

Well, the ghettos of America in the 1950's and 1960's were pretty much run and made that way, with the even poorer and more destitute and undesirable colored people being thrown together in places that were even below the ghetto levels of poverty, they were called the projects, and most of the families and people were poor and on welfare. So now you have tens of millions of Black people across the United States living on top of one another in high rise or low rise buildings all poor, Black, destitute, on welfare, with no jobs, no hope, no self-respect, living in death and violence, and no love for one another, living together all lumped up in a ghetto and housing project.

Although my mother's family, her mother and father, her grandmother and grandfather, her great-aunts, her aunts and uncle, her brother and sisters, her nieces and nephews all lived in the ghetto; and although we lived in the projects with my mother; my sister and I had one big thing that differentiated us from the multitude of other real poor ghetto and project kids. We had a grandmother, our father's mother, who lived in a standalone home that her father had built, three miles from Harvard University, on a street off of Massachusetts Avenue, in North Cambridge, Mass and where she lived was not the ghetto.

Although her son, our father, would become one the most infamous and notorious criminals and gangsters in Boston and New England, she did not live in the ghetto and made sure everyone knew that; and my sister and I would have access to her and her home out of and away from the ghetto.

****

CHAPTER 5
THE CHILDREN OF SLAVES - ROBERT AND EFFIE FAULK

White people are always asking, what's wrong with them, what is wrong with Black people, why can't they get it together, the Jews got it together, the Irish got it together, the Italians got it together, the Polish got it together, we all got it together, what is wrong with those Black people. What's wrong with us?

What's wrong with us Black people is that we didn't come over here on the Mayflower or a fuckin Steamship in 1st, 2nd, or 3rd class steerage.

We came to Europe, to Paris, to France, to London, to Liverpool, to England, to Amsterdam, to the Netherlands, to Madrid, to Spain, to Lisbon, to Portugal, to Berlin, to Germany, to South America, to the Americas, to Jamaica, to Bermuda, to Cuba, to the Virgin Islands, to Aruba, to the Dutch West Indies, to Haiti, to Santa Domingo, to Brazil, to Central America, to the United States, to Antigua, to Anguilla, to Barbuda, to the Bahamas, to Barbados, to Belize, to the British West Indies, to Mexico, to the Cayman Islands, to the United States Virgin Islands, to the Dominican Republic, to Martinique, to Grenada, to Guadeloupe, to Honduras, to Montserrat, to Puerto Rico, to Saint Barthelemy, to Saint Kitts, to Saint Lucia, to Nevis, to the Netherlands, to Antilles, to Saint Martin, to Saint Vincent, to the Grenadines, to Trinidad, to Tobago, to the Turks and Caicos islands, to Pelican Island, to San Andres and Providencia, to Nicaragua, to Venezuela, to Guatemala, to Honduras, to Costa Rica, to Panama, to Alta Velo, to Brazil, to Guyana, to Colombia, to Venezuela, to Argentina, to St. Helena, to French Guiana, to Bolivia, to Chile, to Ecuador, to Paraguay, to Peru, to Suriname, to Uruguay to the United States of America, not on a fuckin vacation, but on a slave ship, packed in by the thousands, with naked African women and young girls menstruating all over the slave ship, while being raped by White men over and over and over and over and over and over and over and over and over and over and over and over and over and over and over again and again and again and again and again and again and again.

Babies being born on slave ships, their heads being bashed against the bull works and then being thrown overboard to the waiting sharks. That's how we came to Western Europe and America.

My Great-Great-Great Grandmother, on my mother's side, was on that ship, along with the tens of millions, hundreds of millions of African men, women, boys and girls who made the trip to Western Europe and the Americas in those slave ships over a four-hundred-year span.

She started her day out in a Sierra Leone village in 1829 as an eleven-year-old girl. She was captured and brought to Bunce Island in Sierra Leone, where she was raped, beaten, sodomized, and made to give blow jobs to many White Englishmen, Dutch and Portuguese traders and sailors. Starved, naked, un-bathed, and forced to live in blood, shit and urine, day and night, only being bathed before she was brought outside the dungeons of the castle to service the many more White men who clamored for her affections. Spoken to in words of love and affection by ghost men in languages she didn't understand.

All of this was before she was chained with thousands of other men and women and boys and girls and brought in terror to the slave ship that would take her to her vacation spot and new home in the Americas, where the white monkeys lived. Where she would be beaten, raped, starved, sodomized, and worked to death in Alabama, Florida, Georgia, Louisiana, Mississippi, South Carolina, Texas, Arkansas, North Carolina, Tennessee, Virginia, Kentucky, Washington, DC, and Maryland.

Forced to watch as her daughters were raped, beaten, and impregnated by white vermin and watch as her sons, her slave husbands, were tortured, beaten, terrorized, sexually abused by White men and women alike and humiliated, lynched, burnt, castrated physically, emotionally, mentally, and spiritually of their manhood. Their manhood taken by vicious, inhuman, barbaric and primitive White men, year after year, decade after decade, century after century, to this very day, this very minute, this very second, in relentless poverty and degradation.

Tens of millions, hundreds of millions of African men, women, boys and girls made the trip in these slave ships over a four-hundred-year span. Kept in hundreds of dungeons and castles built and used, up and down the West African coast by the United States of America, Britain, France, Portugal, Spain, Holland, and other Western European nations, to hold and keep these gentle, captured, African farmers and builders, keepers of the land and fishermen of the lakes and oceans, toilers of the land, these gentle African people.

It would seem, that one hundred and fifty-two years after Abraham Lincoln Emancipated the Confederated Southern States Slaves, 99% who because of the strict southern laws against educating slaves, could not read, write or do math, held no land, did not know where they were, had no money, did not have any understanding of the American or European financial system, had no real understanding of the power of money, and held no power over their lives whatsoever. And so with all that against them, you would still think that 150 years after the civil war, that the great majority of African Americans should have been assimilated into the American dream of economic middle class wealth and prosperity.

But, imagine ten million slaves freed and out on the road in the American South for the first time, but not really free, all different skin colors, because of the sexual ferociousness of the plantation slave master, slave farmers and White men in general for African and Black women. There were hundreds of thousands, millions of just about white slaves, high yella light-skinned slaves, light and bright skinned slaves, light brown skinned slaves, brown skinned slaves, slaves of all different colors mixed with the millions of White men who had raped and impregnated the mothers, grandmothers, great grandmothers, great-great-great-great-great-great-great grandmothers of these slaves for over two hundred years in America.

And then imagine, ten million freed slaves. Hated by just about every White person in America, especially in the south. Hated and beaten, maligned, despised, used, abused, spit on, made fun of, talked about, no money, no clothes, no horse, no buggy, no housing, no lodging, homeless, lynched, burned, starving, stinking, unwashed, disrespected, no jobs, no work, no money, segregated against, terrorized, no citizenship, shot, killed, hunted, raped, sodomized, arrested, blamed for theft, and a million things like rapes that they didn't do, then lynched.

Hated by every White man you see, because they can't get over what they had done to us and it made them hate us even more for being in existence, taking up space, trying to take jobs away from decent White folks, breathing the very air that White people breathe, they kept them out, segregated against them. White men passed laws against the Coloreds very existence, until they went back into slavery as sharecroppers with no economic security whatsoever, and no financial knowledge of the White American financial system at all.

My Great-Great-Great Grandmother would have been on that same road, where some slaves went west to find their manhood working on the railroads or becoming what would be called Buffalo Soldiers for the United States Army and others went north on what would be the first mass migration of African Americans in America.

My Great-Great-Great Grandmother who was now forty-seven years old, black skinned as Africa, had birthed eight children, some for her slave masters and some from her husbands, five who had been sold. She went north, walking from the cotton fields of Georgia, with her three all different colored, remaining children, one of whom was my Great-Great Grandmother born in slavery in Georgia and having her second child, my Great Grandmother born in Virginia in 1866.

A freeborn girl named Daisy, who I would know in the fifties as a skittish, tall, skinny old woman, who talked in a high pitched voice and who along with her husband named Daddy Herbert, and her assorted sisters and aunts, had come down through the ages, through Virginia, Baltimore, Maryland, to Boston, Massachusetts along with my Grandmother and her two sisters and one brother, where they would face like millions of other African Americans, thousands of laws passed legally and illegally across the south and north that would stop them from attaining decent jobs, a decent education, decent housing and restricted to a life of poverty inside a city ghetto or rural ghetto, where they and their men, for the least offense, could be lynched, burnt, castrated and their limbs pulled apart for the enjoyment of White people.

There are a tens of tens of millions of White people in America today, whose grandparents, great grandparents, great-great grandparents, great-great-great grandparents had picnics, barbeques, and social gatherings while watching Black men being lynched, burnt alive, castrated and pulled apart, and Black women, disfigured, lynched, burnt alive, and shot numerous times as sport for White men.

****

CHAPTER 6

My mother's family came from my great-great-great grandmother who was stolen out of Africa, and my great-great grandmother, while on that long road to freedom on 1866, gave birth to my great grandmother, Daisy, in Virginia. Daisy, the granddaughter of a tormented, beaten and raped slave woman from Africa and the daughter of a tormented, beaten, and raped woman from Virginia, would live a long life and end her days in Boston, MA.

She would birth three daughters and one son, and have the companionship and marriage of an African American and Native American man, named Daddy Herbert, who would return to her forty year after he had been put out of her life for molesting one of her daughters, my grandmother, Effie Faulk. She would marry another man during that time named Mr. Brown and he would be accused of the same thing by her. She would have the companionship of her three sisters; their mother was my great-great grand-mother and they would all live long lives as I knew my great aunts also.

One of the sisters, Aunt Rosie, a very, very fair and light skinned woman whose father could have only been a white man, ran a house of ill repute and prostitution on Shawmut Avenue in Roxbury, back in the 10's, 20's, 30's and 40's. My mother would take my sister and I to see her from time to time in the 1950's and she was a very sweet, but business like old white looking woman with what looked like growths on her face, and always looked like she didn't take no shit from anyone.

We would walk over from my projects and walk up this road from Madison Park, it was like a short cut to Tremont and Hammond Street where two of my great aunts, Aunt Lillie and Aunt Mamie lived, right around the corner from Aunt Rosie. Aunt Mamie was real, real old and always had a shawl on, she was a short dark woman, looked like what the slaves must have looked like, she, and I would bet on it, looked exactly like her mother, the daughter of the slave from Africa.

Aunt Lillie was a big boned light brown woman who also looked like she meant business. She could look right through you and know if you were a bad kid, but she always offered me and my sister a glass of ginger ale, while she always drank a glass of something, from a green bottle that said Ale. My mother seemed to know them well and to like her aunts very much, and I the great-great grandson of an American Black Slave and the great-great-great grandson of that eleven year old little girl from Sierra Leone, Africa, an American Black Slave, would have the extraordinary privilege at five, six, seven, eight, nine, ten and eleven years old of knowing, talking, being touched, looked at, kissed and hugged, by my great aunts, the daughters of an American Black Slave, the granddaughters of an American Black Slave from Africa.

As I have said, before, I knew their sister, my great grandmother, Daisy, in the 1950's & 60's. She lived on Ellington Street in Dorchester with her husband Daddy Herbert, her son's family and a few second and third cousins of mine. She never touched me like her sisters did and never had much of anything to do with me. She was a strange old lady, skinny and skittish, like a race horse with an extra step of high energy. She had a high pitched voice and speech that I could never understand.

Like all old people like that do, all five would faded away from me, and then I guess they were no more. Anyway, I never saw any of them again after I turned thirteen, they probably all died around 1959-1962. I think Aunt Mamie was the second oldest and my great grandmother would have been 96 or 97 when she died, Daddy Herbert, who I don't remember ever speaking to me, would have been a little younger than her, but like most old people like that, he faded away from my view and I never saw him again either.

My grandmother had two sisters and one brother. They were all very opinionated, uneducated, smart women, who were always arguing and fighting and not speaking to one another. Aunt Adelle who was the oldest was also the darkest along with her brother who was called, Brother. She was also the smartest and whatever she did and however she raised and taught her children, grandchildren and great grandchildren, they thrived and were ambitious people, most of them became successful businessmen and women. I remember her as a dedicated chain smoker who looked, seemed and talked mean, but she really wasn't.

They all lived in the ghetto, in Dorchester, but not in the projects. Aunt Eva was the second oldest, she was a very light skinned woman, which meant that her father was not my Great Grandfather, Daddy Herbert. Daddy Herbert was a dark brown man with what black people called straight Indian type hair, a matter of fact type of man, with a real stone chiseled face, in his 80's and 90's when I knew him. Aunt Eva was mostly a pleasant woman who was married to a nice man I knew as Uncle Al. She like Aunt Adelle, disliked my grandmother and stayed away from her.

I would know and see her more as I got older, I never knew much about her, but she lived in what was then the new Elderly Homes building at Warren Street and Melnea Cass Blvd, in Roxbury, so I would go and see her and Uncle Al from time to time in the mid-sixties. They did not as far as I could see have any children. I liked them a lot.

Uncle or Brother, as he was called by everyone I knew, was my grandmother's younger brother. I knew him pretty well as a child and teenager. He lived up the street from the Whittier Street Housing Projects where I lived, on the corner outside one of the liqueur stores on Tremont Street. Uncle was a dark skinned man who looked like his mother and grandmother and was the same color as my mother. He was a nice man who liked to drink a lot, but married a nice woman named Harriet and had a number of children, one of whom Richard would marry into a family I would marry into years later, thus his children would be my cousins and the cousins of my second wife. They are eclectic, interesting people and for the most part very well educated.

Uncle's main claim to fame as told by my grandmother was that when the women he lived with in the 1980's died, Uncle or Brother was so drunk that he didn't know that she was in their apartment dead for a week. They were all these, children and grandchildren of slaves, is some ways all broken people; but the worst was my grandmother.

****

CHAPTER 7

When you have the type of evil that slavery was then the degradation of that evil slowly manifests itself in the sexual degradation and depravity between master and slave and it worked both ways. When you have a brutalized and predatorily sexually degraded slave, man or woman, then they are bringing that brutality and predatory sexual degradation back to the Slave quarters.

The Slave quarters were not a place of great happiness. Slaves were living in a brutal world of whips, chains, castrations, shootings, killings, lynching's, rapes, and violent death. There was no happiness, no joy, and even though the children and Black concubines of the slave master had it somewhat easier, by working in the big house of on a more skilled job, they still had to live and sleep together in the slave quarters with the field slaves.

The Slave Quarters were a mixture of slaves, all living together, just like in the ghetto or projects of today. A mixture of good and evil, predator and prey, gay and straight, pedophile and God fearing slaves, good and bad. Violence and sex were dominant in the slave quarters, sex because it was the only joy and relief available to the average field slave, and violence because it was the only way for slave men to express their diminished manhood; and just like any poor community in the ghetto or project, everyone lived on top of one another. Think of the slave quarters as the ghetto or projects of today, except there's no jobs in the neighborhoods.

The family life of slaves was diminished by the breaking up and selling off of mothers, fathers and children. It was best not to become too close to one's child, it was better not to bond or love a child or a man or a woman, and so the brutalizing of children, and slaves committing incest with their children and other children, and the fighting and killing of one another was not uncommon. Jealousies, class distinctions and hatred between slaves who were lighter and slaves who were darker dominated slave row, thus the slave quarters became a place of distrust and mistrust.

Some slave quarter households on slave row would have multiple types of children. There would be the mother and she would have some children by the master and some children by the various men she would have during her childbearing years, some men dark-skinned, some men brown-skinned, some men very light-skinned, and so the connection between mother and child and father and child grew distant, the bonding levels of black men and women almost became non-existent and the breakdown of Black families began as early as the 17th century in America, as the children of mothers and the men of mothers were sold to distant plantations, distant cities and different southern states.

By 1800 in America many Black people were not Black, unless they were just brought over from Africa on the Slave ships, more Black people than not, were a mixture of Black and White blood on the plantations and farms of the South and lower South, and along with some Native American blood, there were various colors of blackness, much like you see today. The book and film *The Color Purple,* by the great Alice Walker and *Catfish Row* in *Porgy and Bess*, even though both the musical, the book and film were based on characters who lived in the late nineteenth and early twentieth century, they were not far from the way it was during slavery and even worse because just like in the ghettos and projects of America's urban cities, you had thousands of poor people living on top of one another, feeding on one another in small confined spaces, where physical hunger and sexual hunger were the same thing, and the weak are prey for the stronger and more powerful black and white predators.

As the Nazis in Nazi Germany portrayed to the world that the Jews living in the Jewish Ghettos and those working in the concentration camps were happy, safe and often just normal, well paid skilled workers. So did the American Antebellum Southerner, as in the film *Gone With the Wind*, portray the American Black Slave as a *happy, dancing and singing all day nigger,* their only worry was being *what white folks wanted or needed,* and 70% of white people in America today still can't understand what all the fuss about slavery was, *them niggers didn't pay no rent, had job security, free meals and free clothing,* what was the problem.

Well, the exact opposite in both cases was true, the horror and trauma of everyday living in the Jewish case maybe lasted for ten to fifteen years of oppression, not even one generation of horror, and in the African American

Slave and my descendants' case more than twenty to thirty generations of oppression, one hundred lifetimes of horror, and as in the Jewish Ghettos and Concentration camps where the strong preyed on the weak, sexually and physically, there were Jewish SS troops and collaborators, who contributed greatly to the horror of six million exterminated Jews, and in the Slave quarters, there were Black slaves who worked against the wellbeing of the Slave, by telling the master or overseer of any up-risings, any slave revolts, any conspiracies, any runaways, any abuses against the authority of White people and contributed to hundreds of thousands of lynchings, castrations and killings of slaves, throughout the South for over two hundred years.

You have to remember that North American slavery lasted for two hundred and twenty some odd years and produced the worst in all involved, and as in every community, city, nation and culture across the world, there are good people and there are bad people and because violence, brutality, rape, and death do not usually bring out the best in people, American Black Slavery produced generations of not only intergenerational poverty, and institutional trauma, but also, intergenerational violence; and although religion was used to subjugate the American Black Slave, the American Black Slave used the words of God and the Bible against the slave system, freeing him and herself of slavery long before the Emancipation of Abraham Lincoln. Those slaves were usually able to produce people whose intergenerational belief in God and the words of the Bible sustained them through, slavery, reconstruction, Jim Crow, The Ku Klux Klan, segregation, the civil rights era and today, and church and the preachers and marching for our civil rights became a central theme and way of life for those descendants of Slaves, and those descendants produced the best and brightest African Americans devoted to the Church and its teachings. Martin Luther King, Jr, came from that group of Slaves.

I did not in my mother's family that raised me come from that American Black Slave group, I came from the former. Until, God found me and took me to St. Francis de Sales church and school, there was no church on Sunday, there was no singing in the choir, there was no God at the Whittier Street Housing Projects, 159 Cabot Street, Apartment 157; there was no marching with or mention of Martin Luther King, Jr., My people were too busy with petty jealousies, whose hair was better, whose skin was to dark, whose skin color was just light and right, who was ugly, whose hair was good hair (good hair meaning white peoples hair), who needed to be beaten, who needed the strap, whose head was going to be beaten against the wall, who was better than who, who thought they were better than someone, who was lighter than who and thought they were better than everyone else and who was blacker than who, as in why would Maria Cole marry that black and ugly Nat King Cole.

The conversations from my grandmother, mother and aunts, were pure evil, just old negative slave talk, never instructive, didn't teach their children or us grandchildren a damn thing, and after I left St. Francis de Sales, I never went to church or heard about God again, until my California days in the early seventies, but that's another book. As I said, my grandmother was the worst! Well maybe my mother was, but then she was raised by my grandmother.

****

CHAPTER 8

My Grandmother was a short medium brown-skin woman, with wavy, short, Native American/African hair, good hair as she would call it. She did not look like her mother, except for Daisy's broad African nose, but more like her father, Daddy Herbert. She was born in Boston, Mass, in 1905, the youngest of Daisy's children, did not have a southern dialect and was named Effie Herbert.

Sometime between 1910 and 1915 she was sexually abused by her father, Daddy Herbert, who was found out, and put out by Daisy. He disappeared from family history for forty years. Daisy then took up with a man with the last name of Brown who sexually molested my grandmother and that would be the ruin of her, for her entire life. She would forever be on the lookout, falsely accusing boys of sexually abusing their sisters and men of sexually abusing their children or family members.

In 1924 she met my Grandfather Robert Faulk at a church she and her family belonged to in Roxbury, Mass. Robert Faulk, my Grandfather was born in 1901 to two former slaves of African and Native American blood and heritage, heavier on the Native American on his Mother's side, in Savage Crossing, Suffolk, Virginia. The whole community where he was born, raised and lived was made up of people who were both Cherokee and African American mixed bloods. They had lived in that region of Virginia since the 18th century as slaves, freedmen, as part of the Cherokee nation, and after slavery, as landowners.

African slave and Native American misogamy had been a part of life in North America since the early 17th Century and whole communities of the two cultures living together were prevalent during slavery, after the Civil War, during reconstruction and on into the twentieth century.

****

"Some Native American women turned to freed or runaway African men due to a major decline in the male population in Native American villages. At the same time, the early enslaved African population was disproportionately male. Records show that some Native American women bought African men as slaves. Unknown to European sellers, the women freed and married the men into their tribe. Some African men chose Native American women as their partners because their children would be free, as the child's status followed that of the mother. The men could marry into some of the matrilineal tribes and be accepted, as their children were still considered to belong to the mother's people. As European expansion increased in the Southeast, African and Native American marriages became more numerous."

"The majority of the people with African blood living in the Cherokee nation prior to the Civil war lived there as free black non-citizens, usually the descendants of Cherokee men and women with African blood. In 1866, a treaty was signed with the US government in which the Cherokee government agreed to give citizenship to those people with African blood living in the Cherokee nations who were not already citizens. African Cherokee people participated as full citizens of that nation, holding office, voting, running businesses, etc."

"In the early 19th century, the US government believed that some tribes had become extinct, especially on the East Coast and those without reservations. It did not have a separate census designation for Native Americans. Those who remained among the European-American communities were frequently listed as mulatto, a term applied to Native American-white, Native American-African, and African-white mixed-race people, as well as tri-racial people."

"The Seminole people of Florida formed in the 18th century, in what is called ethnogenesis, from Muskogee (Creek) and Florida tribes. They incorporated some Africans who had escaped from slavery. Other maroons formed separate communities near the Seminole, and were allied with them in military actions. Much intermarriage took place. African Americans living near the Seminole were called Black Seminoles. Several hundred people of African descent traveled

with the Seminole when they were removed to Indian Territory. Others stayed with a few hundred Seminole in Florida."

"By contrast, an 1835 census of the Cherokee showed that 10% were of African descent. In those years, censuses of the tribes classified people of mixed Native American and African descent as "Native American". By contrast, during the registration for the Dawes Rolls, generally Cherokee Freedmen were classified separately on a Freedmen roll, even if individuals had Cherokee ancestry and qualified as "Cherokee by blood."

"This has caused problems for their descendants in the late 20th and 21st-century, as the Nation has passed legislation and a constitutional amendment to make membership more restrictive, open only to those with certificates of blood ancestry (CDIB). Western frontier artist George Catlin described 'Negro and North American Indian, mixed, of equal blood', and stated they were the finest built and most powerful men I have ever yet seen. By 1922 John Swanton's survey of the Five Civilized Tribes noted that half the Cherokee Nation were Freedmen and their descendants."

"Former slaves and Native Americans intermarried in northern states as well. Massachusetts Vital Records prior to 1850 included notes of 'Marriages of 'negroes' to Indians'. By 1860 in some areas of the South, Native Americans were believed to have intermarried with African Americans to such an extent that white legislators thought the Native Americans no longer qualified as "Native American," as they were not paying attention to culture but only race. Legislators wanted to revoke their tax exemptions."

Freed African Americans, Black Indians, and some Native Americans fought in the American Civil War against the Confederate Army. During November 1861, the Muscogee Creek and Black Indians, led by Creek Chief Opothleyahola, fought three pitched battles against Confederate whites to reach Union lines in Kansas and offer their services. Some Black Indians served in colored regiments with other African American soldiers."

****

CHAPTER 9

By 1919 Robert Faulk was a big strapping quiet country boy all of 6' 3" and weighed about 225 pounds of hard muscle from farm and menial work. He had moved to Norfolk, Virginia, from Suffolk, Virginia in 1919 with very little education, but a good heart and strong hands and arms could take a colored boy a long way. Sometime that year, family lore has it that Robert Faulk had some type of altercation with a White woman and just like thousands of other colored boys in the south and deep south, who had to leave town in a hurry before they were lynched for some small, some big, mostly false accusations made against them, he made that long ride North in the night on the bus, to an Uncle he didn't know, a place that he would never feel comfortable with, marry a woman that he never understood, have children that did him no good and Grandchildren that he mostly didn't like, especially me. He was a country boy his whole life.

My grandparents were married in the church on Shawmut Avenue that they met in and began to raise a family right away. They lived in Roxbury, the black ghetto in Boston, Massachusetts. Both were attractive African American-Native American people with very little if any real education, but they were smart, although, somewhat naive colored people, no different than most people they knew. They went to church and lived in a tenement apartment with their young children. Evelyn Faulk, a light brown baby, was born first in September 1925, Robert Faulk, Jr, a brown baby, was next in 1926. My mother Muriel Faulk was born third into this working class family that would beget a history of great violence on December 15, 1928 at Boston City Hospital. My mother had shown some musical aspirations when she was young, but the violence, family and men, would eventually throw her into the housing projects with my sister and me, where she would succumb to a certain insanity and even more violence. The saying 'we were poor but had God', doesn't apply to me. During her birth, there was a problem, and she would not come easily out of the birth canal and as was the custom for the day, the doctor decided to use what were called Forceps to remove her from the birth canal.

****

(Forceps are a surgical instrument that resembles a pair of tongs and can be used in surgery for grabbing, maneuvering, or removing various things within or from the body. They can be used to assist the delivery of a baby as an alternative to the ventouse (vacuum extraction) method.

Obstetric forceps consist of two branches that are positioned around the fetal head. These branches are defined as left and right depending on which side of the mother's pelvis they will be applied. The branches usually, but not always, cross at a midpoint which is called the articulation. Most forceps have a locking mechanism at the articulation, but a few have a sliding mechanism instead, allowing the two branches to slide along each other. Forceps with a fixed lock mechanism are used for deliveries where little or no rotation is required, as when the fetal head is in line with the mother's pelvis. Forceps with a sliding lock mechanism are used for deliveries requiring more rotation.

The blade of each forceps branch is the curved portion that is used to grasp the fetal head. The forceps should surround the fetal head firmly, but not tightly. The blade characteristically has two curves, the cephalic and the pelvic curves. The cephalic curve is shaped to conform to the fetal head. The cephalic curve can be rounded or rather elongated depending on the shape of the fetal head. The pelvic curve is shaped to conform to the birth canal and helps direct the force of the traction under the pubic bone. Forceps used for rotation of the fetal head should have almost no pelvic curve.

The cervix must be fully dilated and retracted and the membranes ruptured. The urinary bladder should be empty, perhaps with the use of a catheter. High forceps are never indicated in the modern era. Mid forceps can occasionally be indicated but require operator skill and caution. The station of the head must be at least +2 in the lower birth canal. The woman is placed on her back, usually with the aid of stirrups or assistants to support her legs. A mild local or general anesthetic is administered (unless an epidural anesthesia has been given) for adequate pain control. Ascertaining the precise position of the fetal head is paramount, and though historically was accomplished by feeling the fetal skull suture lines and fontanelles, in the modern era, confirmation with ultrasound is essentially mandatory. At this point, the two blades of the forceps are individually inserted, the left blade first for the commonest occipito-anterior position; posterior blade first if a transverse position, then locked. The position on the baby's head is checked. The fetal head is then rotated to the occiput anterior position if it is not already in that position. An episiotomy may be performed if necessary. The baby is then delivered with gentle (maximum 30 lbf or 130 Newton) traction in the axis of the pelvis.

The accepted clinical standard classification system for forceps deliveries according to station and rotation was developed by ACOG and consists of:

> *Outlet forceps delivery, where the forceps are applied when the fetal head has reached the perineal floor and its scalp is visible between contractions. This type of assisted delivery is performed only when the fetal head is in a straight forward or backward vertex position*

or in slight rotation (less than 45 degrees to the right or left) from one of these positions.

Low forceps delivery, when the baby's head is at +2 station or lower. There is no restriction on rotation for this type of delivery.

Midforceps delivery, when the baby's head is above +2 station. There must be head engagement before it can be carried out.

High forceps delivery is not performed in modern obstetrics practice. It would be a forceps-assisted vaginal delivery performed when the baby's head is not yet engaged.

Fetal Complications

- *Cuts and bruises*
- *Occasionally, (usually temporary) facial nerve injury can occur*
- *rarely, clavicle fracture*
- *Intracranial hemorrhage sometimes leading to death: 4/10,000 (O'Mahony F, Settatree R, Platt C, et al. Review of singleton fetal and neonatal deaths associated with cranial trauma and cephalic delivery during a national intrapartum-related confidential enquiry. BJOG 2005; 112:619–26.)*
- *Improper twisting of the neck can cause damage to cranial nerve VI, resulting in strabismus.*
- *Mother Complications*
- *Increased risk of perineal lacerations, pelvic organ prolapse and incontinence*
- *Increased postnatal recovery time and pain*
- *Increased difficulty evacuating during the recovery time*

Advantages to forceps use include avoidance of C-sect, reduction of delivery time, general applicability with cephalic presentation. Complications include the possibility of bruising, deformation, rectovaginal fistula, nerve damage, Descemet's membrane rupture (extraordinarily rare), skull fractures, and cervical cord injury.

Maternal factors

- *Maternal exhaustion*
- *Prolonged second stage*
- *Maternal illness; such as heart disease, hypertension, glaucoma, aneurysm, or other things which make pushing difficult or dangerous*
- *Haemorrhage*

- *Analgesic drug-related inhibition of maternal effort (especially with epidural/spinal anaesthesia)*

****

CHAPTER 10

My mother was blinded in her left eye by the use of the forceps and never had any sight at all in that left eye, all of her life. Not knowing enough about the law and not having any insurance they were never compensated for the scarring and loss of an eye to my mother, and so my grandmother was brought home from the hospital, with an injured baby that needed full time care, not only as a baby, but as a patient with a little eye socket to wash and care for. A newborn baby with all the needs a baby needs. A baby living in constant pain and fear and only seeing people from the right side. A baby traumatized from birth, who would live forever with the pain of being disfigured and blind from birth; to a little girl, to her teenage years, to adulthood, to middle age, to old age, her whole life and at some point in her young adult life, begin to inflict even greater pain on those that came from her and loved her

She was a dark skinned baby, as black as her almost a slave grandmother, and much, much darker than her sister and brother and sister to come, dark enough that people would say that she wasn't Papa's child, dark enough to feel unwanted and color conscious her whole life.

I would not know that my mother was blind in one eye, until around the same time that I learned that she was a virtuoso classical piano player, a musician. I would learn this when I was twenty-three years old, February 1974, and I was living in Los Angeles, California and working at the Burbank Studios. There was a white guy, named David, I was working with in the mailroom, delivering mail to the Columbia Pictures and Warner Brother Pictures, directors and producers, who had bungalow suites and offices on the lot; it was a really great job. I had recently gotten in the show business door at the Burbank Studios and didn't get to be as I was trying to be, a David Bowie, "Pretty Young Thing", on Hollywood Blvd., because of the affections of a thirty-year-old Beautiful Black Woman who was the wife of a famous musician who recorded for Warner Bros' Records. She found and discovered me, while riding in her Rolls Royce on Hollywood Blvd.

It would be many years before I would realize just how fortunate I had been, but in the moment I was just having fun living and going where the wind blew and the wind had blown me into Columbia Pictures, Warner Brothers' Pictures and Lorimar Television. So me and David, somehow realized that we had something in common and had taken to going into the screening rooms where there were pianos, at lunch time to write songs. I would play all the melodies and chords on the piano, and sing the lyrics I had written and David being a much, much, better piano player than me, would write out and play all the notes and music and flush the song out musically. Although I had been fooling around on the guitar I had bought when I was thirteen, I really didn't know where all this was coming from and was surprised that this unknown talent was there. So we recorded one of our songs on a cassette, with me singing and David playing, and I mailed it to my mother so that she could see what I was doing out there in Los Angeles.

About a month later, she called me and said listen to this and for the first time in my life I heard my mother playing the piano. That day she played Mozart, Beethoven, Bach, and what I would learn was her favorite, Chopin, and threw some Schubert in to cap it off. I never forgot that day because it was something I didn't know about my mother. I knew that there was something very wrong with her, because of my childhood and my marriage which she had helped to destroy, and I knew that there were secrets that I didn't know about my family and why I felt about them the way that I did, and always wondered why I had always felt alone and disconnected within my own family.

It would take me another twenty years to piece it all together and yet, right now here was some sort of breakthrough. Where was this music coming from, why had she never played the piano before? There had been a piano at my grandmother's Circuit Street house and I had been banging on it for the first ten years of my life, there was even a picture of me at three years old sitting on the piano stool, but no one, in all those seven years of my trying to understand this piano had ever said or shown any interest in showing me, or playing for me, that black piano that sat in my grandmother's house in her den, not once, not ever.

At that time, I still had no idea of what they had been through, what they had seen and why they were so closed off and secretive. It had always seemed to me that something was wrong and this news of my mother's playing piano proved that. A few months later my mother told me that she was going to have a hysterectomy, whatever that was, and that she needed to replace her left eye. Well that sealed it for me, there were secrets here, my horror as a child had come from somewhere and I needed to know why I had gone through all that pain, from her, as a child.

My mother and I during this time while I was in California were trying to have a relationship, and I was learning things about her that I had never known. So when she told me the story of how she had lost her eye during birth, there was interest on my part, but because of my childhood, there was still a distance between us, and I remember feeling no empathy for her, just curiosity as to how my sister and I could have gone all these years, and not know, from anyone in my family, no one, that my mother was blind in one eye; and how was it that I could have lived with her all of those years and not noticed the disfigurement around her left eye and I realized the first time I saw her without her glasses on, that growing up I had never seen her without her glasses off, and without her glasses off, you could not tell that one eye was not as large as the other eye and that there was something wrong looking with the left eye and that there scarring around that eye.

Even after I knew all the secrets, I always tried to help and excuse my mother for all the pain she had inflicted on me and yes, on my sister also, because my sister had to witness all of that as a younger child, all the horror I was going through, she had to go through it also, and I knew as we got older that she was even more destroyed than I could have ever been. I tried desperately to have my mother love me as a mother, and did all I could for many years, because I saw and knew her pain and I was willing to take her pain as mine.

She grew up thinking of herself as not as pretty as her mother and her sisters, whose skin was lighter, and relished in her long African-Native American hair, as if it was all she had. At twenty she would meet my father, and birth me at twenty-one, be married, and eventually move into the projects on welfare, a beaten and depressed woman who's dreams of success would be lost forever and while my mother's moods while raising my sister and me were often dark because of her color, her blindness, her brother, her mother and my father, she did give us values. She did teach us how to respect people, to have manners, to always be grateful for what you have, and never to take things for granted. Because of her, I always sympathized with the underdog and saw the beauty in everyone, and I always tried hard to understand her, until one day I couldn't understand her any longer.

The third sister and fourth child was called the baby, my Aunt Phyllis. By the time I would know her she was loud, drunk and high most of the time that I saw her, but, she was also bold, brash, funny, outspoken, beautiful and well loved by everyone who knew her. She fought with men and women, was a bar girl, and a party girl, who loved the Rainbow Lounge, on Mass. Avenue and Tremont Street, and had been married just to get out of the house when she was sixteen. She beat on her young husband, was uneducated and highly opinionated, but worked from the age of sixteen at Raytheon, and retired from that job, when she was sixty-five or seventy with a full pension. She died at seventy-four from hard partying, hard living and hard drinking, although it might have been called something else, and she was the nice one. She loved her son Philip and when she was younger she might have forgot about him from time to time and neglected him, as she was living her life and having fun, but she never abused him or hurt him in any physical way. She loved him with all of her heart until the day she died and he loved her also.

Things were as they were during the latter part of the 1920's and 1930's. They were neither very poor nor poor. The thing was that Papa as he would be called by his children and grandchildren worked. He worked in a tailor shop and learned the art of tailoring and sewing. He was a quiet man, a tailor, and worked and took care of his family all through the Depression. That was his claim to fame and would be repeated often by my mother. That they ate when others didn't during the Depression, because Papa worked. He worked at that tailor shop for forty years, this poor Indian-Black boy from Suffolk, Virginia, day after day, year after year and had no idea what was going on in his home.

They moved from the small tenement apartment on Shawmut Avenue, in Roxbury to a rented seven room house on Circuit Street, in Roxbury. The house at Circuit Street was located off the street, in the back of a string of apartment buildings that lined the street. You walked down steps crossed over a bridge and the house was at the end of the dead end alleyway. Near the end of the bridge was a stairway that led down to a large amount of tenement housing at the bottom on both sides left and right of the bottom stairway. At the top of all of this life and property was this seven room house, hanging at the end of the alleyway, across a small bridge, with a long porch attached, and six African American-part Native American people inside.

The deal with the landlord was that Papa would take out all the garbage cans from the all the tenements and apartment buildings, down at the bottom of the stairs and at the top of the stairs and put them all out on barrel days. He did this for twenty-five years, through winter, summer, fall and spring, for twenty-five years, every week, week after week and went to work six days a week; this quiet country boy, who had escaped a hanging in the south. For doing this he only had to pay $75.00 a month for a seven room house, that had a large kitchen, a large front room that had bay windows overlooking the city underbrush and trees that grew up from the bottom landscape, windows where my mother and father would take wedding pictures in front of on their wedding day in 1952. There was the den off the living room, where the piano was, in the basement was the oil tank and the turtles, and upstairs there were four bedrooms, where during the early fifties, me and my cousin Philip would stay from time to time and where my mother and her sisters and brother grew up.

****

CHAPTER 11

But Papa didn't know the horror that was going on in his own house. During slavery, at the plantation or on the farm, slave row, or the slave quarters, as I have stated before, was similar to what passes for the ghetto or the housing projects in American urban and rural cities today. The slave quarters were run like a prison, just like the projects, where violence is a way of life for men, women and children, and as violence became a way of life for people who lived in the ghetto, so did child abuse, child sexual abuse, children killing children, children killing men, children killing women, men killing children, women killing children, become a way of life in the slave quarters, the same as it is a way of life in America's ghettos and projects. Nothing has changed, and every so often the White man, the perpetuator of the violence, the hit man who set all of this up in the first place, will come into the slave quarters, I mean the ghetto, and kill a few people too.

So violence and beatings and whippings have been a part of the American Black Culture since we were violently raped, beaten and whipped out of Africa. In the African culture as well as the Native American Culture the leadership of the family and tribes were dominated by the males. In the Black slave culture, because of the total emasculation of the male, the selling off of the male slaves from their families, and the fact that male slaves could escape slavery more easily by running off alone, the leadership in the slave culture became dominated by a women matriarchy and this would continue to this very day in the ghettos and projects of America. Women would raise children alone, without a strong male influence on the children. Black men are often chastised by the White system for not being with their offspring, and made to feel at fault, but it was the White Man's system during the five hundred years of slavery who began the practice of separating Black Men from their families.

The White system would also have you believe that the Africans that they conquered and enslaved by the usage of their guns and cannons were the warrior class of Africans. In truth the opposite is true. 95% of the hundreds and hundreds of millions of enslaved Africans taken out of Africa over a five-hundred-year period, were already docile African planters, farmers, fishermen and builders. People who were already tillers of the land, builders of their cities and villages, and fishermen of the seas, lakes and oceans of Africa. The White people of Western Europe and America, took these strong African men who loved their families, land, country and seas and turned them into weak, subservient, castrated and emasculated men whose only usage and joy was being worked to death and having sex with women.

This went on, and on, and on, and on, and on, and on, and on, and on, and on, and on, and on, and on, and on, and on, and on, and on, and on, and on, and on, for five hundred years, for five hundred long fuckin years, think about that, in five hundred years from now it will be the year 2115, 2215, 2315, 2415, 2515, in five hundred years it will be the year 2515, think about how long that is from now, and how much life will have changed in that time, space travel and time travel will be as common as riding in a car is today. Think about how long that shit is.

Think about how much damage the White people of Western Europe and America did to West Africa, Africa, Africans, African Americans, people of African descent all over the world over a five-hundred-year period, through slavery and the colonization of Africa. The damage, destruction, hatred and self-hatred continues to this very day, and of course, White people do as they always do and say, *poor Africa, poor West Africa, poor Black people, why can't those people seem to get it together, why can't they be more like us,* never thinking that it might take another five hundred years to wash the stench of the White people of Western Europe and America off of our skins and out of our hair.

Well Papa, although a quiet man and by nature a peaceful man, was also a strong man of a determined nature and just a good ol country boy his whole life, who loved to stand on the corner and talk to his friends. The only personal time that I can remember spending with him outside of the time he took me and my cousins Philip and Cornell on a fishing trip to the long wharf at City Point in South Boston where good ol country boy Papa loved to go fishing and catch all kinds of Atlantic Ocean fish, and where I failed miserably that one summer day in 1962 and caught only a starfish, and was laughed at the whole time by my one year older cousin, Philip, who liked to joke around a lot like his mother. I was never asked to go fishing with my grandfather again. And the only other time was when he and I spent a moment together in the basement of the Circuit Street house where good ol country boy Papa had two huge tanks full of the biggest turtles I have still ever seen in my life. They smelled real bad and it was the only special moment I can remember of being with my grandfather, alone, ever. And just like I didn't like working on cars with my father, I guess he saw that I thought his turtles smelled bad and that I wouldn't touch them and that I was also a horrible fisherman and had no aptitude for the things that he liked. To me he became just somebody I saw on Thanksgivings and Christmas, who although I liked him, he never seemed to take to me.

But, that was okay, because I didn't know how to love him and certainly didn't love any of them except for maybe my cousins, who I always looked forward to seeing. But Papa, well he was a guy I only knew at the head of the table on Thanksgiving and Christmas and he was okay with me, although I always sensed as a little boy, young boy, teenager, older teenager, that something was wrong with him, that he had some type of heavy burden he was carrying. I almost think that he was crying most of the time, but he stayed with the family and his children through it all, and did more than the best he could to take care of and keep a home for his children and then his grandchildren. But, just being there doesn't make you a hero, if your there and your family is falling down all around you, and you don't see it and don't do anything to stop it or prevent it, you can't rise to hero status. Papa was a good man, who had married a bad and troubled woman.

****

CHAPTER 12

My grandmother was the matriarch of the family, she was the leader and had all the say and caused all the damage. One of the things that I heard as an older child my grandmother say constantly, was that she liked children when they were babies, up until two years old, after that they were nothing but trouble. On the outside things looked great, Papa had a job that provided food and a home during the depression, the kids were scrubbed and dressed well, and my mother had piano lessons and was proving to be a classical music, piano genius. She could play Beethoven, Bach, Handel, Chopin, all the classical music, from memory with just one sight reading. At seven years old she was a musical prodigy. At seventeen years old she played before Arthur Fielder and the Boston Pops at Symphony Hall on Massachusetts Avenue in Boston and had been doing concerts in and around the Roxbury and Boston Community in the 1940's for a number of years, and had become a community household name.

In my mother's late teens her piano teacher was Anna Bobbitt Gardner, a well-known Roxbury and Boston figure in the music and arts community. Her first teacher had been the lesser known Mrs. Cook, who had taught her the fundamentals of music theory very well, but lacked the contacts to take Muriel further. People I would talk to later in life, including Anna Bobbitt Gardner, who openly cried when talking about my mother's musical ability, would say that she was the best pianist of classical music they had ever and would ever hear or see play in their lives.

Boston Pops conductor, Author Fielder, had asked her to play with the Boston Pops, and that's when everything turned into shit and the horror began. My aunt Evelyn was given singing lessons, and there is a wonderful photo, program and write-up of Muriel and Evelyn together in concert, my mother playing the piano and Evelyn singing, they made all the local Boston Black Newspapers and the Faulk sisters were becoming known for their musical abilities and life was good for the Faulks. My aunt Phyllis was given tap dance lessons and my Uncle Robert Faulk, Jr. was given trumpet lessons. My mother would say that *he was the best trumpet player to have ever come out of Boston*, but unfortunately that would not be what he would become famous for.

Yes, life on the outside looked good, they were taken to church from time to time, and the Faulk family were well known in the Black community as a family to watch. They were a model Black family. The first sign that something was wrong was when Papa was accused of sexually molesting his oldest daughter Evelyn by my grandmother. The details of what happened are hazy, but Papa was never the same again, and was never close with his two oldest daughters again. This seemed to give my grandmother a free rein to then become the main discipliner of her children and that's when the beatings began and my grandmother's mental illness or schizophrenia truly began.

****

CHAPTER 13

The beatings were given with the leather part of the strap. The strap was usually a man's leather belt and was usually the length of a good size man's waist or about 3-31/2 feet long and was used the same way that the African American slaves had been whipped by their White masters. You were told to undress and you were whipped and beat naked. For the least infraction the girls and Robert were whipped and severely beaten while naked, sometimes they ran naked all over the house with my grandmother chasing them down, beating them and beating them and beating them, year, after year, after year, after year, after year. The boy, Robert, and this was stated by my mother, just so you know how severely he was beaten, over and over, and over, again; this was stated by my mother, who had damaged me to the point of severe trauma, almost beyond repair by her beatings of me, she said that, *eventually mother was beating him with the belt buckle and all we would hear was Robert screaming, and screaming over and over again and mother would be sweating heavily while she was beating him.*

The beatings went on forever, year after year, until each child had been psychologically and emotionally damaged and *"the strap"* would pass down to my mother to beat on me with, and to Evelyn for her first two children, Roberta and Cornell.

Phyllis would get pregnant at fifteen and ran out the house and get married at sixteen and live her life mostly and happily in the bottle, never until she was much older living very far from the Rainbow Lounge on Mass Ave and Tremont.

My mother would eventually go insane and suffer severe schizophrenia and depression for the rest of her life.

Evelyn would eventually throw her four-year-old daughter against a wall in New Mexico, the daughter would be taken to a hospital and have the bone removed in an emergency operation from her skull and until this day wears a steel silver plate in her head, but that still didn't deter her from using the strap and she would beat her son into severe depression and schizophrenia, whereby by the time he was fifteen he had taken to dressing effeminate and seeking the comfort of men and prostituting himself, and would be a drug addict and crack addict for most of his life.

My sister would need a lot of therapy for the first forty years of her adult life and be very confused of her sexuality. After having her vagina probed continuously by doctors from the age of four to see if she was being sexually abused, which she wasn't, (certainly not by a six, seven, eight or nine-year-old little boy), and by continuously being told that she was not to go near boys or men. She would be continuously confused as a teenager reaching puberty as to whether she liked or should like boys, until she with the help of some girls in high school make a decision, and then still confused would try to date boys and men who really liked her for years. Well into her early twenties and with more therapy she would decide and know finally that she preferred the company of woman and was gay.

And me, well you know my story, with oh, so much more to come, but unlike my Uncle Robert, who would go completely insane by the beatings, I was able to handle my alcoholism and drug addiction from the beatings and abuse, by the use of more drugs and alcohol, until I was self-medicating myself totally. A living breathing functional alcohol and drug addict, who would find a hiding place in the greatest place for drug addicts and alcoholics in the world, the 'music and entertainment business'.

And, so while we all looked clean and scrubbed on the outside; on the inside the children and then the grandchildren were being destroyed by the woman and then the women in our lives.

****

CHAPTER 14

I first met Uncle Robert when I was ten years old in 1960. There had been a great deal of consternation and noise within my family that the man who was the cause of my misery, having been the person that everyone had been visiting the day I was first accused by my grandmother and mother when I was seven years old, of *bothering* my sister, was coming home from the prison hospital.

I met him at my grandmother's new apartment on Ellington Street. Papa had contracted something called cancer and couldn't move the barrels anymore and the landlord had gone up on the rent, so they had to move from Circuit Street in 1959-1960 to Ellington Street. They now lived on the same street that my great grandparents lived with my second cousin, Richard Herbert, who was Uncle or Brothers son, and his family.

Uncle Robert was a very big man about 6' 4" and weighed well over 250 pounds of hard muscle. He had a thick neck, broad shoulders, a big chest, huge hands and the biggest forearms, I had ever seen. It was said that while in the hospital, he had squeezed a man's arms so hard that blood had poured out of his arm pores.

I'm thinking that it must have been Thanksgiving or something like that, because I and my cousins were eating at the little kids table, and all the adults including this new person that I had never seen before were sitting and eating at the big table and we all had our good clothes on. He had a woman with him whose clothes, hair and look said that she came from the 1930's. She looked to me like that ghost woman named Fay Wray that was on TV with King Kong, except that she was a light skinned Black woman. He called my grandmother "The Creature", which I always, right from the beginning thought was weird, because I was calling my mother, "The Monster", in secret.

Uncle Robert was cool and I and my cousin Cornell liked him and as we got older, we used to go up his apartment on Blue Hill Avenue and smoke a little weed with him. I also, after I got a little bit older, used to smoke some weed with and fuck another of his girlfriends. They had adjoining apartments.

But the thing was, in January 1949 when he was twenty-three-years-old and my mother was just twenty-years-old and on the cusp of breaking big as a musician; a classically-trained pianist, who had just played for Arthur Fielder. Well, my mother's brother, Uncle Robert who was already a convicted felon on parole, went on a big crime spree. There was a nationwide police hunt for him. He was in all the national newspapers and he became international news, just before my mother and her music could, and ruined whatever chance she had in life.

Finally, the police cornered Uncle Robert on Massachusetts Avenue and Columbus Avenue near the Rainbow Lounge. And in a big shootout with the police, he wounded a police officer, shooting him in the leg. When cornered, Uncle Robert tried to kill himself and instead he shot himself in the head and blew his eyes out. He did 12 years in Bridgewater State Prison Hospital blind.

My mother's family was disgraced, embarrassed, and humiliated. They were ostracized in the Roxbury Black Community, all their hopes and dreams dead, all their friends gone, all their lives torn apart forever, all the rest of their lives lived in shame and secrecy. All their money instead of going to more piano lessons and music concerts for Muriel, went to pay for her brother's defense attorney, psychiatrists, hospital bills, appeals and upkeep in Jail.

The policeman would lose his leg to amputation, Uncle Robert would face attempted murder, armed robbery and rape charges amongst many other things. "The Creature" somehow knowing that her insanity and brutal, horrific treatment of her only son was somewhat responsible for what had happened to him, would devote the next twelve years to getting him out of Bridgewater State Hospital. Although she and the family would always blame this ordeal and horror on Uncle Robert's use of Marijuana. And poor Papa having no choices but to go along with what had happened to his little family, would be thrown out of his church for stealing church funds to help support his only son and namesake's defense. Which worked out because instead of Uncle Robert doing hard time for all that he had done, he just did the twelve years in a cushy hospital setting, with bars at Bridgewater State Prison Hospital.

When she was a child my mother was a piano genius, able to play Beethoven, Bach, Handel, Chopin, all that classical music from memory with one sight reading. At seven she was a musical prodigy. At 17 she played at Symphony Hall in Boston. At 19 she played before Arthur Fielder and the Boston Pops. The black girl who in the forties played classical music so brilliantly now stopped playing piano when she was 20-years-old. There are numerous press clippings of her in a white gown playing concerts in Boston and Roxbury. I still sometimes meet people in the Roxbury community who talk about Muriel Faulk with tears in their eyes, as they describe her musicianship and piano playing.

****

Here is some of the work of "The Creature"

Oh, by the way, "The Creature" was summoned down during the manhunt to where Uncle Robert was holed up at Columbus Avenue and Massachusetts Avenue in Roxbury/The South End, and she could be heard on the bullhorn begging her son to come out, to come out and give himself up, to come out with his hands up, and was on the premise when she and everyone around the manhunt area, heard the gunshot go off that would blind her only son forever.

MARIHUANA CRAZED ADDICT—ONE MAN CRIME WAVE
Name: Robert Faulk Jr.—**Location:** - Boston Mass - **Date:** - Jan 1949

The Portsmouth Herald from Portsmouth, New Hampshire

> 'Maniac 7 Shoots Hub Cop, Himself in Wild Manhunt BOSTON, Jan. ... explanation from the parole board of why Robert Faulk, Jr., 22, described by police, ... through alleys a half mile to hole up in a Massachusetts avenue apartment house.

> BOSTON, MASS. January 1949. After staging a series of beatings, robberies and shootings, Robert H. Faulk, Jr., shot and seriously injured a police officer who was trying to arrest him, and then shot himself through the head, causing total blindness. Wide publicity given to this case attributed the crimes to marihuana, and the judge commented about the influence of marihuana on Faulk. **- Article MARIHUANA; The New Dangerous Drug (pamphlet) by Frederick T. Merrill 1950 version**

> 1949 Boston - Male Assaulted woman; held up auto co.; beat woman stole $3 and jewelry; beat Miss C. stole $75; negro shot Sgt. Cullinen, fled thru back alley; trapped by Sgt. Cannon, so shot self in head, blinded. This started concerted drive Boston vs. marihuana; several major violators arrested. **- Article by James C. Munch; "UN Bulletin on Narcotics"-1966 Issue 2**

> 1949 - Male Stole gun from employer, held up, shot salesman in the stomach for not following instructions; attempted rape clerk; stole $75; Police tracked him down, so he 'shot himself. **-- Article by James C. Munch; "UN Bulletin on Narcotics"-1966 Issue 2**

> 1949 - Robert Faulk, - M - Stole gun from employer, held up shot salesman stomach for not following instructions; attempted rape clerk, stole $75; police tracked him down,

so he shot himself. - Death **-- 6th conference report - INEOA 1965**

Shot salesman for not obeying orders in $75 holdup while under influence of marijuana. **--- The Truth about Marijuana - Stepping Stone to Destruction June 1967**

1949 - Robert Faulk, Boston - male - Assaulted woman; holdup auto company; beat woman and stole $3 and jewelry; beat Miss C., stole $75; Negro shot Sgt. Cullinen, fled thru back alley; trapped by Sgt. Cannon, so shot self in head, blinded. This started concerted drive Boston vs. marihuana; several major violators arrested. - Hospitalized - arrested **-- 6th conference report - INEOA 1965**

On January 10, 1949-, Robert Faulk assaulted Mrs. Mildred Y., stole a gun, and held up his former employer. On January 15, he entered a salesman's car while it was stopped in traffic, and when the salesman didn't follow directions, shot him in the stomach. On January 21, he broke into a home, stole some money, and beat a seventy-eight-year old woman severely. On January 22, he entered a cleaning shop, attempted to rape the clerk, and stole $75. An aroused police force tracked him down, and cornered him. Faulk shot one officer and then seeing that he was trapped, shot himself. Each of these crimes was attributed to marihuana intoxication.

-- The Traffic in Narcotics by H.J. Anslinger and William F. Tompkins 1953

Assaulted woman, held up auto company, beat up two more women, took total of $78 before being trapped. **---- The Truth about Marijuana - STEPPING STONE to DESTRUCTION**

June 1967 NEWSPAPER ACCOUNTS:
Nashua Telegraph
[S- Jan 24, 1949 pg. 1] "2,000 Police Seek Armed Robber"
[S- Jan 26, 1949 pg. 9] "Hero Officer May Lose Leg

Thru Operation"
[S- Jan 27, 1949 pg. 10] "Surgeons Hold Out Hope for
Shot Policeman"
Christian Science
[S-Jan 25, 1949] - "Parole of Boston Bandit Defended
by Board Chairman" [Key-finder - Case #29]

****

CHAPTER 15

When I was twelve, in November 1962, a knock came on our project apartment door, it was Randy Waller or Charles Waller. My sister and I would call him Charles and my mother would call him, Randy. Charles was my mother's last boyfriend before she had married my father, and he had just been released from prison. He had gone to Circuit Street and the people there told him that my grandmother had moved, he found her and she told him where we lived in the Whittier Street Housing Project.

My mother opened the door and let him in, I could see that she knew him and was familiar with him. He was light-skinned, very fair with curly hair, and I thought, although I hadn't seen him in six years, I thought that he favored and sort of looked a lot like my dad. I found out over time that Charles came from a well- known lower Roxbury family, *"the Wallers"*.

My mother had not had a real boyfriend for a few years and spent most of her time backslapping me with the back of her hand in my face, and tormenting me. Her last boyfriend had been a detective with the Boston Police Department. He was real Black and my grandmother made fun of him all the time, calling him the re-tective and mentioned to my mother a lot about how Black and ugly any babies would be if she married Johnny.

Johnny was real nice and I and my sister liked him a lot. He had a car and loved to take us all out for rides. Hardly anyone we knew had a car so it was a special treat for us, plus he liked us and liked my mother a lot. He had a real easy smile and laughed and joked all the time, even making my mother laugh and I could tell that she liked Johnny. They even gave a party together at the house and when they went into her bedroom, I could tell that she was happy when she came out the bedroom and I kind of figured out that had something to do with how she began to treat me a lot better.

During the time that Johnny was around there were no beatings, no accusations, no mental breakdowns, no sadness. He was a big dark skinned man, who moved real easy, with confidence, and seemed to really love us. But, "The Creature" was at work, whispering in my mother's ears constantly, that he wasn't a real detective, that if he was why would he want her, that he was too black, it went on and on, whenever we went to my grandmother's house, I would always hear her talking about Johnny.

Johnny liked music and he had bought us a small record player and a lot of nice things like that. He was also talking to my mother about getting married and moving us out of the projects. I learned later, as I got a little older, that my mother always did the wrong thing, always made the wrong decisions, always went contrary to what was right and always went the wrong way. It was her nature; it was who she was. In fact, the only time I ever saw her really happy, I mean laughing happy, treating me nice happy, authentically happy, was the time Johnny was around, and then one day as fast as he had come into our lives Johnny was gone. And, since everything that went on in our tiny project apartment, happened in our even tinier project kitchen, which was two feet from the front door, my sister and I saw everything that went on in the apartment during the fourteen years that we lived there.

We were in the kitchen when daddy was dragged out by the police, we were in the kitchen when Charles arrived and we were in the kitchen when Johnny was let go. The day before my grandmother, who never came by the Whittier Street Housing Projects to see us, she preferred to go by the Lenox Street Projects to see Aunt Evelyn and her children, my mother always said it was because she didn't really like her because she was black, anyway, she came by and talked to my mother about Johnny and got my mother to say that she would get rid of him.

That day when Johnny came by and knocked on the door my mother whispered to us not to say anything and Johnny kept knocking on the door. Finally, in a voice I had never heard her use with Johnny, she said to him, "What do you want?" Johnny kept saying, "Muriel it's me, Johnny." Finally, after telling him to go away a few times, and I remember this distinctly, she slipped some of his records under the door and told him to go away, that she never wanted to see him again, and we never saw Johnny, a kind and decent man, a real working man, something we would never see our mother with, again. I heard him picking up his records and that was that. Oh, and the accusations, beatings and my own personal horror with my mother, "The Monster", began again. It was just before my ninth birthday and for about three months I knew what it was to have a real mother, to see her laugh, to have some fun with her and then it was over, never to surface again until Randy Waller knocked on the door and it was opened in 1962, when he unsuspectingly walked from the stench of prison into Muriel's living hell.

The thing was that Randy was a World War Two Army veteran, who was fifteen or sixteen when he enlisted in 1945. He never saw combat, but after the war was over, he was beaten senseless by a few White army men while stationed in Germany. Over a period of time he became a 100% percent disabled American Veteran, with a check every month.

And I guess as Randy would always say, *everything was okey-dokey*, until one night in August 1949, when it wasn't okay, and Randy and three friends decided to *'beat and kick a man to death'* in Washington Park, where the Shelbourne Community Center and The Malcolm X Park is today, at Washington Street and Malcolm X Boulevard in Roxbury, near the old Egleston Street Station. They got away with it, until Randy couldn't live with it any longer and turned himself and his two friends in, two years later in 1951.

Because he became a witness for the State of Massachusetts and was proven to be medically incompetent and because of his head injury and beat down in the Army, he was only sentenced too eleven years at Bridgewater State Prison Hospital. And you guessed it, he was in the same prison, at the same time, as good ol Uncle Robert, and because of the medication and God knows what else was going on in there, he became institutionalized, drug addicted and crazy as a fuckin bedbug.

"Bridgewater State Hospital, located in southeastern Massachusetts, is a state facility housing the criminally insane and those whose sanity is being evaluated for the criminal justice system. It was established in 1855 as an almshouse. It was then used as a workhouse for inmates with short sentences who worked the surrounding farmland. It was later rebuilt in the 1880's and again in 1974. Bridgewater State Hospital currently houses 395 inmates all of whom are adult males. The facility was the subject of the 1967 documentary *Titicut Follies*. Bridgewater State Hospital falls under the jurisdiction of the Massachusetts Department of Correction."

****

RANDY WALLER AND
THE DEAD MAN IN WASHINGTON PARK

COMMONWEALTH vs. JUNIUS T. VAUGHN, JUNIOR.

329 Mass. 333

October 6, 1952 - October 30, 1952
Suffolk County

Present: QUA, C.J., RONAN, WILKINS, SPALDING, & COUNIHAN, JJ.

At murder trial, the opinion of a medical expert when he first examined the body of the victim, as to how long he had been dead, was admissible although the question to the expert did not request any grounds or reasons for the opinion. [335]

It was not error at a murder trial for the judge to refuse to strike out, as irresponsive to a question to a medical expert calling for his opinion as to how long the victim had lived after he received a crushed liver, the answer that the victim's "death was not immediately caused by crushing of the liver." [335-336]

No error appeared at a murder trial in the admission of an unimportant question asked at a police station by a police officer of the defendant which contained a statement by a third person, and the answer by the defendant which was in the nature of an admission although it denied the third person's statement. [336-337]

At the trial of an indictment for murder by assaulting and beating, evidence of multiple injuries inflicted upon the body of the victim and of a description by the defendant to a police officer of an attack made upon the victim by the defendant and two others with whom it could be found he acted in concert warranted a verdict of guilty of murder in the first degree. [336-337]

Under G. L. (Ter. Ed.) c. 265, Section 2, as appearing in St. 1951, c. 203, if the jury in a murder case decide that the defendant is guilty of murder in the first degree and are divided as to whether to recommend that the sentence of death be not imposed, the verdict which must be returned is simply guilty of murder in the first degree. [338]

The provision added to G. L. (Ter. Ed.) c. 265, Section 2, in the revision thereof by St. 1951, c. 203, that in "no event shall a person convicted of murder in the first degree be eligible for parole," was not an ex post facto law forbidden by art. 1, Section 10, of the Federal Constitution as applied to a defendant tried under the revised statute for a homicide committed in 1949 and sentenced to imprisonment for life upon a verdict of guilty of murder in the first degree with a recommendation by the jury that the sentence of death be not imposed. [338-339]

A murder case did not remain a "capital case" within G. L. (Ter. Ed.) c. 278, Section 33E, as amended by St. 1939, c. 341, after a verdict of guilty of murder in the first degree with a recommendation by the jury under c. 265, Section 2, as appearing in St. 1951, c. 203, that the sentence of death be not imposed and the imposition of a sentence of imprisonment for life. [339]

INDICTMENT, found and returned on August 10, 1951.

The case was tried in the Superior Court before Murray, J.

Samuel H. Cohen, (Patrick F. Murphy with him,) for the defendant.

John F. McAuliffe, Assistant District Attorney, (Donald P. Brennan with him,) for the Commonwealth.

WILKINS, J. The defendant was convicted of murder in the first degree in the killing, by assaulting and beating, of Roger Brown on August 11, 1949, in an area known as Washington Park in the Roxbury district of Boston.

The jury recommended that the sentence of death be not imposed, and the defendant was sentenced to life imprisonment. G. L. (Ter. Ed.) c. 265, Section 2, as appearing in St. 1951, c. 203. The case is here on appeal under G. L. (Ter. Ed.) c. 278, Sections 33A-33G, as amended. A second indictment charging assault with intent to rob Roger Brown, on which the defendant was likewise convicted, was placed on file. The indictments also named one Waller as a defendant, but he was not brought to trial.

There was evidence that Roger Brown, who was a man of small stature living near the park, had gone for a walk with his dog after 10:30 P.M. on August 10, 1949. It was a very warm evening. The park was crowded. About 11 P.M. he was observed by three relatives sitting on a park bench apparently asleep, with his dog lying on the ground beside him. When they repassed the spot thirty-five minutes later, the bench was empty. About 11:20 P.M. a police officer had seen him sitting on the same bench. The dog returned home alone a little before midnight. Early the following morning the body of Brown was found on the ground in the park. A trousers pocket was turned inside out. At 8:25 A.M. he was pronounced dead at the Boston City Hospital. Examination disclosed broken ribs and cartilages; deep bruises with dull laceration over the right side of face, forehead, and nose; fracture of the nose with dislocation; and crushed liver.

The defendant was arrested at his Roxbury home on April 20, 1951. At the police station he admitted taking part in the robbery and assault with Waller and one Mixon. At the park he pointed out to the police the exact spot where the body was left.

On August 18, 1949, the defendant left his employment in Boston and went to New York with Mixon. He returned to Boston about September 17, 1949.

1. Many assignments of error have to do with rulings on evidence, all but one during the testimony of Dr. Timothy Leary, the medical examiner. They are but briefly argued, and all are wholly without merit.

(a) The first assignment, in so far as it has been argued, has to do with one question asked Dr. Leary on direct examination. The witness had qualified as a medical expert, and had testified that he first saw the body at the hospital on August 11, 1949, at 9:05 A.M. He was asked, "At 9:05, on August 11, 1949, had you formed an opinion as to how long the victim had been dead?" Subject to the defendant's exception, the witness answered, "Yes." In answer to a later question he answered, "Hours." There was no error in his testifying to the results of his own observations. Commonwealth v. Russ, 232 Mass. 58, 74. The question could not fail to be understood to refer to his examination of the body of the deceased. It was not an essential requirement that the question call for the grounds or reasons upon which the opinion was based. Commonwealth v. Johnson, 188 Mass. 382, 389. Greene v. Cronin, 314 Mass. 336, 342-343. Wigmore, Evidence (3d ed.) Section 675.

(b) The second assignment of error presents a similar question. Dr. Leary had testified on direct examination that he had an opinion as to how long the victim had lived after he received the crushed liver. It was then admissible to ask him how long. His answer was, "Well, in my opinion, death was not immediately caused by crushing of the liver." It was not error to refuse to strike out the answer as not responsive.

(c) The eighth assignment of error concerns the same type of question asked during the direct examination of Dr. Leary. There was no error.

(d) The sum total of the defendant's argument on the third assignment consists of the bald citation of one case from a foreign jurisdiction; and on the ninth and tenth assignments of two Massachusetts cases each. There is no attempt to show their pertinency by a statement of any kind. Assuming that these are a sufficient argument on these questions of evidence to meet the test of our rules, no error in the rulings appears. Rule 15 of the Rules for the Regulation of Practice before the Full Court (1952), 328 Mass. 699. Boston v. Dolan, 298 Mass. 346, 355.

(e) The sixth assignment of error has to do with a question and answer of trifling importance contained in the stenographic transcript of a conversation at the police station between a police officer and the defendant. The defendant described the attack upon the deceased which he said was made by Waller, Mixon, and himself. All three approached the deceased. Some one of the three struck a blow, and the man crumpled up and fell to the ground. The defendant hit him twice with his fists on the side of the face, and kicked him once in the side. He could not remember who kicked the deceased in the face. The defendant pulled out one trousers pocket, but it had nothing in it. If the deceased had had anything, the defendant was going to take it. The deceased was not moving when they left him, but the defendant did not know whether he was unconscious or dead. The defendant then told the police officer that a day or two later he asked Randy Waller if he knew what happened to the man in the park. Waller replied, "Maybe nothing happened, they must have found him." He then said that at his house they read the newspapers, one of which was the Traveler. Q. "So that if (Page 337) Randy said, that a couple of days after this assault, that he and you read in the Traveler that the man you beat up in Washington Park, that the police believed that he had been hit with an automobile, would that be true?" A. "No, sir, I am going to say one thing, I didn't read it in the paper." This question and answer given at the police station were objected to on the ground that the question contained the statement of a third party which the defendant denied. In this court the defendant relies upon Commonwealth v. Kosior, 280 Mass. 418, 422, and Commonwealth v. Polian, 288 Mass. 494, 496. Those cases are not controlling for the reasons pointed out in Commonwealth v. Grieco, 323 Mass. 639, 641-642. What is more, the defendant was not harmed by the newspaper evidence, which did not affect the really vital issue of the assault and the killing.

2. There was no error in denying the motion for a directed verdict which related to so much of the indictment as alleged "with intention to murder him and by such assault and beating did murder and kill said Roger Brown." The multiple injuries which the jury could have found had been inflicted upon the body of the deceased, and the defendant's statement at the police station, which we have outlined above, were enough to permit the jury to find the defendant guilty of murder in the first degree. Commonwealth v. Devlin, 126 Mass. 253. Commonwealth v. Devereaux, 256 Mass. 387, 391. Commonwealth v. Bartolini, 299 Mass. 503, 516. Commonwealth v. Galvin, 323 Mass. 205, 217. Commonwealth v. McGarty, 323 Mass. 435, 440. There were in addition other similar statements of the defendant which we need not set forth. It could not have been ruled that there was insufficient evidence to convict the defendant of acting in concert with Waller and Mixon. Commonwealth v. Riches, 219 Mass. 440, 442. Attorney General v. Tufts, 239 Mass. 458, 494. Commonwealth v. Venuti, 315 Mass. 255, 260.

3. The defendant's suggestions in his brief respecting the charge raise no new point. They fall short of being an (Page 338) argument, as required by Rule 15 of the Rules for the Regulation of Practice before the Full Court (1952), 328 Mass. 699.

4. The defendant's motion for a new trial was denied. Under this the defendant argues two matters.

(a) The judge charged: "If the jury decide the defendant is guilty of murder in the first degree and the jury is divided in any way as to whether or not the recommendation that the death penalty be not imposed, the verdict of the jury is `Guilty of murder in the first degree' and nothing else. . .. If the jury is divided, not unanimous in any manner, in any way, by any count, as to whether or not the recommendation that the death penalty be not imposed, then the verdict of the jury which is to be returned is guilty of murder in the first degree, and nothing else." The defendant's argument, which is based upon Andres v. United States, 333 U.S. 740, 748, was completely answered in Commonwealth v. McNeil, 328 Mass. 436, 441-442.

(b) The fifth ground of the motion read: "Chapter 203, Acts of 1951, is unconstitutional and the sentence of the defendant thereunder is illegal and deprives him of his constitutional rights." This statute, which provided for the first time in this Commonwealth that a jury might recommend upon a verdict of murder in the first degree that the sentence of death be not imposed, also introduced into our statute law the provision: "In no event shall a person convicted of murder in the first degree be eligible for parole." At the date of the murder G. L. (Ter. Ed.) c. 127, Section 154A, inserted by St. 1935, c. 225, as amended by St. 1939, c. 451, Section 53, contained the following: "In every case where a person is confined in any penal institution . . . under a sentence for the term of his . . . natural life, the parole board, acting as the advisory board of pardons, shall, within sixty days after the expiration of fifteen years of such sentence, consider carefully and thoroughly the merits of such case on the question of extending clemency, as provided in section one hundred and fifty-four in the case where a petition for pardon or commutation of sentence is referred to it by (Page 339) the governor, and all the provisions of said section shall, so far as pertinent, apply."

It is pressed upon us that this is an ex post facto law enacted in violation of Section 10 of art. 1 of the Constitution of the

United States. "It may be said, generally speaking, that an ex post facto law is one which imposes a punishment for an act which was not punishable at the time it was committed; or an additional punishment to that then prescribed; or changes the rules of evidence by which less or different testimony is sufficient to convict than was then required; or, in short, in relation to the offence or its consequences, alters the situation of a party to his disadvantage." Duncan v. Missouri, 152 U.S. 377, 382. Murphy v. Commonwealth, 172 Mass. 264, 268-270. Commonwealth v. Phelps, 210 Mass. 78, 79-80. See Commonwealth v. Bellino, 320 Mass. 635, 641-642. "But an act plainly mitigating the punishment of an offence is not ex post facto; on the contrary, it is an act of clemency. A law, which changes the punishment from death to imprisonment for life, is a law mitigating the punishment, and therefore not ex post facto." Shaw, C.J., in Commonwealth v. Wyman, 12 Cush. 237, 239.

The declaration of permanent ineligibility for parole is not an ex post facto law as applied to the defendant. At the time of the murder his rights under a conviction of murder in the first degree were confined to a mandatory sentence of death. G. L. (Ter. Ed.) c. 265, Section 2. He would not have had the benefit of G. L. (Ter. Ed.) c. 127, Section 154A, inserted by St. 1935, c. 225, as amended by St. 1939, c. 451, Section 53. In the absence of executive clemency, he could never have received parole. Now that he has been made the beneficiary of a statute permitting imprisonment for life, he cannot complain that the benefits were not even greater.

5. Strictly speaking, this is not a capital case. See Commonwealth v. Coggins, 324 Mass. 552, 556. While, therefore, we are not permitted to exercise the power vested in us by G. L. (Ter. Ed.) c. 278, Section 33E, as amended by St. 1939, (Page 340)

c. 341 (Commonwealth v. Cox, 327 Mass. 609, 614), we see no harm in stating that we are of opinion that there has been no miscarriage of justice.

Judgment affirmed.

CASE CLOSED

****

CHAPTER 16

And after all that, when Randy gets out of Bridgewater State Hospital, my grandmother, who got rid of the Detective, sends Randy Waller over to our house, mainly because like my dad, the criminals, criminal; he was light-skinned with curly hair. It didn't matter that these men were murderers and prison inmates, they were light-skinned with curly hair, and that's all that mattered to her. But, what Randy didn't know was that he had just jumped out of the frying pan into a kettle full of boiling water, because for the next seventeen years he was tortured by my mother, as she wanted control of his 100% disability check that, his stepmother, because of his incarceration, medical and mental problems, controlled.

It was horrible, the only good thing about it was that it got her off of me. Her seventeen-year obsession with getting control of Randy's check was so intense, that she hardly noticed that I existed anymore and I had no more trouble from her at all, until, one day, when I was fourteen, after what was probably the twenty-fifth time Randy had been taken out of the house for going crazy and put in the VA hospital for evaluation and treatment. She must have begun to notice me again and decided to accuse me of something that I hadn't done and pulled out *"the strap"* to beat me naked with the plug end of an iron chord.

I somehow figured out that I was bigger than her and tried to kill her by throwing her out of our fifth floor project apartment at the Whittier Street Housing Projects, 159 Cabot Street, Apartment 157. I had no more trouble out of her after that.

Now Randy wasn't a bad fellow, I mean all he did was stay high on medication and pills all the time, sit in a chair and smoke Kool cigarettes all day, stare at my sister and me with his tongue hanging out, and go in my mother's bedroom with her a lot. But, he also gave my sister and I spending money from time to time, he paid the rent, he bought food, gave us birth-day and Christmas gifts and even though I was making my own money, his was good too.

I remember that he tried to make things a lot easier than they had been before, and he always had a smile, even if it was a dopey smile, and always said something nice to us. He was concerned and he was there as the man of the house. So my sister and I grew up with him and my mother got paid for going in the bedroom, even though she didn't like to. He was the man I lived with from twelve-years-old until I graduated from high school and went into the Air Force at eighteen-years-old. Christmas, Easter, birthdays, holidays, our school graduation photos, my first marriage photos, he's there; and except for whenever he got sick and had to go back to the hospital, he was there for us, until 1977, when after all that, my mother put him out. She married him in 1965, but my mother, *"The Monster"*, never, and I mean never, I mean never, got control of his money, his disability check, from his step-mother, ever.

So on Thanksgiving Day and Christmas Eve, we would all be together, sit-ting at the table, the adults at the big table, the kids at the little kids' table, and make believe that Grandma aka *"The Creature"*, had not put cousin Phillip's head through a wall and that Doctor Trays had not been called and that my cousin had not suffered a severe trauma from that, and that, some people had said, something had happened to him and made him a little slow mentally because of that;

That Grandma aka *"The Creature"* had not severely beaten and destroyed her son turning him into an insane maniac, serial rapist, and attempted murderer, who had tried to commit suicide by shooting himself in the head, blinding himself for life and had served eleven years in Bridgewater State Hospital Prison, blind;

That my cousin Roberta wasn't sitting there with a silver plate in her head because her mother had attempted to kill her;

That I wasn't sitting there being mentally and physically abused and destroyed by my mother aka *"The Monster"*;

That my sister wasn't sitting there being mentally abused and sexually con-fused by her mother;

That my cousin Cornell wasn't being mentally and physically abused and destroyed by his mother;

That my Aunt no matter how beautiful, funny, loud and opinionated she was, wasn't a raging alcoholic;

That the nice man sitting there from 1962 through 1977, smiling and high out of his mind, wasn't a murderer who had served twelve years in Bridgewater State Prison Hospital;

That my mother's career as a classical pianist had not been destroyed and now she was on welfare living in the projects and abusing her children;

That my Aunt's singing and college career (she had been going to the Boston Conservatory for Music when the crime spree occurred) had been destroyed and now she was on welfare living in the projects and abusing her children.

The man who didn't know what was going on in his own house, aka Papa; the child abuser aka *"The Creature"* aka Grandma; the child abuser aka *"The Monster"* aka mother; the alcoholic aka auntie; the child abuser aka the attempted murderer aka Auntie; the serial rapist, aka the attempted murderer, aka robber, aka home invader aka armed robber aka Uncle; the murderer aka Step-Father; the abused Children aka the Parents; the abused Grandchildren aka the Cousins; all products and children, grandchildren, great grandchildren, great-great grandchildren, great-great-great grandchildren of that slave from Sierra Leone. Products of that sexually, physically, emotionally, mentally and spiritually beaten and destroyed American Black Slave Woman from West Africa.

And if I tell you that this was just another normal Black ghetto family, would you believe it? Well believe it. We were just another normal ghetto family and I was just another American Ghetto Boy, a product of American Black Slavery.

The reasons I, a physically, emotionally, psychologically and mentally abused child, didn't turn out like Uncle Robert, and was able to function and somewhat succeed in life, was because I learned how to use drugs and not let drugs use me. The eight months that I would spend with my father were crucial, not only did he teach me things that a poor boy would need to know, but he taught me how to make that abuse work for me, how to hide the violence and anger that was inside of me, and only channel it when necessary and needed on individuals and the world and how to get away with it; and girls were giving me so much pussy, that I didn't need to rape them. I actually used to time the amount of time a new girl or woman that I had just met would take to pull her panties off for me. I believe that the shortest amount of time, that I timed, was eight seconds. And the most important thing was that, when I was a child I had a couple of secret weapons named Grandmére and Papa Ray.

****

CHAPTER 17
THE CHILDREN OF SLAVES - ROBERT AND MARY SMITH

Since this is essentially the story of an American ghetto child and an American Black slave, then it's also a tale of two very different families and two cities, Roxbury/Boston and Cambridge. We have covered the Roxbury/Boston and we have covered my mother's family the Herberts and the Faulks. The Smiths, the LaBerges and the Roses, my father's family, all at some point lived or grew up in Cambridge, Massachusetts. All were the children, grandchildren, great grandchildren, great-great grandchildren, great-great-great grandchildren and so on of African, American Black female slaves and their French, English, White American and Portuguese rapists.

Since we already know that most American Black slaves originated from West Africa, the Roses' descendants being from Cape Verde slaves off the coast of West Africa, I shall not go into greater detail than I did with the Faulk's and the Herbert's.

My Grandmother who I called Grandmére was born in 1899 in Cambridge, Mass. She was the granddaughter of American Black slaves from two very different backgrounds and experiences in America. Her mother, my Great-Grandmother, Mary LaBerge, was born in 1876 in Lynchburg, Virginia. Mary LaBerge's mother, my Great-Great Grandmother was originally from New Orleans and spoke French. Her family had become Mulattos, Octoroons and Quadroons by the continued and consistent raping of female Black slaves from Africa from the early 18th century onward. By the mid-18th century the women and men were highly regarded and prized Black light-skinned slaves used primarily for sexual liaisons with White men.

Black slave women and light-skinned Black slave female children were constantly and consistently used, abused and raped by White men to breed the slave masters and other White men's children; the Black light-skinned children, the children from these liaisons, were then sold for a quite lot of money as house slaves, prostitutes, child prostitutes, and much, much worse in Louisiana, Alabama and Mississippi.

The market term for young Black light-skinned female sex slaves was fancy girls. It was the most notorious and profitable segment of the slave trade in White America, Western Europe and Africa, and had been for going on for centuries. The lighter the skin of a Black slave the more money they were likely to bring. A female Quadroon was a one-fourth black and a mostly white looking slave woman and the marketplaces in White America, Western Europe and Africa were well stocked and supplied with the offspring of the raped and beaten dark Black women slaves.

One fancy girl could be sold for a knocked down price of $8,000, when at that time the going price for an average slave woman was $600, and the largest market in the entire world for Mulatto, Octoroon and Quadroon, fancy girls, was New Orleans. If you were in New Orleans and went to one of the hundreds of brothels, you could be serviced and fucked all night by a Black slave with blonde hair and blue eyes.

My Great-Great Grandmother's family had been slaves under French rule in New Orleans since the early 18th century, and after the Louisiana purchase, they were slaves under American rule, and by the end of the Civil War they had gone from being prostitutes and breeding slaves for White men, to well read, industrious free people of color, who spoke French as a first language and English as a second language and understood who and what they were very well.

Slavery in New Orleans was different under French rule than slavery in most areas of the upper or lower South. The French owners were very comfortable in their sexual liaisons with their Black female slaves, often taking financial responsibility for their mistresses and offspring by sending the Mulatto children of these rapes or sexual liaisons to France for their education and making them legal heirs. This system produced a huge third caste, that of mixed-race Creoles. The term Creole, in Louisiana, referred to Whites and Blacks with French or Spanish ancestry or culture as well as free Blacks or slaves of mixed race.

These upper-class Black Creoles, Mulattos, Octoroons, Quadroons, also flourished and by 1850 nearly 85 percent of Black Creoles possessed the skills to be classified as clerks, teachers, doctors, and skilled workers. Educated Black Creoles, Mulattos, Octoroons, Quadroons free and slave alike did very well, not only as fancy men and women of pleasure, prostitutes and pimps; but also as merchants, and dominated the trades of carpentry, cabinetmaking, masonry, cigar manufacturing, and plastering. These Creole, Mulatto, Octoroon, Quadroon mixed race, Black slaves, and free middle-class blacks, also distanced themselves as much as they could from the Black African slave culture.

Under White American rule, despite the assimilation of the Black Creole, Mulatto, Octoroon and Quadroon communities into French society, discriminating and racist laws were enacted, and the decision of the Supreme Court of the United States of America in *Dred Scott* v. *Sandford*-1857, called the Dred Scott Decision, impinged upon their freedom by ruling that neither free nor enslaved blacks had any constitutional rights. By the start of the Civil War, the new laws restricting the mobility, movement, freedom, and education, of free blacks, Creoles, Mulattos, Octoroons and Quadroons in New Orleans and across the upper and lower south were legislated. But the mixed race Creoles, Mulattos, Octoroons and Quadroons were so entrenched in New Orleans society, politics and business, that the new laws hardly made a dent in their lives at all.

The mixed race Creoles, Mulattos, Octoroons and Quadroons also formed secret societies, fraternities, and clubs and had many organizations and events that put them solidly into the mainstream of White American society and politics. One of the events mixed sex, politics and business so well that even in the early 1960's my Grandmére was still telling stories told to her by her aunts about the *Quadroon Balls of New Orleans,* which would be a prelude to *the Black Cotillion Balls* of the early 20th Century through mid-1960's.

The Quadroon Balls were social events designed to encourage mixed-race women to form liaisons with wealthy White men through a system of concubinage known as plaçage. The balls were elegant and elaborate, designed to appeal to wealthy and socially placed White men. Although race mixing had been prohibited by New Orleans law, it was very common for White men to attend the balls and mingle with the city's quadroon female population.

The principal desire of quadroon women attending these balls was to become placed as the mistress of a wealthy white gentleman. These arrangements were a common occurrence, because the highly educated, socially refined quadroons were prohibited from marrying white men and were unlikely to find Black men of their own status.

A quadroon's mother usually negotiated with an admirer the compensation that would be received for having the woman as his mistress. Typical terms included some financial payment to the parent, financial and/or housing arrangements for the quadroon herself, and, many times, paternal and financial recognition of any children the union produced. Some of these matches were as enduring and exclusive as marriages. A beloved quadroon mistress had the power to destabilize white marriages and families, something she was much resented for.

The system of plaçage' had a basis in the economics of mixed race. The plaçage' of Black women with White lovers, could take place only because of the socially determined value of their light skin, the same light skin that commanded a higher price on the slave block, where light skinned girls fetched much higher prices than did prime field hands. The quadroon balls were the best among severely limited options for these near-white women and a way for them to control their sexuality and decide the price of their own bodies.

The most a mulatto mother and a quadroon daughter could hope to attain in the rigid confines of the Black/White world was some semblance of economic independence and social distinction from the slaves and other blacks. Many mixed race women were successful in actual businesses and political maneuvering when they could no longer rely on an income from the plaçage' system. They had developed enough business knowledge by accumulating information, property and wealth from the process of marketing their own bodies to wealthy White men.

✳✳✳✳

New Orleans:

New Orleans spent nearly a century under European rule before the United States purchased it. Jean Baptiste Le Moyne, Sieur de Bienville, the governor of the French colony of Louisiana, founded the city in 1718. In 1767 it was ceded to

Spain. France reclaimed sovereignty in 1800, and three years later Napoleon I sold all of the Louisiana Territory, including New Orleans, to the United States.

From the first years of French rule, slaves labored in New Orleans and its surrounding plantations. In 1721 more black male slaves than free white men lived in the city, and, until the massive European immigration of the 1830s and 1840s, nonwhite residents formed the majority. A large number of slaves arrived in New Orleans between 1719 and 1731, most of them abducted directly from Senegal. The influence of African culture, therefore, was stronger in Louisiana than in the Eastern British colonies.

New Orleans became nationally important as a slave market and port, as slaves were shipped from there upriver by steamboat to plantations on the Mississippi River; it also sold slaves who had been shipped down river from markets such as Louisville. By 1840, it was the largest slave market in North America. It became the wealthiest and the fourth-largest city in the nation, based chiefly on the slave trade and associated businesses.

Slave traders were men of low reputation, even in the South. In the 1828 presidential election, candidate and later President of the United States of America, Andrew Jackson, came under heavy attack as a slave trader who bought and sold slaves and moved them about in defiance of modern standards or morality. He was not attacked for just merely owning slaves and breeding slaves used in plantation and prostitution work.

Sexual abuse of female slaves was partially rooted in a patriarchal Southern culture which treated black women as property or chattel. Southern culture strongly policed against sexual relations between white women and black men on the purported grounds of racial purity, but, before the late 18th century, the many, many tens of thousands of mixed-race Black American slaves and slave children showed that white men had taken extreme and extraordinary advantages of Black slave women.

Wealthy planter widowers, notably such as John Wayles and his son-in-law, President of the United States of America, Thomas Jefferson, took slave women as concubines; each had six children with his Black mistress, Elizabeth Hemings and her daughter Sally Hemings, the half-sister of President of the United States of America, Thomas Jefferson's late wife, respectively. Both Mary Chestnut and Fanny Kemble, wives of planters, wrote about this issue in the antebellum South in the decades before the Civil War.

Sometimes planters and farmers like the first President of the United States of America, George Washington, used mixed-race slaves as house servants or favored artisans because they were their children or other relatives. The breeding of light-skinned slaves between White men and Black female slaves was a highly prized and profitable institution in America.

The slave owner's exploitation of the black woman's sexuality was one of the most significant factors differentiating the experience of slavery for males and females. The white man's claim to the slave body, male as well as female, was inherent in the concept of the slave trade and was tangibly realized perhaps nowhere more than on the auction block, where captive Africans were stripped of their clothing, oiled down, and poked and prodded by potential buyers. The erotic undertones of such scenes were particularly pronounced in the case of black women.

Throughout the period of slavery in America, white society believed black women to be innately lustful beings. Because the ideal white woman was pure and, in the nineteenth century, modest to the degree of prudishness, the perception of the African woman as hyper-sexual made her both the object of the white man's abhorrence and his fantasy.

Within the bonds of slavery, masters often felt it their right to engage in sexual activity with black slave women. Sometimes, female slaves acquiesced to advances hoping that such relationships would increase the chances that they or their children would be liberated by the master. Most of the time, however, slave owners took Black Female Slaves by force.

For the most part, masters made young, single Black female slaves the objects of their sexual pursuits. However, they did rape married Black slave women, also. The inability of the slave husband to protect his wife from such violation points to another fundamental aspect of the relationship between enslaved men and women. The paternalistic language of slavery, the restrictions of slave law, and the circumstances of slave life created a sense of parity between Black wives and Black husbands.

A master's control over both spouses reduced the black male's potential for dominance over his wife. Married slaves, whose union was not legally recognized, held no joint property in common. What is more, labor segregation by sex and the frequency with which male slaves were sold meant women were not only left to raise their children alone, but also to rely on female friends and relations above husbands.

In consequence, Black slave women were autonomous in ways that white women could not be. Like the attention the master sometimes aimed at female slaves, the perceived "freedoms" of the black slave woman sometimes provoked the resentment of White wives. At the same time, the agency conferred on female slaves also helped to reinforce the notion that Black Females were inherently depraved.

Whenever possible, Black slave women manipulated their unique circumstances in the struggle for their personal dignity and that of their families. As often as Black men slaves, Black women slaves rebelled against the inhumanities of slavery.

Like their ancestors and counterparts in Africa, most slave women took their motherhood seriously. They put their responsibilities for their children before their own safety and freedom, provided for children not their own, and gave love even to those babies born from rape and violence. For their experience and knowledge as caregivers, elderly women were among the most revered slaves on Southern plantations. For enslaved men, escape to freedom was the most promising avenue for preserving masculine identity and individual humanity. For the slave woman, faced with the double onus of being black and female and the added burden of dependent children, womanhood and personhood were easier gained within the slave community.

The demand for slaves increased in Louisiana and other parts of the Deep South after the invention of the cotton gin (1793) and the Louisiana Purchase (1803). The cotton gin allowed the processing of short-staple cotton, which thrived in the upland areas. It made possible a new commodity crop in northern Louisiana, although sugar cane continued to be predominant in southern Louisiana. The northern area of the state became another outpost for the "Cotton Empire", which also encompassed neighboring states such as Arkansas, Mississippi, Alabama, Georgia, and Texas. A brisk domestic slave trade developed; tens and tens of thousands of black slaves were sold by slaveholders in the Upper South to buyers in the Deep South, in what amounted to a significant forced migration.

Early in 1811, while Louisiana was yet the U.S. Territory of Orleans, the largest slave revolt in American history began about thirty miles outside of New Orleans (or a greater distance if traveled along the twisting Mississippi River), as slaves rebelled against the brutal work regimens of sugar plantations. There had been an influx of Haitian slaves, free people of color, and refugee French planters following the Haitian Revolution (1791-1804), which was likely a contributing factor in the revolt. The 1811 German Coast Uprising ended with white militias hunting down black slaves, peremptory tribunals or trials in two parishes, St. Charles and Orleans, execution of the rebels, and the public display of their severed heads. In Orleans Parish, the heads were placed in the Place d'Armes, today's Jackson Square.

****

CHAPTER 18

Into this world my Great-Great Grandmother was born in 1847. She was a Quadroon of French, English, White American and African ancestry. By the time she was twenty-five in 1872 she had birthed two children through her liaisons with prosperous White men, had accumulated a sizable amount of property and money and had made a decision to sell her property's and to move further north to better the educational opportunities for her young daughters. There was also talk that the great Reconstruction of the South that began after the Civil War when Union Soldiers occupied the Southern States, was going to come to an end soon, and much like the Jewish people in Nazi Germany decades later, those that could get out of Germany years before the door closed on the German Jews, got out in the early 1930's. And so those people of African descent that could get out of the Deep South, got out years before Reconstruction ended.

As was the case in most migrations to the north, relatives, usually males, proceeded the rest of the family north and would settle in various places to see how they would be received by the general population of that particular city. Around the year 1869 some relatives left New Orleans for the sole purpose of establishing a trail that could be followed by the family utilizing a series of homes, churches, institutions and people that would help guide those leaving the deep south during the later years of the Reconstruction Era, much like the underground railroad did for escaping slaves.

A man that was very instrumental in helping People of Color of means relocate further north, and a person that my great-great grandmother would have known, was an extraordinary Octoroon himself. His name was P. S. Pinchback and he would become the first African American to hold the Governorship of an American State.

****

Pinckney Benton Stewart Pinchback (born Pinckney Benton Stewart; May 10, 1837 – December 21, 1921, became the first person of African descent to become governor of a United States of America, State. A Republican, Pinchback served as the 24th Governor of Louisiana for 15 days, from December 29, 1872, to January 13, 1873. He was later elected to the state legislature, serving in 1879-1880.

Pinckney Benton Stewart was born a free child in May 1837 in Macon, Bibb County, Georgia. His parents were Eliza Stewart, a freed slave, and Major William Pinchback, a white planter and his mother's former master.

William Pinchback, who also had a legal white family, freed Eliza and her children in 1836; she had borne six by that point and two had survived. She would have four more children with him. The parents were of diverse ethnic origins; Eliza Stewart was classified as a mulatto, and had African, Cherokee, and Welsh and German European ancestry. William Pinchback was ethnic European-American, of Scots-Irish, Welsh and German American ancestry.

Their mixed-race children were thus of majority European-American ancestry. Shortly after Pinckney's birth, his father William purchased a much larger plantation in Mississippi, and moved there with both his white and mixed-race families.

Pinckney Stewart and his siblings were considered the "natural" or illegitimate children of their father. But they were brought up in relatively affluent surroundings and treated as his own. The children were raised as white. In 1846, Pinchback sent Napoleon and Pinckney north to a private academy in Cincinnati, Ohio. In 1848, when Pinckney was eleven, his father died.

Fearful that the Pinchbacks might try to claim her five children as slaves, Eliza Stewart fled with the children to Cincinnati in the free state of Ohio. Napoleon at 18 helped keep the family together but broke down under the responsibility. At 12, Pinckney left school and began work as a cabin boy on river and canal boats to help his family. For a while he lived in Terre Haute, Indiana, where he worked as a hotel porter. During that time, he still identified as Pinckney B. Stewart. He did not take his father's surname of Pinchback until after the end of the American Civil War.

In 1860 at the age of 23, Stewart married Nina Hawthorne, a free woman of color. Like Stewart, she was "practically white" in appearance. They had four children--Pinckney Napoleon in 1862, Bismarck in 1864, Nina in 1866, and Walter Alexander in 1868. Two others had died young. Bismarck's name reflected his father's admiration for statesman Otto von Bismarck of Germany, whom he considered to be one of the world's greatest men. His mother Eliza Stewart lived with Pinchback and his family from 1867 to her death in 1884.

The Civil War began the following year, and Stewart decided to fight on the side of the Union. In 1862 he quietly made his way to New Orleans, which had just been captured by the Union Army. He raised several companies for the Union's all-black 1st Louisiana Native Guards Regiment, which was garrisoned in the city. A minority of men were Louisiana free men of color, part of the educated class before the war who had participated in the state militia; but most of the Guards were slaves who had escaped to join the Union forces and gain freedom.

Commissioned a captain, Stewart was one of the Union Army's few commissioned officers of African-American ancestry. Like Stewart, these officers were mostly of mixed race. Most of them were drawn from free people of color in New Orleans before the war; unlike him, they were usually of colonial French and African descent. He became Company Commander of Company A, 2nd Louisiana Regiment Native Guard Infantry, made up mostly of escaped slaves. (It was later reformed as the 74th US Colored Infantry Regiment, of the United States Colored Troops). Passed over twice for promotion and tired of the prejudice he encountered from white officers, Stewart resigned his commission in 1863. In a letter of April 30, 1863, his sister Adeline B. Saffold wrote to him from Sidney, Ohio, urging him to follow her example:

If I were you, Pink, I would not let my ambition die. I would seek to rise and not in that class either but I would take my position in the world as a white man as you are and let the other go for be assured of this as the other you will never get your rights.

At the war's end, Stewart and his wife moved to Alabama, to test their freedom as full citizens. Racial tensions during Reconstruction resulted in shocking levels of violence as whites tried to re-establish social dominance and suppress black voting. Stewart returned with his family to New Orleans.

After the war in New Orleans, Stewart took his father's surname of Pinchback. He became active in the Republican Party. In 1867, Pinchback organized the Fourth Ward Republican Club in New Orleans soon after Congress passed the Reconstruction Acts. That year he was elected to the constitutional convention. In 1868 Pinchback was elected as a State Senator. He became senate president pro tempore of a Legislature that included 42 representatives of African-American descent (half of the House, and seven of 36 seats in the Senate). (At the time, the population of African Americans and whites in the state was nearly equal.)

As Senate president pro tempore, in 1871 Pinchback succeeded to the position as acting lieutenant governor upon the death of Oscar Dunn, the first elected African-American lieutenant governor of a U.S. state.

Pinchback also contributed to the political discussion after acquiring the biweekly newspaper, the New Orleans Louisianan. He published this until 1879.he was appointed as director of the New Orleans public schools, established for the first time under Reconstruction.

In 1872, the legislature filed impeachment charges against the incumbent Republican governor, Henry Clay Warmoth due to disputes over certifying returns of the disputed gubernatorial election, in which both Democrat John McEnery and Republican William Kellogg claimed victory. Trying to support a centrist fusion government at a time of divisions among Republicans, Warmoth had supported his appointed return board, which certified McEnery as winner.

Republicans opposed this outcome, and appointed their own returns board, which certified Kellogg. The election had been marked by violence and fraud. State law required that Warmoth step aside until his impeachment case was tried. Pinchback took the oath as acting governor on December 9, 1872, and served for about six weeks until the end of Warmoth's term. Warmoth was not convicted, and the charges were eventually dropped by the legislature.

After his brief governorship, Pinchback remained active in politics and public service in Louisiana. From 1868, campaigns and elections in Louisiana were increasingly marked by Democratic violence. Historian George C. Rable described the White League, started in 1874, as the "military arm of the Democratic Party." The paramilitary group used intimidation and violence to suppress black voting and run Republicans out of office.

As an outcome of the controversial 1872 election, four US Congressional seats from Louisiana were also contested, including Pinchback's seat in the at-large position. He was the first African American elected to Congress from Louisiana.

In early 1873, both the Republican William Kellogg-allied state legislators, who had a slight majority, and the Democrat John McEnery-allied legislators elected US Senators. Pinchback was elected by the Republicans and presented the Senate with his credentials. The Democratic candidate also presented credentials. As the 1872 gubernatorial contest had involved the national government, Congress was initially reluctant to assess these issues. The contested claim was not settled for years, and by that time, Democrats controlled Congress.

Holding out for the Senate seat, Pinchback conceded the House seat to his Democratic opponent. But the 45th Congress (1877-1879), which finally decided the issue, was Democratic majority, and it voted against Pinchback. The Senate did give him compensation of $16,000 for his salary and mileage after his protracted struggle to take his seat.

Pinchback had a longstanding interest in education of blacks and was appointed to the Louisiana State Board of Education after the Reconstruction legislature established public education in the state for the first time.

Overall, the mid to late 1870s marked an acceleration of the reversal of the political gains which African Americans in Louisiana had achieved since the end of the Civil War. In 1877, Democrats fully regained control of the state legislature after the withdrawal of federal troops as a result of a national Democratic compromise marking the end of Reconstruction. Most blacks were totally disfranchised by a new state constitution in 1898 and were effectively excluded from politics for many decades.

Pinchback served as a delegate to the 1879 state constitutional convention; he and two other Republican African-American delegates were credited with gaining support to establish Southern University, a historically black college in New Orleans, which was chartered in 1880. Pinchback was appointed as a member of Southern University's Board of Trustees. The college relocated to the capital, Baton Rouge, in 1914.

In 1882, the national Republican administration appointed Pinchback as surveyor of customs in New Orleans, a politically significant position in which he served until 1885. It was his last.

Continuing to be active in the African-American community, Pinchback had joined the Comité des Citoyens (Citizens' Committee), which set up the New Orleans civil-rights challenge of Homer Plessy to state segregation in public transportation. Interstate trains were covered by federal legislation and supposed to be integrated. The case went to the U.S. Supreme Court as Plessy v. Ferguson. The Court ruled in 1896 that the state's providing "separate but equal" accommodations to African Americans was constitutional. This was a setback for African Americans; in practice, white-dominated legislatures and authorities generally underfunded black facilities, from train cars and waiting rooms to everything else.

Pinchback moved with his family to Washington, DC in 1892. Wealthy due to his positions and settlement on the Senate seat, he had a large mansion built off Fourteenth Street near the Chinese embassy. At that time, the oldest son Pinckney was established as a pharmacist in Philadelphia; the younger three ranged in age from 26 down to 22 and were still living at home. The Pinchback family was part of the mixed-race elite in Washington; people in this group had generally been free before the war, and often had formal educations and had acquired property. The Washington Post covered his housewarming reception and many high-ranking guests.

By his death in 1921 in Washington, DC, Pinchback was little known politically. His body was returned to New Orleans, where he was interred in Metairie Cemetery.

It would not be until 1990 that another African American served as governor of any U.S. state. In 1990, Douglas Wilder of Virginia became the first to be elected to office (and the second African-American state governor). Deval Patrick of Massachusetts was elected governor in 2006 and served from January 2007 to January 2015. David Paterson of New York became the fourth African-American governor on March 17, 2008, when he succeeded to office following the resignation of Eliot Spitzer.

****

CHAPTER 19

And with the help of that great man and politician, P. S. Pinchback, my Great-Great Grandmother Lucy LaBerge and her two daughters and some others of her lineage made up of male and female Octoroons and Quadroons, left New Orleans around 1874, and went on that great migration to the north, to Lynchburg, Virginia. Why Lynchburg? I have no idea.

Property was bought, roots were set up and in 1876, Lynchburg, Virginia, Lucy LaBerge would have another daughter and name her Mary. Mary would be a lot darker than her mother which meant that her father was a brown skin man. Mary looked like something between a Mulatto and Octoroon girl. She would be well educated and grow up with all the class and refinement of her mother.

She was probably a snob, just like her mother and just like her daughter, my Grandmére would be. But, they were snobs in the way that they would want to succeed and want those around them to succeed, they believed not only in the finer things of life, but they believed in the betterment of their race, of their people. They were followers of all the great Black men and women orators and heroes of their day, such as Frederick Douglas and Sojourner Truth and were very social beings, beautiful and in command of their lives and the people around them.

They would be vastly different people then my mother's family in that although their ancestral slave family members had been abused and raped by White men earlier in their family history, they had not been beaten and treated as horrifically as my mother's ancestral slave family members had been, and thus had thrived as slaves and were thriving as freed slaves in America by the middle of the 19th Century.

They were also well read and very well educated people who believed that education, Black social clubs, fraternities, social organizations and the right connections were the key to survival and success for the Colored People of America. They would also believe in teaching not beating, they would believe that success was a virtue not something to be jealous of, they would believe in success and not failure and they definitely believed in God, and the church as a sanctuary for People of Color.

They also believed it seemed, that diluting the lightness of their color on their descendants was also a necessary ingredient for them in their march forward to the 20th century. Because both Lucy and Mary whether it was love or fate or God's will, or just the fact that when they could they did, both choose men that were darker than them and in my Great-Grandmother Mary's case, she chose a man that not only was darker, but whose skin was as Black as hers was light. So it would seem that they were not color conscious light skinned people, because when they could of their own free will and validation they both choose dark Black men of Color to marry and have children with.

****

CHAPTER 20

Mary LaBerge as a young girl of fifteen years old in 1891, Lynchburg, Virginia, was wise in the ways of politics, business and real estate, and had already set her sights on a slightly older boy named Robert Smith. Robert

Smith, was born in 1874 in Lynchburg, Virginia. His parents, parents, parents, parents, parents, parents, parent, had been kidnapped from West Africa and made field slaves by White men with guns and cannons, and worked to death in the most horrific conditions possible, in Virginia, for over One Hundred and Fifty Years, until the Emancipation Proclamation of President Abraham Lincoln in 1863, and the end of the Civil War between the North and the South in 1865.

My Grandmére would tell me when I was a little boy in 1961, sitting with her in the house that Robert Smith had built in 1895-98, at 10 Clarendon Avenue in North Cambridge, Massachusetts, the house that she had been born in, as she took her drink and a puff on her Parliament cigarette. She would talk and tell me stories about her mother and father and she would say that her father said that his wife Mary was everything to him and he was everything to her. Mary would not live long enough to see how extraordinary he would become, but he would say to my Grandmére that he was everything he was, because of her.

To see them together these two children and grandchildren of American Black Slaves must have been a thing of wonder, both so different, yet both so beautiful, one an upper class light-skinned daughter of privilege and some wealth, the other a dark skinned son of the soil, of the land.

Mary was a no-nonsense girl, who began to teach, even though Robert was being schooled in one of the Freedmen Bureau's Reconstruction Schools that had sprung up all over the south, to teach the slaves and especially the children of slaves, how to read and write. She began to teach Robert all the things she had learned from her mother and the schools she went to; about finance and business, about real estate, how to buy it and how to sell it, she began to teach Robert the rudiments of social interacting, how to dress, how to talk, how to make the right friends, say the right things, do the right things, and filled his head with the wonders of the world, and all the places that they would and could go. That even though they were in Lynchburg today, that tomorrow they could be anywhere they wanted. They became strict followers of Booker T. Washington and followed his every word and believed in his philosophy of self-improvement for the Negro. They believed that self-worth and hard work would as Booker T. Washington said, save them. They would come to believe together that cleanliness, orderliness, discipline, dedication, organization and education would as, Booker T. Washington said, make them acceptable to White people, so that White people who wanted to destroy and kill every nigger in America, would see, as Booker T. Washington said, that they still needed us to work for them and provide for them all the services that they needed in agriculture and technical work, all the things that Booker T. Washington would build Tuskegee University to do for the Negro to be of and in service to White people.

****

TUSKEGEE UNIVERSITY

Tuskegee was founded on July 4, 1881, as the Tuskegee Normal School for Colored Teachers. It was part of the expansion of higher education for blacks in the former Confederate states following the American Civil War, with many schools founded by the northern American Missionary Association. A teachers' school was the dream of Lewis Adams, a former slave, and George W. Campbell, a merchant and former slaveholder, who shared a commitment to the education of blacks. Despite lacking formal education, Adams could read, write, and speak several languages. He was an experienced tinsmith, harness-maker, and shoemaker and was a Prince Hall Freemason, an acknowledged leader of the African-American community in Macon County, Alabama.

Adams and Campbell had secured $2,000 from the State of Alabama for teachers' salaries but nothing for land, buildings, or equipment. Adams, Campbell, and M. B. Swanson formed Tuskegee's first board of commissioners. Campbell wrote to the Hampton Institute, a historically black college in Virginia, requesting the recommendation of a teacher for their new school. Samuel C. Armstrong, the Hampton principal and a former Union general, recommended the 25-year-old Booker T. Washington, an alumnus and teacher at Hampton.

As the newly-hired principal in Tuskegee, Booker Washington began classes for his new school in a run-down church and shanty. The following year (1882), he purchased a former plantation of 100 acres in size. The earliest campus buildings were constructed on that property, usually by students as part of their work-study. By the start of the 20th century, the Tuskegee Institute occupied nearly 2,300 acres.

Based on his experience at the Hampton Institute, Washington intended to train students in skills, morals, and religious life, in addition to academic subjects. Washington urged the teachers he trained "to return to the plantation districts and show the people there how to put new energy and new ideas into farming as well as into the intellectual and moral and religious life of the people. Washington's second wife Olivia Davidson, was instrumental to the success and helped raise funds for the school.

Gradually, a rural extension program was developed, to take progressive ideas and training to those who could not come to the campus. Tuskegee alumni founded smaller schools and colleges throughout the South; they continued to emphasize teacher training.

In 1856, Washington was born a slave in Virginia. After emancipation, his family resettled in West Virginia. Washington sought a formal education and worked his way through Hampton Normal and Agricultural Institute (now Hampton University) and attended college at Wayland Seminary in Washington, DC, now Virginia Union University. He returned to Hampton as a teacher. Hired at Tuskegee, the new normal school for the training of teachers opened on July 4, 1881 in space borrowed from a church. The following year, Washington bought the grounds of a former plantation and over decades built the institute there. It has been designated a National Historic Landmark.

The school expressed Washington's dedication to the pursuit of self-reliance. In addition to training teachers, he also taught the practical skills needed for his students to succeed at farming or other trades typical of the rural South, where most of them came from. He wanted his students to see labor as practical, but also as beautiful and dignified. As part of their work-study programs, students constructed most of the new buildings. Many students earned all or part of their expenses through the construction, agricultural, and domestic work associated with the campus, as they reared livestock and raised crops, as well as producing other goods.

The continuing expansion of black education took place against a background of increased violence against blacks in the South after white Democrats regained power in state governments and imposed white supremacy in society. They instituted legal racial segregation and a variety of Jim Crow laws, after disfranchising most blacks by constitutional amendments and electoral rules from 1890–1964. Against this background, Washington's vision, as expressed in his "Atlanta Compromise" speech, became controversial and was challenged by new leaders, such as W.E.B. Du Bois, who argued that blacks should have opportunities for study in classical academic programs, as well as vocational institutes. In the early twentieth century, Du Bois envisioned the rise of the "Talented Tenth" to lead African Americans.

Washington gradually attracted notable scholars to Tuskegee, including the bota-nist George Washington Carver, one of the university's most renowned professors.

Perceived as a spokesman for black "industrial" education, Washington developed a network of wealthy American philanthropists who donated to the school, such as Andrew Carnegie, Collis P. Huntington, John D. Rockefeller, Henry Huttleston Rogers, George Eastman, and Elizabeth Milbank Anderson. An early champion of the concept of matching funds, Henry Rogers was a major anonymous con-tributor to Tuskegee and dozens of other black schools for more than 15 years.

Thanks to recruitment efforts on the island and contacts with the U.S. military, Tuskegee had a particularly large population of Afro-Cuban students during these years. Following small-scale recruitments prior to the 1898-99 school year, the university quickly gained popularity among ambitious Afro-Cubans. In the first three decades of the school's existence, dozens of Afro-Cubans enrolled at Tuskegee each year, becoming the largest population of foreign students at the school.

Washington developed a major relationship with Julius Rosenwald, a self-made man who rose to the top of Sears, Roebuck and Company in Chicago, Illinois. He had long been concerned about the lack of educational resources for blacks, especially in the South. After meeting with Washington, Rosenwald agreed to serve on Tuskegee's Board of Directors. He also worked with Washington to stim-ulate funding to train teachers' schools such as Tuskegee and Hampton institutes.

Beginning with a pilot program in 1912, Rosenwald created model rural schools and stimulated construction of new schools across the South. Tuskegee architects developed the model plans, and some students helped build the schools. Rosenwald created a fund but required communities to raise matching funds, to encourage local collaboration between blacks and whites. Rosenwald and Washington stimulated the construction and operation of more than 5,000 small community schools and supporting resources for the education of blacks throughout the rural the South into the 1930s.

Despite his travels and widespread work, Washington continued as principal of Tuskegee. Concerned about the educator's health, Rosenwald encouraged him to slow his pace. In 1915, Washington died at the age of 59, as a result of congestive heart failure. At his death, Tuskegee's endowment exceeded US$1.5 million. He was buried on the campus near the chapel.

****

CHAPTER 21

Yes, they believed in Ol Booker T. Washington, but they also believed in their own self-worth and Mary had the financial means from her mother, to do that. Over the next few years they put together a plan that would take them out of Lynchburg, Virginia and to a school in Hampton, Virginia, where Booker T. Washington had studied, but, not to Tuskegee, where Booker T. Washington taught. Their plan was not to work for White folks, but to own their own businesses, because they also believed that God blesses the child who got his own. And by 1895 when Robert was twenty years old and Mary was nineteen years old these two "Up From Slavery" children of God, were on their way to Eastern Virginia to study business management, finance, carpentry, bricklaying and fine furniture making at The Hampton Agricultural and Industrial School, later called Hampton University.

****

Hampton Normal and Agricultural Institute – Hampton Institute— Hampton University

Hampton University is a historically black university located in Hampton, Virginia, United States. It was founded in 1868 by black and white leaders of the American Missionary Association after the American Civil War to provide education to Freed Black American Slaves and was called The Hampton Agricultural and Industrial School, later called the Hampton Institute. In 1878 it established a program for teaching Native Americans, which lasted until 1923.

The American Missionary Association (AMA) responded in 1861 to the former slaves' need for education by hiring its first mulatto teacher, Mary Smith Peake, who had secretly been teaching slaves and free blacks in the area despite the state's prohibition law. She first taught for the AMA on September 17, 1861 and was said to gather her pupils under a large oak. The tree was the site in 1863 of the first reading in the former Confederate states of the Emancipation Proclamation, it was called Emancipation Oak. The tree, now a symbol of the university and of the city, is part of the National Historic Landmark District at Hampton University.

During the American Civil War (1861–1865), Union-held Fortress Monroe in southeastern Virginia at the mouth of Hampton Roads became a gathering point and safe haven of sorts for fugitive slaves. The commander, General Benjamin F. Butler, determined they were "contraband of war", to protect them from being returned to slaveholders, who clamored to reclaim them. As numerous individuals sought freedom behind Union lines, the Army arranged for the construction of the Grand Contraband Camp nearby, from materials reclaimed from the ruins of Hampton, which had been burned by the retreating Confederate Army. This area was later called "Slabtown."

After the War, a normal school (meaning to establish standards or norms while educating teachers) was formalized in 1868, with former Union brevet Brigadier General Samuel Chapman Armstrong (1839–1893) as its first principal. The new school was established on the grounds of a former plantation named "Little Scotland", which had a view of Hampton Roads. The original school buildings fronted the Hampton River. Legally chartered in 1870 as a land grant school. It was first known as 'Hampton Normal and Agricultural Institute.'

One of the many Civil War veterans who gave substantial sums to the school was General William Jackson Palmer, a Union cavalry commander from Philadelphia. He later built the Denver and Rio Grande Western Railroad, and founded Colorado Springs, Colorado. As the Civil War began in 1861, although his Quaker upbringing made Palmer abhor violence, his passion to see the slaves freed compelled him to enter the war. He was awarded the Medal of Honor for bravery in 1894. The current Palmer Hall on the campus is named in his honor.

Unlike the wealthy Palmer, Sam Armstrong was the son of a missionary to the Sandwich Islands, which later became the U.S. state of Hawaii. He also had dreams for the betterment of the freedmen. He patterned his new school after the model of his father, who had overseen the teaching of reading, writing and arithmetic to the Polynesians. He wanted to teach the skills necessary for blacks to be self-supporting in the impoverished South. Under his guidance, a Hampton-style education became well known as an education that combined cultural uplift with moral and manual training. Armstrong said it was an education that encompassed "the head, the heart, and the hands."

At the close of its first decade, the school reported a total admission in the ten years of 927 students, with 277 graduates, all but 17 of whom had become teachers. Many of them had bought land and established themselves in homes; many were farming as well as teaching; some had gone into business. Only a very small proportion failed to do well. By another 10 years, there had been over 600 graduates. In 1888, of the 537 still alive, three-fourths were teaching, and about half as many undergraduates were also teaching. It was estimated that 15,000 children in community schools were being taught by Hampton's students and alumni that year.

In 1878, Hampton established a formal education program for Native Americans. In 1875 at the end of the American Indian Wars, the United States Army sent seventy-two warriors from the Cheyenne, Kiowa, Comanche and Caddo Nations, to imprisonment and exile in St. Augustine, Florida. Essentially they were considered hostages to persuade their peoples in the West to keep peace. At the end of the warriors' incarceration, Pratt convinced seventeen to enroll at Hampton Institute for a fuller education. Altogether, seventy Native Americans, young men and women from various tribes, mostly from the Plains rather than the acculturated tribes that had occupied Virginia, joined that first class. Because Virginia's aristocrats sometimes boasted of their Native American heritage through Pocahontas, it was hoped that the Native American students would help locals to accept the university's black students. The black students were also supposed to "civilize" the Native American students to current American society, and the Native Americans to "uplift the Negroes."

Hampton Normal and Agricultural Institute became simply Hampton Institute in 1930. With the addition of departments and graduate programs, it was accredited as Hampton University in 1984. Originally located in Elizabeth City County, it was long-located in the Town of Phoebus, incorporated in 1900. Phoebus and Elizabeth City County were consolidated with the neighboring City of Hampton to form a much larger independent city in 1952. The City of Hampton uses the Emancipation Oak on its official seal.

****

Mary LaBerge-Smith - 1897 or 1898

Robert Smith - 1897 or 1898

****

CHAPTER 22

As you can see by their photos, taken at the time of their graduation from Hampton Agriculture and Industrial School or their marriage in 1897 or 1898, when Mary would have been twenty-one or twenty-two and Robert would have been twenty-three or twenty-four years old. They were quite formidable, industrious, handsome, beautiful and determined people. Yet, they would have been living in a world of segregation, racism and Jim Crow Laws, their whole lives, as most lives of the colored people of the United States of America, their whole lives would have been pre-ordained to live in segregation and die in segregation, and live in 70% of the White people of America's hate and fear of American Black people called racism.

They would have to eat, live and work in segregation with White people believing that they were superior and the colored inferior. They would go to segregated beaches, as all colored people did in America, like Buckroe Beach in Hampton, which was the colored part of Bayshore Beach, separated by the Whites only sign and fence which ran all the way to the water's edge. Which reminds me that all the way up to the 1970's in Boston, Mass., Black people could not, as they could not on all of the major beaches in America, could not and better not, put their foot on the South Boston beaches at City Point, and in Virginia up and down Hamptons Road and at Virginia Beach, blacks could clean the segregated town's hotels, but they couldn't stroll on the boardwalk or go onto the beach until the 1960's when the city of Virginia Beach was integrated.

Yes, their whole lives were ordained as all Colored people in the United States of America lives were, to live in the hate, fear and prejudice of 70% of the country's White people. But from 1895-1898 they would try do something that would save themselves, their children, and their great-great grandchildren from a life of institutionalized racism and segregation, of a life lived and died in an American Black Ghetto.

****

CHAPTER 23

In the great African American migrations north, after slavery, after reconstruction and in the early 20th century, the one distinct factor in every family was, as has been discussed, that a family member or those family members went ahead as scouts to strange places, strange cities and would get whatever jobs they could find, work hard and send letters and money back home to try to get more family members out of the south. Sometime in 1896, after his freshman year at Hampton, Robert Smith traveled by train to visit a few family members from Lynchburg and St. Petersburg, Virginia, who had left the south in the late 1870's and early 1880's and were making a fine life for themselves in a Northern city called Cambridge, Massachusetts.

These family members would welcome Robert, make him feel at home and show him their life in Cambridge, Mass. Life for Black People in Cambridge, Massachusetts in 1896 was an enlightening experience as opposed to life in the south, or as opposed to life on Mars or Jupiter, as opposed to life in Virginia. Life in Cambridge, Massachusetts in 1896, was so vastly different then life had been in Virginia for Colored people, that it must have been an exhilarating and unique experience for Robert Smith. The fact that his relatives from Lynchburg by way of St. Petersburg, Virginia, by way of Boston, Mass. to Cambridge, Mass, were doing very well, making a living and making something of themselves in the Fayerweather Street, Concord Avenue area of Cambridge, less than three miles from Harvard Square, where the jobs of maintaining and up-keeping the homes of the well to do, and working for the Harvard University elite were plentiful and not only paid good, but paid dividends in friendships and contacts. My great grandfather would have seen a city with somewhat liberal views and beliefs.

Although not perfect, Cambridge was even at that time and had been for two hundred years and fifty years the Athens of America. Founded in 1636 in Cambridge, Massachusetts, and built by Colonial White and Black Indentured servants and Black slaves and funded for over a century by the sale of Black slaves and Rum, *Harvard College,* which eventually became Harvard University, was the oldest institution of higher learning in the United States. For centuries its all White graduates had dominated Massachusetts' clerical and civil ranks, and in the 19th century its stature would become national, then international, as a dozen graduate and professional schools, including: the Harvard University Graduate Schools of Medicine, Law and Business, as well as the Harvard Graduate School of Arts and Sciences, were formed alongside the nucleus undergraduate College. Since the late 19th century Harvard had been one of the most prestigious schools in the world, its library system and financial endowment larger than those of any other, all based on the labor, products, and profits of slavery that was woven into the University's very fabric.

But by 1850, Harvard Medical School had accepted its first three African American students, one of whom was Martin Delany. Harvard would later rescind the invitations due to pressure from white students. In 1869, George Lewis Ruffin was the first African American to earn a degree from Harvard Law School. Ruffin would become Massachusetts' first African-American judge. In 1869, Harvard would award its first degree in dentistry to an African American named Robert Tanner Freeman; and by 1870, Harvard College, after two hundred and thirty-five years, had graduated its first African American student, Richard Theodore Greener, who went on to a career as an educator and lawyer. In 1895, W.E.B. Du Bois earned his Ph.D. in history from Harvard, the first African American to do so. Robert Smith would have known about W. E. B. Du Bois and admired him. In 1896, Booker T. Washington received an Honorary Master's Degree from Harvard University; Robert knew about Booker T. Washington, as you know, and followed his philosophy, doctrine and teachings much more than he did Dr. W. E. B. Du Bois, but only because the love of his life Mary, did; but his soul burned for W. E. B. Du Bois's philosophy and doctrine. And by 1912, Carter G. Woodson, would become the second African American in the United States of America to earn a doctorate in History, with a Ph.D. from Harvard University. Carter G. Woodson would go on to found the *Journal of Negro History* in 1916 and inaugurate Negro History Week in 1926, which would become, Black History Month.

****

CHAPTER 24

I'm sure it didn't take long before Robert Smith decided to take, with the blessings of his family, this grand idea to one day be a part of this great adventure, in this wonderful town, where the opportunities seemed endless for a man of great expectations such as he. So with the blessings and finance of Mary LaBerge and her mother, the newly married, Mrs. Lucy Woodson, he purchased a plot of land at Ten Clarendon Avenue, right off of Massachusetts Avenue, one mile from Fayerweather Street and Concord Avenue. A prime piece of land right off of Massachusetts Avenue, the central artery, and a straight route, to Harvard Square, only three miles away. Through Central Square, past the Massachusetts Institute of Technology (MIT) and to the Harvard Bridge, also known locally as the MIT Bridge or the Massachusetts

Avenue Bridge, over the bridge and into Boston, Massachusetts, a distance of only ten miles. And with the stroke of a pen, my great-grandfather, one step removed from slavery, one step removed from the horrors of southern sharecropping, one step removed from being shot dead in a southern city, one step removed from being lynched for looking at a White woman, one step up from the fields, secured him and his beloved Mary's future and the future of his descendants or so he might have thought, but as the saying goes, only God knows our futures.

For the next two years, Robert and Mary, studied, lived and worked in the Hampton, Virginia area during the fall, winter and spring and in the summers they would travel to Cambridge or more specifically North Cambridge and work on building their home with family and friends. Other friends and family members had migrated to New England from Virginia and had bought plots on Clarendon Avenue, so the summers were spent happy and well in North Cambridge building their tidy three story homes.

Most of these former slaves and the children of slaves were excellent tradesmen. Robert's father had been a master carpenter, as well as a tiller of the tobacco fields during slavery in Lynchburg, and had taught his son the trade also; and along with the skills he was learning at Hampton, Robert was becoming a very highly and in demand architectural consultant for the homeowners and because he was natural leader, he was able to gain the respect and trust of his family and their friends as a man of honor a man that one should listen to.

New friendships were made, coalitions and business ideas were discussed and formed, a new age had dawned in America, a new technology, phones, electricity, the age of enlightenment for colored and white alike had arrived, at least in this small part of the world, in Cambridge, Mass. It seemed as though the Civil War fought to end slavery and gain the freedom of the American Black Slave was successful and that the Negro was on his and her way to assimilating into America.

But, not so. In the real America new laws were being enacted to suppress the voting rights of these freed slaves and their children, as one Mississippi official in 1890 said, "The plan is to invest permanently the powers of government in the hands of the people who ought to have them, "*the White people of America*". The Ku Klux Klan was on the rise and the lynching of a Negro was a precept, a pastime and a call for a picnic for White people. But, on Clarendon Avenue, Fayerweather Street, Concord Avenue and hundreds of other streets and avenues of such around the country, you would never know that America was still an extremely dangerous place for Negroes in 1897, as it would still be for their African American descendants in 2015.

****

CHAPTER 25

During late 1897 or early 1898, Robert Smith and Mary LaBerge proudly graduated from Hampton Agriculture and Industrial School and were immediately married. Mary would have been twenty-one or twenty-two and Robert would have been twenty-three or twenty-four years old on their graduation and marriage days. These were the two happiest days of their young lives. Their home in North Cambridge, Massachusetts was built and ready for the two creative, intelligent, well educated, business minded young adults and the third happiest day of their newly married life was when they traveled to Boston and Cambridge and stepped over the threshold of their new home at Ten Clarendon Avenue, North Cambridge, Massachusetts. It must have been the happiest of days when in late February 1899, they looked out the window from their sanctuary, at the land that they had purchased, the house that they had built, and looked out into the winter snow, the winter wonderland of Clarendon Avenue and heard the bustling noise of Massachusetts Avenue in the warmth of their new home. As Robert Smith embraced his newly pregnant wife, Mary Smith and they loved each other so much while looking out the window of their small, but elegant living room, while making plans for the arrival of their baby, their first child, that coming November.

During my great-grandparents' first year living in Cambridge they purchased two more plots of land on Clarendon Avenue and began the first stages of what would become a very lucrative business, buying land and building and selling homes. This business would eventually become one of the largest African American owned real estate concerns in Massachusetts, with Robert Smith owning properties in Cambridge, Arlington, Lexington, Somerville, Roxbury, Dorchester, Oaks Bluff in Martha's Vineyard, and The South End in Boston.

In 1966, I can remember my father and I walking into an office on Warren Street. It stood right up the street from the Twelfth Baptist Church on

Warren Street, it was a storefront office, right off the street. I had seen and walked by this storefront office for my entire fifteen-year-old life.

I remember that my father and I walked in and a real tall older man greeted him warmly. After they had talked, I remember that the older man handed him an envelope and looked at me. He came over, and bent a little ways down and said, you know that your great-grandfather founded this business, don't you? I knew that it was a real estate business, but, I didn't know what that meant that my great-grandfather had founded this business, and my father never explained it. But I would find out in twenty-one years.

In 1978 my Grandmére died and Papa Ray died in 1981. My father inherited the house at Ten Clarendon Avenue and ran the house into disrepair and a pretty good size tax debt.

He called me one day in 1986 and said that he owed Sixteen Thousand Dollars in back taxes on the property and that the city was going to foreclose on the property. I told him that I would pay the back taxes, but I wanted him to put my sister's and my names on the deed to the property, something I had asked him to do after Papa Ray had died in 1981.

I told him back then that my sister and I would pay the taxes on the property if he would move into the house with his little son, little Freddie, and take care of it. He refused and by 1986 had run the house into severe disrepair and had trashed all three floors, with him and his friends, drug, alcohol, sex and heroin parties. I found broken drug needles all over the floor, all over the house.

There had also been a family myth that Robert Smith had buried his money in the basement and in the walls of the basement. In 1987, after I had paid the back taxes, and after he had put my sister's and my name on the deed, I cleaned the house out, and found all the documents and pictures and heirlooms and real estate papers that would one day, when I was ready, help me tell Robert and Mary's story; and sure enough, when I went to the basement to clean it out, there were holes all over the floor and in the walls of the basement where my father was trying to find this mythical money. What he didn't understand, and would have never understood, was that the riches, the wealth, the treasure, was the house itself; in the history, pictures, documents and stories.

****

CHAPTER 26

During their first year in Cambridge Robert and Mary had put together a consortium of relatives and friends to pool their money together to buy land and property. Eventually, this would turn Robert Smith a colored man, one step removed from American Black slavery, by the fifth year of the turn of the century into a man of means, a man of respect, a man of some wealth. A colored man, who owned a credit union/banking business, where colored people could deposit money, save their money, and get a loan to buy a home.

The people who lived on Clarendon Avenue, Fayerweather Street, Concord Avenue, in Cambridge and North Cambridge went to St. Paul African Methodist Episcopal Church in Central Square, Cambridge, Mass., founded in 1873.

These people believed in helping one another to succeed. They believed that each one should teach one, but the main thing that they all believed in without any reservation, men and women alike, the one thing that they all agreed on, the savior of the race Booker T Washington had told them so; the one thing that could not be discriminated against, the one thing that could not be denied by any man, white man or the boogie man, was education.

A solid education, an education of worth at the best colleges and universities available and from these people would come doctors and lawyers and professors, and teachers and businessmen and dentists and professionals of all types, for generations to come. These former slaves and the children of slaves would intermarry within their various families and pave the way for their future generations, their future descendants. Well, Robert and Mary were no different, everything they were doing was for their children to come, and their children's, children to come and because they believed in themselves and in their convictions and virtues, spiritually, mentally and physically, they knew that with God's help that they and their race would persevere. Thus was the thinking of the enlightened American Black man and woman of the late 19th and early 20th century.

****

CHAPTER 27
THE GRANDCHILDREN OF SLAVES
BURLEIGH SMITH

So on November 5, 1899, into this world my Grandmére was born. Robert and Mary Smith named their baby girl, their daughter, Burleigh, Burleigh Smith. And as far as 99% of the tens of millions of poor and struggling colored people in the United States of America were concerned, she was born into the lap of luxury, at Ten Clarendon Avenue, North Cambridge, Massachusetts, to two of the best and brightest colored people in the world. The love she felt from her mother and father when she was born would have to last her for the next seventy-eight years, until the day she died, because the following year her mother would go straight from breast feeding her newborn baby girl to being pregnant again in May 1900.

At that time and for many years thereafter doctors did house calls and babies were delivered at home by midwives or and doctors and as shown by certain documents there were an inordinate amount of doctor's visits during the later months of Mary Smith's pregnancy in 1900. There is nothing to explain it, but in December 1900 Lucy Woodson and her two daughters are at Ten Clarendon Avenue, and there is nothing to explain why on a December day or night 1900 while delivering her second child, a son, Mary Smith at the age of twenty-four died in childbirth.

I do know that a prevailing sadness shown over that sweet house for many years and that Robert Smith, never married again. I do know that Lucy Woodson and a daughter moved to Ten Clarendon Avenue and for many years helped raise my Grandmére and her brother. My great-grandfather, Robert Smith, would never get over the loss of his beloved wife, the mother of his children, never, and until the day he died he mourned her loss.

My great-grandmother, Mary Smith, had known and fallen in love with Robert Smith when she was fourteen, and in their short life together, in just ten years, she was able to change the preordained, the predestined life of a Black man and woman in the south. By her will, her courage, her strength, her determination, her grace, and with her knowledge and love of education and with her mother's blessings, she was able to change the course of Robert Smith's life forever and even in her untimely and horrific death through childbirth, give her life and her love forever to her children, to her husband, all the way up to me.

It would not be easy, because through the years so much would be lost, her ideals would not pass down to my father, nor to me. I would remember my Grandmére telling me stories about her mother and how she died in childbirth, when I was a child, and as children do, you listen, but sometimes forget how important it is. But once I found her again, I realized how this young African American woman, a child, a grandchild, a great-grandchild of American Black Slavery, had made it possible for her descendants to try to have a chance at a different life, a better life. So, just as the stories of Robert and Mary told by my Grandmére would one day save me, I give her life, her story, and their love to you, who are mine.

****

CHAPTER 28

When I was about eleven years old my Grandmére wanted to take me on a train trip with her to Ohio to visit her brother. It would have been, except for going to her house in Cambridge, my first trip outside the ghetto, or anywhere. My mother and her mother, my grandmother, said no. My Grandmére begged them, I remember it till this day, because I wanted to go with her so badly, but they said no. I remember my mother and grandmother discussing it, and the reason they didn't want me to go was, *'Burleigh thinks she's something'*, that was it. *'Burleigh thinks she's something'*. That's why they wouldn't let me go.

My Grandmére tried to tell them that it would be good for me, that she would take good care of me, that she wanted her brother and his family to meet me; my Grandmére was always trying to do things like this that would help me, give me a since of the world, show me the nice side of life. But, my mother and grandmother disliked her and her ways. It was a big deal with me for a while, and I remember being upset, but it passed and life went on. I never did meet her brother, and for some reason, as far as I knew, he never visited the house he grew up in.

Soon after Mary Smith had passed on, Lucy Woodson and her daughter moved into the house to help take care of and raise my Grandmére and her brother. My Grandmére was raised in the bosom of love and knew only the best of everything. Her grandmother and aunt, spoke to her in French and her father spoke to her in English, so by the time she could talk she was fluent in both English and French. On Clarendon Avenue she had plenty of relatives and cousins to play with, some of whom many years later my sister and I would know. When we would visit Clarendon Avenue, after we got older, there would often be visiting a cousin my Grandmére's age, who my Grandmére said was cousin Romaine. Cousin Romaine was really something and you could tell that my Grandmére looked up to her. Cousin Romaine, and you could tell that like my Grandmére was once a very attractive lady. They would sit and speak French together, and express themselves in grandiose ways, waving their hands around and laughing a lot, while they sipped their Dewars White Label Blended Scotch Whiskey and smoked their cigarettes.

You could tell by watching them, that they were something from another era. When there were People of Color who were wealthy and lived as we thought White wealthy people lived. You could tell by watching them that they were from a place where Black people had manners and class and were successful, and the ladies were very light skinned like my Grandmére and Cousin Romaine were and beautiful and spoke French and were quite exquisite and very lovely young women.

You could see their youth when they talked, you could easily see where they came from and who they were. You could see them as they must have been in 1915, 1920, 1925, 1930 and 1940. I will always miss watching them. I will always miss Cousin Romaine smothering me with kisses and saying sweet things to me in French as she hugged and smothered me with kisses and smiles and smelled like perfume, cigarettes and good liqueur.

****

CHAPTER 29

Grandmére was sent to the best schools and given the best education, she was spoiled and thought that everyone lived like her or at least thought that they should live like her. She loved her life and until the day she died she lived her life as she was, a Cambridgian, a colored woman born and raised in Cambridge, a woman of class, culture, education and a good upbringing and proud of that. I loved my Grandmére and I loved everything about her, I loved who she was. While Burleigh was being raised and taught all that a young lady should know about polite New Orleans and Cambridge Colored Society, her father, Robert Smith was building his small real estate empire and auctioning and selling the fine furniture he made. He was known for his fine furniture making all over New England and people, Black and White, came from all over to purchase his hand made and hand crafted furniture.

It was a skill that he loved and I sometimes wondered if while his hands were cutting the edges of the wood or smoothing the wood down, if he was thinking of his Mary and talking to her, thinking about her. Every piece of furniture at Ten Clarendon Avenue was made by Robert Smith and was used by every descendant of Robert and Mary Smith that lived or stayed there, and that would include me. When I cleaned out the house, in 1987, I was able to rescue a number of pieces of furniture that my great grandfather made. A 19th, early 20th century handcrafted bed that my Grandmére slept in was also the bed that Robert had made and he and Mary had slept in. A number of 19th century bureaus and dressers, a late 19th century bed that I had slept on whenever I had visited my grandparents, and many antique table and chairs, there was even a Victrola, an RCA Victor Talking Machine.

I remember that the house, except for the debris that was knee high, was as though my Grandmére and Papa Ray were still living there, and would be coming home soon. It was a heartbreaking situation for me, but I cleaned out the house and got rid of the debris and moved on.

My great grandfather's real estate business and credit union flourished and he was able to by a beautiful home on Martha's Vineyard at Oaks Bluff. By the photos that I was able to rescue from the house, it looks like my Grandmére and her father, brother, grandmother, aunt, and assorted other relatives and friends spent a great deal of time at the Oaks Bluff house and beaches at Martha's Vineyard for many years during the summer and had many great times. They were very socially inclined people who were well liked and admired by their friends and all who knew them.

Burleigh Smith - 1917
Eighteen Years Old

****

CHAPTER 30

At sixteen years old, my Grandmére was introduced to Boston and Cambridge Colored Society and I'm sure that was the highlight of her life up to
that point. At eighteen she was very proud of belonging to a knitting circle
that knitted sox and gave teas for the World War One colored soldiers in
1917-1918, and she would often talk about the great service that she and
the other young ladies of her circle did for the colored servicemen going
off to war in France. When she was twenty-one years old her father sent
her to Paris to study at the Sorbonne, The University of Paris, her mother

Lucy Woodson accompanied her and they stay abroad for a summer while my Grandmére studied Art History and Costume Design. Many years later, even when I knew her, she often worked as a mannequin dresser at Bonwit Teller in downtown Boston.

But, Grandmére's main thing to do as a young girl and young lady was to act as her father's hostess at home and to socialize and be attractive at the many parties that her father gave, and she became very good at it. She gave many settees at home and was quite in demand as a dinner partner for many a young man of her social group, but, my Grandmére had a couple of serious flaws. For many years since she had been a young girl she had been going down to the Cape, to New Bedford and then to Martha's Vineyard.

On the way to the Island, over the years, she had met many new friends outside of her social group in Cambridge. These young people lived in the Cape area, in New Bedford and on the Island. She was a beautiful young woman and well known as a party girl in Cambridge and down the Cape. She loved a good time, usually drinking more alcohol than she should have. I'm sure that her father, grandmother and aunt would have been more than a bit worried about her and although they loved her very much, would have attempted to restrict her movements and outside friends, by getting her to marry one of the many suitable and eligible colored men of her social group. But a few things happened between 1922 and 1924, when my Grandmére would have been twenty-three to twenty- five. Her grandmother, Lucy LaBerge Woodson took sick and died in 1922.

This was the same Lucy LaBerge who had begun the process of moving her family out of the deep south in 1874 and had lived long enough to have seen her daughter Mary continue the migration, but had also lived long enough to have to bury the daughter she loved. She had raised Mary's daughter, her granddaughter and had enjoyed seeing the success her finances had brought to her daughter's husband, but she had died not seeing her granddaughter married to the right family, with children of her own to continue what she had begun.

There must have been a great deal of sadness at Ten Clarendon Avenue, a great deal of sorrow. My Grandmére and her brother were losing the only real mother they had ever known and their father was losing his dearest friend, his mother-in-law, the mother of the only woman he had ever loved, a woman he had known since he had been fourteen years old. A woman who had in his time of great need, come to Cambridge and helped raise his children. The woman who had believed with her daughter in the greatness of my Great-Grandfather.

There was a great sadness at Ten Clarendon Avenue and Lucy LaBerge Woodson was mourned by her family, her many friends and all who knew her, from Cambridge, Massachusetts, to Lynchburg, Virginia, to New Orleans, Louisiana. But Lucy had done her work and Mary's children had been raised well and so she died with a clean and good soul. My Grandmére was twenty-three years old and the two most important people in her life were gone. Now it was just her, her father, her aunt and her brother.

During this time, Burleigh joined the National Association of Colored Women's Clubs (NACWC). Organized in 1896. The objectives of the NACWC were as follows: To promote the education of women and children, to raise the standards of the home, to improve conditions for family living, to work for the moral, economic, social, and religious welfare of women and children, to protect the rights of women and children, to secure and enforce civil and political rights for the African-American race, to promote interracial understanding so that justice may prevail among all people.

The NACWC was a great society of women united for service to raise the standards of the home and extend their service to help make better communities. The activities and contributions of the club women help develop the quality of the life for all people, especially those in the African-American community. The NACWC adopted the motto "Lifting as We Climb" with the intention of showing "an ignorant and suspicious world that our aims and interests are identical with those of all good aspiring women." The NACWC established an ambitious and forward-thinking agenda that focused on job training, wage equity, and childcare. The organization raised funds for kindergartens, vocational schools, summer camps, and retirement homes. In addition, the NACWC opposed segregated transportation systems and was a strong and visible supporter of the anti-lynching movement. In 1912 the organization began a national scholarship fund for college-bound African-American women. During that same year, it endorsed the suffrage movement, two years before its white counterpart, the General Federation of Women's Clubs.

****

CHAPTER 31

Burleigh in the 1940's and 1950's would serve as a Vice President of the organization. She would belong to many, many colored social organizations through the years and would count among her many friends Melnea Cass. Melnea Agnes Cass was an American community and civil rights activist. She was deeply involved in many community projects and volunteer groups in the South End and Roxbury neighborhoods of Boston and helped found the Boston local of the Brotherhood of Sleeping Car Porters. Miss Cass also assisted women with voter registration after the passage of the Nineteenth Amendment. She was affectionately known as the *"First Lady of Roxbury"*.

Melnea Cass became my Grandmére's lifelong friend and together they began a lifetime of volunteer work in the local, state, and national level. They contributed their services to the Robert Gould Shaw House, a settlement house and community center. Their community activities over the years were numerous and varied: The Harriet Tubman Mothers' Club, the Sojourner Truth Club, they helped form the Boston local of the Brotherhood of Sleeping Car Porters, which is how and where Burleigh would find her lifelong partner, husband and friend, my grandfather, Papa Ray. During World War Two they helped organize the Women's Community Service Organization, and they were of course lifelong members of the National Association for the Advancement of Colored People (NAACP).

****

Founded February 12, 1909, the NAACP is the nation's oldest, largest and most widely recognized grassroots-based civil rights organization. It's more than half-million members and supporters throughout the United States and the world are the premier advocates for civil rights in their communities, campaigning for equal opportunity and conducting voter mobilization. The NAACP was formed partly in response to the continuing horrific practice of lynching and the 1908 race riot in Springfield, the capital of Illinois and resting place of President Abraham Lincoln.

Appalled at the violence that was committed against blacks, a group of white liberals that included Mary White Ovington and Oswald Garrison Villard, both the descendants of abolitionists, William English Walling and Dr. Henry Moscowitz issued a call for a meeting to discuss racial justice. Some sixty people, including W. E. B. Du Bois, Ida B. Wells-Barnett and Mary Church Terrell, attended the meeting and helped found the organization. Early members included my Great Grandfather, Robert Smith and Joel and Arthur Spingarn, Josephine Ruffin, Mary Talbert, Inez Milholland, Jane Addams, Florence Kelley, Sophonisba Breckinridge, John Haynes Holmes, Mary McLeod Bethune, George Henry White, Charles Edward Russell, John Dewey, William Dean Howells, Lillian Wald, Charles Darrow, Lincoln Steffens, Ray Stannard Baker, Fanny Garrison Villard, and Walter Sachs, and hundreds of other African Americans and European Americans.

Echoing the focus of Du Bois' Niagara Movement began in 1905, the NAACP's stated goal was to secure for all people the rights guaranteed in the 13th, 14th, and 15th Amendments to the United States Constitution, which promised an end to slavery, the equal protection of the law, and universal adult male suffrage, respectively. The NAACP's principal objective was to ensure the political, educational, social and economic equality of minority group citizens of United States and eliminate race prejudice. The NAACP sought to remove all barriers of racial discrimination through the democratic process.

The NAACP established its first national office in New York City in 1910 and named a board of directors as well as a president, Moorfield Storey, a white constitutional lawyer and former president of the American Bar Association. The only African American among the organization's executives, W. E. B. Du Bois was made director of publications and research and in 1910 established the official journal of the NAACP, The Crisis. Today, The Crisis Magazine, one of the oldest black periodicals in America, is a respected journal of thought, opinion and analysis, the magazine remains the official publication of the NAACP and is the NAACP's articulate partner in the struggle for human rights for people of color.

In time, The Crisis became a voice of the Harlem Renaissance, as Du Bois published works by Langston Hughes, Countee Cullen and other African American literary figures. Now published quarterly, The Crisis is dedicated to being an open and honest forum for discussing critical issues confronting people of color, American society and the world in addition to highlighting the historical and cultural achievements of these diverse peoples.

With a strong emphasis on local organizing, by 1913 the NAACP had established branch offices in such cities as Boston, Massachusetts; Baltimore, Maryland; Kansas City, Missouri; Washington, D.C.; Detroit, Michigan; and St. Louis, Missouri. A series of early court battles, including a victory against a discriminatory Oklahoma law that regulated voting by means of a grandfather clause

(Guinn v. United States, 1910), helped establish the NAACP's importance as a legal advocate. The fledgling organization also learned to harness the power of publicity through its 1915 battle against D. W. Griffith's inflammatory Birth of a Nation, a motion picture that perpetuated demeaning stereotypes of African Americans and glorified the Ku Klux Klan.

NAACP membership grew rapidly, from around 9,000 in 1917 to around 90,000 in 1919, with more than 300 local branches. Writer and diplomat James Weldon Johnson became the Association's first black secretary in 1920, and Louis T. Wright, a surgeon, was named the first black chairman of its board of directors in 1934. The NAACP waged a 30-year campaign against lynching, among the Association's top priorities. After early worries about its constitutionality, the NAACP strongly supported the federal Dyer Bill, which would have punished those who participated in or failed to prosecute lynch mobs. Though the bill would pass the U.S. House of Representatives, the Senate never passed the bill, or any other anti-lynching legislation. Most credit the resulting public debate-fueled by the NAACP report "Thirty Years of Lynching in the United States, 1889-1919"-with drastically decreasing the incidence of lynching.

Johnson stepped down as secretary in 1930 and was succeeded by Walter F. White. White was instrumental not only in his research on lynching (in part because, as a very fair-skinned African American, he had been able to infiltrate white groups), but also in his successful block of segregationist Judge John J. Parker's nomination by President Herbert Hoover to the U.S. Supreme Court. White presided over the NAACP's most productive period of legal advocacy. In 1930 the association commissioned the Margold Report, which became the basis for the successful reversal of the separate-but-equal doctrine that had governed public facilities since 1896's Plessy v. Ferguson.

In 1935 White recruited Charles H. Houston as NAACP chief counsel. Houston was the Howard University law school dean whose strategy on school-segregation cases paved the way for his protégé Thurgood Marshall to prevail in 1954's Brown v. Board of Education, the decision that overturned Plessy.

During the Great Depression of the 1930s, which was disproportionately disastrous for African Americans, the NAACP began to focus on economic justice. After years of tension with white labor unions, the Association cooperated with the newly formed Congress of Industrial Organizations in an effort to win jobs for black Americans. White, a friend and adviser to First Lady--and NAACP national board member--Eleanor Roosevelt, met with her often in attempts to convince President Franklin D. Roosevelt to outlaw job discrimination in the armed forces, defense industries and the agencies spawned by Roosevelt's New Deal legislation.

Roosevelt ultimately agreed to open thousands of jobs to black workers when labor leader A. Philip Randolph, in collaboration with the NAACP, threatened a national March on Washington movement in 1941. President Roosevelt also agreed to set up a Fair Employment Practices Committee (FEPC) to ensure compliance. Throughout the 1940s the NAACP saw enormous growth in membership, recording roughly 600,000 members by 1946. It continued to act as a legislative and legal advocate, pushing for a federal anti-lynching law and for an end to state-mandated segregation.

By the 1950s the NAACP Legal Defense and Educational Fund, headed by Marshall, secured the last of these goals through Brown v. Board of Education (1954), which outlawed segregation in public schools. The NAACP's Washington, D.C., bureau, led by lobbyist Clarence M. Mitchell Jr., helped advance not only integration of the armed forces in 1948 but also passage of the Civil Rights Acts of 1957, 1964, and 1968, as well as the Voting Rights Act of 1965.

Despite such dramatic courtroom and congressional victories, the implementation of civil rights was a slow, painful, and oft times violent. The unsolved 1951 murder of Harry T. Moore, an NAACP field secretary in Florida whose home was bombed on Christmas night, and his wife was just one of many crimes of retribution against the NAACP and its staff and members.

NAACP Mississippi Field Secretary Medgar Evers and his wife Myrlie also became high-profile targets for pro-segregationist violence and terrorism. In 1962, their home was firebombed and later Medgar was assassinated by a sniper in front of their residence following years of investigations into hostility against blacks and participation in non-violent demonstrations such as sit-ins to protest the persistence of Jim Crow segregation throughout the south.

Violence also met black children attempting to enter previously segregated schools in Little Rock, Arkansas, and other southern cities. Throughout the south many African Americans were still denied the right to register and vote. The Civil Rights Movement of the 1950s and 1960s echoed the NAACP's goals, but leaders such as Martin Luther King Jr., of the Southern Christian Leadership Conference, felt that direct action was needed to obtain them.

Although it was criticized for working exclusively within the system by pursuing legislative and judicial solutions, the NAACP did provide legal representation and aid to members of other protest groups over a sustained period of time. The NAACP even posted bail for hundreds of Freedom Riders in the '60s who had traveled to Mississippi to register black voters and challenge Jim Crow policies. Led by Roy Wilkins, who succeeded Walter White as secretary in 1955, the NAACP, along with A. Philip Randolph, Bayard Rustin and other national organizations began to plan the 1963 March on Washington.

With the passage of major civil rights legislation, the following year, the Association accomplished what seemed an insurmountable task. In the following years and into the 21st century, the NAACP has been focused on disparities in economics, health care, education, voter empowerment and the criminal justice system while also continuing its role as legal advocate for civil rights issues. While much of NAACP history is chronicled in books, articles, pamphlets and magazines, the true movement lies in the faces--the diverse multiracial army of ordinary women and men from every walk of life, race and class--united to awaken the consciousness of a people and a nation. The NAACP will remain vigilant in its mission until the promise of America is made real for all Americans.

****

CHAPTER 32

My Grandmére's social consciousness would stay with her all her life and even under great adversity, from the pain my father and her drinking would cause her, she would always find a way to help someone, have a kind word for everyone, and her faith in God's eternal love and guidance would be with her forever. But for now, she was content to tend to her social obligations and be the woman of her father's house and then in 1924 just like that, without any warning, without any sickness, without a word to her, without telling her what to do, how to take care of everything, how to take care of herself, how to live without him. Her father, the illustrious Robert Smith, who had walked out of Lynchburg, Virginia with his beloved Mary LaBerge Smith, thirty-one years before, died, just like that, at fifty years old in 1924, without telling her.

****

CHAPTER 33

When I was a child starting at about nine years old my Grandmére was allowed to come to the projects and visit my sister and me. She would come and bring her own tea bags and teacup. I remember this because it would infuriate my mother and she would be angry and talk about it long after my Grandmére had left.

One time when she visited she brought a bank that looked like the solar system with the round part of the bank where the coins went as the sun and steel rods sticking out from the sun as planets orbiting it. She instructed me on how to use the bank, what it was for, and how important it was to save any money that I got. Soon after I began to put my paperboy coins and dollar bills in it and soon after I began to notice that my bank was being robbed by my mother. It took me a few months to realize that the only reason my mother was letting me keep the gift from my Grandmére was so that she could take money from it whenever she wanted to.

Another time when she came she wanted me to learn something called the 23rd Psalm. She gave me a small Bible and read the prayer with me for a while and the said she would give me a dollar if by the next time she came, I could recite it from memory. The next time that she came I recited the Lord's Prayer, The Twenty Third Psalm, "*The Lord is my Shepherd; I shall not want. He maketh me to lie down in green pastures: he leadeth me beside the still waters. He restoreth my soul: he leadeth me in the paths of righteousness for his name's sake. Yea, though I walk through the valley of the shadow of death, I will fear no evil: for thou art with me; thy rod and staff they comfort me. Thou preparest a table before me in the presence of mine enemies: thou anointest my head with oil; my cup runneth over. Surely goodness and mercy shall follow me all the days of my life: and I will dwell in the house of the Lord forever.*"

Another time when she came, she brought me a red transistor radio in a brownish leather cover. I was ten years old and it was the most important gift that I would ever receive. A Transistor Radio in 1960 was the latest thing, it was like getting a smart phone is today. My Grandmére gave me the Transistor Radio as a secret. When my mother went into her bedroom she told me not to tell my mother that I had it. Transistor Radios were small and could fit in your pocket, it also had an earplug that went from the radio into your ear and the first time I put the earplug in my ear and turned the radio on, the world of music entered my head for the very first time. My mother hardly ever changed my bed or changed my sheets or pillow cases so I kept my Transistor Radio under my pillow at night, where I lay on it and listened to Arnie "Woo" Ginsberg at WMEX all night long for three years, until my mother found it and threw it out. But that Transistor Radio would be the beginning of my music career.

Another time just before my Grandmére came when I was still ten years old, I learned that I would be going, for the first time, back to Cambridge with her to stay with her for a week. When she came, she was as she always was so happy to see me, and with her was this little black puppy. She told me that the puppy was mine, but that he would have to stay at her house, but that he was mine and when I stayed at her house I would have to take care of him. And then, for the very first time, my Grandmére and I walked out of my apartment together. It was in the winter, because I remember that I had a coat and hood on and that she wore a coat that was furry and shiny, and with my puppy which I held, we walked across the courtyard to Tremont Street and up Tremont Street where all the Trolley Cars and Electric Busses converged. It was a short walk from the projects and we rode up Tremont Street together towards Downtown Boston. I remember that we got off the bus and went underground to the train and on the train I remember my Grandmére asking me had I decided on a name for my puppy and I told her that I wanted to call him Paws, because he had big feet for such a little dog and she laughed and smiled and said that was a good name. I can still see us together in the train window opposite us as we are riding together all three of us, and I see my Grandmére with her arm around me and I'm bundled up in my coat and she is holding me close and at that moment I know that she is the only person in the whole world who truly loves me.

We get off the train together and for the first time I am in Harvard Square, Cambridge with my Grandmére. We wait for and get on an Electric Bus that will take us up Massachusetts Avenue to another the Electric Bus Depot, we get off the Electric Bus, and walk about three short blocks up Massachusetts Avenue and take a right onto Clarendon Avenue. We walk close together and it is the first house on the street, on the right hand side as you walk up from Mass. Ave, and turn right. We walk up the steps to the front door together and we are at Ten Clarendon Avenue, and she unlocks the door opens it and I am home with my Grandmére and my new puppy, Paws.

Ten Clarendon Avenue, North Cambridge, Mass. The front room. - 1953

On the parlor chair is my Grandmére, (Mrs. Burleigh LaBerge-Smith-Rose-Chisholm), sitting beside her is my Papa Ray. (Ralph Chisholm). Sitting directly behind her is Grandmére's friend from up the street on Clarendon Avenue, (Mrs. Alexis Audet). Sitting behind her on the couch is my mother. (Mrs. Muriel Faulk-Rose). I am very happy in the front and I am two years old.

****

CHAPTER 34

Ten Clarendon Avenue when I knew it in the fifties, sixties and seventies was probably much as it was when my great grandparents lived there. It was a small tidy house, one of a few dozens like it on the street, a clapboard type house with shingles, all architecturally designed and built by my great grandfather. When you walked in the door you walked into a small foyer, to your right was a large mirror with five hangers for coats, to your imme-diate left there was a stairway that took you to the second floor and then a stairway up to the attic, in six years that stairway to the attic would be the cause of my banishment from the house, straight ahead was the kitchen where Papa Ray who was a head chef on the Boston to Chicago train line, loved to cook.

My Grandmére was known to hardly ever cook, because Papa Ray, who was a world class cook did all the cooking when he was home. In the kitchen was a small green kitchen table, a stove, a small 50's style refrigerator and a sink area facing the house next door, to the immediate left when you walked into the kitchen was a door that led to the basement. There was a very well stocked pantry in the kitchen on the right side of the kitchen table and to the left of the kitchen table that was against the back wall, was a small foyer that led outside to the porch. I can still hear the chimes on the porch, because that's how I always knew I was at my Grandmére's house, I had been hearing those chimes since I was a little baby, a little child, and those chimes always told me that I was somewhere safe.

The chimes hung down from an overhang on the porch and there were at least fifty of them, they were beautiful, I love chimes to this day. During my one week in the summer when I would visit my Grandmére, I used to sit on the porch and take a deep breath. It was similar to when you're in combat and then you go on R&R and take a deep breath before you have to go back in to combat, well that's what it was. Although I never told her, I think my Grandmére knew what was happening to me in the projects, at my mother's apartment. I think she knew that I was slowly being destroyed and she was trying her best to save me. The 23rd Psalm, the Transistor Radio, the bank, her love and her home were all her ways of trying to fight off what was happening to me, and in ways that I wouldn't know even until this very day, it worked. As I've said before, most Black ghetto kids' grandparents lived in the ghetto right along with them, the thing that saved me, the thing that showed me another life, another way, was that my Grandmére didn't live in the ghetto.

****

CHAPTER 35

When my Grandmére and I would walk down the five steps from the porch to the backyard we would be in her favorite area of the house. On one side of the backyard was her tomato, vegetable and flower garden and on the other side was her well-manicured lawn and patio area. She would have on her colorful garden clothes and floppy hat and work long hours in her garden. She and I would pick fresh tomatoes and radishes for our lunch and talk together. It was a beautiful garden, her pride and joy. My Grandmére gave me a party at her house for my tenth birthday. It was held in the garden and all my Cambridge cousins, my sister and my Roxbury cousins were invited and came.

Before I left with my Grandmére, my mother had told me that she thought that my father was out of jail and that I was not to speak to him or go anywhere with him, should he be there. Well, all during the party I felt like someone was watching me and then I saw him, he was peeking behind a wall at me, just looking at me. I made believe that I didn't see him, but I was so happy to see him, and I could tell that my Grandmére was happy that he was seeing me. I was ten-years-old and I hadn't seen him in four years, but I had to keep making believe that I didn't see him and he couldn't approach me because of something called a court order. But, he was there and that's all that mattered. It would be five years and I would be fifteen-years-old in 1966 when I would see him again. But for now he was there and my tenth birthday party outside in my Grandmére's garden was something I will always remember.

She loved having settees and parties in her backyard. But, my Grandmére's everlasting and forever main claim to perpetual and eternal fame, with all of Cambridge and Boston, was that, Rose Kennedy had personally selected Burleigh Smith Rose Chisholm to host in her home and garden, teas and lunches in Cambridge for her son, Jack Kennedy, when he ran for the office of Senator from Massachusetts in 1952, which he, of course, won. The photo of her, Senator and soon to be President of the United States of America, John Fitzgerald Kennedy, and Rose Kennedy in her garden would be the first thing you saw when you entered her home. Among her peer group in Cambridge and Boston, Burleigh would become famous for those Rose Kennedy Teas; and until the day she died, boy, did she work it for all it was worth. Grandmére would say, when she was drinking her Dewars White Label Blended Scotch Whiskey and smoking her Parliament Cigarettes, *I remember when Rose said to me…*, or *Jack was just so funny when he asked me how did I get my tomato's so plump.*

When Papa Ray was on the road, we would sit there together in the living room with the soft couch, chairs and cabinet that her mother and father had sat on and the photos in the cabinet that her father had taken in the late nineteenth century and early twentieth century, photo albums that I could never get enough of looking at. The photo cabinet was next to the dining room and the dining room table that her father had made that was next to the kitchen, and Grandmére would sit and tell me all kinds of secrets and stories about her life.

Sometimes she would get up and slowly and sadly make her way to the steps and grasp the hard dark wood banisters that her father had built and pull herself up the stairs one step at a time, so that she could take a nap in the bed that her father had handmade. Upstairs at the top of the stairs it opened into a rounded area with the bathroom on your left, Papa Ray's room to the left of the bathroom, my Grandmére's room straight ahead and my room when I was there in between their bedrooms.

Every room in the house, the hallways, the staircases, except for the kitchen, had different styles of wallpaper on the walls, with a hard dark brown wood at the door openings and around the edges of the walls and staircase. The attic was pretty bare except for the treasures I would find and a cot where I guess my Dad slept when he was between women and not in jail. That same attic would be the scene of my disgrace some years later.

The house was simply beautiful, and although not as big as some houses in Cambridge could be, it was big enough that my Housing Project Apartment could fit in the kitchen and dining room, with room for the bathroom, and that was plenty big enough for me. But, this was not my true life. For 51 weeks out of the year I was in the projects at my mother's house, 159 Cabot Street, Apartment 157, The Whittier Street Housing Projects. I was just there a week in the summers of 1960, 1961 and 1962, and assorted visits during the years. In 1963 and 1964 I was at Adams Pond Boy Scout Camp with Mr. Hector, and by the summer of 1965 at fourteen-years-old I found girls and the gangs found me.

****

CHAPTER 36

There must have been a great deal of consternation, trauma and sadness upon the sudden death of Robert Smith, my Great Grandfather, he had succeeded against great odds and built a small fortune, but his daughter didn't know how he had done this and his many business partners and credit union shareholders didn't know what to do about Burleigh, who it looked like was going to inherit everything.

Burleigh although adverse in the ways of giving money to charities and social organizations and spending money on her many parties and fineries, simply did not know how to run a business and make money. She was twenty-four, soon to be twenty-five, not married and now she was totally alone. In the course of her twenty- four years she had lost her mother, her father and her grandmother and except for her aunt who was now in her sixties, she was alone and expected to bury her father and tend to his business and his partners.

The loss of her father was devastating to one and all and he was mourned in death as he was celebrated in life, as a great man, a father, a man of principal, a great businessman, a carpenter, a creative wood loving spirit. As the son, grandson, great-grandson, great, great-grandson, great, great, great, great, great, great-grandson of American Black Slaves, who had toiled, lived and died under the lash in the tobacco fields of Virginia for one hundred and fifty years. As a man who in his short fifty years had provided homes, land and businesses to family, friends and people all over the Greater Boston, Roxbury and Cambridge area, a man born to American Black Slaves, with nothing, who would rise to the heights of Cambridge, Boston and Martha's Vineyard-Oaks Bluff Colored Society.

So now there was a burial to be had and Burleigh did the best she could do under these terrible conditions. A child having to bury their parent isn't unusual but she was only twenty-four and all the people she had known and depended on, except for her aunt were gone, and she would do for her father what he had done for her, her best, and she buried her father from St. Paul African Methodist Episcopal Church in Central Square, Cambridge, Massachusetts with all the aplomb her father deserved. Colored people and White people who had respected her father's business acumen came from all over New England to pay their final respects and then after he was laid to rest, Burleigh for all practical purposes was alone at Ten Clarendon Avenue.

****

CHAPTER 37
THE GRANDCHILDREN OF SLAVES
THE SOCIALITE & THE CAPE VERDEAN

There was some effort made to include Burleigh in the business dealings, and Burleigh made some effort to learn the business, but after a year she had enough and found her way back to what she enjoyed most, socializing and charity work, with an emphasis on the socializing. At the age of twenty-five, in 1925, Burleigh was a very attractive, even beautiful young woman, she was between 5' 4" and 5' 6" inches tall and never weighed more than 117-125 pounds. She had long wavy hair and the most beautiful smile you could imagine. She was smart, quick, inventive, haughty, intemperate, loved to laugh, drink, party, and was a total snob. She could be kind and very considerate to those who truly needed her, but had no love, no quarter, for those she felt, especially those, uneducated, uncouth, common, loud, stupid, illiterate, unwashed, poor, begging and ignorant, Colored People, who she felt should and could do better for themselves. Not realizing that when she drank she was uncouth, a little loud and common.

Unfortunately, she had a quick temper and a quicker mouth for those she felt were beneath her and deserved her contempt. She had inherited property and some wealth, was Colored Rich and the houses she lived in at Ten Clarendon Avenue and visited at Oaks Bluff, Martha's Vineyard were all paid for and all hers. Yes, Burleigh was quite something and she knew it. But, in the eyes of her social group, her peers, she was an unmarried woman and alone, with no children, twenty-five years old and all felt that something needed to be done about Burleigh Smith. But, and I'll take a minor stretch here, Burleigh, being the forerunner of my father and me, if she was anything like my father and me, she was looking for some hot passionate love, some real sex, and she was finding it lacking in the grad school, medical school, pre-law, second year law school, going to be business men, doctors, lawyers, boys and men of her social group, and because of that, her hot behind would cause a ripple that would be the undoing of all that Robert and Mary Smith had done and that would be her, my dad's, mine, my sister's and those of mine to come, dilemma and undoing. Something I would have to try, and not quite get there, but try and then get there ninety years later. But, for now Burleigh was hot-blooded, and that thirst was not going to be quenched in the society pages of Colored Boston, Cambridge or Oaks Bluff.

While socializing with her friends down the Cape in New Bedford, Massachusetts, she met a young man from Falmouth, Massachusetts named Frederick Rose. He was a beautiful Cape Verdean, as were many of her friends in the New Bedford, Cape Cod area, and he was as far from her social class in Cambridge, Boston and Oaks Bluff, Martha's Vineyard as you could possibly get.

****

Of the Cape Verde or the Republic of Cabo Verde, 499,413 inhabitants and some 500,000 people of Cape Verdean Ancestry who live in the United States, mainly in New England, the largest segment is defined as mestiço and 81% of the population of Cape Verde is also classified as such. The great majority of the current Cape Verdean populations descend from the mixing of the Portuguese that initially settled the islands from the 15th century onwards and the Black African Slave Women brought from the African mainland, primarily West Africa, to work as slaves.

In Portuguese-speaking Africa, the term mestiço is used officially to describe people of mixed Portuguese and African ancestry.

In 1442, the head of the Catholic Church, Pope Eugenius IV gave Portugal the right to explore Africa. This right was 'exclusive', which meant that no other countries were allowed to explore and exploit Africa. The Portuguese were exploring the coastline of Africa, but it was costing them money. They wanted to protect their new discoveries, especially from the Spanish, who were also starting to explore Africa. At this time, leaders of the Catholic Church in Europe were opposed to the Islamic religion, practiced by Muslims. Southern Spain was occupied by Muslims, and the Catholic Church felt threatened by this. Pope Nicholas V in 1452, as part of the fight against Islam, gave the Portuguese king the right to enslave people who were not Christian. This was used by the Portuguese to enslave Black Africans.

Cape Verde or officially the Republic of Cabo Verde, is an island country spanning an archipelago of 10 volcanic islands in the central Atlantic Ocean. Located 350 miles) off the coast of West Africa, the islands cover a combined area of slightly over 1,500 square miles.

Portuguese explorers discovered and colonized the uninhabited islands in the 15th century, the first European settlement in the tropics, ideally located for the

Atlantic slave. According to Portuguese official records, the first discoveries were made by Genoa-born António de Noli, who was afterwards appointed governor of Cape Verde by Portuguese King Afonso V. In 1462, Portuguese settlers arrived at Santiago and founded a settlement they called Ribeira Grande now called Cidade Velhas, Ribeira Grande was the first permanent European settlement in the tropics. Diogo Afonso is credited with the discovery of Santo Antao, Sao Vicente and Sao Nicolau.

To encourage settlement and investment, the colonists were given exclusive trading rights along the Portuguese-controlled West African coast and its rivers in 1466. The Colonists took slaves from the African Mainland to develop the land and by 1582 there were over 25,000 slaves working the land on Santiago and Fogo.

The Cape Verde Islands played a pivotal role in the transatlantic Slave Trade. European colonization of the new world required a labor force to exploit the land and was a ready market for the cheapest labor of all, slaves. Along with goods, the Portuguese also had exclusive rights to the trade in slaves from the West African coast. Apart from this legal necessity for the slaves to pass through the Cape Verde slave markets, the Islands also offered slave traders several advantages over direct trade with the African coast. The hardship of imprisonment and the sea journey from the African mainland would have already killed many of the weaker slaves, meaning that a higher proportion would survive the cramped Atlantic crossing. Secondly, the slaves that were for sale in Ribeira Grande would have received some domestication by the whip and learned some Portuguese. The traders also avoided having to trade directly on the African coast with the perils that would have entailed. Initially, the Slave Trade made Ribiera Grande rich and it became the first European City in the tropics.

The first Portuguese Settlers on the Cape Verde Islands, who were mostly White males, mixed with the Black African Women Slaves that they had brought to work the land on the Islands and for the first two hundred years of Cape Verdean Slavery, from 1462 to 1662, White Males brutally, horrifically and savagely raped and sodomized hundreds of thousands of Black African Slave Women. In the Middle East and Asia, it took a Black African walking out of Africa mixing with Neanderthal Man, sixty thousand years to mutate to a lighter color and in Western, Northern and Eastern Europe it took a Black African walking out of Africa mixing with the Neanderthal Man and other early humanoids, one hundred thousand years to mutate into a White person. In Cape Verde it only took two hundred years for the Portuguese to turn a whole country into primarily light skinned African people. The Spanish and Portuguese White men would brutally, rape and sodomize millions of Black African Slave Women and do this in numerous, numerous, countries including Santo Domingo, Brazil, Puerto Rico, the Dominican Republic and Cuba, in this they were no different than the French, the English, the Dutch, the Germans, the Italians, and most Western European Countries, except Ireland.

Lancados, children of Portuguese slave traders were used as middle men on the mainland of Africa and facilitated the capture and trade of Black Africans to Cape Verde. These Africans would have been brought to Santiago or Fogo where they were, presumably, then sold and/or transported to the Americas.

Cape Verde was once the hub of the slave trade. White Slave traders from the America's would travel to the islands and purchase slaves who were "seasoned" or baptized and given Christian names. Cape Verdeans participated in the trading and transportation of slaves, as well, mostly to the Caribbean, Central and South America, although there are records of some who transported the slaves to North America.

On the island of Maio, salt was being mined and sold on the open market. Passport records exist of men traveling to the island with numbers of slaves who were actually identified by name. Slaves were used in the mining of salt primarily, until Manuel Antonio Martins established his salt mines on the island of Sal which included the first rail system in Africa by the early 1800's. This rail system was also built by enslaved Black African men.

Ribeira Grande – later called Cidade Velha – became the most important slave trade harbor for a century. In addition, cane sugar and rum was produced and exported, cotton cultivated and processed and meat was sold from the livestock in Maio as supplies for the slave ships.

A new territorial dispute broke out after the discovery of America in 1492. With the mediation of the Pope and the Catholic Church in 1494, the competitors of Spain and Portugal agreed on a new boundary line in the treaty of Tordesilhas: 370 sea miles west of Cape Verde from the North Pole to the South Pole. The territory to the east of the line was granted to Portugal and the region to the west of the line to Spain.

In 1493 Pope Alexander VI divided the world between Spain and Portugal. A line was drawn on the map down through the Atlantic Ocean. Portugal was allowed to explore and trade on one side, in the 'old' world and Spain on the other, in the 'new' world. This was designed to stop the two European countries from competing over parts of the world that they wanted to explore and trade with. Spain had the Americas, where Africans were needed to supply the labor. The Spanish could not go to Africa to buy enslaved Africans. The agreement stated that only Portugal was allowed to trade with Africa. Spanish landowners in the Americas had to buy from Portuguese or other slave traders. The first slaves were intended for the goldmines on the Spanish-owned Caribbean island of Hispaniola (which is now divided into the countries of Haiti and the Dominican Republic).

The Spanish government in 1518 introduced the asiento, to supply the new colonies with slave labor. The asiento was a licence to supply a given number of slaves. The Spanish authorities sold the asiento to the highest bidder, and the money went to the Spanish king and queen. The merchant who bought the licence could buy slaves in Africa and sell them in the Spanish Americas. They hoped to get back the money they spent on the licence, and make a good profit. The merchant could also make money by selling shares in the licence to other merchants. Any Spanish licence holders had to arrange delivery of the enslaved Africans by Portuguese traders. This was because Spanish ships could not legally go to Africa, as only the Portuguese could trade there. As Spain and Portugal were at that time on good terms, arrangements for the purchase and sale of slaves were easily made between the two countries.

The asiento, or licence to sell slaves, was often sold to foreign merchants rather than Spanish. It went to whoever was prepared to pay most money to get the licence. Often this meant that Portuguese, Dutch, German, British or Genoese merchants were supplying slaves to the Spanish colonies. From 1550 to 1595, the official records show that 236,300 enslaved Africans were imported into the Spanish-owned parts of South America. The number was probably much higher, as more were smuggled in by slave traders who did not hold a licence to supply slaves.

The numbers of enslaved Africans needed rose as the new colonies developed. More land was cleared for sugar plantations, new areas were found where gold and silver could be mined.

Often, the merchants who bought the asiento were, for some reason, unable to supply the slaves required. In 1676 a group of merchants in Seville in Spain (including women investors) bought the asiento or licence. They found that they could not supply the number of slaves agreed and withdrew early from the contract. The Cadiz Slave Company, from Spain, bid for the asiento in 1767.

They agreed to supply 80,000 slaves per year to the Spanish plantations. They also found that they could not buy enough slaves each year to fulfil the contract.

In 1713, war between Britain and Spain was ended. By the terms of the peace agreement, Britain took over the asiento. Britain was given the contract to supply the Spanish colonies in South America with slaves for 30 years. The contract was later sold by the British government to the newly-formed, British-owned, South Sea Company. This company had been formed to sell merchandise to the Spanish colonies. The contract was to supply 40,800 slaves each year for 30 years. They also had to pay the King of Spain 33½ pesos (the peso was worth about 4/6d or 22 pence) for each slave supplied, plus an advance of 200,000 pesos. The Company was made up entirely of London merchants. Bristol's merchants were put out by this exclusion from a profitable trade. There were Bristol people who invested money into the South Sea Company though. One was Mary Baker, who owned £300 worth of the company (about £ 15,000 today). Another Bristol investor, Abraham Elton II, also owned shares.

Bristol merchants felt excluded by the South Sea Company's contract to supply slaves to Spanish-owned colonies in the Americas. However, they were still involved in this part of the slave trade. The demand for slaves in Spanish-owned South America helped to set the level of Bristol's slave sales in the 1730's and early 1740's. The British-owned Caribbean island of Jamaica was a convenient place for slaves to be brought to and sold from. British slave traders would supply slaves from Africa to the Spanish colonies in South America, via the island of Jamaica. Many Bristol merchants traded with Jamaica. This meant that many enslaved Africans were shipped to Jamaica in Bristol-owned ships, and later sold on to the Spanish colonies in South America. The Bristol merchants were probably selling slaves to Spanish America illegally, because the South Sea Company was supposed to be the only supplier.

In the 1730s, sugar prices were low. If sugar was not selling well, plantation owners were not likely to be buying more slaves. Yet Bristol slave traders were importing record numbers of enslaved Africans into Jamaica. This suggests that selling slaves on to Spanish merchants through Jamaica, kept Bristol involved in the slave trade.

Some Bristol ships traded directly with South America, without selling their slaves in Jamaica. The Pilgrim in 1787 left Bristol for Africa and Buenos Aires, in Argentina. At Bonny, or along the West African coast, the captain purchased 421 slaves. The Pilgrim then sailed directly from Africa to Montevideo in Uruguay and Buenos Aires and returned to Bristol via Santander in Spain.

In the late 18th century, Britain acquired the colony of Demerara, now part of the country of Guyana, on the north coast of South America. Merchants in Bristol joined the new trade to Demerara's sugar plantations. Between 1770 and 1807, twelve Bristol ships took slaves to Demerara. The ship the Alert made 3 voyages with a few thousands of enslaved Africans in 1796, 1800 and 1804. The ship the Swift also made three voyages between 1800 and 1804. The Minerva in 1802 was reported to have 1000 prime Chantee (Asante), Fantee and Coromantee African slaves on board.

It is estimated that about 100,000,000 enslaved Black Africans arrived alive in the Americas over the whole period of the transatlantic slave trade from the 15th century to 1807.

****

CHAPTER 38

Frederick Rose was a very, very handsome young man with swarthy, olive tone skin. A sinister, some would say sexy wolf look on his angular face. He oozed danger and looked like he had an attitude that said, 'I could give a fuck'. He was a light-skinned Portuguese *mestiço*, a descendant of Black African Slaves, probably about 6" 1', because my father was 5" 11', of hard muscle, in the prime of his youth. He was very handsome and in the only photo I ever saw of him, he had a hat on. The back of the photo said 1926 and I found it on the floor in the attic at my Grandmére's house in 1987. I knew it was him because he looked exactly like my dad, Frederick B. Rose and a little like me. So as soon as I picked the picture up off the floor I knew that it was him, the mystery man, the man nobody, that was still living, had ever seen. The man that had my Grandmére still crying out softly and talking about him, to me, forty years later and I would bet that the second before she died, it wasn't Papa Ray or my Dad or me she was thinking of. I would bet it was the first Mr. Rose, 'that's who she called him'. I bet in that last second of her life, it was the first Mr. Rose that she had her last thought about.

He had been a whaler, like his father and his father and his father before him. He was a seafaring man, a man of Nantucket, of Cape Verde, of New Bedford, of the High Seas; a man who knew his way around the ladies in a few countries, and he was still just twenty-four-years-old.

****

Before the American Revolutionary War, New England whaling ships were sailing off the Cape Verde Islands and picking up crewmen from the Islands and from the West Coast of Africa. A large population of the best harpooners, steersmen, and all round whale men had for long been Portuguese-speaking Africans....In almost all the crews, the African figured very prominently and those from Portuguese West Africa proved particularly outstanding as whalemen. These crewmen, known collectively as Bravas, usually far surpassed all others of whatever racial or national origin.

Yankee and Quaker whaling ship owners, known for their frugality, actually preferred to recruit men in Cape Verde where the men worked hard to save what they could while on board the vessel and they could be hired for much less money than American seamen. Furthermore, they made a disciplined crew."

For a poor boy in the drought stricken Cape Verde Islands, obtaining a berth on an American ship was a dream come true. Already during the first decades of the nineteenth century, three-eighths of the crews of the Nantucket whaling ships were "mestiço."

The shanty town where they lived on the outskirts of the town of Nantucket Island came to be known as "Guinea-Town" or "New Guinea" after the Guinea Coast of West Africa. From about 1825 to 1875, an average of 100 whaling ships per year called at the Cape Verde Islands for supplies, men, and recreation.

The white whalers in turn often contracted venereal disease on the Cape Verde islands; hereditary syphilis was reported in Brava, Fogo, Sao Vicente and Saotiago. Already in 1885, John Rich aboard the Nancy out of Boston wrote, we diverted ourselves with the inhabitants of the islands. The chronicler of the voyage of the ship Hannibal spoke of negro women who talked to us many smutty English words making lascivious, indecent gestures with their bodies, which were all naked. The 1849 logbook of the Mattapoisett records the crew went ashore drinking spirits and playing with the wenches. The author of the journal kept aboard the Chili found the rest of them in a little shanty discussing the merits of the aquadients. The Captain of the Richmond finding them intoxicated and very disobedient and threatening to kill the first man that came to rescue them. The whalers frequently took aboard escaped slaves and criminal fugitives which greatly upset the Portuguese authorities.

Whaling itself was horrific for the whales and their calfs with whole whale foetuses being torn from their mothers' bodies and a brutal, bloody and risky occupation for the whalemen. Until the beginning of the twentieth-century, whaling was considered an admirable occupation. Oil was needed for light and lubrication; baleen was needed for skirt hoops and corset stays. That whales had to die to provide these and many, many other things are a fact of seventeenth, eighteenth and nineteenth century life.

The head of the sperm whale was very valuable. It was separated into three parts: The "case," at the top of the whale's head. Tons of the purest oil was scooped from the case with buckets. This oil, known as spermaceti, hardened into a white waxy substance that was worth three to five times more than other whale-oil. Up to 500 gallons of the liquid wax might be scooped from the head of a large sperm whale. The "junk" or lower half of the forehead, which contained more oil, was cut into horse pieces and tried out separately. Although oil from the junk was not as valuable as the spermaceti from the case, it was considered superior to the rest of the whale's blubber. The jaw and teeth were saved for scrimshaw carving by the crew.

An enraged eighty-five foot whale could smash a small whale boat to kindling, killing the crew instantly or dumping them into the sea to be drowned or to be eaten by sharks. Accidents were frequent aboard whaling ships, and the Cape Verdean 'hands' did not always escape injury.

The mate in charge of one of the whale boats dropped from the Pedro Varela with a crew of greenhorns was a Black man. When we get up 'long side the whale, he shouted, those of you out here for the first time'll want to jump overboard on the side opposite the whale. Well don't do it! STAY IN THE BOAT! The mate steered the frail craft so as to come up behind the big sperm whale, over the dangerous flukes (tail) of the whale. In the bow, the boatsteerer, a Cape Verdean named Antonio, stood poised with the harpoon, ready to hurl it. Suddenly the whale spouted a jet of water and moved to dive. Antonio drove his harpoon deep into the whale and let out a shout of Fasto! The mate gave a quick command Stern All as all crew members pushed hard on their oars to get away from the whale. The tail of the whale rose and flukes smacked the water where the whale boat had been a few seconds before.

The whale surfaced and started to tow the boat at an incredible speed. Whalemen came to call this spine chilling experience a Nantucket sleigh ride. Frequently, boats were overturned as they were pulled through the waves or a man might catch his hand in the line being let out and lose it. The boatsteerer continuously poured water over the rope to prevent the wood from burning and stood by with an axe to cut the line if the whale decided to dive. After half an hour of being towed miles away from the mother ship, the whale slowed down and the whale boat quietly rowed up to the giant sea monster to hurl the fatal lance.

The whale instantly became enraged and smashed his flukes several times against the surface of the water trying to destroy his attackers, before he dove again. The mate directed the crew to look down in the water; suddenly the enormous head appeared below the surface a hundred feet from the boat Stern ALL! The crew pushed hard as the boat jumped back and the whale shot out of the water directly in front of the skiff. The mate plunged another lance into him, as they maneuvered the boat out of the whale's path. The whale made one more attempt to smash the boat but this time the mate's lance reached the lungs and the water slowly turned red.

After killing the whale came the drudgery. "Of all the ungainly things to tow," said one whaleman, "a dead sperm whale is the worst. You could stick your oar two or three times into the same hole in the ocean before making any progress." Then the blubber had to be stripped off the whale before the sharks got to it. This was also dangerous work. The blubber was then boiled in large kettles aboard ship. For each whale killed, the men had to toil for several days cutting, stoking the furnace, covered with the whale oil, choked with smoke.

Whaling was also monotonous work, in addition to being dirty and dangerous. For weeks, even months, no whales would be seen. The crew would repair the gear and carve scrimshaw to pass the time. During the periods of calm, food and water became foul and fights among the crew often broke out because of the heat. Captains were reluctant to enter major ports for fear that their crews would desert them. They often stayed away from home port several years. One Cape Verdean who spent four months on a whaler received only twenty-five dollars for his work after the expenses for the shoes, clothes and tobacco supplied to him on the ship had been deducted. The net earnings per voyage of foremast hands in twenty-three voyages made by three representative vessels during the years 1836-79 was only $30.47.

Many Cape Verdean seamen also looked for work in the expanding textile mills of New Bedford, but others returned to sea where, by all accounts, there was relatively little racial discrimination aboard the whalers and a man earned recognition for his skills.

By the latter half of the nineteenth century, anyone who completed his first voyage to the satisfaction of the captain had little difficulty in shipping out as a harpooner on his second voyage. Harpooners ranked as officers and it was easy to advance to mate. Many mates could not even speak English or navigate with a sextant, but were given the rating of an officer.

The Cape Verdeans were universally regarded as "hardworking, honest seamen." When all others abandoned the old sailing ships, the Cape Verdeans bought the decrepit vessels out of their earnings as seamen and kept patching them up with loving care. Eventually, they came to own almost all that remained of the New Bedford fleet, either by purchase or by default. In some cases, they received the ships as outright gifts and "sailed them all over the earth with their own crews and made a modest profit by whaling in the old and tried manner."

Theophilus Freitas of Sao Nicolau was captain of the Pedro Varela for her last voyage in 1918. He was also mate on the Charles W. Morgan which frequently stopped in Cape Verde for provisions and seamen and now remains preserved in the Mystic, Connecticut, historic seaport. The list of Cape Verdean whaling captains of courage and perseverance must include the names of Teofilo Gonzales, Luis Oliveira, Jose Senna, Julio Fernandes, and Jose Perry. Joseph Gomes wrote an autobiography of his whaling adventures, Captain Joe, in 1960.

By 1925 the whaling industry was essentially over. In late August 1924 the whaling ship 'Wanderer', the last square rigged, three masted vessel to leave New Bedford on a whaling cruise was wrecked off Cuttyhunk Island in a fierce gale and ran aground just fourteen miles from New Bedford. In late 1925 the Schooner 'John R. Manta' returned with only 300 barrels of sperm oil, as opposed to a successful whaler from the late 19th century returning with 73,707 gallons of whale-oil; 5,348 gallons of sperm oil and 30, 012 pounds of whalebone (baleen). That cargo from the 'John R. Manta' was the last whaling oil or whale bone brought to the New Bedford port and was the end of whaling from New Bedford.

The invention of the electric light bulb, by Thomas Edison, effectively helped bring the whaling era of the early 20th century to an end. But notwithstanding the heroics and constant risk to these underpaid Cape Verdean Whalemen, they methodically killed an estimated hundreds of thousands of the largest and most magnificent of God's creatures on Earth.

For more than a century, the headquarters of this global oil business had been a little island some 24 miles off the coast of southern New England called Nantucket. One of the defining paradoxes of Nantucket's whale ship owners was that many of them were Quakers, a religious sect stoically dedicated to pacifism. At a time when most seamen were notoriously dissolute, the Quaker ship owners of Nantucket viewed their brutal calling as a pathway to both spiritual and financial fulfillment. Combining rigid self-control with an almost holy sense of mission, these were what Herman Melville would call Quakers with a vengeance.

****

CHAPTER 39

Burleigh Smith was a tenacious woman, who when she saw something she wanted, she got it; and she wanted Frederick Rose, the first Mr. Rose. I'm thinking that she must have called him Freddie in the fall of 1925; because when she called my father Freddie, it always sounded to me like she was calling for someone else who wanted her. My Grandmére, would tell me that she never understood what he was saying, that he spoke some kind of Portuguese and that he barely understood what she was saying. But as the saying goes, the language of love is universal and Burleigh Smith of the Cambridge, Boston, Oak Bluffs' Smiths was falling in love with a handsome Cape Verdean New Bedford Whaleman.

There is not a lot to know about the first Mr. Rose, but if he didn't speak English, then he was illiterate as far as reading and writing in English, and if he couldn't read or write in English, then he couldn't make any money in Boston or Cambridge. He could work in one of the many hotels in Martha's Vineyard, because a lot of Cape Verdean men chose the tourist trade down the Cape, New Bedford and the Islands after the whaling days were over; but Mr. Rose was an adventurer, a man who was used to the open air and the freedom that salt air and cold or warm breezes gave a man; and he would not be a man that could be tied down to a set and pat job, an office job, a job carrying bags, a job sitting down all day, a job period.

But he could make love to a woman all day, all night, every day, every night, all week, all the next week and the week after that. 24 hours a day, seven days a week, all day, every day. He could make you laugh and drink with you, and talk about his country, his home and how beautiful you are, and how soft and wonderful you feel, how you taste, how you feel at night, how you feel in his arms, how good you feel inside, how good you feel all over. He could make you feel like a woman, like nothing else ever felt like that, like you were the only one, like you were the Queen of everything, the Queen of his heart, like you were his angel, like you should marry him. And Burleigh said yes, yes, yes, yes, all in love, all in passion, all in lust, to a man who couldn't speak English and could hardly understand her, yes he could make Burleigh scream and shout, and tell you what it's all about, but he was a man to who could not and would not find a job.

Burleigh tried. She talked to her father's friends and partners, men in her social group who had businesses, to her downtown Boston department store friends, everyone she knew, but nobody liked him, especially her social circle and he couldn't even speak English. It was like, *Oh Burleigh, we want you to get married, but we didn't mean to that.* Her friends warned her against him, her cousin Romaine said years later in French to me, *he was beautiful, you know, but what could you do with him except fuck him.*

It was just after I had been honorably discharged from the military and I went by to see my Grandmére a week before I was to get married to Betty Jayne. Cousin Romaine was there sitting in her favorite seat next to Grandmére and they were reminiscing about the ghost who was my grandfather, while smoking their Parliament cigarettes and drinking their Dewar's White Label Blended Scotch Whiskey, and she leaned over and said that to me out of the clear blue sky.

I had heard the story many times before and it all ended with *and he never came back.* Usually my Grandmére at that point would be a little drunk. Crying softly and slowly she would get up from her chair, hold on to her chair arm, the wall and then fall into the banister on the stairway and pull herself up the steps, one at a time, to pass out onto her bed at the top of the stairs.

****

CHAPTER 40

My sister and I started going over together to see Grandmére when I was twelve and she was ten years old. Until now I never knew how much she knew about what was going on with my mother, sister and I in the projects, but I look back and see that she must have known something and instead of confronting my mother with what she thought was going on, she decided to use an indirect approach on trying to save us. While at Ten Clarendon Avenue she began, as she called it, training us for a better life.

She began by teaching us how to hold our forks, spoons, silverware and the proper way to eat our meals. She would have us sit up straight at all times. My sister had rounded shoulders and walked slouched over with her head down and she would put a book on my sister's head and have her walk around the house properly. She would teach us French and how to pronounce and say our words properly in English and French. She would show us pictures of her mother and father, her family, and tell us stories about them, she said that her father had been a great businessman and that we could be to. She taught us how to read better, how to listen better, she told us that our education was very important and that listening to people who have something to say, something to teach you was very important. She fed us well and cared for us with love. She was tender with us and made us feel as though we were brother and sister.

Often Papa Ray would come home from off the road. He was a Head Chef on the New York Central Railroad-Boston to Chicago Line, and he would bring square pats of butter stuck on a paper sheet, steaks and onions, with potatoes and green beans and make us a wonderful dinner with his special gravy over everything.

Papa Ray had been born in South Carolina, and I learned later had graduated from a Southern 'Historically Black University' with a degree in Chemistry and a degree in Chemical Engineering. And just like many Black men in the United States of America who could not find a decent job at a professional skill they had studied in College, tens of thousands of Black men in the United States of America, were able to find work as porters and chefs, serving White people on America's great Train Rail Lines. Jobs as waiters and baggage handlers, the *'boy, get over her and carry this bag for this fine White woman'* jobs.

Papa Ray told me while doing his cackling laugh, while ranting on about white people after he had retired in 1969 with a watch from the New York Central Railroad, after having served White people their meals as a waiter and chef for over thirty-five years, that he and the other cooks used to spit in the fine White people's food while they were cooking it. Papa Ray said he loved watching White people eat the food that he cooked for them.

****

CHAPTER 41

On July 11, 1971, my first son was born and my first wife, Betty Jayne and I brought him home to our Stratton Street Projects apartment, right across from Talbot Avenue and Franklin Fields, near Blue Hill Avenue in Dorchester. I had just started my city job, July 2nd, 1971. It was a patronage job given to me by Boston City Councilman Thomas A. Atkins, the first Black City Councilman to run and win a City Council seat in the history of Boston and the first Black man to run for the Mayor of Boston. I had worked for Mr. Atkins from the moment he had announced that he was running for Mayor of Boston, as a Boston city neighborhood researcher at his City Hall office, to his personal neighborhood advance man and then as Precinct Captain of Dorchester and Mattapan's Ward 10. My jobs with the City of Boston Brookside Park Family Life Center in Jamaica Plain and the Mary Mahoney Family Life Center in Roxbury were my rewards.

Since I would begin my freshman year at the University of Massachusetts/Boston, the job was my second priority. Mr. Atkins had told me that my first priority was going to my college classes and that he wanted me in school full time and that my work schedule would revolve around my university class schedule, and so it did. I came into work early, went to classes, came back to work after 5:00pm and worked until 8:00pm at night.

By that September I decided that I was going to buy a home for my family and began to save as much money as I could. By January of 1972, I found a real estate company and began to actively search for a two or three family home. That June I found a beautiful three family home owned by a Portuguese family on Whitfield Street in Dorchester, Massachusetts. I had saved up about, and this would include, my VA disability money, some of my financial aid and grant money for going to school and my job money, four thousand dollars. The owners who said that they liked me agreed to pull the home off the market and wait while I raised the rest of my down-payment money. By October with the money I had saved and a new infusion of financial aid and grant money given to me in September by the government for going to school, I had saved up eight thousand five hundred dollars and with my GI Bill I was ready to close on a home.

****

CHAPTER 42

On October 5th, 1972, Betty Jayne and I went downtown to the Bank that was giving us a Mortgage. We were in a high rise building, in a huge boardroom, with our realtors, the sellers and the bank officers and had signed all the papers and turned over a check for $8,700.00, when one of the bankers said that we were less $1,765.00 for our closing costs and everyone, including my wife turned and looked at me. It took me only micro-seconds to understand that the only one who would or could help me at that moment was my Grandmére. I had never asked her for any money before, in fact I had never asked anyone in my family for any money at all and I knew that sum of money would be out of everyone's range. Even if they had wanted to, and I couldn't think of any who would want to even if they could, except maybe Grandmére.

So I immediately got up from the table, excused myself from everyone, and called my Grandmére and told her what was happening. She had always told me to never ask anyone for money unless it was life or death. Well, there was no thought about it, no let me think about it. She said, *Hurry up and get out here to Cambridge and I will have a check for you.* That was it. I went back into the meeting and said to my wife and everyone there, that I would be right back. I rode the elevator down to the street, walked on over to City Hall and the Government Center, got on the T. and rode it on out to Harvard Square. Got on the electric bus and rode it up Massachusetts Avenue to the bus depot and walked over to Ten Clarendon Avenue.

My Grandmére and Papa Ray were waiting at the door with big smiles. Grandmére had a check and said, "Hurry up, I called the Bank across the street and they're waiting for you." They both hugged me and told me they loved me and how proud they were of me. I thanked them, hugged and kissed them and I went across the street to the bank. While I was in the Bank getting a cashier's check made out to the Mortgage Bank, the bank manager came over to me and started talking about my grandparents and how much he admired and liked them. He told me that they had been banking there for forty years. I didn't know that and thanked him for his kind words, he gave me the cashier's check, patted me on my shoulder and said, *good luck.*

I got back on the bus to Harvard Square, took the train to the Government Center, ran all the way to the building, rode the elevator up to the Mortgage

Bank's floor, got off, hurried to the boardroom and gave the cashier's check for $1,765.00 to the realtors. A total of $10,465.00 that day. Everyone smiled, my wife hugged me and said thank you, the realtors and the sellers were proud and said so. The final papers were signed and the bankers and my wife and I closed the deal.

At twenty-one-years old I had bought my first house, a three family home in Dorchester. That's who my real Grandmére was. That's what she was all about. The other Grandmére was a little sad and lonely, because of all the people she had lost, and she was always, always, always, so disappointed in my father, and just maybe, just maybe, like ol dad and me, she liked *'dat old evil liqueur'* a little too much.

But, that October day, 1972, I will always remember, because of how proud she was of me, how bright her smile was, how warm her kiss was as she handed me the check to buy my first home, and how much I loved her. I had big plans for my future, but as I've always said, *'There's your plan and then there's God's plan'*, and so my future would be very different than the one I imagined that day.

During my time in 1970's Los Angeles, I paid Grandmére back a little at a time and then in 1976, I had a small windfall and paid my Grandmére back the rest. She never once refused a payment no matter how small and always told me I was a good grandson.

I love that lady until this very day. I prayed for her soul and did a couple of Novena's after she died in September 1978, because I figured she might be in Purgatory and need some help. I did get to see her again in February 1979 five months after we buried her. She was with my Great-Grandfather, her father. They told me that everything was going to be okay. That same month I met Maurice Starr and Michael Johnson; and that March, Marcia Tappin; and that June, Prince Charles Alexander; and that December, Yvonne Willis.

****

CHAPTER 43

But this was 1926 and Burleigh was about to be married no matter what anyone said and that summer she married Frederick Rose in the Cape area. All of their Cape Verdean friends attended as well as Cousin Romaine and a few of her Cambridge and Boston friends. It did not make the Colored Society pages in the Cambridge or Boston Colored newspapers and it certainly wasn't anywhere as extravagant as her coming out party at sixteen, but it didn't matter to Burleigh, she was a young woman in love and that's all that mattered.

Mr. and Mrs. Frederick Rose moved into Ten Clarendon Avenue and so a New Bedford, Cape Verdean Whaleman, the ghost that no one alive has ever seen, lived, ate, walked, slept and made love, in the house that Robert and Mary had built. And even though Burleigh and others had been teaching Freddie how to speak English better, he could not get or keep a job, and because Burleigh was used to men like her father who worked hard and were successful, once he moved into the house and a little of the romance was over, Burleigh began to impress upon him that he needed to work. But the whaling days were over and the only type of work available to a man like him, a man who lived by the law of the sea, a man of the Atlantic Ocean, was down in New Bedford. And so the months went on and by December, Burleigh realized that she was pregnant.

As the pregnancy progressed Burleigh's temperament grew worse. She was already at best a self-indulged, headstrong young woman and probably needed to be at the house on Oaks Bluff, but it was winter and she didn't want to take the chance and ride the waves over to Martha's Vineyard. She preferred to stay in Cambridge and hope by her persuasiveness, some would say nagging, that she could persuade one of her father's friends to give her husband a job. But, nobody that she knew wanted to hire him and so by March 1927 the marriage was becoming an intolerable situation for both newlyweds.

The day it all happened was like the day before. They were both upstairs in the main bedroom fighting and arguing, he in his gruff Cape Verdean Kriol-English speaking voice, Burleigh, pregnant, shouting and not giving him an inch. And then he hit her and picked her up like she was a flower. Just like he had done a hundred times before, usually to lay her down on the bed and make love to her. He brought her out to the second floor rotunda, where the steps were, and threw her ass down the stairs.

My Grandmére would say to me over and over and over and over again, thirty-two, thirty-three and more years later, over and over again, as she poured herself another drink of Dewar's White Label Blended Scotch Whiskey and took another drag on her Parliament double filter tip cigarette, me being eleven-years-old, sitting on the floor watching her, while she was drinking and crying. Just before she pulled herself up from her chair and made it to those same steps and crawled up them, like I would do and ol dad would do thousands of times on our own steps through the years, deep in our own bottle of misery or pleasure, and we, just as she, would pass out on the bed or somewhere, she would say in the same weepy, crying slur, *and then he threw me down the stairs, and I told him to get out and he left and I never saw him no more.* And when she said, *no more*, the tears would just flow. My Grandmére was crying for a young man she hadn't seen in over three decades, but I know now, that three decades is just an instant, and we cry hardest for those that we remember, love, and miss the most.

****

CHAPTER 44
THE GRANDCHILDREN OF SLAVES
THE END OF THE CAPE VERDEAN

And that's it, there is no more. Nobody in my family ever saw the first Mr. Rose again. I'm sure at some point Burleigh and her family, friends and Cape Verdean friends tried to find him, but nobody ever saw or heard from him again. My guess is that he returned to Cape Verde and my Grandmére and the unborn child he left behind became a memory he forgot. Until as old men do, he remembered and wondered about her sometimes. Maybe he remembered stepping over her on his way out the door, and maybe when he had too much to drink, he told his children about his wondrous and adventurous life as a whaleman and the woman he had loved a long time ago in America. Not knowing or maybe not caring that the woman cried for him her whole life and that her last words, when she told his story were, *and I thought he would come back.*

She and the baby survived the brutal attack. My father Frederick Burleigh Rose was born healthy (he looked healthy, he seemed healthy, but something inside was broken) on July 1, 1927 to a disheveled, unbalanced, mentally and emotionally destroyed woman whose labor pains were eclipsed by the horror and heartache at being left alone, beaten, and abandoned by the man she loved, and whose child she had just birthed. And not only had her husband abandoned her, but so had most of her Boston and Cambridge society friends.

The *'I told you so'* crowd had been long gone and the *'poor Burleigh left alone with a new baby'* crowd was just getting revved up. Her only salvation was her mother's sister, who had taken care of her during her pregnancy and was prepared to care for and help raise her sister's daughter's child. And then, of course, after a few months, sensing her even greater weakness, the vultures descended and persuaded her to sign away, for a large amount of money, her shares in the credit union and most of the properties and land her father had built. She would retain Ten Clarendon Avenue forever, and the Oaks Bluff home up until the early forties; and Grandmére always said it wasn't such a bad deal because the coming Depression of the 1930's wiped them all out anyway.

After a few years Burleigh had regained her health, strength, tenacity and most important, Colored Society Status, and she and her good friend Melnea Cass who had remained by her side were working with the Boston Local of The Brotherhood of Sleeping Car Porters Union.

****

From 1868-1968, the African-American railroad attendant's presence on the train became a tradition within America. By the 1920's, 20,224 African-Americans were working as Pullman Porters, train personnel, cooks, baggage handlers, etc. At that time, this was the largest category of black labor in the United States of America. Working for the Pullman Company was, however, less glamorous in practice than it appeared. Porters depended on tips for much of their income and thus on the generosity of white passengers who often referred to all porters as, "Boy" or "George", the first name of George Pullman, the company's founder.

Porters spent roughly ten percent of their time in unpaid "preparatory" and "terminal" set-up and clean-up duties, paid for their food, lodging, and uniforms, which could consume up to half of their wages, and were charged whenever their passengers stole a towel or a water pitcher. Porters could ride at half fare on their days off — but not on Pullman coaches, and they were never promoted to conductor, a job reserved for whites despite frequently performing some of conductor duties.

The porters had tried to organize since the beginning of the century. The wages and working conditions had been below average for decades. For example, the porters were required to work 400 hours per month or 11,000 miles—whichever occurred first to receive full pay. Porters depended on the passengers' tips in order to earn a decent level of pay. Typically, the porters' tips were more than their monthly salary earned from the Pullman Company. After many years of suffering these types of conditions, the porters united with A. Philip Randolph as their leader.

Finally, having endured threats from the Pullman Company such as job loss and harassment, the Brotherhood of Sleeping Car Porters (BSCP) forced the company to the bargaining table. On August 25, 1937, after 12 years of battle, the Brotherhood of Sleeping Car Porters was recognized as the official union of the Pullman Porters. Protected by the union, the job of a Pullman Porter was one of economic stability and held high social prestige in the African-American community.

****

While at one of the meetings, Burleigh met a handsome southern man of distinction. A man who held high values and even higher convictions. His name was Ralph Chisholm. Born in Beaufort, South Carolina in 1905, he was a brown-skinned well educated man from South Carolina. He loved to read, tell stories and talk about his beliefs and convictions, but most important to Burleigh he was working a well-paid Colored man's job, and Burleigh by 1934, with a growing child and an elderly aunt at home needed to find a man with a secure job.

****

CHAPTER 45

Ralph Chisholm's father was Henry James Chisholm. Born into slavery in Charleston, South Carolina in 1865, he died a freed man in Boston, Mass, 1941. His mother Essie D. McGill Chisholm, born the daughter of an American Black Slave in Charleston, South Carolina in 1878, married Henry James Chisholm in Beaufort City, South Carolina in 1898. Henry James Chisholm's father was Henry Murrell Chisholm who had been born an American Black Slave in Charleston, South Carolina in 1836 and died a freed slave in Boston, Mass., in 1906. Henry Murrell Chisholm married Amelia Chisholm who was born an American Black Slave in Charleston, South Carolina in 1865 and was the mother of Henry James Chisholm. She died shortly thereafter and he married Susan Ann Robinson in Charleston, South Carolina a few years later.

The end of the Civil War brought a lot of changes. One of the changes was the release from slavery for the entire Black Chisholm family who had been living in bondage for over a hundred years to the White Chisholm family in Charleston, South Carolina. Henry James Chisholm grew up in Charleston with his father, his stepmother, Susan, and his half brothers and sisters, Mary, Frank, Henrietta, Harriet, and George. Henry James married Essie McGill in 1898. Their first children Luther 1899, Theodore, 1902, and Ralph 1905, were born in Beaufort, South Carolina. By 1906 they moved back to Charleston at 164 Line Street and Henry went to work for the Charleston Navy Yard as a shipwright. In 1909 their daughter Edith was born, then Ernest in 1915 and in 1917 their last child John was born.

Henry's youngest son John remembered his father leaving early in the morning and coming home late. He worked very hard at the Navy Yard and became a master craftsman. Eventually a Navy Admiral had Henry removed from the ship yard to work on his personal yacht. He felt that Henry was the best craftsman around to remodel his yacht. Henry James Chisholm retired in 1931 and died ten years later on March 11, 1941. Eventually all the children: Luther, Theodore, Ralph, Edith, Ernest and John would migrate to the Boston-Cambridge area. Ernest would go to work for the New Haven Railroad as a chef taking up the same career choice as his older brother Ralph. The brothers and their one sister remained close their whole lives, with Ernest not living more than four blocks from Ten Clarendon Avenue on Cameron Avenue in North Cambridge. Their children Ernest, Jr. and Pamela Chisholm would be childhood friends of mine and I would see them often when I visited Gandmere and Papa Ray.

****

CHAPTER 46

After a two-year courtship Burleigh and Ralph Chisholm were married in 1936, when my father would have been nine years old. Burleigh continued her social organization work and joined the Order of the Eastern Stars. Ralph joined the Freemasons; and together through the 1930's and early 1940's they enjoyed a robust life with family and friends. Ralph was on the road four, five, sometimes six days out of the week and was home often on the weekends. When I began to know who my grandfather was in the 1950's, the first thing I knew was that he had a big black satchel bag and when he would come in from the road, when I was there, he would leave it in the foyer near the front door and come and greet me with a hearty, *hey there young fellow how you doing.*

I loved him. He was a good and gentle man, who just hated most White people with a deep passion. Some, like the bank manager, I think he liked. But what I think, was he just hated pompous, ignorant, stupid, racist White people and there were many, many, many, many, of them for him to hate.

****

CHAPTER 47
THE GREAT GRANDCHILDREN OF SLAVES
THE BLACK ERROL FLYNN

They were a good match, my Grandmére and Papa Ray. Papa Ray was a short tidy man about 5' 7" or 8" inches. One of those guys who looked good in their clothes and never gained any weight. He had a prominent nose, sharp eyes, and a slight temper, especially when he saw Burleigh drinking too much. He was what is called a teetotaler.

But something was wrong at Ten Clarendon Avenue. It was said that by the age of ten, my father, by white people standards, was the most beautiful boy anyone had ever seen. More handsome than his father, the ghost who was a New Bedford Whaleman, and even more beautiful than his mother, the colored socialite.

His nose was long and straight, his lips thin, but supple, like his French ancestors. His skin was a very light, olive, swarthy complexion like some Portuguese ancestor. His body was lithe and strong. His mind quick. His eyes fierce like his African ancestors. He would one day be as Billy Dee Williams was called the *Black Clark Gable*, he would one day grow to be and look like the *Black Errol Flynn*. A real swashbuckler, a real pirate. A man who was as comfortable in a State Prison as you are in an armchair, a man who could shoot and kill another man, as easy as you go get a glass of water.

At ten-years-old something was wrong, something seemed broken; items went missing, jewelry went missing, other kids' toys were stolen and lies were made and said. Was he born broken? Was he born evil? I don't know. I consider that I was made broken. Broken by my mother. Broken by my environment. Not born broken and if I believe that, then maybe he was made broken. But I never heard how. What did his mother do to him, what made my dad broken? You don't all of a sudden, become evil. You don't just become broken and evil at twenty-years-old. You begin your journey of evil as a child, you think like that and begin to live with lies as a child and the evil just gets bigger with you.

You know that you're different because you can't really love anyone. You can't really love anyone, but yourself. But I know that my father loved me, I always felt that he loved me. I knew that he didn't love many people, if any, but he was good at pretending, and I always felt a real kinship with him. Maybe he sensed that I was broken too, or maybe he sensed that I was more broken and dangerous than him.

Anyway he never hurt me or thought that he did, except that one time in November 1972 when I was at my most vulnerable. My first wife Betty Jayne had left me. I had been drinking all day, and when she came home from school at 9:00 at night, I beat her ass bad and put her in the hospital. Not only for having found a boyfriend at Northeastern University, but for telling me what the fuck was I gonna do about it.

So dad came up to my new house on Whitfield Street on the pretext of comforting me. I was all broken up because I thought that she might leave me for having beat the living crap out of her. When he left that night after drinking with me, one hundred and fifty dollars that was in my dresser drawer, and my Super 8 Movie Camera, projector and film footage reels with all the film shit that I had taken of Betty Jayne, my new son, all kinds of family stuff, that I had taken between 1971-1972, went with him. I didn't really see that as hurting me, just that there was an opportunity and he couldn't help himself. To show how much he loved me, though, he gave me back the film footage in 1987 after I had paid the back taxes on Ten Clarendon Avenue.

No, I don't know if he was born or made broken by his mother, like I had been. I just know that he did not and would not ever love his mother as she wanted and needed him to. He did not like her ways. He did not like her. He did not want her life and he did not and would not ever know, and neither would I ever know, why. I just knew that I loved everything about her. I just loved how she taught me to be polite to people, to say thank you, and as I got older I realized that you could hide who you really were in good manners.

****

CHAPTER 48

Some say at fourteen-years-old that my father was seduced by an older woman who lived on Clarendon Avenue. Which I could relate to. When my father had gone back to jail again, I had been willingly seduced by my first bottom lady, Rosa. She was twenty-three-years-old and by the time she was through with me, I knew everything there was to know about a woman inside and out, in every crevice, in every place, in every hole, you could imagine and more that you don't wanna know.

I always thought of that as a good thing. It certainly didn't make me broken, so I never got why my father was broken. Did it happen when he was thrown down the stairs along with his mother by his father? Maybe he thought it was her fault. Because it definitely wasn't that he was born poor, with shit and flies all over him. He was born and came home to Ten Clarendon Avenue for God's sake. It wasn't entirely the lap of luxury, but it was as far away from the ghetto in Roxbury as you could get, and if you were a kid living in the projects of Roxbury, well, it looked like the lap of luxury to me.

Why my father left the sanctuary of the Wealthy Colored Society, into which he had been born, turning his back on his cousins, his family in Cambridge, just as they would eventually turn their backs on him, I never knew to ask him *why*. But what I do know is, that by the time he was fifteen, his mother had sent him to a military academy, where he was thrown out in six months. And I do know that his early friends were some Italian kids from Somerville, Massachusetts where he learned to speak fluent Italian and meet his first Wise Guys and do his first B&E jobs. A few years later, before he would be touted as the King of Crime in the 1950's Boston Newspapers, he managed to do his first 1-2 1/2 years in the Billerica House of Corrections by the time he was nineteen. Breaking my Grandmére's heart and most importantly her social standing.

She would always be well liked, and well thought of by the ladies of her social circle, but she would never achieve the presidency, which she badly coveted, in any one of the many social organizations she belonged to. She always blamed Freddie for that, but then my Grandmére was conveniently forgetting her little drinking problem.

****

CHAPTER 49
THE GREAT GRANDCHILDREN OF SLAVES
THE KING OF CRIME & MURIEL FAULK

He got out after a year and settled into a routine that would stay in place for the next eighteen years: Jail, Cambridge, Somerville, Roxbury, Jail, Cambridge, Somerville, Roxbury; becoming famous around town in the right places in Boston and New England as a young up-and-coming criminal who could be trusted to do some necessary things for the Mafia Big Boys.

By the age of twenty-one when he embarked on his second 1-2 and a 1/2 years' tour of the Billerica House of Corrections, he would always call it '*going on vacation*', he would meet Joseph Barboza, a New Bedford Portuguese gangster and lifelong friend. Another lifelong friend and major intro into the big leagues, would be Phil DeCarlo, a Made Man, affiliate and relative of the Patriarca crime family of Rhode Island, Boston, Worcester and the rest of New England, who while I was riding in the back seat of my father's car on my way back from Los Angeles and Boston's Logan Airport for Papa Ray's funeral in 1981, threatened to shoot and kill me if I mentioned one more fuckin time my four sons. Phil had five daughters and was a little touchy that I had all boys. Something about his manhood and shit like that. We all, including my dad laughed, although I could tell by my father's eyes in the rear view mirror that I had better keep my fuckin mouth shut.

Both of these guys I would meet and know well when I was fifteen, along with my dad's main crew: Roy, a real smart B&E guy and Arnie, Dad's strong arm guy, who I already knew because he had a girlfriend in the Whittier Street Projects. Walter was his main man and heroin shooting buddy and crazy as a bedbug. Ol dad would be talking and finessing you and good old Walter would creep up behind you and pump two in your head. This was my dad's crew along with three other bad motherfuckin guys, who you never, ever, wanted to meet or know. All these guys treated my dad with the deepest respect. It was always like they knew who he really was. To me he was just my father, who laughed a lot, sang Frank Sinatra songs and thought that the Beatles, the Rolling Stones and Marvin Gaye were sissies. I always had fun with my dad.

A month after my dad got out of jail in July 1949, he met my mother at a house party in Roxbury, Mass. By August 1949, my mother, Muriel Faulk was at the very beginning of what would be a bad life. Her sister Phyllis had just had her one and only baby at sixteen years old in June 1949. Her other sister Evelyn had dropped out of Shaw University in North Carolina, and the cause of all of their upcoming and future misery and misfortune, their mother, '*The Creature*', was at the ending of a long and horrific trial carried in every newspaper and radio station in the country.

Her son Robert's new name now known by everybody in Boston, Roxbury, the ghetto, New England, her neighbors, her friends, known to her family, now known worldwide as that "*That Insane motherfuckin Nigger Rapist Criminal, Robert Faulk, Jr.*'.

And now *'The Creature'* and her son *'That Insane motherfuckin Nigger Rapist Criminal, Robert Faulk, Jr'*, were at the beginning of a twenty-five-year stretch at the Bridgewater State Hospital for the Criminally Insane.

So, in August 1949, Muriel Faulk, at twenty-years-old, once a promising, pretty, one eyed, proud, talented, music prodigy, known throughout Boston and hopefully soon the world, as one of the greatest Black Pianists of Classical Music in the World, was now reduced to an, all to new low for her, of going out with some nothing, going nowhere, about nothing, Roxbury girls. Drinking and smoking, to some low-life house party in Roxbury, where she was going to meet the prettiest of all the pretty boys ever in the history of the whole world and soon to be the King of Crime in Roxbury, Freddie Rose.

By January 1950, as her former boyfriend Randy Waller had beaten and kicked some guy to death in Washington Park. As her brother was serving twenty-five years in Bridgewater State Hospital Prison for the Criminally Insane. She was on her back, as the just out of jail, and soon to be King of Crime was shooting his semen with me in it, up into her vagina. Where I would have to fight and beat out millions of other spermatophytes in order for me to be able to write this fuckin book.

****

Sperm refers to the male reproductive cells and is derived from the Greek word sperma (meaning "seed"). In the types of sexual reproduction known as anisogamy and oogamy, there is a marked difference in the size of the gametes with the smaller one being termed the "male" or sperm cell. A uniflagellar sperm cell that is motile is referred to as a spermatozoon, whereas a non-motile sperm cell is referred to as a spermatium. Sperm cells cannot divide and have a limited life span, but after fusion with egg cells during fertilization, a new organism begins developing, starting as a totipotent zygote. The human sperm cell is haploid, so that its 23 chromosomes can join the 23 chromosomes of the female egg to form a diploid cell. In mammals, sperm develops in the testicles and is released from the penis.

The mammalian sperm cell consists of a head, mid piece and tail. The head contains the nucleus with densely coiled chromatin fibres, surrounded anteriorly by an acrosome, which contains enzymes used for penetrating the female egg. The mid piece has a central filamentous core with many mitochondria spiraled around it, used for ATP production for the journey through the female cervix, uterus and uterine tubes. The tail or "flagellum" executes the lashing movements that propel the spermatophyte.

The spermatozoa of animals are produced through spermatogenesis inside the male gonads (testicles) via meiotic division. The initial spermatozoon process takes around 70 days to complete. The spermatid stage is where the sperm develops the familiar tail. The next stage where it becomes fully mature takes around 60 days when it's called a spermatozoan. Sperm cells are carried out of the male body in a fluid known as semen. Human sperm cells can survive within the female reproductive tract for more than 5 days post coitus. Semen is produced in the seminal vesicles, prostate gland and urethral glands.

Although the human male semen contains millions of sperm, the human female egg will admit only one. The other ones will soon die and be absorbed.

****

CHAPTER 50
THE GREAT-GREAT GRANDCHILDREN OF SLAVES
THE ROSES

My Dad. Frederick B. Rose and me - 1952

We are taking a picture beside my Grandmére's rose and tomato garden, at Ten Clarendon Avenue in Cambridge, MA. With us is Neguinha, she is a puppy and is the first dog I knew. I am one-year-old, almost two-years-old and my father is about twenty-four-years or twenty-five-years-old.

And so, thus I was born, not hatched, on a rock in deep Outer Space, on the left lower side of a sphere called the Milky Way Galaxy, in a Solar System on a planet called Earth, from inside a woman, pushed out at 11:47 p.m., October 11, 1950 and would first see and be held by my mother, and then be held and seen by my Grandmother (*The Creature*) and Papa and my Grandmére and Papa Ray the next day, all of us descendants of American Black Slaves.

I would go home to my Grandmother's house and in six months when my father got out of jail again, he would bring my mother and me to live with him at my Grandmére's house in Cambridge and I would hear the chimes at Ten Clarendon Avenue, chime and ring for the first time.

My father would go back to jail in late 1951, my mother would move back to her mother's house. He would come out of jail in mid-1952, marry my mother and move us to Townsend Street in Roxbury. They would conceive my sister in October 1952. Ol dad would become the King of Crime for robbing banks and payroll trucks, pimping and selling cocaine. Being the innovative early fifties drug dealer that he was, a man way ahead of his time, and go back to jail in late 1953. This time on a 3 and a ½ to 5-year stretch at Walpole State Prison.

Ol dad was always very proud of being a well-dressed, well connected, well known criminal and always said that they never got him for the really big things he did, just the small shit. He was smart like that.

Dad was a criminologist and liked everything about crime. He loved telling crime stories. He loved the Brinks Bank Robbery and the Lufthansa Airlines-LaGuardia Airport robbery stories. He truly loved the Mafia. That was like making the big leagues to him. Associating with his Mafia friends was like a badge of honor for him. It was like me getting production deals with Virgin Records and Atlantic Records in the 80's. It was a big deal.

I often wondered if one of the reasons that he found my mother attractive, outside of her 5' 8", tall, lithe, strong black body. Her long legs, her black, long, '*Indian*' hair. And no, it wasn't because he loved her piano playing, because he never heard her play the piano. No, it wasn't just all that, but, just maybe, it was because her brother was the most famous black criminal of his time, I mean worldwide famous, and Freddie, just maybe liked being known as "That Insane Bad Motherfucker, Robert Faulk, Jr's, brother-in-law". Just saying.

Anyway, he would come out of jail and live with us at the Whittier Street Housing Projects in mid-1956, for a few months, where he would be led out by the police in the shiny things in early 1957, and my mother would soon after begin to hurt me badly, because as she would say forty-five years later, "She was hurting and liked hurting Freddie's son".

And after all that Robert and Mary Smith had done and been through to stay away from racism, segregation and poverty. To stay out of Black Ghettos imposed on and created by America's White City Governments to segregate Black people from White People and to squash a slave mentality that had been put upon them and their ancestors by four hundred years of White Male Terrorism, White Male Supremacy, Slavery, Jim Crow and Segregation against Black people in America. Well now, thanks to, of all people, Grandmére, the Cape Verdean Whaleman aka the New Bedford Ghost, and of course good ol dad, the once and forever, King of Crime; Robert and Mary Smith's, great grandchildren were officially back on the plantation, oops, I mean the Ghetto, and worse, in the housing projects, and we would have to use every means possible, as children, to fight and dig ourselves out of a situation where every day, every night, you fight against the dark smelly hallways of death and the people who put you there, just to know that you're alive and not dead inside. But, all that would do for me, was to make me smarter, stronger, more stubborn, more tenacious and more courageous.

****

CHAPTER 51
THE GREAT-GREAT GRANDCHILDREN OF SLAVES
THE END OF THE BEGINNING

I would live my life and laugh at death a million times as a child and millions more as a man. I would refuse to allow myself to become a victim. I would fight every step of the way against the evil in my life and while laughing out loud, fuck every girl, every woman, I could find. And then always find one moment, one second of joy in a bottle, in a drug, in some weed, anything, and laughing all the way, finding everyone and anyone I could possibly find to aid me, to save me, to fuck me.

Because of our Grandmére, my sister and I would always know that we were more than our poverty, more than the projects, more than our mother's abuse, more than our father's life of crime, more than our mother's family, more than our father and mother, more than the White system; that we were Robert and Mary Smith's Great-Grandchildren, with a choice, with a chance, and that, at the end of the day would help us to eclipse our birth and our circumstances and put us on our chosen paths. It would take time, but we would eventually make it to a new beginning.

And although I would never escape what my mother and grandmother, my family, my sister, did to me as a little boy, a child. The horror of being called a child molester, a pedophile at the age of six-and-a-half-years-old, being accused, beaten and tortured for it and other things made up by a schizo-phrenic, mentally-unstable mother, over and over and over again, until I was twelve-years-old, would stay with me until this very day, this very second.

It's like I always want to know why, although I know why, my grandmother was a sick, depraved monster and my mother was simply evil. I still always want to know how they could do that to their son, their grandson. Did they believe what they were saying about me? Did they think that about me? Did my aunts, who knew what was happening to me, did they believe that about me? Did my cousins believe that?

There have been apologies from my mother through the years, but not one person in my family, except my sister, has ever talked to me about what happened to me and how it affected my life. And although the man I am now has accepted my mother's apologies and through the years I have done all I could to help her and hope for her love. The little boy inside of me won't, can't and will never accept her apologies. Because he sees and knows, no matter what she says, that she has not changed at all and is still an evil monster. As I have said before, sometimes it's not just the stench of institutional American Black Chattel Slavery that destroyed the ghetto, the housing projects. Sometimes it's just plain old ordinary, *'dat old black magic called evil'.*

****

CHAPTER 52
THE GREAT-GREAT GRANDCHILDREN OF SLAVES
THE BEGINNING OF THE END

When I was twenty-four and living in Los Angeles, I lived with a woman and her two-year-old daughter. One day soon after we started living together she said that she was going out on some errands and would I look after the child. Because it was a one-bedroom apartment, the child was still sleeping in a crib in the bedroom. From the moment she left I was paralyzed, in trauma and in great fear. I had lived my life always making sure that I was never alone with a child. It didn't matter, boy or girl, I just never wanted to be alone with a child, I was scared of them. I sat literally paralyzed in one place until she came back.

I have lived my whole life and can count on four fingers, maybe, the times that I have found myself alone with a small girl child. Luckily I had all boys, but I didn't spend much time with them as little boys either. I have a great fear of children and never really bonded with any of my children. I now have grandchildren and went out with my granddaughter for the first time alone recently. It was hard for me, but the father of the child is a son that I did not see from the time he was a baby until he was twenty-five. But he has shown so much love and forgiveness to me and his mother over the last twelve years, that I have overcome so much through the sheer love of him, his wife and my grandson. So I overcame my fear, took the little girl out, and we had the greatest time.

Because of what my mother, grandmother and sister did to me as a child, it's always been hard for me to give and receive love from people. I always hold back something, probably out of fear. But, my Grandmére had unconditional love for me, and my grandchildren have unconditional love for me, my wife seems to sometimes have unconditional love for me, that son who has never wavered once in showing me what love is, has conditional love for me and I accept that, because he needs my unconditional love even more than I do.

So, I have walked through life with all of this on my back, and I'm still walking thanks to some great people and friends I found along the way.

THE AUTOBIOGRAPHY OF AN AMERICAN GHETTO BOY

VOLUME TWO

THE EARLY YEARS

CHAPTER 1
The PAPERBOY AND MELVIN B. MILLER
1956-1965

1

I started selling newspapers when I was six-years-old in 1957. An older kid from outside the projects told me about an orange truck that would park over at Madison Park at 6:00 at night, and the man would sell a ten cent newspaper to any kid who was there for five cents, and we could sell it for ten cents. I picked up all the old Pepsi Cola and Coca Cola bottles I could find, washed them out, took them to Al's grocery store, made two dollars and that night I went over to Madison Park and bought twenty newspapers for one dollar.

I had an instinctive knowledge that told me I could sell these newspapers to the people I knew on my side of the projects. I knocked on people's doors and when asked who I was I announced myself as the "paperboy", People that I knew opened the door and said hi to me and bought the newspaper from me. I noticed that some people gave me a dime and some people gave me a quarter and said keep the change. Some people would have a dollar and ask for change, if I didn't have the change I would take the dollar and tell them I would be back with their change, and I always came back.

At the end of the night, I had over four dollars and learned something about money and making a profit that I didn't know before. The next night and the next night and the next night and the next night, for six years I met that man at Madison Park, his name was Abe, and I guessed after a while, that he was making some money on the side by picking up extra copies from the Record American Newspaper headquarters and selling them to kids.

2

By the time I was eight-years-old, I owned two buildings in the projects. I was a true ghetto hustler and I would sell my people in the projects, the Record American newspaper at night during the week, and the Boston Globe on Sunday morning, run their errands and run their numbers after school. At that time, I didn't know the words investment and profit, I just knew I was making money and could buy the extra things I needed, like school supplies, candy and food for my sister and me to eat. The only problem I had, was that my mother would sometimes take my money for things she needed and that would include my "investment" money, so that meant I wouldn't have enough money to get all the newspapers I would need for all my customers.

By the time I was eleven-years-old my customer base was about three hundred newspapers a night and my territory stretched from the projects to the bars on Tremont Street, like Slades, where the Boston Celtics, Bill Russell, Sam Jones and Satch Sanders, would buy a newspaper from me for a dollar and get their shoes shined for fifty cents. I was all purpose, had my newspaper business going strong and had built my own shoeshine box, stocked with one color, black, and some rags. It might have been the worst shoe shine you ever got, but my customers never complained.

I also had as my territory the bars like Shanty's at Northampton Street, which meant if I'm there at the bar selling you your newspaper and you're drunk and everything, then that newspaper plus your shine is two dollars. At that time, I could go uptown to Kresge's and Woolworth and get things I needed for school, and other necessities. With that and my deal at Al's, I was able to keep me and my family one step ahead of the kind of poverty that smelled bad. I loved my newspaper boy sack. It hung around my neck, and loaded up with newspapers and my bat, made me feel secure. I loved reading and selling the Record American and the Boston Globe newspapers.

3

When I was twelve I learned about a job carrying newspapers at the Christian Science Monitor on Massachusetts Avenue near Huntington Avenue, near Northeastern University. I applied and got the job, it might have been my first job where I got a check. The job was this. The Christian Science Monitor people had their own subscription base and all you needed was a bike. They provided you with your own territory. So all I had to do was show up after school, Monday through Friday, report in, punch a clock and pick up my customer tablet, it had a gray silver metal cover and had my customers for the day; old, new and canceled in it. it was a real job and I loved it. I could drink all the free chocolate milk and sandwiches I could drink and eat and the people there were real nice.

My territory was the Upper South End from Dartmouth Street and Tremont Street to downtown Boston and ended at the Cinerama Theater on Tremont Street where I would watch snippets of the latest movie, like it's a "Mad, Mad World", I would time my arrival at the theater so that in a few days I could see the whole movie. Some of my customers never saw me, I would usually have a hundred or so rolled up newspapers in my sack and just put the newspaper through the slot of the South End Brownstones I visited, some knew me, like the Cinerama Theater manager, and would greet me and at Christmas I would get a tip.

I made twelve dollars a week and to me whether it was riding my bike in good weather or riding the bus and walking in snowy or rainy weather it was pretty easy and interesting work for a twelve, thirteen and fourteen-year-old. The thing was also, I could be sporadic there and could work for six months and then take off for a month or two as long as I gave them ample notice. The guy who was the manager of us boys, liked that I was mostly dependable, honest and strong, meaning I could handle the route. He always looked out for me and I in turn gave him my best work. I thought about joining the Christian Scientist Church then, and a few times over the years, but I always remembered my promise to Father Paul Francis and the Catholic Church.

4

I loved newspapers, newspapers were helping to save my life, so that day when me, Anthony and Ronald were walking up Ruggles Street from the projects to go Uptown to Woolworth and get a banana split with our newspaper money, I had no idea that the two older guys standing at Ruggles and Washington Street, right outside Woolworth, what we called the Dudley Street Station area, doing what looked to my experienced eyes, trying to sell or give away newspapers; that they would become my business partners and that one of them would mentor me and become my friend for life, he would become like my father, my surrogate father.

Mel Miller and his brother Jack Miller were from Roxbury, the other Roxbury, the up the hill, people doing good Roxbury, and grew up in a large home on Harold Street, across from Walnut Park, in a very nice area and were Harvard Law School graduates, but on that Saturday morning, I didn't know that. I just saw two guy's struggling to sell their newspapers. Now, I'm a professional newspaper boy and when I saw that, I decided to help them. I said to the one who looked like he was trying the hardest, I looked at him and said, "Mister, Mister, I can help you, would you like for me to sell your newspapers for you".

The man looked at me and his eyes twinkled and he said a hearty, "sure, how many would you like". I told him my name and he told me his, and on the spot I made my business deal with him. It was the same deal I had with the Record American Newspaper guy, the paper was ten cents and my cut was five cents, except here for the first time I'm learning what the word "consignment" would mean to me later. The man gave me fifty newspapers and my friends fifty newspapers each. He gave us the newspapers with no money up front and we were supposed to bring his five cent cut back to him.

That day I did not go to Woolworth, I went down to the projects and began selling his newspaper and so did my friends. I was a professional newspaper boy and proud of that. What I learned after a few days was that this newspaper could be sold for a week or longer, that it wasn't a daily like the record American, and that I could make money with it for a longer time. I learned when I went home and read it, that it was a new newspaper and that nobody had ever heard of it, but, I saw that this was something new, something I had never seen before, something I had never heard of before, it was a Negro Newspaper, with Negro news, with Negro people inside and outside on the cover, it had Negro ads, and talked about Negro things, I had never seen this before in my life, but I knew it was something important and something that I wanted to be a part of.

5

I remember knowing this and feeling excited about it, the papers name was the Boston Banner and I began knocking on people's doors and announcing myself as the "Boston Banner newspaper boy", the paper cost a dime and most people gave me fifteen cents, so I was making money with it and people seemed to like it because after my papers ran out in a few days, I noticed that people in the projects were coming up to me asking me when

I would have the new paper for them. I had saved out the man's cut and began looking for him to give him his share and to get more newspapers. I would go up to Dudley Street Station every day after school and look for him. Every day I looked for the man, and every day I would put his cut, I had made about eight dollars, including tips on the fifty newspapers and his cut which amounted to two dollars and fifty cents, in my pocket, and then one day about two weeks later I saw the man in Dudley Street Station and said "Mister here's your money".

It took the man a moment to remember me and he gave me that twinkle in his eyes, smiled and said, "well you came back", and from the day forward, my whole life I had a mentor, a friend and often a father in Melvin B. Miller, The Publisher and Editor of the Bay State Banner; and I had connected another dot that would begin to save my life. It would take time and my mother, the gangs, alcohol, the drugs and life, would eat me up for a long while, but he would find me again and again and again and then one day when I had the music together, Mel Miller and his entertainment editor, Kay Bourne, would be there for me with the Bay State Banner, and his kind words and encouragements would begin to kick in.

What I learned was that I had to do the living, that God would provide, but I had to do the living. I had to take charge of my life and even if there were opportunities, I had to take them, I had to listen, I had to hear that ship come in and hear that voice say *get on board* and try desperately to stay alive.

CHAPTER 2
ST. FRANCIS DE SALES
1959-1964

1

I was 8-years-old, and in the third grade at Asa Grey Elementary School. I had already started working and had a number of jobs in the project, and certain territories around the project that I covered. To my right facing Tremont Street, from the projects, and across the street was the laundry room where I took our clothes to wash and dry, there was liquor store where I got people's alcohol for them. Then, to the right of the projects there was a similar scene where I went to Slade's to sell my newspapers and shine Bill Russell's and other Celtics' shoes. And then it was over to the Lenox Street projects where my cousins lived and other people I knew from school, so I would visit my cousins with my mother from time to time, and then just up the street from there at Northampton Street was where all the clubs were – Shanty's Lounge and a number of other clubs where I sold my newspapers and shined shoes. So that was pretty much my territory outside of the projects, and across the street on Ruggles Street in back of the Ruggles Street Baptist Church where all the ghost people went, was the Asa Grey School.

Then, there was Madison Park on one side where we played at from time to time. In the summer the park had the biggest grasshoppers and all the stray dogs lived there and in the winter the snowplows would plow all the snow into Madison Park and make big mountains of snow with valleys and hiding places to have snowball fights, and then up on Cabot Street was the Cabot Street Gym, and at Cabot Street and Vernon Street was Al's grocery store.

Now Al's grocery store was important because that's where I had established credit for me, my mother and sister so we could eat, but I had never been beyond there; I had never gone beyond Al's store because it wasn't necessary; but I did know that a lot of ghosts lived up in that area. So I wasn't sure what was there, but one day, it was in the winter time and I had my sled, and just beyond Al's store was this home – this sort of—something I hadn't seen before. It was one story and it was brick and it was across the street from a field which looked down into the Health Unit Park. Across the street from where we lived on Cabot and Whittier Street was the Health Unit where we went to get our teeth pulled; and there was a make shift baseball court on cement in that small park on one side and a basketball court on the other and in back of it was a place to wade in the water in the summer.

These were all the things I could see, when I went a few steps past Al's grocery store. They were all part of the field below. On this particular day, I had no reason except that I was used to doing it, and it was my job to knock on people's doors and ask them if they wanted me to go to the store for them. It was a way to make money and I had been doing it for about 3 years. The house was just beyond Al's grocery store and I, with my sled, took a chance. It was probably around November 1958, and I went up to the gate, it was surrounded by a fence. I opened the gate and went up the walkway to the steps and saw there was a doorbell there and I rang it. And a woman came to the door and opened it up and God entered my life, right away. It was an immediate situation. It was immediate – nothing else mattered, I remember the rush to this day.

2

I understood exactly what this woman was. Although I had never seen anything like her before; but it was a ghost woman and she had on black, and her head and hair was covered with something black and white. And she asked me "what did I need?" She didn't ask me what I wanted, she asked me what I needed. I had never seen her before and she had never seen me before, but she asked me what I needed. I asked her if she wanted me to go to the store for her; then she looked at me and smiled and came back and said no, not right now, but for me to come back later.

So I went away and didn't know what to make of it, and on another trip to Al's I came back and I knocked on the door and rang the doorbell and asked the same ghost if she wanted me to go to the store for her. The ghost said no but she had something for me that she had been saving and wanted to know if I wanted it. It was near Thanksgiving and what I learned was that these people gave away turkeys. So she handed me a basket with the turkey and some other things in it and I took the basket home and gave it to my mother. And I would come back to that house, and sometimes I would go to the store for them, and sometimes they would give me more food stuff.

By now I was inside the house. I would come to the door and they would open it up and I would go inside the house and stand there and they would talk to me. There would be a number of women ghosts and they would just talk to me. And so, I would go to Al's for them sometimes and get what they needed and bring it back; and they would give me food and sometimes a dollar. I would take the food and the dollar home. One trip was the most important trip to that house, because it changed my life. The women ghosts parted and in front of me stood a colored man. He had on what I now knew was some type of a uniform. It was black and had a white collar so I kind of knew what this was by the pictures I had seen in the hallway. This was a colored man and he asked me some questions.

He asked me my age, what I did, where did I go to school, things like that, what grade I was in. And then he asked me a question which I found strange and that was, *would I like to go to school there?* And I didn't know what that meant because I didn't know there was a school there. But somehow I knew I should say yes, so I said yes. He smiled at me and said he'd have to talk to my mother. Well my mother was crazy, so I didn't know why and if he needed to talk with her at all; but he certainly could talk to me. Wherever he wanted me to go, I was ready to go right now, because that was just how it was for me. I was willing to go anywhere from where I was. And, so I said, "Well, I don't know, I'll have to ask her." Then I left. So I went back to the projects, which were right down the street, more or less, and I didn't say anything because my mother was crazy and I didn't know what she might do.

3

So life went on, and about Christmas I went back up there and they gave me another turkey and invited me in; and the colored man came and asked me if I talked to my mother. I said yes and he said, *well what did she say? I said, well I'm not sure. I didn't understand her, but I think she said yes.* And he said,

I'm going to need to talk to her, and at that point I didn't know what to do because my mother was crazy and I certainly didn't want him to meet her. But he was a little forceful. He said, *I need to speak to your mother, where do you live?* He said, *You live down the street, don't you?* And he motioned down to the projects where I lived, and I said yes. So he said, *I need to know what your address is and I need to talk to your mother.* And I said, *okay.* Then he said, *can you come back tomorrow?* And I said, *okay.*

So I didn't go back; actually, I didn't go back the next day or the next day, or the next day, either. Christmas came and went and it was now going to be 1959. And I didn't know what to say to the people up the street and one day I went to Al's to transact my business with Al. And after I transacted the business with him, I said, *can you hold my bags?* He said, *okay,* and I went around the corner to the building again and knocked on the door and the ghost woman answered the door and she said come in and she called for the colored man. The colored man came and he said, *Are you ready for me to see your mother? I want to go see her now.* I said, *okay, come on,* and so he came with me.

We stopped at Al's and he took one of my bags and we walked down to the project to my address 159 Cabot Street, apartment 157. And of course the elevator was broken and we had to walk up the five flights of stairs and I knocked on the door and my mother opened it; and there I was with the colored man. And the colored man introduced himself as Father Paul Francis. I didn't really know his name, but that was his name. That's what he said to my mother and he said he'd like to talk to her about me going to school and so he came inside our little project apartment. And there was no place for him to sit because we didn't have a dining table or chairs so he just stood there. When you walked in the door you walked right into the kitchen and the stove, with the chicken grease popped all on the wall, was right in front of you and to your left was just a small cabinet and so that's where he stood there. There was no place else for him to stand or sit.

So he just stood there and he asked my mother if I could go to the school up the street; and she—I couldn't believe it—she was actually nice to him. She smiled at him and she said, *well you need to tell me more, what is this about?* And he explained to her that it was a Catholic school, a Parochial school, and that they would like for me to go there. And she looked at me and she said, *do you want to go there?* I said *yes* and she said *okay,* (and that's when it first hit me that maybe she was just crazy on me when nobody else was around, that she just hated me, not everybody else.) The colored man said, *okay, he's coming then. I need some information. When does he graduate?*

He knew the grade I was in; and I guess I had given him some other information about Asa Grey.

4

The thing was, I was in the third grade at Asa Grey and I would be graduating the next May or June, and I was scheduled to go to the Sherwin School and from the Sherwin School you went to reform school and then jail. Everyone knew that. The Sherwin School was basically a reformatory for the surrounding projects and the ghetto kids who lived in the area tenements. Everyone who went to the Sherwin went to jail. They went to reform school and then jail. It was a matter of fact…it was where everybody went. There was nothing at the Sherwin School. There wasn't anything there to learn, you just went there. Everybody was either bad when they came in or turn bad afterwards. Eventually, the school was burned down by Johnny McAvain around 1964 or 1965.

So, at this time it was 1959. I was 8-years-old and I still don't know what's going on but I knew that something important was happening and the colored man said so. And so I go up there again. They gave me food, they gave me money for going to the store for them, they talked, they were nice people. I liked the ghost women and I liked the colored man. They were real nice and so they find out that I'm graduating in June and that in September I'll be going to the Sherwin School. They have all my information, they have everything they need and life goes on in the projects and I continued my work in the projects, my buildings and my deal with Al goes on. And all the things that are necessary for me to do, I do. It was summer now and it's June. When we graduated from ASA Grey in June, we were marched over to the Sherwin School to register for the fall.

The Sherwin School was just up the street from ASA gray across from Madison Park; so we were marched into Madison Park and over to Sherwin and up the stairs because we had to register there. It was a registration process and I'm in line to be registered for the Sherwin School for the following year, which began the 4th grade all the way to the 8th or 9th grade. So while I'm standing in line, my mind goes to the people at the house and how they said that they would be coming for me, to get me, and take me with them; because I didn't want to be there. I didn't want to be there at the Sherwin School with these kids. I knew that I didn't want to be there. I felt that I didn't belong there.

It was just something in me that I knew that day. And I'm standing in line with the other children and I'm 8-years-old and I'm waiting, and then all of a sudden it was like I was seeing an aberration. One of the ghost women comes up the stairs, her black robes are flowing. I can still see her today. And she walked up the stairs and she looks at me and says my name and takes my hand and walks me down the stairs, out of the building, across Madison Park, up Cabot Street, past Al's to what I now know is called the rectory. And the colored man, who I now know is Father Paul Francis, takes my hand and walks me out and around the bend to what is St. Francis de Sales Parochial School, where I will spend the next five years. And he takes me inside and they register me for September; and I now would be going to St. Francis de Sales Catholic School. So that's the beginning of me, of my life with God, and learning about God, the Catechism, the Catholic Church and myself.

5

St. Francis de Sales, which I began in September of 1959 when I was 8, I would be 9 that October, I began in the fourth grade. It was like a new world to me. It was full of ghosts in black and white, and full of ghost kids who were Irish and Italian; and from what I saw, a sprinkling of other colored kids like me. I think there were probably 5, 6 or 7 from the project where I lived. I didn't know them well in the projects, but I later learned who they were and I would know them well for the next five years -4th grade, 5th grade, 6th grade, 7th grade, 8th grade.

And the best thing about that school was, since we were poor, there were only a few changes of clothing that I would need. I had to wear a blue blazer, white shirt, a clip on tie, and blue or gray pants. So there were very few clothes needed for that situation; the most important things were underwear and shoes, and because there were always holes in the one pair of shoes that I would get a year, I would always be wearing cardboard in them, I would be literally walking on cardboard going to school, but that would be okay, because wearing no underwear or my sister's underwear would be a lot worse.

The main bad thing about going there was that the ghost sisters didn't serve breakfast or lunch and since my mother didn't serve or pack breakfast or lunch for me, I was always sitting in my classrooms hungry as a mother-fucker, but that's where good ol Al came in, Al always kept a package of bread open and would slap together a baloney and cheese sandwich for a poor, hungry, colored child.

In that five years' time, a lot of things happened. The most important thing about that situation was how I got there and what I learned. There were quite a few battles that had to be fought with the ghost kids, but I learned that was a necessary situation. I learned a different value. I learned how to do things well; the ghost sisters were great teachers; they were great people.

One thing I learned from a ghost man named John was how to be an altar boy. He would pay us a dollar to come to alter boy practice and learn the Catechism and learn Latin. The main thing was to learn Latin. At nine years old I became an altar boy for St. Francis de Sales Church in Roxbury on Vernon Street, and would serve Father Paul Francis at the 7:00am Mass. It would be a proud moment always for me, and I remember my mother and sister coming sometimes.

6

The sisters took care of our Catechism and taught us to go to church, and about God and Jesus Christ and all that meant. It was a great time and it was a bad time because as anyone who's been through that experience knows that you go from one place, and then you have to go back to another place; the ghetto, the projects and my mother, who because of all that had happened to her life, was intent on destroying mine. I would go to school with black and purple welts all over my body where she had beaten me with a belt for whatever reason that she could fabricate, I can still see the bruises on my upper arms and body raised up along with the bed bug bites I would constantly have. Bed Bug bites are similar to belt buckle welts, except that at the top of the swollen purple bed bug bite is a small hole that oozes pus and blood out of it.

I honestly believe that if we had a gym period and my bruises had of been discovered, that she would have been arrested for child abuse and that would have been the end of her in my life. I can honestly say that I never learned one damn thing from my mother, all she did was beat on me physically, mentally and emotionally through my whole childhood. Her sickness and madness knew no boundaries when it came to me, her tortures for me were endless and awesome. I was my father's son and she was going to do everything she could do to hurt and destroy me. I would pay forever with her for the sins of my father.

I could read very well by the time I was four and reading became an obsession for me, it became my refuge. Within a book I could be anywhere but where I was and my imagination grew. I learned early as a six-year-old child, that with the noise and clutter of my mother's voice that I could not do homework in our project apartment, she would sweat as she screeched on and on about her color, her mother, my father, the welfare lady, the welfare department, my father, her color, how we were black and ugly and nobody wanted us, I heard that a million times as a child, always complaining, always sad, always hating, always hating me, and there was nothing or nowhere for me to sit and do homework on anyway.

There was no peace and there was no God at 159 Cabot Street, apartment 157, there was only struggle, anxiety, poverty, and my mother's howls at what had happened to her. So I learned to do my homework by reading whole books at a time, all at once and memorizing them and then reading the assigned book with my class and getting A's and B's on my tests.

I learned to read my assigned reading with a flashlight under the covers at night, while listening to a transistor radio that my Grandmére had given me when I turned nine years old. This transistor radio had an ear plug and I kept it under my pillow so that The Monster I lived with couldn't find it. I listened to all the hits with Arnie "Woo Woo" Ginsberg on WMEX. I learned to love music and books with Arnie "Woo Woo" Ginsberg in my ear, after I finished my late night job of killing roaches, and my mother was asleep. And unless her howls brought this monster into my room late at night after 1:00am or 2:00am, where her howls would end in a severe and traumatized beating of me with the belt buckle end of the belt, all the while this monster would be screaming incoherent words at me that I didn't understand, while dripping sweat and hate, I would listen to music and read books into the night.

7

I was unsafe and safe in the unsafe and violent world of my mother and the projects, but all the music of 1959, 1960, 1961, 1962, 1963, the books, the bookmobile, the libraries, the Boy's Club, the YMCA, the Boy Scouts, The Nuns and Priests of St. Francis de Sales and God's love, were all coming in to teach me, to save me and I listened and learned, and what I remember is that *"The Monster"* could not destroy me. I would find these people and places and I would know that the howls and monstrosity of that monster would make me stronger than it, that I was stronger and could defeat it and time would be on my side and that one day I would get out, I dreamed all this when I was nine, ten, eleven and twelve years old, everything I would be, everything I would do, everything I knew I could do, I could do and be, because if I could live through this monster then I could live through anything.

I did this until the prime and always there and consistent enemy and dilemma of the project-ghetto boy/teenager; Post-Traumatic Stress Disorder (PTSD), death and violence both inside and outside of my project apartment caught up with me, and embraced me, and I found alcohol, girls, drugs, and the gangs. They would soothe me and I would feel strong and safe in their embrace and eventually I would go crazy, just like millions of poor, hungry and black project-ghetto kids do every day, but in the end God was stronger, the books were stronger, the music was stronger, the nuns were stronger and God would meet me again when I was eighteen and take me by the hand and show me the way out, and I would begin the long journey to sanity through insanity and come out decades later still insane after all those years, but just sane enough to do some great things.

The insanity of Post-Traumatic Stress Disorder destroyed my mother, her mother, her brother, her uncle, her father, her sisters, her nephews, nieces and her children, but somehow, luckily, my sister and I had a beautiful grandmother, we called Grandmére, who loved and cared about and for us and began to save our lives as soon as we were born and no matter where we had to live, or who we had to live with, we knew that there was a better place because she always said so and we believed her.

Every African American whose family traces back to slavery and has lived through segregation in the south and segregation in America suffered and suffers from Post- Traumatic Stress Disorder's natural inclination to feel afraid. This fear triggers many split-second changes in the body to prepare to defend against the danger or to avoid it. This "fight-or-flight" response is a healthy reaction meant to protect a person from harm. But in post-traumatic stress disorder (PTSD), this reaction is changed or damaged. People who have PTSD may feel stressed, traumatized or frightened even when they're no longer in danger, and that's called paranoia.

PTSD develops after a terrifying ordeal that involved physical harm or the threat of physical harm. The person who develops PTSD may have been the one who was harmed, the harm may have happened to a loved one, or the person may have witnessed a harmful event that happened to loved ones or strangers.

PTSD was first brought to public attention in relation to war veterans, but it can result from a variety of traumatic incidents, such as muggings, rapes, torture, being kidnapped or held captive, car accidents, train wrecks, plane crashes, bombings, *or child abuse.*

8

There's always something different and then you're back at the same place. You're poor always. Your poverty never stops. You're always poor, but I was always, mostly, treated well within the confines of that school. Not everything was always great; there were a couple of ghost sisters who were definitely prejudiced and weren't very happy about having the experience of teaching poor, ugly, colored children, and showed it at times; but the education was formidable. The education was the most important thing that I got. I learned how to read and write and spell and do math wonderfully. It was something exceptional, it was a gift that had been given to me. At the time the gift was being given *did I know that?* Yes. But I also had to live through it, walk through it. And this means, I also had to deal with life there and I had to deal with life at home and in the projects at the same time. So it was and I was, quite formidable in every aspect. It was neither good nor bad, it just was what it was; but I went on and I went every day, all year, every season for five years.

Up the street on Vernon Street was something I also didn't know was there, and that was St. Francis de Sales Church. So between school and church, for the next five years, the church and the school came to be the most important things in my life. I became an altar boy and I learned how to read and write well between the ages of 8, 9, 10, 11, 12 and 13. It was that simple. And up the street from there on Vernon Street, there was a place called the Blessed Sacrament, where I went and there were more ghost Sisters and they taught arts and crafts and you could go there from time to time; and they also gave you food and baskets with turkeys for Thanksgiving and Christmas. And up the street from there, and around the corner from Vernon Street was the Salvation Army, so I learned how to go and eat there too.

And from there I would bring my sister and my mother to the Blessed Sacrament and Salvation Army and we would eat dinner and we would get gifts and they would fix food for us and we had the most wonderful time.

They would give us clothes and baskets of food and all kinds of things at the Blessed Sacrament and the Salvation Army. And up the street from there, was a place called The Society of Saint Vincent de Paul so we would go there and they would give us more clothes. And I brought my mother and my sister there and I showed other kids from the projects these places. I would have a number of people from the projects attend the Blessed Sacrament, Salvation Army and St Vincent DePaul, where we would get free clothes and free food. Every Christmas and Thanksgiving, they would have little parties and social things for us and we would go to them and I learned to like that life and it became part of my social life for all those years. They were wonderful ghosts, wonderful ghost people and it became an important part of and development of who I was; and to this very day I give everything I can, all the money I can give to those good people.

9

While I was at St. Francis De Sales, there were a number of kids from the projects who went there – I think my sister went there for a year, but she didn't like it and she wanted to go back to where her friends were at the Timilty School. Frank Jenkins was there from the projects, Carl Jones was there from the projects, and Carlton McCarthy was there from the projects. So, like I said, we had to wear our uniform for all five years – a white shirt with a tie and blue or black pants…that was our uniform. It was a uniform school and we had to have a blue or gray blazer jacket, and these clothes were bought with a stipend from the school. Our tuition was $10 a year. They had to charge us something so they charged us $10 a year to go to St. Francis de Sales School.

While I was in school, I met and made friends with a number of ghost kids who seemed friendly enough. I had never made friends with any ghost kids before then. I also made some ghost enemies—Richard Brewster, I'll never forget—his father owned the Brewster Ambulance Company, and Kevin Jenna. They were constant adversaries who by the time I would get to be 11 years old and in the six grade, we had a fight and I beat both of them up and that was the end of them. I remember busting Kevin Jenna's nose.

One of the sisters who was prejudiced kept me after school. She was very prejudiced, disliked that she had to teach colored kids. She kept me after school and sent them in the room to deal with me. It was over singing black spiritual songs like "Old Black Joe" that she wanted us black kids to stand up and do, and I wouldn't do it, I refused to stand up and sing it for her and the snickering ghost kids. She left me alone in the room with them, they surrounded me and I suppose I was going to get beat up. But, of course, I was quite something, and surprised them and the prejudiced ghost sister. I can still see her snickering with the ghost kids as my colored classmates were standing there singing, as she called them, "old darky songs".

I had learned that knowing how to fight was necessary when I was about six in the projects. I learned that sometimes you won and sometimes you didn't, sometimes you fought and sometimes you ran, sometimes you stayed alive and sometimes you died, sometimes the kids were older and you fought anyway and sometimes they were dangerous, and you just stood there and looked at them, but you never backed down from a bully, you always stood your ground and looked them in the face. Most kids didn't have guns then, so you could deal with ghetto life like that, you didn't have to worry about some coward pulling out a gun and shooting your ass dead.

So fighting another kid was something that I understood and dealt with very well. There was this fight, a major fight that I had with this Irish kid from school named Thomas Walpole. I'll always remember it. It was interesting because it was a thinking kind of a fight. Thomas Walpole was a year older and much bigger then I was and he was going to beat me pretty bad. I mean he was beating me pretty badly and then I'm thinking there's this wall at my back; and as I was fighting, I was thinking, I remember thinking that if I backed up, because he was hitting me so hard and bad, if I backed up I might be able to do something. And so I did. I backed up, and put my back to the wall and I watched his fist come toward my face. He was planning to knock me out with a very powerful blow to my head. I watched his fist in slow motion and as his fist came, I inverted my head to the right. I'll never forget that day.

You could hear his fist crack against the brick wall. All the kids who were watching the fight heard that sound and I remember just beating him and kicking him all day, he had spit and blood coming out of his mouth while I was kicking him. I'm probably still kicking that motherfucker. I was still kicking him until he stopped making noises. I had quite a few fights at St. Francis de Sales, but that was the fight the kids in the projects talked about for a long time.

10

Most of the ghost sisters were wonderful. In the midst of it all, once in a while, down the hall watching us, was a man who would often pat me on the head and ask me how I was doing. He was a tall ghost man and he had on the same uniform as Father Paul Francis, but he had a hat with a red thing on the top. He was nice, he had a nice friendly face and he always smiled at me. He always seemed to pick out the colored children and be especially nice to us. He always said something nice to me.

His name was Monsignor George Kerr and he was a big fellow, a big man, and I would always smile at him and tell him I was doing fine. And he would pat me on the shoulder and I would see him often. He was always talking to the sisters, talking to them going back and forth up and down the hall with all the classrooms. So it was a good experience and I remember something that was very important. I remember Cardinal Cushing praying with me at St. Francis De Sales Church. He often said Mass there and a few times I was his Alter Boy. I was confirmed in the Catholic Church at 12 years old, I went through my confirmation, together with a few of the project kids. I went through my baptism and turned Catholic when I was about 9 years old and my name became Peter. My middle name was changed to Peter and then when I was twelve, at confirmation, my middle name became Peter Joseph.

While researching Monsignor Kerr, Father Paul Francis and St. Francis de sales Church and school for this book on Goggle, I found this Obituary from a distant relative of Monsignor Kerr, a man I knew as a child, a man I knew from my childhood who walked the hallways of the Catholic School I went to.

When I first read the obituary I couldn't believe what I had just read, I had to read it over and over and then I saw that I had been part of something big, part of a man's belief, part of a man's dream to do something for those who needed help. I slowly began to realize that the day I walked up to that rectory door and knocked and rang the bell for the first time and the Nun saw me that there must have been a lot of prayer and conversation behind the door after I left, that the beginning of the dream and wish of Monsignor Kerr and Father Paul Francis had just walked up to the door and that through God's divine province, that the will of God was at work, that God's will was going to be done and that the first colored child to go to St. Francis de Sales School had just walked up to the door, on his own.

While reading the obituary, I would know what I always knew to be true, that we have to save ourselves, that the life you save may be your own. That I had begun to save myself as a little child, and that Monsignor Kerr, Father Paul Francis, the good Nuns of St. Francis de Sales Church and Parochial School and God's love would always be inside of me, no matter how far I would stray, that the love of God, if I listened would always be there.

After I read the obituary I wondered if Monsignor Kerr had remembered us, his little colored kids, and while reading more about him, I knew that he had remembered us and had prayed for us all of his life. Through the years, as I got older and all the hustle and bustle of my young man work in the music business was through and I was living in Los Angeles, I had time to reflect on my youth and I began to remember those wonderful people I had met as an eight year child, who had begun to save my life a very long time ago, and although I had no idea at that time that I had walked into a situation that God had planned for me, I began to pray for their them and their souls, and although I thought of them often and even found Father Paul Francis in a nursing home and talked to him on the phone, he did not remember me he said, and that to me meant that he had saved so many children that we were all as one to him, and even though I never saw any of them ever again, I remember them and their love and teachings to this very day.

From: Betty
Subject: Rt. Reverend George KERR, Obituary, 1983
Date: Wed, 30 Nov 2005 09:34:50 -0500

> Hello,
>
> I had recently discovered that people who subscribe to "The Boston Globe" (home delivery) are able to search the archives of the GLOBE (news items only) for free. I just signed up to be able to do this—this morning, and, was browsing around a little.
>
> I found this obituary from 1983 and thought it might be interesting to researchers:
>
> RT. REV. GEORGE V. KERR, 63; BECAME ALL-AMERICAN IN LIFE'

Author: By Edgar J. Driscoll Jr. and William P. Coughlin Globe Staff

Date: 01/24/1983 - Section: RUN OF PAPER OBITUARY

Rt. Reverend George V. Kerr, chaplain of the Massachusetts House of Representatives for nearly a quarter of a century and pastor of St. Francis Xavier Church, South Weymouth, died of lung cancer at 12:10 p.m. yesterday in his summer home in Falmouth. He was 63. Msgr. Kerr had been ill for the past six months.

Monsignor Kerr, who had been Roman Catholic chaplain of the House since 1959 and was coordinator of its chaplain services, was a former Boston College All-America football player who played guard on the famous Boston College football squad which came up from behind to win, 19-13, over the Tennessee Volunteers in the Sugar Bowl game of 1941.

In a Boston Globe column in 1965, Will McDonough wrote of Monsignor Kerr as the "righteous reject" at Boston College who reported to then coach Gil Dobie wearing three sweaters and two overcoats to weigh in for the team at 185. When it was later discovered that his true weight was only 165 pounds, he was told he "was too slight for a football scholarship."

"It's the story of a youngster who went from sixth team to All America; from curate to monsignor," who at the time of the column was to be honored by Sports Illustrated magazine as a "man who has become All-American in life through his 25 years after graduation."

Monsignor Kerr became pastor of the South Weymouth Church in 1979. Before that he was pastor of St. Francis de Sales Church, on Vernon Street, Roxbury, a church he saved from the wrecker's ball. He was named administrator of the Roxbury church in 1958.

At the time, the then 89-year-old church was in serious disrepair and could not be supported by its poor membership, which once had numbered 17,000 persons but had dwindled to fewer than 300 families.

Richard Cardinal Cushing, though he did not want to, was seriously considering tearing the church down when the then Father Kerr, by now no stranger to comeback victories in life and an aide in the Catholic Charitable Bureau, volunteered to try to save the old church and all its traditions. It was August 1958.

"I'd never give it up," Father Kerr reportedly told Archbishop Cushing. "You've got the job," the archbishop told the priest.

Father Kerr immediately set out "running and writing" to raise funds, and within a year, the church, where the famous Irish tenor John McCormack once sang and prayed, was renovated, along with its school (built originally in 1913). In addition, by moving into a room on the second floor of the school, Father Kerr gave his rectory over as a convent for nuns to staff the school since their old wooden convent had been condemned.

It was not long before the number of St. Francis de Sales' parishioners increased. And while he was at St. Francis de Sales, Monsignor Kerr was in the forefront of efforts to put Christian virtues of love, kindness and charity to work in Roxbury's streets on behalf of the black community.

As a pastor, he spoke out often in behalf of black causes, describing "integrated schools as anchors for present and future generations."

Before coming to Roxbury, he had served as assistant director of the Catholic Charitable Bureau of the Boston Archdiocese for three years. The broad-shouldered and once dark-haired 6-footer had been stationed as a curate at St. Mary's Church, Dedham, from 1945 to 1953. Then he was made administrator of St. Linus' Church, Natick, where he served until 1955.

Monsignor Kerr was born in Philadelphia on Feb. 14, 1919, the son of Mr. and Mrs. Felix Kerr. Brought up in Brookline, he was a graduate of St. Mary's High School, where he was a star athlete in football, baseball and basketball, and of Boston College, Class of 1941. He was graduated from BC Cum Laude, with a scholastic average of 90, and was voted the most talented in his class.

Years later, Frank Leahy, the famous coach of the BC national championship team in the monsignor's senior year, said of him:

"I sincerely believe he is the greatest all-around

scholar-athlete that I have ever coached and I feel convinced that he would compare favorably with the finest in history at any school."

On the occasion of the 25th anniversary of the Sugar Bowl win, Monsignor Kerr told a large dinner gathering, sponsored by the Boston College Varsity Club:

"A man may glitter athletically on the gridiron, and he may twinkle intellectually in the classroom. But unless his conscience sinks deep into the subsoil of religious faith and shoots its antennae up beyond the stars and space, that man will miss alike the music of Divine inspiration and the thunder of Divine command."

In 1962, when a new $50 million football stadium was proposed for the city and a Greater Boston Stadium Authority was formed, former Governor John A. Volpe appointed him to the board with the then Boston Patriots President William H. Sullivan Jr. of Wellesley Hills and Robert M. Jenney of Brookline. Monsignor Kerr had been at Boston College when Sullivan was athletic director there.

At a birthday party in the monsignor's honor in 1968, while he was chaplain of the House of Representatives, Volpe lauded the clergyman for his compassionate work in his Roxbury parish and his dedication in state government.

"Fortunately," he said, "to the extent that brave men, good men, spiritual men, like Monsignor Kerr, create a refuge of faith, a center of light in areas of darkness, to that extent they are lifted up from despair, and others are strengthened as examples of good citizens and successful Christians."

That same year Mayor Kevin H. White appointed the clergyman to a six-man committee for an in-depth study of student racial unrest in the Boston public schools.

In the 1970s Monsignor Kerr was the eye of a political storm on Beacon Hill when members of the House questioned his $8400 annual salary as chaplain and called for a system of rotating clergymen of other faiths to say the opening prayer. It was then that he was made "chief" chaplain and established a rotating schedule for other clergymen to deliver the daily prayer.

As for the salary, he said he had never sought increases and that he always turned his paychecks over to his St. Francis de Sales parish to aid the poor.

The popular and dynamic monsignor prepared for the priesthood at St. John's Seminary and was ordained by then Archbishop Cushing at the Cathedral of the Holy Cross in the South End on June 29, 1945. He was named Papal Chamberlain in 1959 and was elevated to the rank of Domestic Prelate by Pope John XXIII in 1964.

During his years in the priesthood Monsignor Kerr had served as director of the Archdiocesan Nocturnal Adoration Society and as chaplain for the Cecilian Guild, the Boston Press Photographers Assn. and the Caritas Guild.

Monsignor Kerr leaves a brother, Peter Kerr of Jamaica Plain, and a sister, Mary Kerr Lynch of Hyde Park as well as nieces and nephews.

His body will lie in state in the rectory Tuesday from 2 to 4 p.m. and 7 to 9 p.m. and in the church from 9 a.m. to 9 p.m. on Wednesday.

A funeral Mass of the Resurrection will be concelebrated with more than 30 concelebrants Thursday at 10 a.m. in St. Francis Xavier Church, South Weymouth. Homilist will be Rev. Msgr. Francis Dolan, a longtime friend.

Betty (near Lowell, MA)

P.S. I am descended from an extended KERR family who arrived in Everett and/or Malden, MA, in the 1870's, coming down from Quebec, Canada! I believe there are still relatives in that area, but I don't know their current addresses. I just lost an uncle, George Raymond KERR, last month.

circa 1955

Rev. Paul R. E. Francis

Reverend Paul R. E. Francis entered into eternal life October 16, 2011. Father Francis was born in Belize, formerly British Honduras, June 16, 1915. He was raised in Belize and attended St. Johns College before entering the seminary at the Pontifical Urban University Rome. Father Francis was ordained December 22, 1941, and his first assignment was in Belize City. He moved to New York in 1952 serving parishes in Brooklyn and Manhattan. **He transferred to the Archdiocese of Boston in 1958 serving at St. Francis de Sales in Roxbury** and the Cathedral of the Holy Cross in Boston. His next assignment was as associate pastor of Sacred Heart Parish, Weymouth, from 1969 until 1982. Father Francis then served as pastor of St. Theresa's Parish in Revere until he moved to Regina Cleri Residence, Boston, in 1988. For many years, Father Francis continued to assist at St. Gerard Majella in Canton and St. Bridget in Abington. Father Francis was the devoted son of the late George and Bernice Francis; beloved brother of the late William Francis, Gwendolyn Smith and Sister Barbara Marie Francis; and is survived by his loving nephews, Norman, Paul, Andrew and Franklin Francis; and nieces, Karen Francis and Ann Belizaire. Father Francis will lie in repose Wednesday, October 19, at Sacred Heart Church, Weymouth, from 4-7 p.m. and at Regina Cleri Residence, 60 William Cardinal O'Connell Way, Boston, Thursday from 2 to 4 p.m. Relatives and friends respectfully invited. Funeral Mass Friday at the Sacred Heart Church, Weymouth, at 10 a.m. with principal celebrant Sean Cardinal O'Malley, O.F.M. Cap. Burial in St. Francis Xavier Cemetery, Weymouth. Donations in memory of Father Francis may be made to Regina Cleri Residence, 60 William Cardinal O'Connell Way, Boston, MA 02114. Arrangements by the Clancy-Lucid Funeral Home, Weymouth.

CHAPTER 3
DEAD IN THE PROJECTS
MRS. PARKER - 1961

1

Living next door to us, when I was eleven years old, was a lady named Mrs. Parker. I never really noticed Mrs. Parker, but she must have been there awhile because I never saw her move in. But I noticed her from time to time and when I saw this lady she always had a white uniform on. She lived directly next door to me on the 5th floor. Her apartment was on our side of the floor; her door opened next to my front door, which was where you walked into my kitchen.

When you came down the stairs from the elevator that stopped at the third and sixth floor when it was working, you had to walk down the stairs. Then you went straight to into my apartment and if you went left, you went to Mrs. Parker's apartment; but if you went right, you opened the door to a small hallway, which was my back door and which went into our little living room, in that hallway was another door and that opened into the living room door where probably the last remaining white people in the Whittier Street Housing Projects lived and then you opened another door, into another hallway which opened into the poor white peoples kitchen, the white people were still living there as of 1962, so they must have been real, real, poor.

I think they moved around 1964 and the apartment remained vacant for many, many, years, thereafter, and there was another door which went into another hallway, which was the kitchen entrance into that apartment next door to me, and the back door to another apartment, and then you opened the door into the other side of the building, where Mrs. Parker's back door opened into the living room and was another door with another apartment that opened into someone's kitchen area. All this was on the fifth floor and it was the same for every floor in the projects as it was on the 5th floor, and so on each floor there would be four families.

2

Mrs. Parker was one of those quiet people. There was never any noise from her apartment and she seemed like a nice lady. One day when I was eleven years old Mrs. Parker became very important to me and did something for me that would change my life. Her son, Tommy Parker, must have been about six or seven years older than me. I know this, because she came and knocked on my door one day and she said *'I want to give you something.* She had a couple of boxes full of toys and clothes, and all kinds of things, she said that Tommy was going into the Army.

The box reminded me of the boxes my sister and I had been getting from Globe Santa since I had been five years old. Every October the welfare lady would give us sheets of paper and we had to write to Globe Santa what we wanted for Christmas. She would collect them and sometime in December every year, Globe Santa who lived at the Boston Globe Newspaper, would bring boxes of toys to all of us colored project kids at the Annunciation Road Projects, the Lenox Street Projects, the Orchard Park Projects, the Columbia Point Projects, the Mission Hill Projects and the Whittier Street Housing Projects where we lived.

Globe Santa himself would deliver the boxes around the middle of December, I would try to catch him bringing the boxes year after year. I never did see him and by the time I was ten I gave up at seeing Globe Santa deliver my box. Anyway, there would be over one hundred boxes, in the middle of the project courtyard in the middle of December on a Saturday, and hundreds of kids like me would come running out to get our boxes. The project maintenance men were in charge of helping Globe Santa get our boxes to us and those kids whose mothers had something going on with any of the twelve maintenance men got their boxes before anyone else. My mother always failed at getting a maintenance man to like her, so we always had to wait while the maintenance men called our name, building number and apartment number.

3

There were a lot of fights over those boxes, though nobody ever got killed, but, a lot of kids boxes got stolen and they would be crying and shit, but there was nothing anybody was going to do, because we all wanted our boxes and nobody was going to share their box, because most of the time these were the only presents we were going to get, except for the other Santa Claus stuff we got from the church, Salvation Army, St. Vincent de Paul and the Blessed Sacrament.

The boxes were real big and you needed a parent to help carry it, so along with us kids out in the courtyard would be plenty of mothers, and so Globe Santa day would turn into a big party day and celebration in the projects. Everybody would be happy, except for the kids whose boxes were stolen. We would get our box and drag it up to the fifth floor, because the elevator was always broken and drag it into our apartment, and on Christmas Day we would open it.

The Globe Santa toys were great. I got a microscope set one year, a stamp and coin collection set another year, a chemistry set another year and plenty of cap guns and holsters and games and all kinds of great stuff. My sister would get dolls and games and girl stuff. I learned many years later that the people of the City of Boston and vicinity were responsible for Globe Santa, that Globe Santa was actually the donations of many, many people, mostly white people who donated money and gifts to the Boston Globe Newspaper and that Boston Globe made sure that underprivileged little colored kids like me in the Roxbury and Dorchester projects and all the poor white kids in the South Boston, Charlestown, Savin Hill and North Dorchester projects could have a Christmas.

That must have taken a lot of money, time and effort from a lot of people, and over the years I became a Globe Santa supporter and donator, so I want to say thank you to the Boston Globe Foundation and to all those people who donated toys and money to Globe Santa between 1956 and 1963 and gave joy to some little kids at the Whittier Street Housing projects in Roxbury. Thank you.

4

At that time, Mrs. Parker gave me the box, Tommy was a quiet, tall, skinny brown-skin kid with glasses. I didn't know him at all. I never saw him in the project courtyard, never saw him hanging out. Anyway, I guess he had always been in there, but I didn't notice him because he wasn't part of the group of kids I associated with or traded comic books with.

I remembered Mrs. Parker was in and out and she smelled good and she always had on a white uniform. So I took the box, and in the box there was a uniform; I looked at it and said to myself, *what is this*? And the uniform was a green uniform, but I wasn't really sure what it was. It wasn't until I found a place, kind of by asking around. It was farther away and so I had my mother take me to the place on Circuit Street near where my grandmother lived and they had this type of thing going on with the uniform. But they said I was too young and that I couldn't start until the next year, but I was told I could join something for little kids. I didn't want to join the little kid thing, I wanted to join the uniform, and so the following year when I turned twelve, I went up the street to St. John's Episcopal Church on Tremont Street. I had learned that there was a uniform there, led by a man named Frank "Fuzzy" Hector.

5

When I was 13 years-old, in 1964 Mrs. Parker while on her way home from what I learned was her nursing job, was found dead in the hallway, down in the basement, blood all over her white uniform, stabbed to death and robbed, down in the basement at 159 Cabot Street. I saw her a few times more after she gave me the box and I knocked on her door one Friday night so that she could see me in Tommy's uniform and she smiled and hugged me hard. I asked her how Tommy was, and she said he was doing fine in the Army.

She had taken an interest in me, it seemed, and like the many casualties and the many dead people I knew who died violently while I was growing up in the Whittier Street Housing Projects, she disappeared slowly from my view. But, she contributed to my life and my going into the Boy Scouts, and I will always love and remember her, because without that box of toys, and those Army Men, and that uniform from Tommy Parker, I would have never found Mr. Hector, who was very, very, very important to me in the development of my childhood and young manhood. From Mr. Hector, I would learn things that I would forget during my gang years, my lost childhood years, but they would come back, and I would remember Mr. Hector in his uniform, a Black man proud to be Troop 14's Scoutmaster, my Scout Master, the ghetto's Scout Master, and I would remember Mrs. Parker, Tommy Parker's mother forever.

Tommy came home from the Army. I remember seeing him and he was always sad, and the thing about Tommy was that Tommy began to look like a black ghost in the projects, because for a long while he could be found wondering around the projects or sitting at the bottom of the stairway at 159 Cabot Street, usually drinking; and I would talk to him about his mother, at the bottom of the stairs in the hallway. I would talk because now I was 14 or 15-years-old and I would talk to him and I knew how sad it was, that his mother was killed like that. And then I would see him with the gang I was in, around Grove Hall, in Dorchester when I was 16 and 16- years-old, from time to time. Tommy was now a heroin addict and I would still talk to him and he would do his heroin in front of me, and I knew how sad it was; and then I went into the military and I never saw him again.

CHAPTER 4
MY BASEBALL CAREER - 1962

1

By my 3rd year at St. Francis De Sales, I had made friends with a big white ghost kid named Francis Walsh, because if there was one thing I loved and he loved it was baseball.

I had loved the Celtics when I was a little kid, shining Bill Russell's shoes and all, but after I got a little older when I was 9, 10 and 11, it was the Red Sox that I loved. I would use my paper boy money and going to the store for people money and go to Fenway Park. A couple of my friends from the projects would go and we would sit up in the bleachers for a dollar on a Saturday afternoon. From time to time I would do that, I enjoyed doing that; and of course by selling the Record American newspaper, I was always reading about my sports heroes, the players from the Celtics and the Red Sox. But, I loved baseball and I was pretty good at it when I played it. I had a baseball glove and a baseball bat that I had bought with my paper boy money; they were very important to me, because I loved baseball.

In school, when we went out to recess I loved playing baseball and I was bad. When I was 11 years old Francis asked me if I would like to join his Little League Team with him and I said sure. Francis said he would talk with his mother about it and he and I and made plans. By this time, I had been going to St. Francis for a few years so I was well aware of who the ghosts were and that they were called white people. It seemed that some of them were nice and some of them weren't. He came with his mother to school one day and she asked where I lived. Francis knew I lived in the projects down the street from school already, but his mother didn't and asked where and how to get there and all that. So we made plans so he and his mother could come to my apartment. Now, of course, as I said before *my mother was crazy* and I didn't know how she would react to anything that I told her or did; so I didn't tell her anything until the last minute. I told her that same day that some kid from the school and his mother would be coming to take me so I could join a baseball Little League team and that I loved baseball.

2

So they came. The mother, as I remember, was a tall gangly woman. Frances was with her, before we graduated he wanted us all to call him Frank instead of Francis. He was a big, huge, nice little kid. They had never seen anything like the projects where I lived. I could tell by their eyes and by the way they looked, that they had never seen anything like they were seeing. They didn't know what they were coming to; but everything went fine and we walked down the stairs and nobody bothered them and I went out and we got into their car.

Where we were going was the Mission Hill Projects, which was near other projects where I lived. One was the Lenox Street Projects, one was the Orchard Street housing projects, another was the Cathedral Street Projects, across the railroad tracks going up Ruggles Street across from Tremont Street was the Annunciation Road Projects and the Heath Street Projects, and in back of that going up the hill a bit was what was called the Mission Hill Projects.

The Mission Hill Project was in back of the Mission Hill Immaculate Conception Church. It was mainly just like our projects, except it was full of ghost people, 99% white, so I knew we were going to the Mission Hill project because you had to sign up there to play baseball in the Little League, but I wasn't sure that Francis and his mother knew what they were doing.

3

Francis and his mother were pretty much just nice people and so they didn't think anything about it. But the minute I walked in the door there was a loud bustling noise and there were a lot of those ugly white ghost's people staring at me. We walked in and all of a sudden it became like a gauntlet of all these white men and women ghosts and they were talking loud. Then there was just a lot of them coming from everywhere; I'll never forget and I heard Francis mother saying *we are just trying sign up for the Little League.* And we went in and she walked past the door and we were sitting there and a man said *don't let that nigger in;* and it didn't dawn on me that they must be talking about me. But they were, and it went on and on, and their voices got louder and louder, more and more; and the mother was getting scared. I could tell that by her eyes and how she was trying to hold on to her son and me.

The crowd just kept saying *get that nigger out of here* and we started backing out; and before we knew it somebody spit on me and then somebody else spit on me, and somebody else spit on me. I guess everybody spit on me. I think there might have been at least 200 White people there at this point, yelling, screaming and pointing at me, *get that nigger out of here,* and calling *me nigger, nigger, nigger, nigger, nigger, nigger, nigger, , nigger, nigger, nigger, nigger, nigger, nigger, nigger, nigger, nigger, nigger, nigger, nigger, nigger, nigger, nigger, , nigger, nigger, nigger, nigger, nigger, nigger, nigger, nigger, nigger, nigger, nigger, nigger, , nigger, , nigger, , nigger, , nigger, nigger, nigger, nigger, , nigger, and nigger,* again and again and again and again and again and again and again and again and spitting on me. And the mother just started running and pulling us, running and crying; and we got to the car and she was crying. She didn't understand. But, I understood what was going on. I had seen them before and heard them before, but never like that before. And she drove me back to my mother's house at 159 Cabot Street, walked me up to the 5th floor, screaming and crying. I don't know what she said, she just yelled something and she kept saying *I'm sorry.* I walked back into the apartment and took off my clothes and spit was in my hair and face. I was just full of spit; and Francis' mother rushed out crying.

My mother closed the door. Frances and I had to go to school together, but he never mentioned it. He never mentioned it in school, he never said anything about it and we never played baseball together again. I never tried to join the Little League again and I never played baseball again. I never went to Fenway Park again either, and that was the end of my baseball career.

CHAPTER 5
THE BOY SCOUTS OF AMERICA
1962-1965

The Boy Scouts of America is one of the nation's largest and most prominent values-based youth development organizations. The Boy Scouts of America provides a program for young people that builds character, trains them in the responsibilities of participating citizenship, and develops personal fitness.

For over a century, the Boy Scouts of America has helped build the future leaders of this country by combining educational activities and lifelong values with fun. The Boy Scouts of America believes and, through over a century of experience, knows that helping youth is a key to building a more conscientious, responsible, and productive society

1

The green uniform I met that Friday night in October 1962 at St. John's Episcopal Church on Tremont Street in Lower Roxbury, was a big boned seemingly tall, but short, but kind of tall, stocky, husky, heavy set, light brown skinned Black man with a big mustache, a stern kindly face, a booming voice and he was exuberant about me and the other Black kids from the surrounding projects and ghetto. I had just turned twelve years old and was meeting for the first time the man who for the next two and a half years would guide me and give me his greatness, his knowledge, his confidence, his belief, his patience, and take me to places I would never have gone without his love, care and attention to ghetto and project boys like me.

His name was Frank "Fuzzy" Hector, he had run track for English High School, trained at the Tuskegee Institute in Alabama and became a part of the 99th Fighter Squadron the all-black unit that distinguished themselves fighting the German Air Force and the United States Army Air Corps' institutional racism. He was a Tuskegee Airman, a gunner and radio operator. He was a World War ll hero,

2

The 99th Fighter Squadron, earned three Distinguished Unit Citations (DUC) during World War II. The DUCs were for operations over Sicily from 30 May – 11 June 1943, Monastery Hill near Cassino from 12–14 May 1944, and for successfully fighting off German jet aircraft on 24 March 1945. The mission was the longest bomber escort mission of the Fifteenth Air Force throughout the war. The Tuskegee Airmen shot down three German jets in a single day. Forty-three P-51 Mustangs led by Colonel Benjamin O. Davis escorted B-17 bombers over 1,600 miles into Germany and back. The bombers' target, a massive Daimler-Benz tank factory in Berlin, was heavily defended by *Luftwaffe* aircraft, included Fw 190 radial propeller fighters, Me 163 "Komet" rocket-powered fighters and 25 of the much more formidable Me 262s, history's first operational jet fighter. African American Pilots Charles Brantley, Earl Lane and Roscoe Brown all shot down German jets over Berlin that day.

For the mission, the 332nd Fighter Group earned a Distinguished Unit Citation. The 332nd also flew missions in Sicily, Anzio, Normandy, the Rhineland, the Po Valley and Rome-Arno and others. Pilots of the 99th set a World War ll record for destroying five enemy aircraft in under four minutes. Individual pilots of the 332nd Fighter Group earned 96 Distinguished Flying Crosses. Their missions took them over Italy and enemy occupied parts of central and southern Europe, including Germany. Their operational aircraft were, in succession: Curtiss P-40 Warhawk, Bell P-39 Airacobra, Republic P-47 Thunderbolt and North American P-51 Mustang fighter aircraft.

Mr. Hector was 38 years old when we met and a fifth-generation Bostonian, who had grown up Upper Middle Class in Roxbury and was living in a massive home on a side street off of Warren Street, up the hill in an Upper Middle Class cul de sac called Elm Hill Park, right across the street from where my future wife, Yvonne Rose, was born and raised. After the war Mr. Hector attended Suffolk and Northeastern Universities, married a woman named Edna who he was married to for fifty years, became an account executive with the Boston Beverage Co., distributors of Seagram's liquors, for 30 years, and was raising two son's Chris and Derek Hector. He would later form a local Massachusetts Chapter of the Tuskegee Airmen, become its first President, and go into the Boston Public Schools and talk to kids and as each Tuskegee Airman would pass away Mr. Hector and the other Airmen would be there, at attention, snapping a final salute to a Lonely Eagle.

3

I did not know anything that I have written and would not know nothing about this man until many decades later, all I knew on that October Friday night of 1962, when we met, was that, Mr. Hector was the Scoutmaster of Boy Scout Troop 14, Boston's and maybe Massachusetts only Black Boy Scout Troop. He wore the green uniform and was quite possibly the greatest man of many great Black men and women that I would ever meet; and I was standing there looking up at him in Tommy Parkers old Boy Scout Uniform, that I had personally taken across the street to the laundry mat on Tremont Street and washed, dried and ironed myself, wearing my freshest sneakers.

He told me that they met on time, from 7:00 p.m. to 10:00 p.m. every Friday night, that my membership dues were $10.00 a year and he handed me what was to be my bible for the next two and a half years, "The Boy Scout Handbook", one of the greatest books ever written, which I read cover to cover, maybe a hundred times over the next two and a half years.

The first thing he taught me was the Boy Scout oath: *On my honor I will do my best to do my duty to God and my country and to obey the Scout Law; To help other people at all times; To keep myself physically strong, mentally awake, and morally straight,* and motto: *A Scout is trustworthy, loyal, helpful, friendly, courteous, kind, obedient, cheerful, thrifty, brave, clean, and reverent.* One month later, after I had performed many tasks given by the Boy Scout Manuel to Mr. Hectors satisfaction and recited my Boy Scout oath and motto, on a Friday night with my mother there I was Inducted into the Boy Scouts of America with a special Scout Induction Ceremony.

4

The preparations included 2 candles and candle holders, Scout badges, Troop flag and one lighted candle placed in the center of the ceremony table. **Scoutmaster**: *This flame is the Flame of Knowledge. You new Scouts have shown me that you have a hunger for knowledge by fulfilling the requirements of joining our great troop. The Scouting program offers you a special kind of knowledge that will serve you well as you walk the sometimes difficult Road* to Manhood. **Scoutmaster**: *The Flame of Knowledge never goes out as long as there are people on the earth who seek knowledge. Its light guides seekers to higher understanding.* The Scoutmaster picks up the 2nd candle from the table and lights it from the first.

Scoutmaster: This *candle represents a Youth who seeks knowledge. It represents each of you scouts here today because you seek to travel on the scouting path and learn our ways.* **Scoutmaster**: *Tending this flame is a big responsibility.* The Scoutmaster hands the candle to the closest scout. **Scoutmaster:** *Pass this candle from scout to scout until you have all held it, never letting the flame go out. Just as you receive this flame from another scout, you will receive much knowledge from other scouts in your troop. Receiving the knowledge is only half of the challenge. Just as you pass the flame to another scout, you will be expected to pass the knowledge you gain on to other scouts that follow you. As you become a more experienced scout, rising through the ranks of Tenderfoot, 2nd Class, and 1st Class, your flame will grow stronger, helped along by these scouts around you. When you are ready, you will become the teacher rather than the student and will help new scouts keep their flame burning. You will only excel and grow if you take your responsibility seriously. Scouting will give you more than you can possibly imagine, but only if you fulfill your commitment to your patrol and your troop.* When the last scout has the candle, the Scoutmaster takes it from him.

Scoutmaster: *Remember, this flame is your new search for knowledge about our scouting ways. As you are just beginning, it is not yet strong.* Scoutmaster puffs out the candle. **Scoutmaster:** *See how easily the Breeze of Laziness extinguishes it? If you put off your responsibilities, or don't bring your Scout Handbook for requirements sign-offs, or let other scouts carry the load, your small flame will fail. Luckily, the flame of Knowledge in our troop is strong, very strong. You can relight your flame at any time by participating and concentrating on the Scout Law. The more you participate and the more effort you put in, the stronger your flame becomes and more difficult to extinguish. At some point, your flame will become a burning ember deep in your heart that will be impossible to ever put out.*

Scoutmaster: *It is my pleasure to present each of you with your Scout badge to show that your flame is burning and you are on your way to higher ranks. Notice there is also a small pin. Present this pin to your parent now and have them attach your badge on your left shirt pocket. In our troop, it is customary to attach the badge upside down until the scout has performed a good deed.*

Quickly return here when you are finished. The program continues when all have re-assembled. **Sr. Patrol Leader**: *Scouts, gather around our troop flag and take hold of the flag with your left hand. Make the Scout Sign with your right hand. Troop number 14, Stand at attention! Troop number 14. Scout Sign! New scouts, please lead the troop in the Scout Oath. Troop 14, join me in congratulating these new Scouts of Troop 14!*

5

It was the happiest day of my life up until that point. I remember being so proud, so happy to be there with Mr. Hector and my new scout friends. When I turned twelve, I also began working for the Christian Scientist Monitor Newspaper during the day after school and only did my Record American Newspaper route from Mondays to Thursdays so that I would have Fridays off for my Boy Scout meetings. Eventually after a year, when I was thirteen, I reduced my paper route to just selling the Boston Globe Sunday Newspaper and doing the Christian Scientist Monitor, so I could devote more time to my scouting activities during the week, but for now, I was finally a full fledge scout a Tenderfoot Boy Scout of America and I took my duties and oath very seriously.

Every Friday night from 7:00 p.m. to 10:00 p.m. Mr. Hector became a father, a teacher, and a man to me. I don't ever remember him interfering or being in our regular lives, but every Friday night he would be there in the basement of St. John's Episcopal Church waiting for us, ready to take us young boys on another journey towards our eventual teenage and manhood. I was very lucky to have found him and the things he taught me and showed me have lasted to this very day.

Mr. Hector taught us many things on how to be boys, how to be men, and how to be prepared. He taught us discipline, organization, dedication, how to be dedicated to something, how to finish a project, how to hold our heads up high, how to do our best, how to live by the scout oath and creed, how to not let one another down and he was absolutely one of the most important people who I would ever meet. But Mr. Hector would have to learn how to love me, as well as, maybe sometimes dislike me.

6

Because of my environment, my mother, the projects, my family, or the boogieman, I had developed a Dr. Jekyll and Mr. Hyde personality, which meant that one day I was this way and the next day I would be another way.

In micro-seconds I could change from a quiet, shy, unassuming child into a ferocious animal fully adapted to the harsh demands and realities of the projects and the ghetto. I was impulsive, hyperactive and paranoiac as well as thoughtful, concerned and attentive. I would be a real mess and cause Mr. Hector endless embarrassments and he would learn to dislike me, but I was real intelligent, real competitive and real adventurous and those were the things that Mr. Hector would learn to love.

One time he took us to an Air Force base, Hanscom Air Force Base in Bedford, Massachusetts. Whenever we would go anywhere, Mr. Hector would always give us the *don't embarrass yourselves, me, the Boy Scouts or our Race* speech. Meaning that since we were the only Black Boy Scout Troop that anyone might or would ever see, that we shouldn't embarrass him, ourselves or Troop 14.

So we were up at Hanscom Air Force Base to learn about air conditioning and refrigeration and to take a tour of the base and I wondered off from the group and climbed into a helicopter. Unknowing to me the helicopter door had locked, and I started pushing buttons and flipping switches and turned a key and the helicopter blades started turning and the helicopter started to try to lift off the ground and some Airmen saw me and the helicopter and tried to open the door, but it was locked and so they tied the helicopter down and ran to get something to break the door down, which they did and another guy managed to reach in and stop the helicopter. At this point there were like a hundred people outside the helicopter and I saw Mr. Hector and the Troop. Mr. Hector was real angry with me and although he didn't put me out the Troop, he was upset and didn't speak to me at all for the next few meetings. Stuff like that I would do.

7

Most of the time though we spent in the basement of St. John's Episcopal Church playing endless and exciting games of dodge ball, which everybody loved and helped release a lot of excess energy a twelve, thirteen and fourteen-year-old Ghetto kid like me might have. The rule was that we always had to wear our uniforms to meetings, so sometimes, more often than not, our uniforms would be looking pretty shabby after the dodge ball games. But, Mr. Hector didn't care about that as long as we wore our uniforms to meetings and when we had to go somewhere that they were clean, pressed and starched.

So we played hard between 7:00 p.m. and 8:30 p.m. and then Mr. Hector would put the younger scouts with the older scouts so that we could prepare and learn how to tie knots and ropes, which was real important, and lots of other stuff that was in the Boy Scout Handbook, so that we could advance in rank. One of the more important things in Scouting was the attainment of Merit Badges and that was where Mr. Hector would learn to love me.

8

Taken from the Boy Scout Handbook - *Boy Scout merit badges give scouts the opportunity to investigate around* 120 *different areas of knowledge and skills. The merit badge program plays a major role in the scouting advancement program and participation can begin as soon as a scout registers with a troop. Each scout can explore topics from American Business to Woodworking as he has interest. The only limitations are his ambition and availability of adult merit badge counselors to offer instruction.*

Merit Badge Process: *A scout decides he would like to earn a specific merit badge. He obtains approval to begin the merit badge from his Scoutmaster. The Scoutmaster identifies possible merit badge counselors. The scout identifies another scout, buddy, or family member that will be his partner to attend all meetings with the counselor to follow safe scouting guidelines. He then contacts the counselor to begin badge work. The counselor reviews the requirements with the scouts and they decide on projects to complete and a completion schedule. The counselor provides expertise, advice, guidance as needed until the scouts have completed the requirements. The merit badge counselor certifies completion of requirements and the merit badge patch is presented at a court of honor or troop meeting.*

Required Merit Badges: *A boy scout can begin taking merit badges as soon as he joins a troop, but no merit badges are required for advancement until he receives his First Class rank. Advancement to Star, Life, and Eagle all require completion of merit badges, service, and demonstration of responsibility. To reach Eagle rank, a scout must complete a total of at least 21 Boy Scout merit badges listing them in his handbook, 13 of which come from the Eagle-required badge list.*

9

During the winter of 1963, I wanted to earn a Merit Badge in Camping, one because I had never gone camping before and two because I wanted to go camping. I had a sleeping bag because I was a member of the Boys Club near Dudley Street in Roxbury, and they had always had sleep overs in the gym during the winter and outside with movies in the summer. I had been a member of the Boys Club and the YMCA on Huntington Avenue, near Boylston Street since I had been eight and nine years old and treasured my Boys Club Card which was a hard piece of red shale. Like the public libraries where I practically lived at, they were places where I not only could go and hide from my mother and get away from her madness, but they were places where I could learn things, read all the books I wanted, play sports, ping pong, play pool, swim and have friends who came there and people I knew who worked there that didn't live in the projects.

Both the Y and the Boys Club had wonderful swimming pools and I loved not only to swim, but, I loved to compete in swimming matches and I could almost always win in my age group all the time. I loved winning. I mean I loved competing and winning. I totally loved it!! The Boys Club and Y would give me all these little trophies and ribbons when I won or came in second and I would hide them in my room. Some of the kids' mothers would come to the matches and watch them, but the reason why I was there was to get away from mine, so I hardly ever told her about the matches and when I did it was after the fact. It was like, "Oh look what I won", and she would hardly look at it.

I was so good at swimming, competing and winning, that the Boys Club and the Y would fight over me to swim exclusively for them and the swim meet people and instructors would tell my friends at the Y or Boys Club to tell me to make sure I came to this match or that match, it was a lot of fun. Anyway, I had bought a sleeping bag with my paperboy money when I was a real kid and now I was going to buy a bigger boy sleeping bag, the type that Mr. Hector said that I needed with extra padding and he said I needed cooking utensils, a tent and he went over the handbook with me and the regulations, requirements and items I would need to have and know to get the Merit Badge. He also put with me an older scout named Oscar, who became a good friend of mine.

So I bought my sleeping bag and cooking utensils and Randy who had just moved in with us, bought my tent, clothes, boots and other items I needed, he was always good like that. Mr. Hector's sons Chris and Derek were very helpful and made sure that I was fully prepared to achieve my goal of getting my first Merit Badge.

10

We started out that February of 1963 at Oscar's house and myself along with Oscar and five other scouts going for various other Merit Badges like Camping, Hiking and Cooking were driven to a starting point in the Blue Hill Mountains near Milton, Massachusetts. Mr. Hector had told me that it might be possible for to get a cooking Merit Badge, also, if I did certain things in starting a fire, properly using and handling my utensils and following the requirements in cooking my meals in our campsite. So we began hiking up a trail into the Blue Hills and after about a four hour hike we decided to set up a camp in an open area with few trees around.

It was a little cold, and the requirements were two days and two nights, but we were all hardy Boston Ghetto boys who were used to the cold. That afternoon and early evening we had a lot of fun pitching our tents, setting up our camp, setting our camp fires, digging our latrines and doing all the requirements necessary to get our Merit Badges. That night after a lot of joking and playing around and after we had all enjoyed fixing and eating the meals we cooked, we settled in our tents and sleeping bags and went to sleep.

Oscar's screams woke me up and when I went to peek outside my tent and see what was going on, I couldn't see anything, and all I knew was that I was colder than I had ever felt before. It seemed that Oscars screams had woke everybody up and a lot of the kids were crying, I guessed they were all having the same problem I was and that's when I first noticed something about me, something that I had always known as far back as I could remember, something I knew I had, but didn't know what it was. I was calm, it was like everything slowed down and I could see everything that was happening real clearly and what was happening was that a Nor'easter, an unforeseen, unpredicted, major Snowstorm, a Blizzard, was blowing through Boston and New England and we were buried up to our tents in the mountains in snow.

I had slept in my clothes, parka and boots and after a while I managed to dig myself and my scouting partner out of our tent with my half shovel, saw that the other four tents were buried in snow, and made my way over to Oscar, who was still screaming and then I saw why. Oscar had for some reason fallen asleep with his feet hanging outside his tent, and when I made my way into his tent his sleeping bag was open and he was half in and the lower half with his legs and feet were hanging out. It looked like his feet had become frostbitten.

11

It was always so cold in a Boston winter that you had to be real careful, because frostbite could sneak up on you anytime, before you knew it, and your hands or feet would be in some deep shit. I had a tendency to play outside long after I should have and when I came inside I would have to put my hands in the oven to warm them up and that could be some painful shit. So I knew that Oscar was in deep shit and he needed some help right away.

The other kids were beginning to dig themselves out and I said that I was going for help, right now. What I knew then, and what I've always known since I was a child, was that because of the type of mother I had and throw in the environment that I lived in, I was always under stress, I was always under pressure, it was like I thought that's how everyone lived, under stress, so stress and pressure were normal to me. It was like in my Dorchester High yearbook, some kid said that I was 'calm under fire' and that's what it was, I ate stress for breakfast, the more stress the more pressure on me the calmer I was, without stress, I would fuck shit up, because I was bored. So I learned early that I could cause people enormous stress and I could take enormous stress, I could give and take shit pretty easily and then one day forty years later I couldn't take shit anymore and I was done.

But this was March 1963 and my friends needed me to be cool, because they needed help and the stress and whatever the problems were felt good to me, I could deal with this. I told my fellow scouts that we needed to try to build a fire as close to Oscar's feet as possible and I told them that I was going for help, right away. I knew that to wait would not be good, because what for, nothing was going to happen, but get worse, and besides we and nobody else knew where we were. So I just started off the way we came in, so I thought.

12

The Timex watch my Grandmére had gotten me for my twelfth birthday had told me that it had taken us about four hours of walking to get where we were and I thought I would be walking at least that long and in this much snow probably much longer to get back to the road we came in. Well, that didn't happen. God and fate kicked in and I went the wrong way and must have walked the direct opposite way that we came in and after walking about an hour I came out to a ridge and looked down upon a road. I went down the ridge to the road and just started walking up the road following the tire tracks that had been made in the snow; and after about a half an hour, a Massachusetts State Police car drove up and stopped. The Massachusetts State Policeman with the big hat got out the car and said, *"We've been looking for you".*

While I sat in the patrol car, he radioed in that we had been found. What I found out later was that Mr. Hector had called the police and other state agencies as soon as it had begun to snow, alerting them that we were out there, somewhere in the Blue Hills and had given our starting point as a reference. While I sat in the warm patrol car other police cars came and an officer handed me some hot chocolate and candy bars.

They walked into the woods following my footsteps and in a couple of hours had brought Oscar and everyone out. We were taken to a nearby hospital, checked out and examined. Oscar stayed, and the rest of us were driven home by the Massachusetts State Policeman with the big hat. When the State Police car arrived at the Whittier Street Housing Projects there were a lot of project people hanging out around my building in the snow and what I found out later was that we had been all over the news as missing children and that a lot of people had been looking for us.

Everybody, including my mother, were happy to see me; and my picture, for the first time, was taken for the newspaper. There was a write up in one of the newspapers that I sold and I was a legend in the projects for about two weeks. At a ceremony on a Friday night, Mr. Hector awarded us our Merit Badges and I got two Merit Badges, one for Camping and one for Hiking. Although he didn't make a big deal about it, I could tell that Mr. Hector was very proud of me; but that, unfortunately, wouldn't be the last time that Mr. Hector, me and State Policemen would interact. And although Oscar would be okay, with no severe frost bite, he would always walk a little funny after that, but at least he was walking.

13

I would have many more camping trip adventures and outings with Mr. Hector and Troop 14, but none would be better than our sorties to Adams Pond Scout Camp in Barnstead, New Hampshire. The first time I learned that I could go to the camp, it became the most important thing to me in my whole life and since it would be the first time I would be going to camp and the first time I would be going anywhere outside of my Grandmére's house and outside of Boston, I couldn't wait to go.

There were a lot of things to do to get ready. Clothes had to be labeled with your last name and you could only bring so many pieces of each item, three pairs of sox, four pairs of underwear and tee shirts, lots of stuff like that, and I had to buy what I found out was the second and third most important things you needed when going to Boy Scout Camp, and maybe any camp, was mosquito lotion and a mosquito net. The mosquitos were so big up at Adams Pond Scout Camp that all night long all you could hear was this tremendous ruckus and noise of hundreds of mosquitos so huge, that when you shined your flashlights on them, you could look in their eyes, staring back at you, outside of your mosquito net, drooling, salivating and hungering for your blood, thirsting to get inside and bite you, and drink your blood. God ever forbid that your mosquito net had a hole in it and you didn't know it.

One of the funniest things I can remember was one of the scouts, screaming in terror one night. He must have woken up and found a few hundred mosquitos in his cot with him, biting him, drinking his blood, and he jumped up breaking down his cot, mosquito net and tent, running off into the woods dragging it all behind him. It was funny. I'm telling you, patches for mosquito net repair were right there behind mosquito nets as the most important things you need at camp, especially when you're sleeping in a tent. But the most important thing, the number one thing Mr. Hector wanted us to care about, was our Boy Scout Uniforms.

14

From the Boy Scout Handbook—*The tan and green Boy Scout uniform is a well-known symbol of American scouting. Scout uniforms are an important part of the Boy Scouts of America program and one of the methods of scouting. Each boy gets to be part of a group demonstrated by their uniform and each group has a personal sense of identity. The scout uniform is also a display case for a scout's individual accomplishments, Merit Badges and recognitions. We wear the uniform to associate ourselves with the principles to which we are committed— character development, citizenship training, and physical and mental fitness.*

All scouts in the program wear the same uniform with the major differences being the badges each scout has earned and the troop specific neckerchief. The uniform is not intended to hide our individuality, but it is a way we give each other strength and support. The official scout uniform consists of hat, shirt, red

or yellow neckerchief, pants, belt, and socks. Having all scouts consistently uni-
formed for meetings and outings makes for a much better adventure.

The Scouting movement is built on positive values. As we wear the uniform
scouts stand together and encourage each other to live by those principles. Scouts
and adults alike should take pride in belonging to this program and wear the
uniform correctly. Placement of insignia and patches on the uniform is very
important. The Boy Scout Handbook and the Boy Scout Association Insignia
Guide discusses all the uniform patch placement and other insignia use. Merit
Badge placement on the sash is up to the scout. The Merit Badge sash is worn
draped over the right shoulder and left hip. the Merit Badges can be displayed
in rows of two or three and there is no required ordering of badges.

During my two and a half years with the Boy Scouts I never had another
Boy Scout Uniform except the one that Mrs. Parker had given me, Tommy
Parker's uniform. I played in it, hiked in it, went on outings in it, learned
in it, went to meetings in it, went to Adams Pond Scout Camp in it. I
absolutely loved my uniform and wore it with pride.

15

Mr. Hector knew that we were poor boys, and couldn't afford all the acces-
sories the Boy Scout Handbook said we were supposed to have including
different uniforms for official duties and different uniforms for recreational
purposes. He knew that us ghetto boys were all in the one uniform does
everything and serves every purpose program, but he did all he could to pay
for everything he could for us, and that included sponsoring and finding
sponsors for our outings and Adams Pond Scout Camp. He did everything.
He secured our camp site, paid each boys fees, our meals, our recreational
time slots. He paid for our transportation up to the camp and back home
and never asked us for anything in return, except that we come to our Boy
Scout meetings on time and that we always do our best and be the best
scouts we could be.

Before we went to Adams Pond Scout camp, Mr. Hector trained us well. He
showed us how to give the Boy Scout salute in unison, how to march and
walk together, how to eat together at meal times, how to conduct ourselves
and act around what he said, except for us, was an all-white boy scout camp,
and that was the beauty of Mr. Hector. He might have had to give us 'the
speech', but he made sure that we were fully exposed to their Boy Scouts of
America White World and had access to all that they thought was theirs. He

made sure that we ate with all the White Boy Scout troops and made sure that they competed with us and judged us in the competitions fairly and he didn't take any shit from the other scoutmasters or camp officials about us. He totally believed in us and believed we could do no wrong. But, of course, he somehow forgot about me.

16

Adams Pond Scout Camp was like a magical place for me. It was like a Disneyland, a place I would never get to, but better. A place where we could do all the things we loved doing as Boy Scouts and adventurers. The camp occupied 900 acres on Adams Pond and offered us scouts *swimming, boating, canoeing, small boat sailing, plus motor boating and water skiing.* The camp offered *tent campsites, an activity field for athletics, a dining hall and patrol outdoor cooking sites with a full service quartermaster center with stoves, chef kits and patrol boxes, high adventure programs, extended backpacking and canoe trips, two archery ranges, two handicraft centers, a track and trailblazer road.* The waterfront offered: *fishing, kayaking, windsurfing, water basketball, water polo, lifeguard and first aid training, water volleyball, open swims, the mile swim, snorkeling and rowing.*

Field sports activities included: *rifle shoot, shotgun trap shoot, field archery, target archery, volleyball and Frisbee.* At the Handicraft Center they offered: *leatherworking, basketry and woodcarving.* The Scoutcraft Center included: *pirate's breakfast, Dutch oven cooking, utensilless cooking, tin foil cooking, knot instruction, orienteering treasure hikes, low impact camping, lashing and rope making instruction, wilderness survival skills and pioneering projects.*

At the Nature Center they had: *nature hikes, star hikes, conservation projects, nature canoe jaunts, tree identification, scavenger hunts, bird watching and day hikes.*

And finally the most important thing to me was that Adam's Pond Scout Camp offered a 36 Merit Badge Achievement Program that included: *Archery, Art, Astronomy, Athletics, Backpacking, Basketry, Camping, Canoeing, Climbing, Emergency Preparedness, Environmental Science, First Aid, Fish and Wildlife Management, Fishing, Forestry, Geology, Hiking, Leatherwork, Lifesaving, Mammal Study, Motor boating, Nature, Orienteering, Pioneering, Reptile and Amphibian Study, Rifle Shooting, Rowing, Shotgun Shooting, Small Boat Sailing, Soil and Water Conservation, Sports, Swimming, Waterskiing, Weather, Wilderness Survival and Wood Carving.*

17

That 1st year July 1963 at Adams Pond Scout Camp my intentions were, and I had already applied for and got my requirements from Mr. Hector to get my Swimming, Cooking, Canoeing, and Archery Merit Badges, and to swim the one-mile swim meet. When we arrived at the camp we were led to our campsite. It was called the Mohawk Camp Site and had eleven tents and twenty-one cots set up in a circle. There were twenty of us boys and Mr. Hector, so there were two boys to each tent and Mr. Hector had his own tent. In the middle was a huge campfire pit where we would cook our breakfast and evening meals and it was also used for those scouts going for their cooking and Camping Merit Badges.

We were going to be there a week and on the third day I was scheduled to be tested for my Swimming Merit Badge, which consisted of me performing two laps of the freestyle stroke, the backstroke, the sidestroke and the butterfly stroke and then after a ten-minute break swimming five laps freestyle, all of which I could do and was pretty good at except for the butterfly stroke, I always had problems with my breathing with that stroke. On the fourth day I was going up for my Archery Merit Badge and would be practicing for an hour each day. That same night I would be going for my Cooking Merit Badge and on that Saturday I would be swimming the One Mile Swim Competition and going for my Canoeing Merit Badge. I was a pretty strong, resolute, stubborn, somewhat confident and competitive twelve-year-old kid, so I didn't think I would have any problems and wasn't worried about anything except for the Butterfly Stroke and Archery which I really wasn't that good at, but on a good day I could hit the bulls eye all day, but on a bad day I couldn't even hit the target. So it would be hit or miss with that.

18

I was not scheduled for anything that second day and after breakfast when Mr. Hector went to take care of some business with the camp officials I decided to explore the area and see what was going on, sort of get the lay of the land. I walked out of the campsite down the road a while checking out the other campsites and a white scout who was doing the same thing I was doing hooked up with me. We were about the same age and we talked about the camp and stuff.

As we were walking along we spotted a body of water and walked over to it and started walking along the edge and throwing rocks in the water to make them skip. As we walked along some more throwing rocks and talking we spotted a rowboat along the edge in the water surrounded by bushes and I decided that we should get in it and pretend that we were sailors.

Well, before I knew it, we had pushed off from the edge of the shoreline and were enveloped in a current that was moving us fast from the edge of the lake deep into the middle of the lake and yes, you already have guessed it, the rowboat didn't have any oars in it. So there we were, this white kid I had just met and me, trying to paddle with our hands and make it back to the shoreline without having any success, after a while we saw that we were stranded far from land and decided that our only recourse was to start yelling for help, which we did.

19

Someone did hear us and people started showing up at the shoreline and soon what looked like firemen showed up and then the New Hampshire State Policemen with the big hats showed up and soon there is a very large crowd and soon I can see that Mr. Hector has shown up, I guess once they had determined that there was a black scout in the middle of the lake, they knew who to go get. Finally, a boat came out and they secured a tow line to the rowboat and towed us back to shore.

Mr. Hector, and I never use this word, but Mr. Hector was pissed off. He all but snatched me and dragged me back to the campsite, lecturing and complaining about me all the way back. But, I will say this he stood up for me and made sure that I got the same punishment as the white kid, which was none. I was able to compete for my Swimming Merit Badge which I aced, my Archery Merit Badge which I failed, my Cooking Merit Badge which I passed, the One Mile Swim where I came in first in my age group and where I'll never forget Mr. Hector being all proud and giving me the biggest hug as I dripped water all over him, and my Canoeing Merit Badge which I passed also. As I've said, Mr. Hector had a love, dislike relationship with me, but that week up at Adams Pond Scout Camp, I made him, except for that one incident, proud, and he presented me some weeks later with my two new Merit Badges to be added and sewn into Tommy Parkers Boy Scout Uniform.

20

During the next year I would get my First Aid and Stamp Collecting Merit Badges and that next summer, 1964, up at Boy Scout Camp again, when I was thirteen, I would come in first in my age group at the One Mile Swim. That same night I convinced a group of fun loving adventurous scouts like me, in my troop, to raid another troop's campsite. We did and pulled down their tents and made a lot of mischief. The camp officials and the New Hampshire State Policemen with the big hats came to our campsite to talk to Mr. Hector, and when they left Mr. Hector called me into his tent where he was even more pissed off then the year before and told me to *pack my bags and hike back to Boston.*

The next morning, I did. My scout brothers were all sad and commiserating around me while I was packing and putting in as much as I could in my backpack. I started out and walked to the road, turned left and started walking towards where I though Boston would be. After about five hours of walking, a camp transportation van pulled up to me and Mr. Hector was in it. He told me to get in and drove me back to the campsite. I would cause no more trouble up at Scout Camp and go on to get my Rowing Merit Badge and ace my Archery Merit Badge test with five bullseyes.

21

My Boy Scouts of America career with my Merit Badges, my Red Neckerchief and Tommy Parkers Uniform would last until April of 1965, and I would have many more adventures with Troop 14 and Mr. Hector. That April I would quit the Boy Scouts and join the gangs, never looking back and effectively ending my childhood.

And so in the space of seven years I would seek and find for myself four men and some sisters who would begin to save me and change my life: Melvin B. Miller, the Publisher of the Bay State Banner, a Boston Latin School Graduate, a Harvard University Graduate, a Columbia University Law School Graduate, an Assistant U.S. Attorney for the District of Massachusetts, a man who I would befriend at the beginning of his career, and learn the fundamentals of running a business from. A man of great generosity and kindness, who would befriend me and listen to my advice as a child; Frank "Fuzzy" Hector, a family man, a man of the highest principals, a Tuskegee Airman, a Boy Scout Scoutmaster a great, great man, who would teach me organization, discipline and dedication; Father Paul Francis and Monsignor George V. Kerr, two men who would begin to save my life as a child using the love of God and education as the primary instruments; The Sisters of St. Francis de Sales School who would care for me and educate me like I was a child of God, which I was, and my Grandmére' and Papa Ray who would show and give me unconditional love all their lives.

And so with the Catholic Church, The Boston Public Libraries, The Boy Scouts of America, The Boys Club of America and the YMCA, I would have, and would need all that they had taught me, because my father would be getting out of jail soon and he would have something else to say and show me.

CHAPTER 6
AGASSIZ VILLAGE - 1965

1
AGASSIZ VILLAGE IS A CAMP FOR AT-RISK CHILDREN

An overnight summer camp experience for thousands of children since 1935!

Agassiz Village was founded in 1935 at its present lakeside location in Poland Maine by Mr. & Mrs. Harry E. Burroughs. Then, as now, Agassiz gave children the opportunity to escape the hardship of their daily lives. Originally the camp served boys who worked as newsboys, bootblacks, or other street vendors. The boys learned basic job skills, practiced school subjects, experienced outdoor living, and developed many life skills.

By the age of fourteen I had stopped going to the Boy Scouts. I was becoming more affiliated with gangs. I was smoking and had taken my first drink, which changed my life because with drinking alcohol I saw that everything was possible. I understood who I was and drinking changed me and made everything possible to me. I could be who I was. I saw my salvation in this bottle of alcohol and it would and could destroy all the pain inside of me that I had been feeling for many years; but unknowing to me, God was still working with me and would work with me for many years as I went down and up and down and up and up and down in life with drugs and alcohol.

So Agassiz Village was a place that you got sent to if you were causing problems within the home and nobody knew why. My mother had gone to the welfare department and said that I was a problem child because I had tried to throw her out the fifth floor window, that's why. She, of course, didn't tell them what she had been doing to me all those years in that apartment since I had been a little child. I was out of Saint Francis de Sales Catholic School and had been going to public school, English Annex it was called, up near Egleston Station, near Jamaica Plain; and I wasn't really going to school a lot. Instead, I was fooling around, doing a lot of things like: finding alcohol, getting high, drinking, and smoking cigarettes, probably all that you do when you live in the ghetto and live in pain, or fuck it, live in pain anywhere.

So I went to Agassiz Village and while I was there something happened that would enlighten me. I was used to fighting in the projects with Black kids and in school with mainly White kids. It was what I did and I enjoyed it. I enjoyed hand-to-hand personal combat, especially with kids a little bigger than me. I found that fighting with kids that weren't as big as me was less formidable and wasn't a challenge. So I liked to fight you if you were bigger and I didn't like you, I didn't like fighting kids I liked. I enjoyed being hit and I enjoyed hitting a kid back. So, at this camp, there was this white kid, and I guess I must have stepped in line. I mean at all the camps that I went to, I was a little weird because I was a weird type of kid, but I always found things to do that were outside the realm of the rules. I didn't adhere to rules really well. At this particular time at Agassiz Village, this Irish white kid from Savin Hill said, *Well you know you're not supposed to step in line like that!*

I looked at him. He was bigger and it was an immediate invitation to fight, which meant that in fighting, I never said anything, I just hit you. That's what we learned in the projects; there was no sense in talking about it. So I just hit him and we started fighting and it was good. But I didn't like him, so that night I snuck out of my bed and snuck into the kitchen area of the camp and found a knife; and came back into the bunk area and stood over his bed. I had made a decision that night that I wanted to stab him and mess him up real good. I wanted to kill him. But I decided not to do it that night, and I hid the knife so I could use it later, if necessary.

The White kid came over to me the next day and told me it was the best fight he had ever had. We were all ghetto kids. He was from the White ghetto in Savin Hill and I was from the Black ghetto in Roxbury. We were all real poor ghetto kids up there, so I liked him after he came over. He said it was a great fight and that he enjoyed it; and then he said let's be friends. Cool. I was good with it. It was 1965 and so something was happening. More life went on and one of the camp counselors must have told me to do something, which I must not have liked. I don't remember it real well, but I do remember that I got my knife, and I pulled my knife on him, and I circled him; and I swiped the knife at him and did a lot of other things and caused a big ruckus up there. The police had to come and wrestle me to the ground, all kinds of stupid shit was going on and they sent me home.

What I learned from that experience and what was enlightening to me was that I was a violent, broken, angry motherfucker and I wanted to kill and could kill someone else besides my mother; and knowing that my life was going to go in that direction was okay with me. I was now ready and ready now to be real. I just felt that my life was always going to be fucked up and I had better get ready for it, and used to it.

CHAPTER 7

DEATH IN THE PROJECTS
1965-1969
THE DRUG STORE ROBBERY – PART ONE

1

This story about the drugstore robbery is only important because most crime committed by kids in the ghetto is not thought out, it happens in the spur of the moment, nothing is really planned, it's just there's an opportunity and you just do it and it's not that important to anyone outside the ghetto unless you die.

Shit happens so fast in the ghetto, that you're dead five days before you know you're dead, and you're in jail five years before you know you've really fucked up, and you're doing life without parole. Kids die in the ghetto because there's no thought about, oh I'm going to die if I do this shit, kids die all the time, but, you're always thinking, not me, so you do stupid shit, real stupid shit, that you never think you will die over.

You do that drug deal with another asshole, never thinking that asshole is gonna rip you off, shoot and kill you; you do that drug rip-off because you think, 'I can get away with this shit; you pocket a cigar from a store, because you think no police is gonna blow my head off for doing this light shit; you talk back to a police because he ain't gonna pull out a gun a shoot you dead in the street; you rob the store down the street, because you ain't gonna die that night; you do all kinds of stupid, fucked up shit all the time in the ghetto, because you either don't give a fuck, or fuck, life is so fucked up and full of shit and poverty and low class jobs and shitty apartments and no fuckin car and everybody you know from miles around is all fucked up and sometimes your just high and fucked up and sometimes there just ain't nothing else to do but fuck up somebody else's life.

Sometimes for a young poor black teenager, after a lifetime of poverty and abuse, living in the ghetto or projects, life isn't worth living, fuck it.

2

When I was fourteen during the spring and summer of 1965, I just stopped going to the Boy Scouts. I don't think there was any reason, except I just stopped going. Maybe it was girls, maybe it was the gangs, maybe I was growing up and I wanted something else. I dropped my childhood friends and started hanging out with another group of boys from the projects.

That summer instead of going to my Grandmére's house for a week or Adams Pond Scout Camp, I went to a camp called Agassiz Village and got thrown out and then got a job with an organization called ABCD or Action for Boston Community Development. It was a new program, started by the City of Boston to help Inner City kids. My job was to, along with other kids, clean up the neighborhood vacant lots and condemned buildings. It was good outside work and I enjoyed it. A lot of the kids were from outside the projects and lived in the tenement buildings that surrounded the projects, some of the kids lived in other parts of my project and I knew them by their faces, but, all of the kids myself included were kids who saw this as something different that we were a part of, something big that we could belong to. We were all 14 and 15-year-old ghetto and project kids trying to grow up, trying to figure it out and if you were working for this program, you were still a good kid, working for a paycheck, learning how to collect a check every two weeks for doing a job that you were proud of. It was like a real job, except that it was also about our love for the Roxbury community. It might have been one of good ol Lyndon Baines Johnson's War on Poverty Programs.

I remember that our supervisors were nice Black and White politically-orientated liberal college kids, who supplied us with rakes, shovels, garbage bags and gloves and every day we would meet and sign in at a different vacant lot or building that we were to clean up or clean out that day.

When it happened, we were at the top of a vacant building, cleaning up the rubbish and debris, and had been working together all day. We were sweaty, a little tired and alone.

3

Her name was Renee, she lived across the street from the projects in one of the tenement apartments on Tremont Street and was a sweet, pretty, tall, skinny, brown skinned girl. She was not a 'home girl', she was a 'round the way' girl. Round the way girls were all skinny, had long legs and could outrun most boys. They were exotic and beautiful young girls of twelve to fourteen-years-old and there were hundreds of them in and around the projects that summer of 1965.

When we kissed the first time, we looked at each other; when we kissed again, we kissed with our eyes closed; when we kissed the third time, we kissed with our eyes open, our lips just touching, and smiled at each other. I had reached puberty the year before and though I sort of knew what to do with it, the only thing I had available was my hand. But, when we kissed again, she allowed me to touch her budding right breast and her smell overwhelmed me, and for the first time, in my first real kiss, I tasted and smelled a woman, although a girl, Renee would one day be a beautiful woman, and in that summer, late afternoon, her eyes, although closed, and it was just a kiss, she said *yes*, and I found my first girlfriend.

We worked together all the rest of the summer. We held hands, talked about silly stuff, made things with our kemp ropes and sang and danced to The Four Tops, The Supremes, Marvin Gaye, Smokey Robinson and the Miracles, The Marvelettes, Martha and the Vandellas and The Temptations, on the little portable radio with batteries, that I had while we worked, that summer of 1965.

At night I sang songs like Billy Stewart's, "Sitting in the Park", with the fellows out back on the benches while drinking and smoking. I had taken my first drink from the bottles of wine that Randy kept in the kitchen cabinet. I kept drinking them and refilling them with water and would take one or two cigarettes a day from his pack. I had tried to throw my mother out the fifth floor window, earlier that summer and so she was leaving me alone. I had also finished my first year at public school, the ninth grade, at English High Annex and was scheduled to go to English High School for the tenth grade that September; and that August we moved to a three-bedroom apartment on the Whittier Street side of the projects at 15 Whittier Street, one of the small buildings in the project, on the third floor, next door to Deleno and his brother and sisters. Deleno would be the first person I knew to go to college, Northeastern University, that's why I was so surprised when I used to see him in Grove Hall copping and shooting heroin, that summer of 1967.

4

One night, shortly after dusk, after I had started the tenth grade at English High, I was across the street from our new apartment on Whittier Street playing basketball by myself at the Health Unit basketball court and I saw about eight guys and a girl walking towards me and getting ready to go into the tall building next to my building on Whittier Street. The girl was staggering and the boys were nudging her along, like in a playful way. Nobody was paying attention to me so I just stood still and watched. As they came closer I could see that the girl was Renee and the boys I knew. They walked into the building, down into the basement, and within about 30 seconds Renee began to scream.

5

Earlier, at the beginning of summer in June, I had been outside playing and another kid came up to me and said, they got your sister in the hallway on the third floor, I knew what that meant and I without a word to the kid ran into my building on Cabot Street, ran up the stairs to the fifth floor, opened the door, grabbed a long fork, the kind you use to lift a pot roast out of the pot, a long fork, with long silver blades and ran down to the third floor and busted through the door into the inner hallway and there they were like roach's crawling all over my sister who was spread out on the hallway floor.

I started yelling and screaming and punching out with my fork and the boys scattered off of my sister, who was just lying on the hall floor, her clothes ripped off and she's just lying there, not making a sound, not even crying and the boys who were just a little older than me started running out the different sides of the hallway.

I chose one and ran after him. We ran down the stairs and out the building into the project courtyard. I chased him around into the middle of the project that day and with the whole it seemed project yelling and screaming at me to catch him, I did catch up to him and with a swoop of my arm and hand, over and down, on the run, I plunged my long bladed fork into his back and became a project legend for two weeks. The police never came and life went on in the projects.

6

The boys that were trying, and I never knew to this day if they had before or after succeeded, because my sister has never talked about it, the boys that were trying to gang rape my sister were a part of a larger project gang that lived on the Ruggles and Tremont side of the project. They had been gang raping young girls in the project for about a year that I knew of. These gang rapes were planned and more than a few of my friends' sisters had been gang raped.

The girls that were being gang raped by these boys were between eleven and fifteen years old and a lot of these girls were turning up pregnant and some of them were being turned out and began to like the big boys pulling trains on them. All of this was happening and nobody was saying or doing anything. So when Renee was pulled into the building and started screaming at 25 Whittier Street, I knew exactly what was going on. But, I also knew that for me to go into the building that night and try to save her would be the death of me, that I would die that night, because the boys that had her were the leaders of the Tremont and Ruggles Street gangs and they were killers.

The leaders of these gangs were 18, 19, 20 and 21 year olds, had all been to jail and had been running the projects for many years. They were the same boys that robbed me of my paperboy money and had held me over the seventh floor roof and threatened to drop me when I was younger, they were the same boys who had gone on a very famous murder spree in Boston and robbed and killed eight taxi cab drivers, they were the same boys who ran the heroin drug trade in the projects, they were the same boys who robbed and killed people for miles around the projects, they were the same boys who had robbed and killed Mrs. Parker. They were young heroin drug users meaning they were not yet fully strung out, and so when they got high, they did not yet, just nod out, they became violent and very dangerous.

If you grew up in the real ghetto, the real projects, in any urban city in America, you know who they were, you remember them, they were the real gangsters, the real killers, the ones the police leave alone, the ones that the police are afraid of, the ones that prey on and viciously rape and kill eleven and twelve year old girls and stab, rob, shoot and kill elderly people, you know who they are, they live right in the ghetto with you, they are evil vicious cowards who destroy your community, who you allow to sell drugs to your children, rape your daughters, steal your lives and your dignity.

They live right with you, every day. You know who they are and you don't do a damn thing about it.

And so, at fourteen and then fifteen I had been living with these bigger boys most of my life, I knew who they were and they knew who I was and so while Renee's screams from being brutally gang raped that night in the basement at 25 Whittier Street in The Whittier Street Housing Projects in Roxbury, Massachusetts rang out into the night, I and nobody else did nothing because we were all scared.

So while Renee was screaming that night, Renee's life was being changed, and Renee would learn to love being gang raped and soon she would love guys coming up to her apartment right across from the projects and pulling trains on her and soon she would learn to love sucking White men's dicks in Boston's Combat Zone alleys. I never really saw Renee after that night, that summer. The gangs had her and she was turned out.

7

Soon after that night I just stopped going to school and began hooking school with other kids in the Fenway. We would hang out there in the marshes and on the benches and drink and smoke cigarettes and sometimes I would hook up with a girl and we would lay in the bushes and grass and fool around. When it started to get cold, we would go up one of the kid's houses whose mother worked and hang out at his or her house for the day.

Soon English High expelled me and life moved real fast after that. The ghetto enveloped me, the alcohol engulfed me, the weed found me, the horror of the projects, of how I had been living, of all that I had seen and gone through finally embraced and pulled me in. I went into shock and had a mental breakdown and wouldn't get out of bed for two weeks. My mother called the welfare department and they sent people to evaluate me medically and psychologically.

When I re-emerged, I was new. It was like my blood had been drained and I like a Vampire awakening, knew who I was for the first time. The things I had already felt were there, were now enhanced and I knew what they were for the first time. The God that I had learned about at St. Francis de Sales had given me strange, visual, colorful dreams of wealth when I was a child and now with prayer (I was now praying for the big boys deaths, as I was always praying for my mother's death) was showing and giving me strange gifts of the power of suggestion, mind reading, invisibility, speed, endurance, courage, wisdom, the ability to be in many places at the same time, the ability to visualize, to have visions, to see the future and the brain and the body that would use these strange abilities, came alive.

The doorway to help the underdog, to help those who needed me, to help the hundreds and thousands of people I would meet on my journey and the heart and courage I would use to attack my enemies and win many battles for others and myself for the next forty-five years, opened up. Some feats you have heard of, and most you haven't, but they would all begin at the Whittier Street Housing Projects that fall and winter of 1965 and 1966.

8

The first thing I did after my transformation and with my new powers, was to align myself with some new friends from the Cabot, Whittier and Lower Ruggles Street sides of the project, the second thing was to process or straighten my hair and I took to wearing a doo rag, the third thing was to go downtown to the knife store in the Combat Zone and buy two long silver switchblades, the fourth thing was to start a psychological war against the big boys by telling everyone I knew that we needed to do something about the big boys gang raping girls in the project, the fifth thing was to with great stealth and courage write the words RAPISTS in chalk all over the projects.

9

In the meantime, in early 1966, I learned from my mother that my father was coming out of jail again and he wanted to see me, and if I wanted to, I could see and meet with him. The last time I had seen my father and spent any time with him was in late 1956 or early 1957 when he had unexpectedly showed up at my first grade class at the Asa Grey elementary school in Roxbury and took me out of class so that we could go to the movies and see *Walt Disney's Song of the South based on the Tales of Uncle Remus,* He got in a lot of trouble for that, as he had just gotten bailed out of jail by my Grandmére' for threatening to kill my mother and grandmother that time he had been dragged out by the police with the shiny things on, but I had never forgotten that day sitting in the movies with my dad eating popcorn and watching the enchanting old darky world of Br'er Rabbit and Br'er Fox with Uncle Remus in the deep south after slavery and during reconstruction. I had never stopped loving my dad, so damn right I wanted to see him and besides I wanted to tell my dad all that you had done to me when I was little boy.

The day finally came early February 1966, it was a cold Boston winter Saturday and I had been waiting outside the 15 Whittier Street building all day, sitting on the benches around the corner. They said he was coming at 11:00am, but it was 12:30pm before a car rounded the Cabot Street gym and made its way down Whittier Street. My brain said, "it's my dad", and I took off leaped over two fences and met his car before it was halfway down the street. Since I didn't know anything about my dad, I didn't really know what he looked like, how he sounded, who he was, if he would like me, I didn't know anything and didn't care. I just knew whoever he was I had missed him, for some reason that I didn't know about.

But, there he was. I didn't recognize him, but I sensed a familiar presence in that car. There was a woman with him and he told me to get in the back. I got in the back and pulled my doo rag off so that dad could check out my process and me real good. The woman said, "Is this him", like I was some smelly, dirty, motherfucker, under her shoe and my dad told her to shut the fuck up. Me and what I learned was his main bottom lady and soon to be wife, never got along from that day forward, but ol dad beat her so bad and so often and fucked with her mind enough for both of us through the years, so I managed to disregard her from that day forward until that miserable bitch died. You should have seen her face when ol dad died in 1989 and she found out that he had signed the deed to Ten Clarendon Avenue over to me and my sister in 1986.

The last time I had seen my dad he was a man of 26 and now he was 36 years old, he looked older and much fatter, but he also looked a little tame and little weary to me, which I was to find out later was just because he had just got out of jail, so all that was just the bad jail house starchy food and the whipped look was the inmate look.

Just about everybody I knew below the age of seventeen had been to Concord reformatory and Lyman Reformatory in Shirley, Mass, I mean all of the Ruggles and Tremont Street gang had been there and most of the mothers' boyfriends in the project were always coming in from or going out to jail. So the projects were run by weary looking former inmates on heroin, and we were all living in jail, everyone I knew was a criminal, and that included my dad and my step-dad. In fact, Billy, one of the big boys' younger brothers had just asked me in January 1966, when I was going to jail. I said soon.

We drove out of the projects to Tremont Street, turned left and drove up Tremont Street, Dad said that we were going to him and Lou's (that was that miserable bitch's name) favorite restaurant. It was a place I knew well, up Tremont going towards downtown Boston in the South End, Lew Changs, a Chinese Restaurant. We went there and I had my first meal with my dad in…; since I don't remember us having any meals together whenever he was around before, which was hardly ever, I'll just say it was the first meal I can ever remember eating with him. And then, that was it. He took me back home and I wouldn't see him again until he came to save my life.

10

By March on my way to Trade High Public School, near the Annunciation Road Projects, where I had ended up in the 10th grade paint department because my cousin Philip went there and I had to be somewhere, I had taken to going into the buildings where the big boys lived in the morning and yelling their names, saying shit like, "D, rapes little girls" or "Mak rapes little girls" or "Stevie rapes little girls", shit like that I would yell out loud in their buildings on my way to school.

This went on until one day near the end of March, one of my new friends, probably the one who was ratting me out, telling the big boys that it was me who was making all this noise in the projects about them gang raping girls, told me that Stevie wanted to have a sit down with me and talk about the shit I was doing and I was so crazy and fucked up on alcohol and weed at this point that I actually believed that I was going to negotiate, a new word for me at that time, actually this was going to be my second major negotiation outside of my deal with Al's grocery store, which had ended because we were now getting these big motherfuckin cans and blocks of welfare cheese, welfare powdered milk, welfare beef, welfare macaroni, welfare butter, food stamps and other welfare food shit from the Boston Welfare Department, so my deal with Al's was no longer needed.

I remember Al shaking my hand and wishing me well when I thanked him that summer of 1965 for the deal and told him that after seven years we could no longer keep the deal because with all the welfare food and food stamps we got, they had cut way back on our welfare check, so we had to go straight welfare. Anyway at fifteen-years-old, I actually believed that I was going to negotiate a deal with the big boys, so that they would stop gang raping the girls in and around the projects.

11

The sit down with the big boys, specifically Stevie, was set for early April at night in the middle of the projects on the benches near the wading and shower pool. Now, Stevie I had known nearly all my life. He was the older brother of about six siblings, one who was about my age, and Billy who was a couple of years older and who I had some type of relationship with. The brother my age, when we were about six-years-old was picking on a real skinny kid named Paul who live around my way in the bigger building on Cabot Street and who was a friend of mine, I had pushed this big boy's brother off of Paul and flipped him over to the ground, at that time his older brothers, Stevie and Billy, came after me and pushed me to the ground and told me not to bother their brother again. So this was how I met those brothers, and like I said, I had known them most of my life that April night when Stevie and I were to meet in the middle of the projects.

Finally, the day came. I don't remember what I did that day, but I do remember what happened that night. That early April night at the Whittier Street Housing Projects was stiller and quieter than it usually was, I remember that it was as though everyone knew something different was going to happen that night. I just knew that something was about to change forever.

As I walked to the middle of the projects I saw Stevie sitting on the bench alone. I walked up to him and sat down. Stevie was a short, built, dark-skinned man, about nineteen-years-old. He shot heroin, raped little girls and robbed, stabbed, shot and killed people. I was a tall, skinny, fifteen-year-old kid, and I was not afraid of him or the other big boys, because I had known them most of my life, from my early newspaper selling days when they used to rob me, and I knew who they were and what they were.

He offered me a drink of alcohol and so we drank together, while he was asking me what I was doing, why was I fucking with them. I started to tell him about Renee, when some other guy came up on us. I was a little drunk by now and heard the guy say to Stevie, "Is this him?" Stevie said, "Yes". Stevie said to me, "No hard feelings, but you got to learn your lesson." He said to the guy, who I didn't know and would never know or see again, "Don't kill him, he fucked up, but he's still one of us." With that Stevie got up and walked off. The bigger, older guy, who I didn't know, stood over me, right in front of me and his fist smashed into my face and broke my nose immediately, his next hit broke my right jaw, his next broke the left side of my face, my cheekbone, the next hit busted my mouth and my lips, the next hits I couldn't feel anymore.

When it was over, I remember hearing Stevie's voice, saying to the guy, "help me with him", and they dragged and carried me over to 15 Whittier Street, up the three floors of steps, knocked on my door, my mother opened it and Stevie said, "Mrs. Rose, here's your son" and dropped me in front of her. The ambulance came, I was rushed to Boston City Hospital, I almost died twice they said, but I was brought back to life. The doctors that worked on me were dedicated people and they saved my life. The police came and interviewed me in the hospital after a week. I told them about the gang rapes in the projects and didn't name any names. They kept asking me who had done this to me and because 'I was one of them', I gave no names.

What I knew was that because it was Stevie, I was alive. He and his brother Billy, had some empathy for me and probably fought for my life in whatever meetings the big boys had about me, because if it had of been up to D. and Mak, I would be dead. They had no love, no empathy for me whatsoever. The police investigated, talked to the project people, the activist people in the projects stood up, had meetings and the big boys stopped gang raping the young girls in and around the projects.

12

I stayed in the house recuperating for about a month and then one day my dad came and walked me out of the projects to his car and we drove off. It would be the first time I would live outside the brick walls of the projects since I was three and I would live with my dad until he would go back to prison. We would have many adventures, some recounted in these pages and some not. I would repeat the tenth grade at Dorchester High that September 1966; Mak would die violently, shot to death a few years later at twenty- four-years old; D. would move to California and find some real black gangsters who would shoot him dead in the streets of Compton in 1973; and Stevie, well he just disappeared and nobody, including me, ever saw him again.

13

I did see Renee again. I was in New York City recording my band *Prince Charles and the City Band* with Prince Charles Alexander at Intergalactic

Recording Studios, 84th Street and Lexington Avenue. It was January 1982 and I had a huge hit out called *Beat the Bush* we had produced and written on a group we called Slyck, that record was getting a lot of radio play and sales across the country, especially in New York City. We were recording a follow-up track and I was staying at the Holiday Inn on Eighth Avenue and Forty Eighth Street in the Times Square area in Midtown Manhattan.

While walking down Eighth Avenue one night on my way to catch the #7 train at 42nd Street over to get the #4 or 6 train at Grand Central Station going uptown, I saw her. I knew it was her, I hadn't talked to her or really seen her since that summer and fall of 1965, but I knew it was her, same cupid pretty face, except she had on this funky wig and looked emaciated, but it was her and she saw me too. We walked over to each other, looked at each other in the middle of the Times Square area on Eighth Avenue, near 42nd Street and hugged and looked at each other closely.

It had been almost seventeen years since that summer we had kissed, held hands and worked for the ABCD summer program; but, my heart felt the same joy as it did that last day I saw her. She had on a short waist rabbit jacket and her wig, short mini skirt and high heel shoes in the dead of a New York City winter said it all. I had on my Burberry coat, leather black pants, almond silk shirt and carried my music industry briefcase. She asked me what I was doing in New York and I told her that I was recording a record in a studio uptown. I asked her what she was doing and she said that she worked across the street at the Peep Show Theater on Eighth Avenue and Forty Second Street. I asked her if she wanted to come with me to the studio and she said yes.

So she locked her arm in mine and we went underground taking the #7 crosstown train to 42nd Street to the #4 express uptown to 86th Street. We didn't say anything to each other on the way to the studio and when we got there I introduced her to my partner and friend, Prince Charles Alexander; my main man and bass singer, Edmond Harris; and Jay Burnett, my recording engineer, as a background singer. Gina G. our main vocalist for the session was already there and ready to go.

14

Jay set up a mike for Renee in the vocal booth, while Prince Charles and I coached Renee on the chant we wanted her to sing with Gina G. When Renee was ready she went into the vocal booth and we turned the track on.

The music played and we cued Gina and Renee and they chanted/sang, in a call and response verse, "He's just a Freak", and Edmond sang, "Video Freak", and the girls sang, "He's just a Freak", and Edmond sang, "Video Freak".

This went on for about six takes, three overdubs and a couple of measures worth that we could use and then those particular backgrounds were done. It still remains after all these years one of the best hours of my life. To see and be with Renee that night doing something that we could have never known we would do, something so outside of what had happened to her, something that seemed to make her happy, is still one of the best feelings I have ever felt. That night at the studio we drank and sang and did a little cocaine and drank some more and sniffed some more cocaine and kissed again, and looked at each other and marveled at what was happening and that night when we left the studio we went back to the Holiday Inn and finally, we concluded what we had begun as fourteen-year-old children in 1965.

15

That June 1982, the record, "Video Freak (Defend It)" came out and I moved to New York City from Boston that month with my wife Yvonne. One day I took the record, it was one of those old "12 inch" disco long playing records from the 1970's and 1980's, and went over to Eighth Avenue and Forty Second Street to the Peep Show Theater and asked for Renee. The manager took me to the back where the naked girls were waiting for someone with five dollars to put it in a machine and they could then go into a room and do their thing for one minute.

Renee was sitting down and stood up when she saw me. We hugged each other and kissed with just our lips touching softly and I held her and looked at her warm brown face, with that ugly wig on, and held her naked body close. I then reached down and handed her a "12 inch" record of "Video Freak", and showed her where her name was on the record. She just shook her head and looked and said thank you. We hugged again and I think I cried a little because it was all I could do. I said I had to leave and walked out, when I turned around just before I turned the corner, she was standing there looking at me and that would be the very last time I ever saw Renee.

I know, I won't lie. I went back there again looking for her and the manager told me that she had quit and he didn't know where she was. I lived in New York City for the next twenty-two years, as well as living in Los Angeles and Phoenix and would often return to New York City all through the years and I would look for her on the trains, walking down the street, in a store, anywhere, but I never found her again, but wherever Renee is, her name is forever on the record, now a cd, and that record, "Video Freak (Defend It)", is still being played today all over the world and she is still singing, "He's just a Freak", forever!

CHAPTER 8
THE DRUGSTORE ROBBERY
PART TWO

1

By October 1967 at sixteen years old I hadn't really been back to Dorchester High School since my father went back to jail and I had to go back to the projects. I was pretty much safe in the projects, but I was hanging with a gang in Grove Hall for companionship. We were all somewhat violent kids looking for trouble and I am usually high on alcohol, weed and bombers and so is everyone I know. I know a lot of kids who have gotten killed. I've been violent with and fought many other kids and other kids have been violent with me; and yet I'm still living, still walking around.

So the Almighty Hawk was with me one night and there was this drugstore we hung out at every day getting stuff. My gang had a territory, and everything in that territory belonged to us. Whether it was girls, stores, money, people or food, it didn't matter, if you were in our territory you belonged to us as a gang. So in this particular gang, which was in Dorchester starting from Grove Hall within a radius of about 3 miles, everything in that area belonged to the gang. We had our headquarters at a Chinese restaurant, directly across the street from Ma Dixon's Country Style Restaurant; the Muslim place and in the center was a barbershop. We knew everybody there and everybody knew who were. The drugstore that we hung out in that was in our territory had prescription pills like bombers and shit like that, so the Almighty Hawk and me decided that we would rob this drugstore up on Washington Street and Columbia Road, and so we did.

One night after midnight around 2:00am we were just hanging out it and we did it. The drugstore was facing Columbia Road on Washington Street, and on the side street going up Washington Street there was a door that led into a basement, which we figured was underneath the drugstore. We were gonna go in there into the drugstore and steal the all the drugs that made you high. The Almighty Hawk who was sixteen also, knew which ones to get, so we up went up Washington Street to the side back door and figured out how to open it. I think the Almighty Hawk had been working on it for a few days. Anyway we got in and went down the stairs to the basement and I opened another door and went up some steps into the drugstore, went into the back rummaged through the drugstore area and found some pills and this and that.

We went back out the way we came in and as we were coming up the stairs we saw at the top of the stairs that people were talking outside. The Almighty Hawk said, *Oh shit, that might be the polic*e! And when they didn't leave, I said, *We better get the fuck out of here! We need to get the fuck out of here! If they come in we're caught; we might have a chance if we can get the fuck out of here!* So we slowly crept up the stairs and we looked at each other and understood what we had to do…something that was gonna take a tremendous amount of energy and strength. We were two 16-year-old street-wise kids and we knew what was out there and what we had to do. As we moved up the stairs we could see them with the lights and we just moved at the speed of sound so fast we could have been just a blur, and we were. We busted through that door into a sea of police cars and policemen and moved past them faster than they could blink, faster than a locomotive, faster than a speeding bullet, like superman and shit, and ran right past them, right down to Washington Street, around the corner, around the next corner. And we were gone.

And I happened to think that in this day of police killings that are so prevalent across the United States is that, what if some policeman had just pulled his gun, took a quick aim and fired at us like they do to black kids who are mostly doing stupid shit, either me or the Almighty Hawk would have been dead that early morning night as so many of my other friends were. In fact, one had been shot dead not more than a block away from where we were doing the same thing in another store a few months earlier. But for some reason, either we were moving that fast, or they couldn't think in time, nothing happened to us, we didn't get shot and killed. But, what I really know is that if a policeman really wants to kill you, because he hates Black people, especially Black kids, he's going to have his gun out in a second and shoot and kill you. So one or two stupid motherfuckers like us would have died for nothing but a few pills to get us high. And so I know that night, no Boston Policeman wanted to kill a Black kid for nothing.

We called ourselves different names. I called us the Grove Hall Gang. At that time if you had a formal name, you were a sissy gang. We were real hard core fighting street gang; we really didn't have a name. At that time, if you were in a gang and had a name that was when you gave parties and stupid shit like that. We got in fights, did drugs, talked shit and had a good time. We we're getting a kick by just roaming the neighborhood and fucking with whoever we wanted. Our leader was Petey. He turned into a hardcore heroin addict, so I had to be the leader sometime. But Petey was the real leader. He killed three people in a gas station robbery, a friend of mines father was one of them, and went to jail for life and died in jail in 1980.

God kept me from heroin. Before I left for the war in 1969, the gang was just starting to get into heroin really bad. Heroin wasn't a drug of my choice because it has too many things necessary to use it, so I would just sniff it. It never really became a drug of my choice because it was just too much trouble. You have to do a lot to get ready for that; there was a needle involved, a spoon involved and you need to involve a wrap. My father was a heroin addict and my father's main claim to heroin was if you stop using heroin you died; so he had told me that and heroin just never appealed to me. But there was one time that I remember that I might've just been drawn that way.

They were in an alley and they were my best friends, more or less. Petey was a bigger kid and he was some type of natural leader, but he liked heroin and when I looked in this alleyway and they had a girl in there with them with some hot pants on and she looked good and she was going to shoot up with Petey and CP. It was on Blue Hill Avenue, actually it was Cheney Street and Blue Hill Avenue and they were all there in an abandoned building and I was near the corner. I had just come from hanging out and I saw CP in there with Petey. They were going to do their thing and shoot up and the girl was in there because after they shot up she was supposed to be sucking their dicks, she was going to give them some head, and I'm looking at that. She was begging me to come back there with them and then we could shoot up and I could get my dick sucked. While I was looking at them, and this was just before I was going to go over, it was in my mind and then I'm not wanting to go.

It was probably about June 1969 and I'm eighteen-years-old. *I'm not sure if I've already been downtown to the Air Force recruiter yet.* I'm just not sure, but I do know that God intervened in my life again. God showed me a vision, that if I shot that shit into my vein that for the rest of my life I would be a scroungy rat-looking junkie, hiding in condemned buildings, shooting heroin, until someone mercifully shot me in the head and ended my life. I thought that my life was worth something more than this thing. Something was changing me at that time. I had been through a lot of things and seen a lot of things; and my father was saving my life again. A number of things were shifting. I was understanding something. Some kind of shift was going on, one way or the other.

It was a few weeks before the White Stadium robbery, when I robbed the stadium with a gun and could have been shot and killed if a policeman had been nearby or someone at the concession stand would have had a gun and they would have started shooting because I had a gun in my hand while robbing the place. And so life was shifting, although everything I knew about life was still going on. Everything was still happening, but it wasn't going to be enough to throw me over to the other side. I was straddling something that was going to end up good or bad. All the way bad or all the way good, one way or the other.

And at this particular time when Petey and CP beckoned me, I made a motion to come. I saw the girl in the hot pants; I wanted that. I liked Petey and CP. We had done a lot of crime together, so I wanted to do that with them too I guess. Then all of a sudden, right before my eyes God showed me the rest of my life, it was a vision. I had a strange situation in microseconds and in that vision, God showed me that if I went in an alleyway with them, I would forever be in that alleyway fumbling around looking for them and shooting up until someone just shot me and put me out of my misery. So in that vision, I became a heroin addict who was eventually killed, and I saw it as clear as you can see anything. I saw that thing, one of many, many visions that I've had in my life. Always a vision has taken me to a good place and I've always followed my visions, seeing them for what they were and they always showed me the right path. There's a good and evil path. It was a good thing and in this case it showed me the evil path; and if I wanted to take that path all I would have to do was go back in that alley and let them tie that rag around my arm and put that needle in my vein and shoot that heroin and that would have been the end of me.

I could have chosen that path I could have easily chosen to go to hell; but God showed me what he showed me. The path I wasn't shown was what would happen if I didn't do that; I was just shown what would happen if I did do that, and I said no. I would have been a different person and that would have done it for me. Heroin would have been my favorite drug.

The gun came from Petey. He gave me the gun. We didn't need guns during that time, I never did. I was very good with a knife; I had always kept two knives. From fourteen years old on, I had a switchblade knife. I had knives that clicked open in micro-seconds. I was really good with a knife. Petey had a small caliber type of gun. Petey was so high when we were robbing White Stadium, and he give me the gun. We were at White Stadium robbing the place and it was underground at White Stadium. The stadium was this place where they played football—high school football games—and the concession stand was under the ground. I guess Petey had made the decision that we were going to rob the concession stand and the Almighty Hawk and he were there with me. Petey was high on heroin and when we got to the concession stand, he got the gun pointed at the people behind the concession stand, but he couldn't move; he froze and all that was coming out of his mouth was off just a loud noise…*AH, AH, AH….*

Petey was making all this loud noise. He was standing there robbing the place and all these white kids were behind the counter at the concession stand serving people. Petey was standing there holding the gun, pointing it at them, so I just took the gun from him. He didn't hand me the gun; I just took it from him and leapt over the counter and jumped down and pointed the gun at the guy behind the counter at the cash register. Then I opened the cash register, grabbed the money and handed the money and the gun to the Almighty Hawk.

They ran one way and I ran the other. I had on flip flops and I was running up the other end of White Stadium tunnel, which opens right into Humboldt Avenue. I got to Seaver Street and there was a bus waiting and I ran up to the bus with my flip flops on and jumped on the bus and sat down. About two or three minutes later the bus was still sitting at the top of the hill and two policeman get on the bus. I looked nonchalant, like every black kid knows how to look when he sees the police. I looked like I was chilling on the bus looking out the window. I had a dead look on my face. I was breathing kind of heavy when I got on the bus, because I had run up that tunnel with flip flops on, but I was just looking out the window, and again some kind of a divine intervention was with me because I was scared and I couldn't show it, and I couldn't breathe because I couldn't look like I was breathing hard. I was just looking out the window and not even looking at the bus driver or police. I was looking out the corner of my eye and saw them say something to the bus driver and the bus driver just looked around. He glanced at me but he wasn't looking at me and back to them again real fast and he shook his head no. I was looking out the window looking at them like nothing's going on here and then I looked and they got off the bus. Then the driver closed his door and began taking the bus route down Seaver Street and it was a white bus driver. He could have said anything; he could have said I had just jumped on. But, he didn't say nothing.

The Almighty Hawk and I later met at my cousin's house—well not my cousin but we called ourselves cousins. His place was on Washington Street. I don't know what happened to Petey that day. But, within a year he had killed three people at a gas station and would go to jail for life. He probably got away that day, but I didn't see him much after that…and soon after I went in the military and never saw or heard from him again.

BOOK TWO

THE AUTOBIOGRAPHY OF AN
AMERICAN GHETTO BOY

VOLUME THREE

THE EARLY TEENAGE YEARS

MURDER - THE LIFE
BY TONY ROSE

A SEMI/FICTION/BIOGRAPHY

A STORY ABOUT ME, MY FATHER AND MASSACHUSETTS' GREATEST
MURDER MASSACRE.

NOVEMBER 13, 1968

I wrote most of this in 1970 and finished it in 1972. It's a semi-fiction-bio story about me, my father and friends one day and night in December 1968 and a semi-fiction-bio story of Roxbury/Boston and Massachusetts' greatest murder massacre.

This short story of my life is very, very graphic.
The people are real, the events are real and the language is real.
It is the life and language that I lived and used as a
child and teenager in the moment and time that I lived it.
Do not read this short story if you are easily offended and sickened
by extreme violence, extreme drug use and extreme sexual matters.

"The Life" is a for the most part a true story about one day and night in the life of me, my father, friends and people I knew when I was seventeen years old in Roxbury Mass., and a composite of the life I led from 14 years old to 18 years of old. I am Dung, Spook and Paisley. My father is Fuller and Frank. Betty Jayne is Betty. The CIA is a part of this story because my father loved to pretend to his ladies that he worked for the CIA, and at some points in my life so did I. It was fun, because for some reason women always believed it.

PART ONE

MURDER

1
PAISLY

"I said, I didn't know, I mean I might go, but well I don't know, I just don't know, Jesus, Fuller you can't expect me to know this soon. Come on man give me a break, listen, I'll tell you what. Tonight about ten or ten-thirty meet me at the corner of Lawrence Ave. and Blue Hill Ave, and we'll talk about it, okay, ya, you know man, we'll just talk about it, and if everything's okay, then I'll go along. But I ain't going to know 'til later, and tonight I'll let you know."

The corner at Devon Street was deserted, except for the two men talking. The cold air was still, and the morning light cast a dimness over the grey deserted storefronts. The avenue was empty of cars, and the men's breath rose in the air. It didn't look as though Christmas was two days away, but this was the Bury, where Santa never came anyways.

The taller of the two men broke away, they slapped hands, and separated in different directions. Just then, a car sped up the avenue and almost hit Paisley, the smaller of the two men. He muttered something about mothers and continued crossing the street. Fuller watched the car almost hit Paisley and wondered about rabbits' feet; then he decided he was hungry.

2
SHIT

"Wake up man, wake up man, wake up, wake up sugar, wake up. You know today's your day to get us some scratch, come on man, come on man all I got is a little bit of shit left, and if you going to stay here you better get on up and get out in them streets and get us some money, put your arm over here and let me joint it for you, this will help you get that early morning start. Come on man! Get your arm over here, shit, I ain't got all day, shit! If you don't want this shit, then say so, so I can pop myself. If you want to get down, then I'll let you have some, you know me, I'm your friend. I always share my shit with you, come on man, will you wake up and get out! Shit, that's right. Move, come on baby, yeah, now put your arm over here, yeah. See? Now hold this while I tie this around, okay? Now, no! Let me stick it in for you, okay? You know mama knows how to put it in, come on. There, see? I was afraid you wasn't going to be getting up. Shit, I got some tricks coming by here, and some of those johns gets kind of scared, they see another man around. They afraid that I'm going to try something, you know how it is sugar. Isn't this shit good, yeah. I can see it is, oops! Shit! Watch out baby, that's right. Ya, just nod nice and easy, now; you just lay back and mama will work on another thing for you, and maybe you can put that, and that needle inside me, okay baby?"

3
HAWK AND SPOOK

Hawk and the Spook were floating down Grace Hall, minding nobody's business but their own. Their high was beautiful today, and they felt at peace with their jones. They went inside the record shop where the man was playing some of that Chicago Blues. The Blues banged against their minds and they hummed simultaneously. They hummed for about 10 seconds, and then, Hawk scratched his private area, and then the side of his face. He then mumbled something about somebody giving him some money. He was about to say it louder, but then he looked down at his shoes, which were untied. A drop of snot fell from his nose as he looked down. The Spook, who was leaning against the counter, scratching his arm, laughed, and we could see that he had three spaced teeth at the top and an assorted eight at the bottom. They hung around the record store for about five minutes, just enough time to dance to the Temptations' new record, which Spook said he was going to buy as soon as he could raise some money from his mother or somebody. They left the record shop and crossed the street to Ma Dixon's.

4
COCAINE

Being nine-thirty, Ma had just opened for the day. Although she was just a little late, on account of she had been forcibly screwed by the two young boys she had brought home with her from Mr. Afro's house the night before so they could share some cocaine and some uppers with her. She didn't mind them screwing her last night, but she had told them that in the mornings, she had to be together, and her idea of being together was not being screwed by two cats all over the place. "Shit," she said, just the thought of it was making her mad. She didn't like to start the day mad and tired. She lifted her dress and pulled out her rim of stuff and took a double, four snorts, two in each nostril, breath of pure, sweet, loving cocaine.

5

DINKEY

"Hey ma, let me have one of them finger lickin' good chicken sandwiches of yours." "And let me have some bean pie with two grape tonics."

"Shit," said Hawk, still scratching at his body; his shoulders hunched, and huddling deep inside his coat, which he had taken off of Dinkey after he had O.D.'d, just before they had taken him to the City Hospital, where he died after throwing up his liver. "Shit, Spook, we got to get us some money, you heard what T.J. said. He said that if we gave him twenty dollars, he'd give' us enough shit to last one day, plus his gun, which he said we could use to make some hits and he'd only take a fourth out of whatever we get, which means that if we made hits of maybe two hundred, then we'd only have to give him fifty, and we'd have one hundred and fifty ourselves. I think I know where we can get some too. You know Dung?" "Um" said Hawk. "You know Dung man, you know, the cat that's holing up with that scroungy junkie whore that blew half of Station Two before they let her go after they busted her and Twinky for hiding in the Greyhound bus station's men's room, charging them white boys five dollars to pee on them. Ha, ha, ha, you know!" "Ha, ha, ha, ha, ya I think I know who you mean." "You boys want anything else? There's either cornbread or regular bread to go along with each order, if you want it. If you don't, that will be 75¢ for the chicken sandwich and 45¢ for the bean pie and two tonics," said Ma.

"Ya", Hawk said, "Let me have some cornbread and a glass of water."

6

CHUCKS

The door behind them opened, and a tall, brown complexioned man, in his late forties came in. He was clean in a Paglorioni handmade, pin-striped suit, with ruffled edges and four pockets. His shoes could have been bought only in New York, and his hair blown out only by Chuck of Chucks Barber

Shop, who could blow your hair out like nobody else could. Fuller walked in, and sat down next to Spook, who was trying to decide if he wanted some cornbread or bread. Ma was serving Hawk his cornbread when she saw Fuller.

7
FULLER

"Hey Fuller! What you think you doing in here, ain't you got nowhere else to eat? What happened to that bitch you was staying with last time you was in town, can't she cook? I run a fine decent place here, for fine decent people to come and eat. I don't need no pushers coming in here eatin', especially if they got the Italian boys looking for them!"

8
MR. AFRO

Hawk and Spook at that moment had a simultaneous thought. The last time they had thought the same thing at the same time, was when they were in Hawk's apartment shooting up, and the same thought hit them, that this shit they were shooting into their veins was no good, maybe Ajax or rat poison. They had jerked their needles out at the same time, and just about drank a quart of milk each. They had done that without a word spoken between them. To test if the shit was bad, they had given it to Tuttle to sell to Haynes who had burnt them a long time ago. Three days later, Tuttle sold it to Haynes, who was grateful, since hardly anybody else would sell to him, because everybody remembered how high the price, and how low the quality of the shit he used to push, when he was pushing. Haynes had become addicted to the shit, and was using more than he was selling. So the big boys had to cut him loose. He was just an out and out junkie now. Haynes had taken the shit home, and told his wife who used to whore for Mr. Afro, that he was going in the bathroom to take a shit. She later told her friends.

9
NEEDLES

"Well, after a while I decided that two hours was long enough for him to take a shit, besides I had to take one too. So I opened up the bathroom door to tell him to stop stinking up the bathroom and to come out. And there he is, staring up at the ceiling, with his needle in his arm, and his mouth open with his pants around his ankles. So's I goes over to him; and I say, Haynes! And I push him, thinking he's nodding; well! He falls off the toilet seat, into the bathtub. I see two turds in the toilet, but then I begin to realize that Haynes is dead. So I untied his handkerchief from his arm, and took out his needle. I got his works together, and went down the hall to Booster's who had said he was looking to buy all the needles, and syringes, and caps he could find. I sold Haynes' works to him for six dollars, and then I came back and called the police."

10

A DOLLAR TWENTY

"Hu, Ma, hey, uh, listen, here's a dollar twenty for Spook's and me's food."

"Ya, Ma, um, look, uh, let me have a paper bag so's I can put my food in it; we got to be going. I just remembered something very important that Hawk and me got to be doing." For the next ten seconds all that was heard was a quick rustle of a paper bag, four very quick steps, and the very heavy closing of the door, behind two very scared junkies.

11

PANTIES

The clean gentleman leaned back against the counter, and watched the two cats leave.

"How you been Fuller? I was thinking that you were going to come to Boston. What are you doing here?" Ma and Fuller went back a long ways, the Baltimore days. "Just come to see you Ma, and to get something to eat."

"What you want?"

"You got any coke?"

"You know where it's at, you just reach under and get some." Fuller put his hand up under Ma's dress and in her panties, he found the vise and pulled it out.

"You sure know how to keep it nice and warm Ma."

"And sweet smelling too." They both laughed.

12

DUNG

Dung tried to reach for his cigarettes. At first he tried just inching his fingers along the sheets, pulling at the sheets until he could pull his cigarettes into his hand. When that didn't work, he tried to raise himself off the bed, and fall close to the cigarettes. When that didn't work he decided to forget the cigarettes for a while, and remove his obstacle.

"Mary! Mary, hey Mary! Come on sugar, will you get off me! Mary!" He tried to push her off, but since they were somehow stuck, plus she weighed seventy-five more pounds than he, it was kind of hard.

"Mary! He shouted in her ear. Mary, will you get off of me."

"Uh," she said.

"Get up off of me, I got to hurry and get out of here, your tricks will be coming in a little while, and I got to see if I can make some money too. So, come on, and get your nasty body off me."

13
MARY

Mary raised her body off Dung, and gently rolled over onto her back. Dung hurriedly reached for her cigarettes, and lit one. He glanced over at Mary who lay with one leg raised, arms behind her head, cooing to herself; and decided to make it, and not come back before she killed him. Mary weighed seventy-five pounds more than Dung, but Dung only weighed between eighty-five to ninety-five pounds, and looked like he had half a day to live. Thus Mary weighed about one-hundred sixty-five pounds, and stood six feet to six feet-one. She was an Amazon, a beautiful, Black, sweaty, hairy piece of honest to God fine womanhood. Looking at her, Dung decided that he couldn't put up with it anymore, she was too much. She was always good for some dope though. That was because Mr. Afro was her sister's pimp, and he'd give it to Elaine anytime, because Elaine was his top whore. He looked at Mary again, and then went to the bathroom.

"Hey Dung, hey Dung, how much of that shit we got left?" Dung swished his mouth with water, and smelled under his arms; he spit the water out.

"We've got two bags, two nickel bags. We got enough to last till this afternoon. You want to get high now, or do you want to get high after your johns leave?"

"I'll get high after they leave; where you gonna get some money from?"

"I don't know, I heard Fuller was looking for someone to go on a job with him tonight. I might go, he said something about seventy-five thousand dollars, some kind of breaking and entering job." Mary lay back and scratched herself. She said, "Sheeeit."

14
BEAT HIM TO DEATH

The day was a bright and cold winter day. The noon sun, yellow and glistening, made some people happy, others could only hope that its light would flicker fast, and the shadows would creep beside it, slowly extinguishing it. Among the brighter souls of the day was Jackson B. DeShields who was blind, and had been ever since his stay at Walpole State Prison, where someone, or something had almost beat him to death with a 10-pound weight in his face. He was blind now, but happy. He called that a lucky break since they had reduced his sentence, and sent him out, not having to report to a parole officer. Jackson had studied brail, and in the six years since his accident had worked himself up to become a leader of the Black community. He was a short wave radio freak, and so, had started the first community communications center, directly responding to the needs of Black people. His organization was called COMM, short for: Communications of Minority Men. Jackson's wife was blind, and they had two children.

15
SOME CAT FROM OAKLAND

"Hello, Conrad, yeah this is Jackson. Yeah, how are you? That's good. Listen, how soon do you think you can get in touch with Frank and Mel; in about an hour? Good. Tell them to be down here at the office about eight tonight, yeah, that's where I'm at now. No, ha, ha, I get to see my wife sometimes, I must see her, we got two kids, ha, ha. How's your wife and kids? That's good, that's good. Who? Fuller? No, but I heard he was in town, what's he up to, yeah, people like him are not welcome in the community. No, my sister went down to Freeport, Georgia for the winter offensive. No, ha, ha, if she makes it back, she should be back by the new year. Yeah, my family. You know, yeah, I told you a long time ago I was from Georgia. No, I came to Boston about twenty years ago. Well listen Conrad, get in touch with them, tell them it's very important, and to be here at eight. Some cat from Oakland, California is flying in, so I'll see you at eight, okay, yeah, later!"

16
PAYSTON STREET

Hawk and Spook, after huffing it down to Payston St., decided to stop in at Chuckie's house. Chuckie lived fourteen houses down Payston St. on the left; if you were facing Payston St. from Blue Hill Ave. Across the street was a gas station; Mobil Gas; next door was a condemned building, in front of the building was a fire hydrant. Downstairs underneath Chuckie, and his six brothers, and one sister, also a mother, lived Darcel Henderson; or, what was left of her.

17
THE PARTY

About three months ago, Darcel, who was twenty-three, had moved to Boston from Connecticut about three and a half years ago to get away from her mother, and to have fun; was just getting off work, when she met this fellow, who wanted to walk with her. He was attractive, and personable, so she agreed. After he walked her home from her job at the Unity Bank, he asked if she was going out that night. She said, *yes*, and gave him the address of the party she was going to. He said he'd see her later.

18
DARCEL

About three months ago, at four A.M., Darcel returned home with her new friend. She was a little high from the rum and cokes she had been drinking at the party; plus, a little high off the anticipation she felt inside her of sleeping with the new friend she had found. He wasn't so big, but she sensed he might be good for the night. She told him to make himself comfortable, and to put some records on the new record player she had bought two months ago. She went into the bedroom and put on her blue laced nightgown, then into the bathroom, which adjoined her bedroom, and washed. She then put on her bikini panties, and perfumed herself. She came out of the bedroom swaying to the sound of The Supremes' record: "Floy Joy". She noticed his look that swept over her body, and felt a sexual excitement inside her. She asked him if he wanted something; "a drink?" He said, "no". She went over and sat down beside him in the dimly lit front room. At first she just turned her head sharply towards him; the blow in the stomach hadn't registered, but then, as he punched her in the head, the surprise gone, she was puzzled and scared. Scared so that she yelled, and said, "What are you doing?" She twisted and screamed, she got up, and he grabbed her arm, and told her to shut up. She screamed, and he threw her onto the floor, and kicked her, and kicked her, and kicked her, and kicked her, and kicked her. After the first ten kicks, her stomach was bleeding profusely, and her spleen was ruptured. After the next twenty, her pubic and vaginal area were smashed. After the next twenty-five, her face was unrecognizable, and her lower jawbone was hanging to the side of what was once her cupid shaped mouth. Four more, and she was dead. Her once pretty frame, now a smashed bloody heap. Her pretty blue laced nightgown was soaked with her blood. The form inside it, was a few minutes into death. He went into her bedroom, and grabbed fifteen dollars from her purse. Moving back to the front room, he gazed at her once, and unplugged the new phonograph. Putting it under his arm, he walked out; very quietly, and disappeared into the night.

19
MAGGOTS

Just as the maggots were feeling confined to the apartment, and starting to climb the walls, and branch into less crowded conditions; Hawk and Spook were climbing the stairs to Chuckie's apartment on the third floor.

20
CHUCKIE

"Chuckie! Hey Chuckie!", Isaac yelled, while Spook banged on the door. "Chuckie!" Bang, bang. "Chuckie!" Bang, bang, bang. "Hey Chuckie!"

Who is it, who is it? Chuckie's mother yelled from behind the door.

It's me, Hawk. And Spook. The door opened.

Chuckie's in the back, his mother said.

21
COURT TOMORROW

"How you been Mrs. Williams?"

"Fine, just fine, but I got to go back to court tomorrow cause of that stupid judge they had there last time. You know how they sent Tommy to the Island for two years, and gave Katherine a suspended sentence? Well they continued my case so's that they could dig up some more evidence against me. I don't see why they didn't let me go, or send me up then. I guess they just likes to see us comin'; you know, and standing up there lying; and they know that we're lying, and we know that they know. Like when I told him Katherine was my only daughter, and I would never have her picking up men, or when he asked me if it was me, who had started my children on shit, and I told him, no! He knew I was lying, and I knew he knew. But, what can you do, that's the way the game is. So now, I got to go back."

22

SOME SAD CAT

"Where's Katherine?" Spook asked.

"She's in the bedroom turning a trick, Mrs. Williams answered. Some sad cat that lives over on Lawrence Ave., I noticed him looking at her all the time, so's I told him he could have her for fifty dollars; it must have taken him a month to scrape together his change. She coughed while she laughed. I don't know, I got to get the kids down to the hospital in the methadone program, 'cause the dope's getting scarce around here. Sometimes I wish I had all girls, 'cause I could sure make some money off them."

23

BURN SOME SHIT

They saw Chuckie sitting in the back getting ready to shoot up.

"Hey Hawk, Spook, what's happening man."

"Nothing much, man."

"You cats want to help me burn some of this shit?"

"Sure, uh, you got some extra works?"

"Ya, here's some here," Mrs. Williams said. She produced a small box and handed it to Spook.

Dope is death; bust a pusher; finger your mother; dope is hell; love your brother…

24

HEROIN

The bag is very neatly wrapped in wax paper, or a somewhat gummier substance. It is placed on a small table in very quiet conditions. The breathing heard, is the same of those anticipating sex. The envelope, or bag is then opened. Your works are pulled out, consisting of a tie, or belt, or handkerchief (anything that will cut your blood) this is tied between heart and needle. The next is your syringe and needle. This is your primary work; it is used to inject your lady into you. The next is your dropper. This is used in some instances as the mover between the water, and dope, and cooker. It is used also as the injector. The next is the cooker, or a bottle top, anything round, and small, also the cooker holder, and with a little water and a match, you can now get laid.

25
STRIPS TO HER WAIST

Chuckie strips to his waist, so do Hawk and Spook. Chuckie's brother Wayne who's thirteen comes in, he strips to his waist. Mrs. Williams strips to her waist. Hawk and Spook look because she has no bra on. Chuckie tipped the bag and half its contents into his cooker, he tapped the other half into Hawk and Spook's. He took his dropper, and dropped five drops of water, five into each of the two Coca Cola bottle caps (cookers). He picked up his belt, holding one end between his teeth, and tightening with his teeth and hands. The belt secure, he ties a tie around Wayne. Spook ties Mrs. Williams' belt, and Hawk and Spook strap each other. Chuckie goes back to the white powder diluting under the water. He picks up his cooker holder attached to the cooker. Wayne lights a match, they all stand around and watch. The powder changes into liquid under the heat of the match. Charlie fingers his dropper. Hawk, Spook, and Mrs. Williams begin their own ritual, repeating step for step Chuckie's rite.

26
DROPPERS

The dropper's rubber is squeezed, and released, the needle sucks up the liquid into the dropper. The dropper is pointed up, and tested. Chuckie stretches out his arm, and balls his fist. The needle seeks a vein; finds one. It probes it, sinks into it, with just the right thrust from Chuckie. The rubber is squeezed slowly, so slowly, slow and easy, just like you make love to a woman, slow and easy, picking up momentum, and then released. Chuckie's blood filled his dropper. He squeezed again, letting it rush him; (Drums pound, a siren-like stillness bangs your heart; I love you, you love me, I love you baby, you love me. This love is true. I love, I love you baby, I love, I love you baby, O yes! I love you, you love me) a heavy sigh, an orgasm.

Belts untied, sweet, sweet, sweet, love. So soft, O yes. "Huh." A deep breath.

27
MRS. WILLIAMS

The process has been repeated by all in the room. Everybody nods happily, with the exception of Mrs. Williams, who had to use the veins of her feet, since her other veins had collapsed one by one. She couldn't rush, and was unhappy. But she waited patiently for it to hit her. She sat with her face over her knees, her oversized tits being squashed by her knees and stomach, rhythmically tapping her syringe while it stuck in her middle vein, the vein that ran from the fourth toe straight up through to the ankle.

28
THIS SHIT IS GOOD

The high hit her -- fast -- and as her lips dropped open, saliva clinging to them, and she took a deep breath from between her legs, and stank, and her daughter was just finishing wiping herself and the husband of Jessie Mae Smith of Lawrence Ave. off, she said to herself, *this shit is gooooooooooooooood.*

29
KATHERINE SLEPT

She nodded; James Smith left. Katherine slept, and the other four sitting around the table nodded. The only movements were scratches. Just as Isaac scratched his mouth and nose, a maggot crawled from the second floor bathroom pipe, in between the opening, and onto the third floor bathroom.

30
CIGARETTE

Dung tucked his shirt in, zipped his zipper, and put his belt into the fourth notch. His new plaid striped yellow shirt, was just made for his old pair of green knit slacks. His cigarette burned in the ashtray on the dresser beside the mirror, where his reflection smiled at himself. In back of his reflection, Mary lay on the bed, turned to the side, facing the door, as the noon sun shone lightly on her face. Dung flipped the ashes from his cigarette, put it to his mouth and dragged on it. The smoke, and the cigarette came from his mouth a second apart, the cigarette before the smoke. The cigarette went back into the ashtray, the smoke hit the reflection and bounced in a diameter;

31
AFRO COMB

Dung was cool. Dung took out his afro comb, and gave twenty up strokes, and ten across strokes to his afro. He went to the bed, sat down and put on his shoes and socks, without awakening Mary, who was still waiting. He decided to waken her.

32
JOHN'S COMIN

"Mary! Mary, hey, Mary wake up! Hey."

"Yeah, yeah, what you want Dung?"

"Is Elaine coming by today?"

"I don't know. Why?"

"Well call her, and ask her to meet me at Shanty's about six or six-thirty, okay? I got a favor I want her to do for me."

"What is it?"

"I'll tell you later; what time them johns comin', if they're comin'?"

"They'll be here; you going now?"

33
WHEN HE DIED ALL HE LEFT US WAS A LOAN

"Yeah, as soon as I hear my new sound." Dung went over to the phonograph he had stolen about three months ago, and put on The Temptations' record: "Poppa Was A Rolling Stone". *Poppa was a rolling stone, wherever he lay that was his home',* Dung sang, *and when he died all he left us was a loan, hey, hey, hey, hey, poppa was a rolling stone, wherever he lay that was his home, and when he died all he left us was a loan um, um, um, um, HEEEEEEY!*

34
IN ABOUT TWENTY MINUTES

Ma Dixon finished hanging up the phone. "Hey Frank, there's some guy who wants you to call him in about twenty minutes, it's very important, he says. I think it was Conrad, your friend; I didn't ask you know, but I did take the phone number. You got a pen? Well its 442-8863. He said you can get him there in about twenty minutes, but after that he'll be at Mel's. He said it was important, so you better call him. If you need change, I got some here. You want some more coffee?"

35
PROBABLY A JUNKIE

"Hello Conrad." The dime clicked. "Yeah, this is Frank, yeah, it's a nice day, look, uh, Ma told me you called, what's up?" Frank watched the door open, from behind it came the most sorrowful mess he had ever seen; some cat with a yellow plaid shirt, and green pants. *Probably a junkie,* he thought.

36
THUMPS

When Paisley left Fuller this morning, he had gone straight home to his wife, and the warm bed she had warmed with her pregnant body. Betty had married Paisley one year ago. She remembered how good and fine he had looked then. He didn't have much of any money, but his sweet whisperings in the night, and the promises to come filled her warm breast and motherly feelings with love. Betty loved life. To her life was living; loving was life. Betty loved Paisley; he was a good man; he had helped make her breasts full of milk. The child inside her was formed now. The feet thumped; kicked; the body turned, and the hands pounded her for more room. Betty would sit, with the pain she would sit, and smile, and hold her stomach, and breathe, and sigh, and raise her head and smile, and her stomach would be round, and firm, and her high soft cheeks would laugh with the smile, and she would look up and think of the life within her. *Life was hard for him,* she thought; having to work as a janitor, hurt him. She loved him, but sometimes it wasn't good enough for him.

37
THE JANITOR

Paisley smelled the warm, soft woman-mother odor of his wife, it did not frighten him. He had smelled it too often, but it did cause a pain, from where he didn't know. His thoughts were frustrating; he only wanted to lie beside this woman, and feel safe. She was safe, he knew she was, she had proven. His thoughts of his conversation with Fuller were another reason for him to forget. He wanted to, he didn't like what Fuller was planning, but he knew that he had no choice. Life for him was an endless existence of nothing; not Betty, or the coming child – but it was endless for what he could not give them.

To live with rats, and roaches, filth, and garbage, from one condemned building to another. To work, work his life away. To not be young anymore, to die after reading about Rockefeller's, or Kennedy's, or Ford's, or motherfuckers, to just barely survive. To have to tell his woman that Lawrence Ave. was it, this was to be their paradise, that the three rooms, the kitchen, the bedroom, the front room, was where their child would grow.

The pee smell of hundreds of other tenants, crawled through his skin. Home, home! He was a man! I am a man, but my woman has to sleep cold, one blanket, her look of sadness in this shabbiness. WHAT IS SO GREAT ABOUT BEING POOR! I want money for my family, I will kill for that money, I will kill for rugs, furniture, a washing machine, tables, chairs, sofas, a T.V., a radio, a house, decency; a breath of fresh air, a right to call myself man.

Yes, I will kill, and kill again. His child was not yet born, but it would be soon, and to come home to this; this! He! He would look at his child in this? He slides in under the cover, he puts an arm over his wife, and draws close. The morning light comes in from a million ways. Her mouth is open, and he breathes, and smells her morning breath. She is brown, and she is soft, her hair is knotty, her eyes are closed, her legs are covered by his, her belly is swollen; she is woman.

38
HIS UNBORN CHILD

There could be no right, or wrong, life to him was wrong. This would be his only chance. If he didn't go, it would be the same nothing. If he did go and fail, the same. But if he succeeded; tears rolled down his face as he thought of his unborn child, he looked over the room, and saw its emptiness. He thought of the huddled form lying next to him, he cried softly and cursed his God. The woman awakened; Betty was her name. She woke slowly listening to the night janitor, lying beside her. She moved her body closer to the male figure, she felt it tightening.

39
I LOVE YOU JAMES

"You alright James?"

"Yeah Betty, I'm alright. How you feeling? The doctors say you could go in any day now. Did we get everything packed?"

"Yes honey, now you get some sleep. I'll have your breakfast ready for you in an hour, then you can go back to sleep." The man tightens his hold around her, telling her he loves her, and everything's alright. He touches her stomach and feels the hard thumps of the baby's movements. She watches, a satisfied radiance glows in her stare. She touches him and says, "I love you James." He puts his head on her breasts, and she cuddles him to sleep.

40

SIX SNORTS OF COCAINE

Ma Dixon closed the restaurant at four-thirty, not only because she had a migraine headache, but also because she felt the urge to be in heat. Both were due to the massive amounts of cocaine she had sniffed that day. *Jingle bells, jingle bells, jingle all the way, O what fun it is to lie in a one horse open sleigh heyyyy*; cough, cough. Shit, this shit is worse each time I sniffs it, but the more you do it, the more you like it, ha ha; *jingle bells, jingle bells, jingle all the way, O what fun it is to lie in a one horse open sleigh*. I guess I'll go over to Mr. Afro's see what's happening there, get me some more coke. Lord have mercy, um, um, um, what a day. First, Fuller comes in looking like he got something going for himself, then Frank gets a call from one of his partners, and flies the hell out of here. Then the police comes by; two of them with Station Two written all over their big fat noses, to their big fat asses; come asking me questions like, have I been hearing anything about a conspiracy, or what type of dope was being sold outside, trying to get familiar with me. Shit after them mothers left I had to take six snorts of my shit. I wonder what's happening though."

41

TWENTY DOLLARS

"Hey Dung, what's happening baby?"

"Yeah where you been hiding man? Ha ha ha."

"Yeah man, we was just getting ready to come look for you, we heard you was staying with that junkie bitch. How is she man, she getting you enough dope? I hope so man 'cause I don't know how else you could stand staying with her, shit that bitch is nasty, whew, I remember when Alfred had her on the streets, one night Alfred gave her some bombers and some smoke, he found her the next morning with the manager of the State Show, said she had turned everyone on in the movies for free; ha, ha."

"But this ain't what we's looking for you for. We was wondering if you, or your whore could lay about twenty dollars on us?"

42
YOU KNOW T.J, MAN

"Yeah man, we need it to get us some action. Dig man, if you do that for us, in about a week, we're expecting some real heavy shit to be comin' in from New York. T.J. told us we'd be among the first he'd cut in, for just a little scratch; so we'd cut some up and give you about half an ounce, which would be like giving you eighty dollars. Okay man? Shit, you'd be making a profit."

"You know T.J., Man, yeah, you know T.J., yeah shit he'd do anything for us, me and Spook his boys."

"Yeah we helped the cat out of a jam once, and the cat remembers. So if you can lend us the bread, man, we would appreciate it."

43
BLUE HILL AVE. AND WARREN STREET

The progressing day had become colder, at five o'clock the temperature was 10°. The three men talking at the corner of Blue Hill and Warren St., were oblivious to the freezing cold. Their only movements were the motions of their hands scratching. The junkies' only thoughts were of junk or money, nothing else mattered. Dung mentioned to Hawk, and Spook that Mary was going to be turning some tricks, and probably would have some money. "I'm going on down to Shanty's I got to meet Mary's sister Elaine. Say why don't you all stop there about eight o'clock, I think something big might be happening, I talked with Fuller, and he told me there was something up that he wanted me to be a part of. I can't tell you too much but come on down, okay?" Dung put his hands in his pockets, pulled out his Kool's, put a cigarette to his mouth, and lit it.

"Why don't ya'll go over to my pad and see Mary. She ought to be finished by now. Tell her I sent you, and that I'll give her back the money tonight, and remind her for me, to get in touch with Elaine."

It began to snow, and snow harder. The three walked towards Dudley down Warren. The snow closed them from view.

44
CIGARETTE SMOKE #2

Mary got up and got ready for work; she brushed her teeth, combed her hair, and put on a body stocking. She threw the magazines off the bed, lit a cigarette, and waited. The time went by, and she smoked another cigarette, she sat there and smoked and didn't wonder anything. At one-thirty she moved her body about an inch to her left. She thought that maybe she had had time to take a bath before, but not now. She sat and waited. She had called Elaine right after Dung had left, and gave her Dung's message; she said she should meet him. She felt bored and tired, waiting was the hardest part. She felt as though she had been waiting all her life, just to wait some more. The smoke circled the room. She rubbed her thighs back and forth, and felt heat, urges stirred within her, and she waited. She had never felt good about herself, she wondered why. She knew she was a slut, and a junkie, but she didn't know why, she supposed she liked it, what else? Of course she did. Nothing thrilled her more than the waiting. She decided to just wait and not think. She waited. In a few minutes there was a knock on the door. She put out the cigarette. She breathed deeply, her body relaxed, she stood, and rubbed her buttocks, she turned the lock and opened the door. Not glancing at the man, she said, "Come in." She went and sat back on the bed; not in the same spot as before. She looked up at the stranger standing before her, and wondered if he was in the Knights of Columbus.

45
YOU WANT IT STRAIGHT?

"What you want honey?" She always wanted to know what they wanted her to do, before she started, it was less complicated that way.

"You want it straight? Or, you know, you got something else in mind?"

46
THE STRANGER

The stranger stood there in his rain or shine, all he wanted to do was fuck, and get the hell out of there. She knew that, but she liked to make it somewhat agonizing for them. She spread her legs and looked up at the stranger, waiting for his answer. His wedding banded hand went to his reddened face, and rubbed it. He croaked, "Straight."

"Okay honey, now you put the money over there and hurry." She watched him go into his pocket and pull out some bills. He fingered a twenty and put it on the dresser.

"Twenty-Five, honey."

47
YOU JUST WANT TO LOOK

Mary stood up as the other five was placed on the dresser. The stranger watched her, very content to let her run the show, his executive leadership was not to be forced on people like these. He watched her slip out of her body stocking. She slipped out of her body stocking, noticing the stranger watching.

"You just want to look honey, or did you come to play?"

She finished undressing. The stranger now remembering; lust overcoming fear.

48
ON HER BACK AGAIN

Mary lay on the bed, on her back again. She felt safe and comfortable on her back. She actually loved being on her back. She watched the ceiling, and watched the stranger take off his undershorts. She laughed to herself at how different they all looked. She watched him as he came on top of her, she lurched her body, and began to work.

49
WAITING

Mary sat on the bed and smoked, waiting. She disliked waiting. She wished that it could happen at once, and be over. She had put her body stocking on after the stranger had left. Speed in leaving was their common trait, after their common goal had been finished.

50
JUNKIES AND WHORES

I wonder what Dung is doing, I wonder where he is, she thought.

Maybe he'll come back this afternoon and lie with me."

She kind of figured she loved Dung, but nobody loved junkies and whores, and whores and junkies didn't love.

51

EIGHTEEN AND BEAUTIFUL

Mary felt her jones beginning to come down on her, and knew she'd need a fix soon. Mary stared into space, needing a fix, waiting for the john. The familiar knock came. May lay on her back, watched the hard breathing stranger come down on her, she began her work. The stranger left. A cigarette lit in her mouth, she reached for her works. Eighteen-year-old Mary, lay on the bed, on her back, naked; with a needle in her arm; *I'm beautiful,* she thought.

And it all rushed her at once.

52

JACKSON

Jackson swiveled around in his chair; "car 2, car 2, go to 24 Syller St. in Dorchester, a possible break and entering." The police calls came rapidly this time of year.

"Conrad, the budget listing for the past year of operations --"

"Car 12, car 12, a disturbance on Bicknell St. in Dorchester, please to go to the scene immediately."

"-- is full of complications as the government sees it. With the new equipment we got in, and the two cars we added, we ought to have gone a few thousand over, but we didn't. So the government is bitching, or was, because we asked for more than we received last year for operations. As they see it we should have asked for less; but--"

"Car 8, car 8, please go to Ruggles St. in Roxbury, gun fire has been reported, proceed immediately."

"-- but with the aid of Curtis Askins, our good friend in Washington, we seem to have got what we asked, and a bit more."

"Car 18, car 18, go to Shanty's Lounge at Northampton Station, a disturbance."

"Those poverty programs will probably be obsolete in a few years, so we have to get all we can for the community now. This money we're receiving will pay our back salaries, and keep us going for at least four years--"

--" Car 5, car 5, a robbery is in progress at The Ebony Clothing Store on Warren Street, proceed immediately; caution is advised; the robbers are armed."

53
COMMUNICATIONS OF MINORITY MEN

The door to COMM opened at eight-ten; the assistant director, Frank Rushing, and street worker Mel Delancy came in. The office of COMM was furnished with an assortment of communication-electronic devices. Frank had badgered with the Federal Communications Committee, to let them start a radio station, or at least, to broadcast from COMM in affiliation with another station. It had taken him eight months before they had consented to the affiliation with WILD on code WXUR. Their broadcasting equipment took up most of the front office. The back consisted of the director's office, the assistant director's office, cubicles for the secretaries, and a lounge area, and conference room for the workers.

54
GOING TO BE HERE FOR AWHILE

"Hey Jack", Frank spoke, "what's this meeting all about? I talked to Conrad and – O! Hey Conrad. How's it going?"

"How are you doing Frank, Mel? From what Jackson's been saying, it looks like we're going to be here a while tonight."

They sat in a semi-circle facing Jackson.

55
SEVENTY-FIVE THOUSAND DOLLARS FROM OAKLAND

"Tonight, probably late, an Edward Thomas from Oakland, is coming in with about fifty thousand dollars in cash, and fifteen thousand in cancelled checks, which we're to deposit in Unity Bank the day after Christmas. The reason for this, is that it isn't our money, or it is, but it isn't supposed to be. As I explained to Conrad before you came, Washington didn't want to give us hardly anything for operations here. We had asked for seventy thousand, which was fifty thousand above what we asked for and got last year."

"Car 52, car 52, please back up car 18 at Shanty's Lounge on Northampton St."

56
A FEW CONGRESSMEN IN WASHINGTON

"Well C.O.P.E. in Oakland asked for and received a grant for four-hundred and fifty thousand dollars. Which means, that there has been, and is, a little crooked dealing going on with our friends in Washington. Frank here, sort of brought it to my attention, when he told me the listings for the poverty agencies in the major cities. Last year's budget for C.O.P.E., nationwide, was one million and a half, which would mean that Oakland was getting half!! I called Curtis, and he checked into it. It seems I was right. The big boys in Oakland, and a few Congressmen in Washington, were planning on helping themselves to the excess money. You see Oakland's budget for last year was twenty-five thousand dollars, and their basic operation has not changed. So that the budget they submitted, and was approved, was fraudulent, and approved under less than honest procedures. Curtis got in touch with a few of those people.

We knew our budget wasn't going to be approved the way it stood, so there was no sense in us reapplying for anything. C.O.P.E. seems to have been favored. Why? It didn't matter. There was no sense in going to the government. Curtis and his agency went to Oakland. They talked with some of the people there and persuaded them that it would be advisable for them to fund us. That's about the whole of it fellows, so a Mr. Thomas is flying here tonight with fifty-thousand dollars, and a few thousand in cancelled checks. The money is to be deposited almost immediately; and Frank you're to start a profit-making organization, which will be part of COMM, but will solicit money from the community, and city. I need not say, that none of this conversation is to be repeated."

57
COFFEE WAS BREWED

"Why the other organization, Jackson?" Mel leaned forward in his chair, thoughts racing against his brain, wondering if he should be part of this. The others shifted in their seats, seeing Jackson, who couldn't see them.

"The reason is so that the money we're to receive tonight can be accounted for. By having an affiliated organization that is profit-making, there can be none, or not many questions asked. Thomas should be here about midnight, or shortly thereafter. So let's get down to the business of rearranging our organization, or organizations."

The chairs scraped, all arose, and coffee was brewed.

58
WASHINGTON, DC

Fuller was seen by a prostitute and a dope dealer individually, and four United States Congressmen while in Washington. Fuller's connections were variable. As a dope dealer, and a prominent one, his connections ranged from the lower to the higher levels. Fuller was also a well-paid internal Government Agent, an assassinator, an organizer of death. Because of Fuller's control of his environment, and his ability to seclude his life, his passion and love for death was his weapon. Washington around the beginning of November was cold and breezy, with a suggestion of wetness in the air. Washington's whitish, grey buildings formed a silhouette in the day's cold. The closeted, sterile compartments of Washington were, for a man like Fuller, heaven. His non-desire for power and his passion and love for death made his arbitration very easy. In fact, he felt himself to be a controlled man. The faces of the men talking to him had no distance, no time, no sculpture; they could have been anyone. His feelings were mute; the head shakes were his only movements.

59
PIMP

Fuller was known to black circles as a pimp and a drug pusher. That he was condoned in these communities, was only second to the fact that he was hated, ignored, feared, and scorned. His power was wherever blacks were. He was the government's enforcer, their death wielding weapon. He sold death in drugs, and made death possible through other means. When Fuller left the compartment, the cigar smoked room with the men shaking their heads, nodding, that all was well; he knew exactly what he had to do. He was that type of man. Fuller was a quiet man, very intense. If one was to describe him, they would say, he was cold and aloof. He was from the streets of Baltimore; the Baltimore of the forties. Dope had always been his life. He lived dope, thought dope, dope, and how to get more. He probably had about three hundred people working for him across the country. Fuller left Washington for Boston, Nov. 16th. His first contact was with James Paisley. Paisley was a good friend of Fuller's, or rather his brother was. Harold, and Fuller, had grown up in Baltimore, they had run numbers together, and eventually sold dope together. Their friendship though strong, was very brief, a total of nine years, or until they were twenty-two.

60
HAROLD WAS DEAD

Harold was found by Fuller in a stolen car; down by the yards, dead, with five clean holes in his head. They had been put on Baltimore's syndicate's shit list, and had been encouraged to leave the state of Maryland. But due to their lack of experience, and the courage of youth, they didn't heed the advice of their betters, and continued to deal in three counties instead of one. Their final consequence was that Harold was dead, and Fuller was running for his life, along with Harold's younger brother, James.

61
CRIME AND DOPE IN BOSTON

They had made it to Boston, where Fuller continued his trade, and raised his friends' brother. James had grown to be unlike his brother, or his adopted father. At twenty-four, he was an honest person, or tried to be, and for some reason he didn't go along with crime and dope. He tried to work at honest jobs, but deep inside, he knew there was no future in that. When Fuller made contact with James on November 18th, James had just got his new job as the night janitor over at the John Hancock Building. They money wasn't bad, but he was constantly worried about Betty, and the unborn baby, he knew that Betty could look out for herself, but he still worried. When Fuller drove off of Blue Hill Ave., and onto Lawrence Ave., and saw 92 Lawrence Ave., he knew that James would be ready.

62
WHERE YOU BEEN

"Hey Betty, look who's here! Hey Fuller come on in, have a seat. Where you been, man." All moving very quickly to the kitchen, where the chairs are.

"Betty, get Fuller some beer. You want some beer, man?"

"No I got something I want to talk to you about James, something important."

63
PREGNANT BODY

"Betty turned her pregnant body around and stared at Fuller. She didn't like the man; she knew what he was. But her husband loved him, and she loved her husband, so she accepted and tolerated him; but only so much.

64
WADDLED TO THE BEDROOM

"What you want to talk to him about, that's so important I can't know."

"Now Betty, come on, go in the bedroom and lie down, and take your nap, go on."

Fuller leaned over the table and yawned; he smiled at Betty.

"Alright!" she said. "Alright!" She slammed down the beer and waddled to the bedroom.

65
WATCHED THE BIRDS FLY

"You got a fire escape? If so, let's use that."

Paisley nodded his agreement and they went out to the fire escape. Paisley's smile went into a deep frown as Fuller outlined what he wanted of him.

I'll just ask you twice; now, and the day I need you. You don't have to answer now, but I'll expect one. I'll see you December 23."

Paisley didn't say anything, he just watched Fuller get up and leave. He watched the birds fly overhead, and thought.

66
GIVE ME TWENTY

Mary heard the familiar knock in her nod. She returned enough to hear someone calling her name.

"Who is it? Who is it?" she yelled. "Who the hell is it!"

"Hawk and Spook."

"Who?"

Hawk and Spook, Dung sent us over." Mary went to the door and opened it.

"Dung?"

"Yeh", Hawk said, while entering. "We asked Dung to do us a favor, and he told us to see you."

"Where's Dung at right now?"

"He should be down at Shanty's, that's where he said he was going."

"Well what did Dung want me to do for you'all?" She looked at each quizzically.

"He said to give us twenty, and he'll see you back tonight."

It was six o'clock, although time had no place in this room. Mary put on a piece of bathrobe, and went to the dresser. She thought, and turned around.

"You all wait, I want to go around to Shanty's, you going – what's your names again?"

"Hawk and Spook", Spook said.

"Ya, well let's go on down to Shanty's, I'll give it to you there."

Isaac and Spook watched her dress. Then they went to Shanty's together.

67
ELAINE

Dung met Elaine in the back room at the back of Shanty's Lounge. She gave him six bags of dope, and a half a Ki of cocaine. Dung fixed himself, and nodded for a while. At seven o'clock, he told Elaine what he wanted her for. Fuller had said she'd get about two thousand. Elaine said she'd be ready about ten-thirty. She excused herself, and went to the side of the room on the left, and waited on the cot for her next customer, which would be her ninth so far.

Not bad for just a little after seven, she thought.

68
SHANTY'S LOUNGE

When Dung left the room and went up front, he saw Spook, Hawk and Mary sitting by a table by the bar. He walked over wondering why Mary had come. They saw him and started yelling. Dung arrived at the table.

"Mary, did you give them the twenty?"

"Well Dung, if it's alright with you, I will."

"Ya, ya, I'll give it back to you this evening."

Dung sat down, and looked at Hawk and Spook. Fuller had told him he'd need two more.

"Hey Benny, what's happening? No everything's alright."

"Mary you sit here. I want to talk to Isaac and Spook."

They got up and began moving to the back.

"Hey Jessie, how's it going?"

"Alright Dung, just hanging in." They walk past chairs, smoke.

"Hey what's happening?" Dung slapped hands with old timers.

"What's happening Willy?"

They walked past and through music, winos.

"Hey man, how you feeling?"

"Alright man, you know."

They walked past junkies, and whores, and laughter, and danger and through smells. The standing-room-only crowd, the mellow lights, the soft swirls, the pretty dresses, the fine women, the *in* men, The Life.

PART TWO

THE LIFE

69
THE BABY KICKED ONCE

Paisley left his house at ten o'clock. Betty watched him go. She held her hands to her stomach, feeling thumps; took a deep breath. He had acted strange that whole day, maybe he was nervous because of the baby. She hadn't completely forgotten Fuller. It bothered her a lot, wondering just what Fuller had wanted with James. James in fact hadn't been acting right for a month. She had caught him brooding, and just sitting, looking out, plenty of times. She drew back from the window and sat in the kitchen. She saw a mouse run down through a crack in the floor. She thought about James; she thought about James, and loved him. Betty raised her body, her heavy body up, she went to the sink, pulled down a glass and poured some water. She was lonely, *very lonely*, she thought. She pulled open her housecoat and gazed upon her breasts swollen with milk. She thought about it, and decided it was time: the baby kicked once very hard, and began his journey; her labors began.

70
THE MAGGOTS ENTER

By quarter of six the maggots had begun to infest the first and third floors. Chuckie's younger brother found them.

"Hey Ma, hey Ma! Look at these, what are they Ma?"

Mrs. Williams looked at what her son was talking about, and screamed for Chuckie. The bathroom was full of them, the walls, the bathtub, the sink, the toilet, floors, everywhere. Some horrible odor was omitting from them.

71
I THOUGHT SHE HAD LEFT

"Close that door Tony! Chuckie where are they coming from, Jesus, Lord have mercy; where!"

"Probably the second floor, Darcel's apartment, but I thought she had left."

"Tony", Mrs. Williams said, "Tony! Take our shit over to Roger's house, Katherine you call the police; and the fire department. Where are you going Chuckie?"

"I'm going downstairs."

72
DARCEL YOU HOME

He had a funny feeling, as he went down the stairs, that smell, it was something he had been smelling for a while. But he had thought it was part of the building. He walked slowly down; very scared now, of what he had no idea. There were two or three maggots lying outside the second floor door. He started shaking. He knocked on the door. He thought he heard a noise inside, sort of a hum. He yelled, "Darcel, Darcel! You home Darcel!" No answer. *It's probably something she left*, he thought.

He decided to kick the door open but he heard noises.

She must be home, he thought. *Oh well, I'll kick it in anyway.*

73
FLIES

He kicked the door in and saw thousands of flies, blocking his view, rushing him. He stood in shock, throwing up all over himself. The only noise was the loud buzzing of the flies, and Chuckie's choked screams. The maggots began their wiggling process towards the open door. The dark blue pile on the floor remained. The fire department, and police came. The apartment was cleaned out, pictures were taken, and Chuckie was taken to Boston City Hospital, still screaming incoherently. Nobody knew what happened; they told the police, nobody had heard nothin'.

74
A TWENTY-TWO AND SOME GIN

Paisley had walked to the corner, he got into the car at Blue Hill Ave., and said, "Okay." Fuller smiled. He handed Paisley a twenty-two, and some gin.

"You'll need both of these." They drove to Shanty's lounge.

75
FOUND IT LACKING IN MEN

About eight o'clock, Ma Dixon had come to Shanty's. She had gone to Mr. Afro's, but had found it lacking in men. So she had gone home to take a bath, and come to Shanty's. She stood at the bar, drinking a little, til someone asked her to dance. She danced and sat down, rubbing her legs together. At ten-thirty she noticed Fuller, and a younger man come in. She watched them get a drink, and they both sat with a woman and three men. Two she recognized, the other she didn't. The other two had been in the restaurant when Fuller had come in. He hadn't seemed to know them then. She wondered about them, but then turned her attention back to the boy she was picking up.

76
LOGAN AIRPORT

At eleven forty-five, American Airlines Jet 110206, lowered onto Runway 11 at Logan Airport. A tall man with sandy hair and grey eyes disembarked from the plane onto the ramp beside the jet. The brown briefcase he carried clashed with his grey suit. But he didn't expect to have it too long. He found a telephone booth. He dialed 436-0072.

77
THE TALL MAN HUNG UP

"Hello, hello Mr. Jackson?"

Yes, speaking."

"This is Mr. Thomas, I'm on my way." The tall man hung up.

78
MEL OPENED THE DOOR

At eleven o'clock, Elaine had gone to the C.O.O.M. Office. She rang the bell. Mel had come to ask who it was. "Elaine", she answered. Mel and

Conrad, both knew Elaine. They had visited her a great many times. Mel opened the door, wide.

79
HOW LONG YOU GOING TO BE HERE

"Hey, how are you doing girl?"

"Alright", she said.

"What you doing over here this late?"

"Nothing, I saw the lights while I was on my way home, and decided to stop by."

"Well come on in."

"Okay. Wait! Let me go home and change. How long you all going to be here?"

"I don't know, Jackson's on one of his things, probably til four or five."

"Okay let me go home, and I'll be back about 12:30, okay? 12:30!"

"Okay," Mel said, "That's fine."

80
COME ON IN

Mr. Thomas had the cab driver let him off at the COMM office. He checked his watch, it was twelve-fifteen. He rang the bell. The door was opened by Mel, who was expecting Elaine.

"Come on in."

81
DUNG RANG THE BELL

At twelve-twenty-eight, a car drove up to the opposite side of the COMM Office. Five men got out, each knowing what was to be done. Dung rang the bell.

82
THE BABY BEGAN HIS STRUGGLE

The pains grew and she screamed, she screamed, and screamed, her body tightening, and shaking. Her water broke. She checked the time. She had been in labor almost, or just two hours. It was time to go to the hospital. It was 12:35. She called City Hospital. An ambulance was coming; they would be ready. She called the number James had given her; no answer, scared, and terrified; the baby began his struggles.

83
JESUS ALL THAT MONEY

"Car 19, car 19, proceed to Slayton Way, couple reports a prowler in the vicinity."

Mel leaped up as he heard the bell. This was no place for Elaine now. Jesus, all that money. No, she couldn't come in now. He ran to the front and opened the door.

84
PRAYED FOR HER BABY

The ambulance came quickly, the attendants helped her into the ambulance; they gave her oxygen. Four minutes from City Hospital Betty prayed for her baby, for her, for James; dear James, he'll be so happy. The ambulance arrived.

85
WHERE'S THE MONEY

The five men entered, yelling, screaming, "Where's the money, where's the money."

Mel was pushed to the back, the five came into the back room, guns drawn.

"What's going on? What's going on? I can't see. Frank, what are they talking about? I can't see, who are they?"

"It's just us Jackson", Fuller said.

"Fuller!! What are you doing?" Fuller stepped over to Jackson; Jackson looked around not seeing.

"Frank, what are they doing?"

"Just be cool Jack, I think they just want the money."

"That's right," Fuller said, "see Jackson?"

"Uh?" Jackson said.

86
TWO BULLETS IN THE HEAD

Fuller put the gun to Jackson's head, left side, and blew his brains out with two shots. There were eight more shots fired in the room. Frank lay dead over the side of the desk. Conrad lived a few minutes more with a bullet in his throat. Mel died instantly with a bullet in his forehead and groin. Mr. Thomas would live for two days in a coma, with two bullets in his head.

The silence filled the bright lighted room.

87
THE BABY'S HEAD IS SHOWING

"Take her up to the delivery room. We'll fill out the papers later. Where's your husband at? Not here! Okay, take her right up."

"Bear down hard Mrs. Paisley, take a deep breath and push, letting out the air. Keep on Mrs. Paisley. The baby's head is showing!! Almost Mrs. Paisley, almost!"

Betty was sweating hard. Her little hands clenched, her mouth quivering; the pain, mixed with love.

88
HE SHOT DUNG FIRST

Fuller put a new clip in his gun. The others watched, silence in a dead room. He watched them, the alive ones, and the dead ones. He shot Dung first, then Hawk, then Spook. Paisley turned.

"Why, what did you do that for!! Fuller why, oh shit." Fuller turned to him. "That's the story right there man, don't you see it. Three junkies try to rob the office here, and everybody dies in the attempt."

"Hey, Fuller, man all these dead . . ."

"Shut up man! Here rub your gun off and put it that one's hand. Come on so we can get."

89
THE BABY'S HEAD CAME THROUGH

The baby's head came through, then it's shoulder.

90
FULLER TOOK HIS OTHER GUN

Paisley took his gun, and put it in Mel's hand, closing it around. Fuller took his other gun, and gave it to Conrad.

91
DUNG STIRRED

Dung stirred.

92
IT'S A BOY

"It's a boy, mother!"

93
HE WAS DYING

He was dying, he knew.

94
THE BABIES CRIES

"Wa, wa, wa, wa", the baby's cries were beautiful to her ears.

95
HEARD VOICES

Dung heard voices, saw a figure.

96
A NICE BIG BABY

"7 lbs 8 ounces, mother. A nice big baby." She smiled.

97
HE RAISED HIS GUN

He raised his gun, took aim, and fired it at the figure.

98
THE WOMAN INSIDE HER

She smiled, she cried, she was happy. The woman inside her, named the boy, James Munroe Paisley the second, she drifted into unconsciousness.

99
FULLER HELP ME

The shot hit Paisley just under his right ear. Dung died. "Fuller, Fuller." Paisley looked up at the ceiling, feeling his blood rush from him. "Fuller help me."

Fuller watched the man.

I can't take you with me like this James. I can't, you know that."

"Help me Fuller, help me, my wife."

"I can't James, I can't"

Fuller shot him quickly.

His son cried; the father he would never know. The father died; not knowing.

100
DUDLEY STATION

The bus left Dudley Station at 1:00am, for its last run. The bus driver was tired, he wanted to go home.

101
THE NIGHT RUN

"Shit", how he hated the night run. He hated driving the bus. "Shit", having to drive this bus night after night was a ball breaker. He was mad tonight, and would let his wife know it when he got home. At 1:05 he picked up passengers on Blue Hill Ave. near Gomes Street. At 1:09 another one at Blue Hill and Payston Street.

102
RAPED AND KILLED

At one o'clock Fuller took the briefcase, and walked to the front door. He had one more death in mind. Betty, Paisley's wife. She could connect him when James was found. Elaine had been raped, and killed, a few minutes earlier, by another agent. Fuller opened the door. The cold air blowing strong, he rushed out into the street.

103
THE BUS

The bus driver was thinking about how pissed off he was about this midnight shift. As he rounded the corner between Gaston Street and Lawrence Avenue, he felt rather than heard the bump.

104
AND THE BRIEFCASE

Fuller rushed blindly into the street. His white coat unbuttoned, the fur caressing his neck. The briefcase under his left arm. He heard rather than saw the bus. He turned sharply and froze. Not a scream, as his face was pushed back into his head. Death came quick, the briefcase was knocked from his arms, was knocked open. The briefcase fell. The wind distributed the money to the community.

THE AUTOBIOGRAPHY OF AN AMERICAN GHETTO BOY

VOLUME FOUR

THE LATE TEENAGE YEARS

LACKLAND AND SHEPPARD
AIR FORCE BASE

JULY 11, 1969 - DECEMBER 18, 1969

1
LACKLAND

Shit was fucked up that June of 1969. Dad was pretending to testify against the Campbell Brothers. Shit was in all the newspapers, I'm carrying two butcher knives, everybody's on heroin and I'm trying to get the fuck out of the ghetto, Roxbury and Dorchester, fast before somebody kills me or I end up in jail. But, I've got a secret weapon and I ain't told nobody about this, yet. My mother had moved from the Whittier Street Housing Projects to the Academy Homes Projects in upper Roxbury in 1967, and I had found this nice girl friend, who lived in a nice house near Columbia Road, in Dorchester.

That summer while visiting Cambridge, my Grandmére and Papa Ray, decided for the first time that I was old enough to stay in their house by myself, so they discussed this with me and they were happy that I was old enough to stay while they went out to a social organization meeting. They went out and, just like any kid, I decided to do some mischief while they were gone and I was in their house alone for the first time. I called my girl-friend and told her that I was going to call my sister and have her bring her to me in Cambridge. It took about an hour and a half; but soon they were there, and up in the attic there was a bed. I think my father used to sleep up there when he was home from jail, which is where he was at the moment.

So I took her up there and I began to take her clothes off and fuck her, which is why she was out there in the first place. This is going to take a while, because she's a sweet thing and I want to make sure I'm getting every bit of that pussy that I can, and then I hear a commotion downstairs and I hear my Grandmére calling my name and she's coming up the stairs calling my name and I've now gotta disengage myself from that pussy and jump up and try to hide my pussy, but Grandmére is a little too fast and catches us in the middle of hiding, and like she's done it a million times before, tells me to put my clothes on and come down stairs and to throw that trash out of her house. (I found out later that she had done it a million times before with my father.)

Anyway, I come down stairs with my girlfriend and my sister is crying and my Grandmére's yelling get that trash out of my house and Papa Ray is looking on in disbelief and so my sister takes my pussy out of the house back to Dorchester and my Grandmére in all the hurt and pain and disappointment in me that she can summon up, tells me that I will not be allowed back in her house ever again, and for me to get out now, (I can still see the look of disgust and disappointment on her face today), and I did, and that's why at sixteen-years-old, just like that, I lost my Cambridge privileges, which was all that I had, all the good that I had. So in 1969 I was still banned from Ten Clarendon Ave. and couldn't go hang with my Grandmére at her house while all this shit was going on and if I could have I would have seen a broken and beaten down Grandmére, because of all the shit that my father had spilled on her with his shit again, and so she was probably distraught about both of us, son and grandson.

I loved her and should have gone by and apologized to her, but I never did. But, she loved me and forgave my disrespect of her and her home and in the seventies we would be good again. My secret weapon day finally came and on July 11, 1969, I got on a bus and went down to the South Boston Navy Yard, went through some medical shit, said an oath and was inducted into the United States Air Force. *I do solemnly swear that I will support and defend the Constitution of the United States against all enemies, foreign and domestic; that I will bear true faith and allegiance to the same; and that I will obey the orders of the President of the United States and the orders of the officers appointed over me, according to regulations and the Uniform Code of Military Justice. So help me God.* And just like that, just like the fuck that, I was gone outa the motherfuckin ghetto, except for my summer trips to Grandmére's house and Adams Pond Scout Camp with Mr. Hector, for the first time ever, and on my way, on my first airplane ride ever, on my way to John F. Kennedy Airport in New York City. I was eighteen-years-old.

2

Some older white kid with glasses had our paperwork and was in charge of us, we had on our civilian clothes and were told to stay together. The ride to J.F.K. Airport was uneventful, except I had never seen the earth from up in the air before, but it felt good, being out of the ghetto and going someplace, I felt like I could do this forever. We landed and were taken to the terminal, where we were given something to eat, most of the kids were white, but we were all a little in shock about how fast all this was happening, so nobody said much of anything to one another. We were taken to another terminal and put on a plane for San Antonio, Texas. It was like wow, two airplane rides in one day, New York City and San Antonio, already I'm seeing the world, already life is changing.

We arrived in San Antonio and were put on a bus that was taking us to a place called Lackland, it sounded like Disneyland and since I had never been to Disneyland I wondered if they had rides and shit like that. We arrived and passed through some big gate that said Lackland Air Force Base near dusk, and were taken off the bus, lined up with a lot of other kids, and that's when I met Staff Sergeant Jansen. Staff Sergeant Jansen was a white guy of medium height, stood ramrod straight in a crisp and creased khaki uniform, wore a T.I. hat on top of his head, had a sharp face, with a flaring pointy nose, wore aviator glasses and chewed gum.

I was 6' 3" 1/2 inches tall and wore the latest in home boy ghetto clothes, I came clean, with bright purple pants, a bright yellow fishnet tank shirt, white fresh sneakers and a picked way out afro, I looked good. Well, Staff Sergeant Jansen came right on over to me like he knew me and started showing me some love right away. He yelled at the top of his lungs, right in my face and said, "Airman, take off them clothes". My brain processed immediately that this was not a threat, that my new name was Airman and that Staff Sergeant Jansen was digging me, because I was so cool. I also realized that he was my new gang leader, except he was white and didn't look like he was on heroin, and that I should do what he said, so I took my clothes off and stood there in the brightly lit dark, in line, with my clothes off.

I learned soon that we were all Airmen, and that Staff Sergeant Jansen liked a lot of other kids too. He had an Italian cool kid that rode with me from Boston take his clothes off too and a few other kids, and then went back to where he had been standing and said for the first time to us, "Attention!"

And because we all had played with army men and seen army movies with John Wayne and all, we knew what to do and we all stood straight, shoulders back, heads up, arms and hands down and back, and a few of us, dicks out.

My new gang leader Staff Sergeant Jansen then began to tell us who we were, we were the 3701 Squadron, Flight 1091 in the United States Air force, and we were all Airmen. He told us a lot of things that early July evening, but the thing that I remember is that he said, that, 'He was our father and mother, that he was going to wake us up and tuck us in, that he was going to make us men, ready to fight for America, that this was his Air Force and that we belonged to him and that, this Air Force, whether any of us liked it or not, was integrated, and that he would tolerate no discrimination bullshit from anyone.' And then he marched us off, for the first of one million times, in cadence. *Step one, two, three, four, step one, two, three, four, your mother is on your left, your right, your mother is on your right, your left, sound off, one two, sound off, three four, sound off one, two, three, four!*

We marched off to get our hair cut, my Black is Beautiful Afro was gone, we marched off to get our boots, underwear, socks and green uniforms, looked just like Tommy and my old Boy Scout uniform, and then we were marched off to the mess hall.

Now listen up, when my sister and I would go over to my Grandmére's house in Cambridge, we were taught personally how to hold our forks and knives and how to properly eat at a table by Grandmére, because we ate like dogs at home, we ate with our hands over our food, our faces down in our food, shoveling food into our mouths, as if someone was going to steal our plate of food. We ate food on a plate so seldom, except at Thanksgiving Dinner and Christmas Eve Dinner at my Grandmother's house, we thought someone would steal it when we did. Food was very important to me, because I was always hungry, always searching for food.

So, here I am in San Antonio, Texas, Lackland Air Force Base and before we get to the mess hall, the dining hall, my personal friend, Staff Sergeant Jansen said to us, "You got three minutes to eat all you can, you better get to it". Well and I'll only speak for myself, I was a starving dog at that moment and rushed in to an all you can eat place for the first time in my life. There were hamburgers, hot dogs, mashed potatoes, bread, pork chops, rolls, all kinds of shit, I couldn't believe it.

This wasn't real, but there was one thing I'll never forget as long as I live, actually two things, one was the ice cold white American pasteurized milk and the other was the chocolate American pasteurized milk. Oh my God, between the food and the milk, I mean milk was a delicacy to me, cold milk was something I never had and I loved milk, white or chocolate, it didn't matter.

The milk was so cold and good that, it's one of the main things I will always remember about the United States Air Force, that wherever I went in service of my United States Government, the food was plentiful and free and free and free, I guess I can't say free enough, as Staff Sergeant Jansen said, "Boys, you got three minutes to eat", and boy could we eat, lips smacking as all of us boys from the ghetto, country, city, suburbs, Montana, New York City, South Dakota, Florida, Mississippi , Boston, Alabama, poor kids, middle class kids, black and white kids bonding over all that food that good ol Staff Sergeant Jansen said we could eat as much as we could in three minutes. It was pandemonium, but it was America at its best. After the first four weeks we could sit for ten minutes and really enjoy the food, it was always there for us.

Staff Sergeant Jansen as promised assigned us beds, did the roll call, and put us to bed in a clean and welcoming barracks. It was a beautiful time. Staff Sergeant Jansen woke us up, screaming at us, calling us names every morning, just like he said he would do. We did 100 pushups, 100 sit ups, 100 of everything every morning, and then breakfast, and then marching and then running, and then more calisthenics and then the mess hall for lunch in three minutes, then marching, then exercise, then marching, then calisthenics, then marching, then running, then all day screaming and yelling by Staff Sergeant Jansen showing his love for us, often when it was raining. Staff Sergeant Jansen would wake us up at 3:00 am screaming and yelling at us and loving us so much that he wanted us to come outside and go for a five mile run with him in the rain and twice Staff Sergeant Jansen woke me up personally and took me outside for a three mile run with him, I could feel the love.

Staff Sergeant Jansen must have known how much I loved the rain. It reminded me of home in Boston, and he must have known that all my life all I had done was run in the projects, run from the big boys, run from my enemies, run after my enemies, run in the hallways, run while playing, run a little track in High School, run from my mother, run after girls, run from the police, run from the ghetto, run from girls, run for my life. Staff Sergeant Jansen loved me so much that when I think of how he had me run up and down the barrack stairs from 5:00 am, up and down, up and down, up and down for seven hours one blessed day, and when every hour, since his office was right up at the top of the stairs, I would pop in his office while still running in place and say, "Staff Sergeant Jansen can I keep running some more?" and good ol Staff Sergeant Jansen would say, *Keep running son, I want to hear those footsteps on those stairs, you're doing fine.*

I couldn't believe that ol Staff Sergeant Jansen was letting me do all this stuff that I loved, pushups, sit ups and God bless me, when he started taking us to classes after the first four weeks of running and running some more, and one of the first classes we went to was how to fold parachutes. That was great, we had a lot of classes with Staff Sergeants teaching us how to be Airmen, and they were all great, but none greater then when Staff Sergeant Jansen said we were going to go up in a plane and he would know who didn't know how to fold their parachute in about two hours.

I couldn't believe that Staff Sergeant Jansen was paying me every two weeks, giving me all the food I could eat in three minutes and now in ten minutes, and all the exercise and sun and rain and cold wet weather I could get, but now he wanted me to do something I had never done before, he wanted me to jump out of an airplane with a parachute on. Jesus, he was the best gang leader, or as he called himself, my Training Instructor Leader that I could ever be with.

I loved Staff Sergeant Jansen and when he took us to this big ol transport plane and said, "This is it, it's time to jump." I couldn't wait. We got on the plane and hooked up and Staff Sergeant Jansen pulled on our parachutes and rigging, making sure we were tight and the pack was right on our backs. Ol Staff Sergeant Jansen was right there with us, he had on a pack and was making the jump with us.

His last words as he patted us on our shoulders and pushed us out of the plane were, "I'm going to know if you didn't pack that parachute right, real soon, go on and jump boys", but ol Staff Sergeant Jansen knew we were going to be alright, because he had personally inspected everyone's parachute rigging and packs himself, so he was just fooling around. It was a great experience and taught me as Mr. Hector had taught me to always be prepared to make that jump, that leap, into the unknown by being prepared to win and that day up in the sky, floating in God's air to God's green and blue earth, I never felt so prepared for life ever, and when I landed, just two seconds outa the ghetto, away from my mother and father and family, I knew things would never be the same for me again. I knew that I could do anything I wanted in this world, as long as I could hear Staff Sergeant Jansen say 'go on and jump boys'.

3

The next two weeks were more of the same running, exercising, and classes; and then came our basic training graduation run. The lead up to this event was very important, it was all we could think about. Most of our conversation after the first three weeks, for those that made it that far, had to deal with being sent back.

Being sent back meant that you had to repeat Basic Training all over again, that your ass was grass. The rumors held that there was an extreme amount of torture involved for those people who couldn't graduate from basic training on time. We lived in fear of this and all of us who could, who were strong enough, worked 200% to assure ourselves that we would not be sent back. There were many rumors of people who had been sent back and to even think of going through all that again, was enough to send some kids into shock.

As much as I was enjoying Staff Sergeant Jansen, I knew that I did not want to spend another six weeks with him. Even though we were boys now, Staff Sergeant Jansen always made sure I had an extra 100 pushups and 100 sit-ups to do every day, I really did not think I could stand another six weeks of Staff Sergeant Jansen showing me all that love and us running and playing together every day, except Sunday. We definitely needed to move on and find other people to work out and have a good time with.

I was ready to move on and knew that there was no way in hell that I was going to be sent back. And finally after six weeks, the Basic Military Training PFT Graduation from Boot Camp Day came. The Air Force's Basic Military Training Physical Fitness Test was a three-event physical performance test used to test our endurance. It was used to measure our physical strengths, abilities, and cardio-respiratory fitness. We were all required to pass the Basic Military Training PFT in order to graduate boot camp and continue on to our next tour of duty, which after six weeks we were all anxious to do.

The three PFT events were 62 pushups in one minute, 70 sit-ups in one minute, and a 1.5 mile run in 8:00 minutes. We had all been performing physical conditioning exercises five days a week and often Staff Sergeant Jansen showed me and a few other kids how much he loved us by having us do five mile runs with him on Saturdays or whenever it was raining. And now that the day was here, I was really going to understand how much Staff Sergeant Jansen loved me, because I was going to be magnificent that day. I only came in third behind one white boy warthog from Idaho and that was only because of the enormous amount of drugs, smoke, Thunderbird Wine, Rum, and other alcoholic beverages I had been sucking down over the last four years. Luckily I only smoked filter brand cigarettes, 'cause if I smoked that Chesterfield shit like ol Dad did, I would have been dead by now with all that running around and shit.

Ol Dad called me a pussy for smoking menthol filter cigarettes, he said I was a fuckin faggot for smoking that shit, but if I hadn't been smoking the filter cigarettes I wouldn't have lasted at Boot Camp; and the other thing that held me back from being first was, and the T.I.'s and Staff Sergeant Jansen got all excited about this, was that, there was this puny white boy kid from Nebraska in my Flight crew and the kid couldn't even do the minimum pushups. Anyway, I saw during the run that he wasn't going to make it. All the brothers were doing fine and the farm and country white boys had no problem; but this white kid, who looked like Dopey in Snow White, wasn't going to make it so as I ran past him once and came back up around him again, I grabbed him by the back of his white tee shirt and pushed him in front of me all the way to the finish line, well under the 8 minutes. Thus the puny little white boy came in second and I came in third.

As I said, the T.I.'s were all excited and Staff Sergeant Jansen said that there was something special about me. He said they looked for shit like that in recruits and that I had some hero shit going on. I told Staff Sergeant Jansen that I just didn't see that the kid would ever make it outa there if he was sent back. Staff Sergeant Jansen said he was going to write it up in my file. I wondered if I was going to get a prize or something. We were almost there and the only thing we were all waiting on was to see who was graduating and who wasn't and to see where we were going next and what our job title would be.

In the meantime, Basic Training was for all purposes over and Staff Sergeant Jansen was giving us a day pass for our last weekend at Lackland and he had some rules we needed to listen to. We could go into downtown San Antonio on the bus and see the Alamo, but we had to be back in Barracks at a certain time on Saturday night and anyone who got some pussy while out on pass and brought back the panties to prove it, would get a day pass for Sunday.

On Saturday afternoon while sitting in the Alamo, in San Antonio drinking a beer and smoking a cigarette with a few of the brothers I saw her, she was hanging out trying to look nonchalant, standing in the Alamo, waiting. I walked on over checked her out and sure enough she was a home girl trying not to look like she was selling pussy in the Alamo.

She was cool and we smoked a cigarette together, had a beer together talked about nothing and got up and walked across the street to a hotel where she was staying, went up to her room and took our clothes off. She was tall and skinny about nineteen or twenty, nothing unusual, looked like any ghetto girl and since this was the sixties she had pride in her hair and wore her hair natural, no white woman looking wig on.

I looked at her and my dick got big and she pulled me down on the bed with her and I entered her and moved with her like we knew each other and this was our sixth time doing it. The pussy was real easy and good, real wet, just slid in and out, easy as pie. We rocked in and out together, she gave a little scream, held me close and we came at the same time. It was a nice and a good memory.

We laid there for a while, smoked another cigarette and talked about nothing and then it was time for me to go. As I bent at the foot of her bed to put my underwear on and then put my dress khaki pants on, I slipped her panties into my pants as I pulled them up, and put on my undershirt and dress khaki short sleeve shirt on and looked at her. She's sweet laying there with her hair sticking up all over her head, I could like this girl, but I got to go and as I open the door and look back at her, covers pulled up, I can still see her today, covers pulled up, she's peeking over the covers at me, looks a little shy now, and she says, *I ain't gonna charge you, cause you cute, but let your friends know that I'm here and it will only be twenty dollars.* I said okay and assured her that I would, I said bye to her and walked out and closed the door and never saw her again, but I can still see her peeking over the covers at me, maybe hoping I'll come back.

One of the things I knew was that girls all had a pipeline to one another and the reason why I got so much pussy back in Boston was that I never told anyone who I was getting pussy from, other guys were always bragging and telling lies about how much pussy they were getting and I never said nothing, and all the home girls knew that, so they were all fighting to give me some pussy because they knew I wouldn't say nothing about the pussy they were giving me, well the same thing in Texas, when the brothers asked me where I went with that girl, I told them she took me on a sightseeing tour of downtown San Antonia. That's why when later that night when everyone was back in the barracks and ol Staff Sergeant Jansen asked if anyone had gotten any pussy and I pulled out home girls panties, the brothers were as surprised as anyone, but the reaction from Staff Sergeant Jansen was not what I expected.

Everyone including Staff Sergeant Jansen just stared at me and then I knew that Staff Sergeant Jansen was just making a joke, just like he had done with the parachutes, and that he never expected anyone to get any pussy, much less bring back some home girls smelly panties. He just looked at me and said to, *'get that thing out of here'*. I felt embarrassed, because I thought I was going to get a prize or a day pass, it's what Staff Sergeant Jansen had said and it was the second time I thought I was gonna get something for what I had done and I didn't get anything.

I was embarrassed, but mostly a little mad that I had gone through all that hiding home girl's panties in my pants for nothing. We went to bed and that was that. On Monday I got my graduation notice, dress blues, shoes, duffle bag, great coat, tie, all that an Airman would need for his next duty and found out that I was assigned to Sheppard's Air Force Base in Wichita Falls, Texas for Jet Fighter Mechanics School, I didn't know what that meant, but I was on my way.

The next day we had a graduation parade and a lot of the Airmen's families were there. I didn't know you could have invited anybody, but I knew nobody would have or could have come anyway, so I was cool. We marched proudly for good ol Staff Sergeant Jansen and made him proud. He shook all of our hands, told us how proud he was of us and when he came to shake my hand, he said *good job*, Airman First Class Rose. I smiled at him and thanked him for all he had done, and went back to the Barracks and grabbed my duffle bag and walked out of the barracks got on a bus with all my travel pay and papers and rode up to Wichita Falls, Texas.

I never saw Staff Sergeant Jansen again, I never saw anyone from the 3707 Squadron, Flight 1091 again, and I never saw home girl again. But, in six weeks out of the ghetto, away from my fucked up family, out of the streets, I had a new name, Airman First Class Rose, and a new life, with pay every two weeks, plenty of food, travel and girls. I was ready for the world, and that's what it's all about, right?

4
SHEPPARD

I arrived in Sheppard, near the end of August 1969, eighteen-years-old, and not knowing anybody. It was great. I have learned in life that fresh starts are the best starts. I was processed in, given my Squadron and flight numbers, given my class structure, times and dates of study, assigned to a Barracks, and learned that this was going to be very different than Lackland. First thing was that this was a school, it was a lot like being, I learned later, like being in college. There was a lot of freedom and basically now, you were treated as a full-fledged member of the United States Air Force.

One of the main things you had to do was salute Officers, the other thing was you had to be impeccably dressed while on duty, while in school, while on base, which was very different then the fatigues we had to wear night and day, day and night in Basic Training, sometimes the same fatigues and underwear for a week at a time, without taking a shower. That was a lot of fun. Well, you couldn't do that here at Sheppard or else risk getting a demerit or written up. Shoes shined, pants creased, shirt pressed; shit, showered and shaved every day.

I arrived at the Squadron Barracks assigned to me and checked in with my Barracks Chief, who was Black, and was assigned a room. Unlike the Barracks at Lackland, which was open bedding with the only room being for Staff Sergeant Jansen, these Barracks had separate rooms with four Airmen assigned to a room. The other distinctive thing that I noticed right away was that there was no Staff Sergeant Jansen, nobody welcomed me by screaming the rules at me, and actually, nobody seemed to be in charge of us at all.

In my room would be me and two guys and it would stay that way the entire time I was at Sheppard. One was a White racist from Chicago, who hated Black people, just like his father did and his grandfather did, and the other was a White good ol country boy from Waco, Texas, who had never had to encounter a Black kid on any terms ever in his life and he didn't know what to make of me, pretty much the whole time.

The White kid from Chicago was short and ugly and tried to get me out of the room immediately and went to the Barracks Chief, who told him to fuck off, he then asked if he could room somewhere else, the Barracks Chief told him to fuck off with that too, and just to fuck with him some more, when I came in the room, he had the top bunk on the right side of the room, so I took his mattress and bedding off and threw it on the floor, and put the bottom mattress and my bedding on top and looked at him. I had learned back in Boston that white racists like him were essentially cowards and never did anything when they were alone and especially if they were short, ugly fucks like this one. So that little motherfucker went over to the other side with Waco, who didn't say shit, and got on the bottom bunk, and that was that.

My classes didn't start for about a week and I went around and learned the lay of the land. It was cool, and there were a lot of brothers there, and as usual at chow, the same as in Lackland, we would all eat together and we got to know one another and know who was going to be friends with who. I met a couple of brothers I liked who were in my Barracks and I would primarily hang with them for the rest of my stay at Sheppard.

Classes started around September 1st and I quickly found out what I was there at Shepherd to train for. Our instructor was an older guy in his fifties, who was alright, and the time passed while I tried my best to understand what an F4D Phantom Jet was and why in hell the Air Force had chosen me to learn this shit.

The instructor said that this was a 40-million-dollar plane and that it was to be all mine, that the pilot and the plane were mine, and that Uncle Sam was giving me a million-dollar education in Jet Fighter Tech Training Technology.

Now, if you knew me, you would know how funny all this is. My father, ol dad, would die laughing if he knew where I was and what I was doing. Ol dad tried many, many times to get me under a car with him, to show me the basics of car mechanics, to show me how to change the car's oil, to install and uninstall a carburetor, to pull an engine, and I hated that shit. I refused to learn and he made fun of me calling me a faggot, not like he meant it though. Ol dad was always fooling around; but when it came to cars, ol dad drove shit boxes that he was always working on, in one way or another. He drove them until they would break down, and he would be as happy as a pig in shit to have to work on it.

He was always trying to show me and I would tell him, "Dad, I'm into poetry and writing songs and reading and shit, I hate working on cars." He would laugh and call me a fuckin faggot. I mean ol dad was a connoisseur of good music and he had a vintage record collection that included Tony Bennett, Sarah Vaughn, Ella Fitzgerald, Frank Sinatra, Dean Martin, you know what I'm saying, all the albums and hits of the 40's, 50's and some 60's, and he did like to read; in fact, during the eight months I spent with him, when we were pimping together, I read all of his Playboy Magazines.

I used to ejaculate all of my cum over the white girl's titties in the middle of the magazine and read all the articles and I loved Shel Silverstein's and Jules Feiffer's shit, and I still think that ol Hef is still one of the coolest guys in the world today. Every time I see Hef, I think about my dad and how much he loved his Playboy Magazines and the Playboy Bunnies. So yeah, dad could read, but I was trying to tell him that I liked reading James Baldwin and Richard Wright and Ralph Ellison and Imamu Amari Baraka and Elijah Muhammad, and listening to Major Lance and Motown Records and The Supremes and Marvin Gaye and Tammi Terrell and Diana Ross and the Supremes and the Temptations and Smokey Robinson and the Miracles and The Beatles and The Moments and Sam and Dave and The Rolling Stones and Mary Wells and The Four Tops and The Delphonics and Sly and the Family Stone and The Hollies and Sam Cook and Elvis Presley and Nina Simone and Dionne Warwick and James Brown and Sonny and Cher and The Zombies and the Beau Brummels and Martha and the Vandellas and Barbara Mason and Junior Walker and the All Stars and Black Ivory and the Soundtrack to Porgy and Bess and The Five Stairsteps and Barbara Lewis, and that my heroes were Marcus Garvey and Stokely Carmichael and Huey Newton and Cesar Chavez and Angela Davis and Fred Hampton and Kathleen Cleaver and Fred Hampton and W. H. "Rap" Brown and Melvin B, Miller and Sam Greenlee and Elijah Muhammad and James Brown and Martin Luther King, Jr. and Frank "Fuzzy" Hector and Berry Gordy and The Black Panther Party and Bobby Kennedy and The Nation of Islam and Malcolm X and Shirley Chisholm and Motown Records and Gil Scott-Heron and Sidney Poitier, and Music and Books, and Bill Cosby and Don Lee aka Haki R. Madhubuti and David Hilliard and Julian Bond and Jesse Jackson and Harry Belafonte and Bobby Seale and Little Bobby Hutton and Jim Brown and Bill Russell and Lew Alcindor aka Kareem Abdul Jabbar and Muhammad Ali and Eldridge Cleaver and Erika Huggins and Elaine Brown.

5

So I thought it was funny that here I was sitting in a classroom with twenty other guys learning how to take care of and work on an F4D Phantom Jet. But, then I realized it must have been all those classes and tests I took at Lackland that said I must of had an aptitude for this line of work in the United States Air Force, because as I was to learn, The United States Air Force was never wrong, and so even though I had never been up under a car in my life, or held a wrench, screwdriver or pliers, here I was getting ready to be trained on how to work on a United States Air Force Fighter Jet.

The instructor laid all kinds of manuals and tech books and pictures and data on us and then he took us outside to look at and walk around the plane. Well, when I first saw her, I was mesmerized. This was no plane, this war machine of pure death and destruction. She was beautiful. If I could have brought her back to the ghetto and shown her to my boys, I would have. I fell in love with her and wanted to mount her right away and fly away with her to kill everything in sight. I wanted to touch her and caress her, and take care of her, and treat her right; and I just knew my good ol instructor was just the man to show me how to take care of this beautiful woman from hell.

She was an extraordinary sexy large fighter jet. A two-seat, twin-engine, all-weather, long-range supersonic jet interceptor fighter/fighter bomber. 63 feet 2 inches long; 38 feet, 5 inches wide; 16 feet, 6 inches high; she weighed empty 30,328 lbs and fully loaded 61,795 lbs, her maximum speed was 1,500 mph, her cruise speed was 575 mph, her range was 1,632 miles; she could fly high in the sky to 60,200 feet and she needed to eat a healthy 1,900 gallons internally; 1,300 externally. She was powered by Two General Electric J 79 -GE-15 Turbofans; 17,000 lbs of thrust, each with afterburner. She could cruise at 585 mph and go to Mach 2.23 at 40,000 feet in six seconds. She was armed with up to 18,650 lbs of weapons on nine external hard points, four AIM-9 Sidewinder and Four AIM-7 Sparrow Air to Air Missiles and a 16,000 lbs External Bomb Load, including general purpose bombs, cluster bombs, TV- and laser-guided bombs, rocket pods, air-to-ground missiles, anti-runway weapons, anti-ship missiles, targeting pods, reconnaissance pods; and could hold and drop nuclear bombs, including the B 28 EX, B 61, B 43 and B 57 of pure fuckin livin hell.

During the Vietnam War the F-4 was used extensively; it served as the principal air superiority fighter for both the Navy and Air Force, and became important in the ground-attack and reconnaissance roles late in the war. In air combat, the Phantom's greatest advantage was its thrust, which permitted a skilled pilot to engage and disengage from the fight at will; and it was designed to fire radar-guided missiles from beyond visual range.

On July 10, 1965, F-4Cs of the 45th Tactical Fighter Squadron, 15th TFW, on temporary assignment in Ubon, Thailand, scored the USAF's first victories against North Vietnamese MiG-17s using AIM-9 Sidewinder air-to-air missiles. On April 26, 1966, an F-4C from the 480th Tactical Fighter Squadron scored the first aerial victory by a U.S. aircrew over a North Vietnamese MiG-21 "Fishbed". On July 24, 1965, another Phantom from the 45th Tactical Fighter Squadron became the first American aircraft to be downed by an enemy SAM, and on October 5, 1966 an 8th Tactical Fighter Wing F-4C became the first U.S. jet lost to an air-to-air missile. Fired by a MiG-21 and like other Vietnam War Phantoms, the F-4Ds were urgently fitted with radar homing and warning (RHAW) antennae to detect the Soviet-built SA-2 Guideline SAMs.

Sixteen squadrons of Phantoms were permanently deployed between 1965 and 1973, and 17 others deployed on temporary combat assignments. Peak numbers of combat F-4s occurred in 1972, when 353 were based in Thailand. A total of 445 Air Force Phantom fighter-bombers were lost, 370 in combat and 193 of those over North Vietnam (33 to MiGs, 30 to SAMs, and 307 to AAA).

The RF-4C was operated by four squadrons, and of the 83 losses, 72 were in combat including 38 over North Vietnam (seven to SAMs and 65 to AAA). By war's end, the U.S. Air Force had lost a total of 528 F-4 and RF-4C Phantoms. When combined with U.S. Navy and Marine Corps losses of 233 Phantoms, 761 F-4/RF-4 Phantoms were lost in the Vietnam War.

The F-4D and E were the most numerously built, widely exported, Jet Fighters extensively used under the United States air defense system.

And my instructor said that I, eighteen-year- old, Airman First Class Rose, had been handpicked personally by the United States Air Force, the United

States Government and the President of the United States of America, good old Lyndon Baines Johnson, to make love to this beautiful woman who was posing as the greatest Fighter Jet ever made. I was being trained to be a tactical aircraft maintainer or commonly known as a 'Crew Chief'. I was a generalist who coordinated the Jets care and would call in the specialists, like avionics or propulsion technicians, when I found a problem. In other words, if my Jet were a patient in a hospital, I, the 'Crew Chief' would be the Jet's primary doctor, coordinating with specialists in radiology, psychology, and the like, as needed

I was ready, and for the next three months my instructor showed me how to love and care for this United States weapon of destruction, as a United States Air Force 'Crew Chief'. As a 'Crew Chief 'my duties would include getting up about four hours before my Jet flew. I would then inspect the Jet for flight, supervise the refueling, Hydraulic refueling and tire changes as required of the Jet. Make sure all the various systems are serviced, I would then hook up the power component and check all internal and cockpit instruments and lighting systems, annotate all documents as required, and then wait for the Pilots.

I was given over 300 hours of classroom training and 200 hours of hands on training. I learned to use every tool available to man and learn what torque meant. It was an every day except Sunday affair, nine hours a day and one half-hour for lunch. It was grueling, but I loved every minute, every second of my training. The other Airmen and I bonded as we were taught that the F4D Phantom Jet was our Jet, that wherever our Jet went, we went, that we were the first and last Airmen the pilot saw before taking off for combat and the first Airmen he saw when he landed. That my job as a United States Air Force 'Crew Chief' was to protect the integrity of the Jet and the Pilot by the day-to-day maintaining of the Jet, including end-of-runway, preflight, post flight, thru-flight, special inspections and phase inspections, diagnosing malfunctions and replacing components, detailed inspection, record-keeping, and administration and included the supervision and coordination of all aspects of the Jet, as well as such varied duties as repair, reclamation, and crash recovery duties.

But, the most enduring aspect of being a Crew Chief was the launch. The launch is what bonded Crew Chief, Jet and Pilot together. The launch sealed the fate of the Crew Chief, Jet and Pilot. The launch made the Crew Chief and Pilot as one. With a salute to my Pilot, I would stand back and watch as my Pilot began and finished his pre-flight, mounted my Jet and climbed in the cockpit.

To begin the launch, I had to clamp the air hose to the Jet to start the engines, disconnect the ground power and pull the chocks, plug in my headset and begin communicating with my Pilot, going through our flight control checks and begin taxiing the Jet out of the parking spot. For me, the real beauty of being with my baby, was on the flight line. The smell of burnt Jet fuel filled the air, and the deafening rumble of the two General Electric J 79 -GE-15 Turbofan engines with 17,000 lbs of thrust sent vibrations of love through my body every time.

I would wave my Jet and Pilot forward on the flight line and we would slowly move me backwards and my baby towards me and slowly we would move to the moment we both were waiting for. Backwards and forward we would move until we reached our launch point and I had set my baby, my Jet on the X and then I would cross my arms, step to the side, like a bullfighter when a bull is charging and just at the point of impact the Matador would step to the side, and let that massive beast charge past at the last moment. And so would I step to the side, five, ten, fifteen, twenty steps to the side and out of the way of this bitch from hell as she turned up her nose, made her noise and began to climax.

I saluted my Pilot, and he saluted me back, and she gave a roar and thrust her body forward and orgasimed with a paralyzing scream, up, up and away into God's blue sky, and with it, a great sense of accomplishment and satisfaction washed all over my body.

6

Sheppard Air Force Base was a small city all on its own located in Wichita Falls, in Wichita County, Texas. It is the largest and most diversified training center in the United States Air Force. Sheppard has been providing instruction in Air Force specialties for more than seventy years. Though the mission had changed several times, Sheppard had always been in the training business since it was officially opened as an active Army Air Corps base in October 1941. The mission was to recruit, train, and educate quality people through military, technical and flight training. The 82d Training Wing's training programs are administered by the 82d, 782d, 882d and 982d Training Groups. The 80th Flying Training Wing is the home of the Euro-NATO Joint Jet Pilot Training program (ENJJPT), the free world's only internationally manned and managed undergraduate pilot training program. Technical training is provided in the major academic areas of aircraft maintenance, civil engineering, electronics, fuels, telecommunications, biomedical sciences, dentistry, health service administration, clinical sciences, medical readiness, nursing and aeromedical education. The major command is the Air Education and Training Command (AETC).

When your duty day was done and it was time to relax, you could bowl, play golf, swim laps, play tennis or maybe see a movie. It had a post office and medical center. It had a Ceramics Shop, Auto Skills Center, three lighted softball fields, three lighted football/soccer fields, a lighted running track and two bowling centers for league and individual play, with 16 lanes each. It had two fitness centers, Basketball, volleyball and racquetball available in both centers. A cardio room, weight room and saunas. It had a Base Library with over 25,000 books, as if you could read anything else but the tech manuals that you were given, and an Outdoor Recreation Center that made available to all service man and woman, hiking, canoeing, hunting, fishing and horseback riding, some of the stuff that Mr. Hector did with us, but nothing that a home boy was going to do now.

It had a picnic area for families and young lovers and a resale store where on base permanent duty staff could buy all kinds of household items. It had a community center for special events, performing arts, meeting rooms for commander's calls, squadron functions and a large ballroom. It had three large swimming pools and a huge base theater where I first saw Paul Newman and Robert Redford in *Butch Cassidy and the Sundance Kid.* It had everything a small city had, but the most important thing that it had was the Chow Hall where the food was twenty-four hours a day, where at any given time, thousands of service men were in and out, coming into training or leaving training, it was a social place where you went to be with your boy's and eat together.

There was breakfast, lunch and dinner and everything in between, the milk was cold, white and chocolate and the food and sandwiches were plenty for a being worked to death home boy. I loved the dining hall at Sheppard and just like at Lackland all the home boys sat together, maybe once in a while a white boy would sit with us or you would have a white friend you would sit with, but it was not the norm, and it was by choice, not a law or rule.

But for real, the really greatest, I mean the greatest place on God's Green Earth and Sheppard's Air Force Base was the Airmen's Club. The Airmen's Club was huge and had a ballroom with pool tables, air-hockey, and a jukebox. It featured Friday and Saturday night Airmen's Club dances, where you could drink as much as you wanted of something called 3.5 Beer and act crazy. The poolroom had five pool tables and this cavernous ballroom had tables and chairs, a large dance floor, and a stage area for live bands. This was the place where you could meet up with your Airmen friends yell and scream and get drunk on a Saturday night or listen to music from the jukebox or someone spinning records. The sound system was loud and made to dance and party with. It was a cool place to be if you liked to be with over a thousand people from everywhere America on a Saturday night.

But, the really and truly, most important thing going on ever in the whole universe, and Sheppard's Air Force Base, was the Women's Air Force (WAF's). They were there in the Airmen's Club in all their most beautiful glory. All over the place, they were there, girls and women, and plenty of home girls from all over the good ol USA and that's where I first saw her, or rather she saw me. She walked over to where I was sitting and drinking with my new Air Force friends, she walked up behind me, tapped me on my back where I was sitting, and looked around at me and said, *you wanna come with me?* I looked at her and just got up and as this new song called "The "Hawaii Five O" Theme", started playing, we walked out of the Airmen's Club to the beat of that song, and I met the girl who would save my life in three years.

7

She was a big-boned, tall, eighteen-year-old girl, with a thick neck and big tits. I liked her immediately, and didn't know what to do. Most of the girls I had knew were either skanks or home girls. A skank was a white girl from South Boston, Malden, Medford, Charlestown, you know, one of the white neighborhoods girls from Boston, who drank until she was sloppy drunk, throw up, and would then suck your dick, or demand to get laid. A home girl was a black girl from Roxbury, and Dorchester, the black neighborhoods in Boston, who got high on weed and drank a little alcohol, but mostly liked to dance and twirl around, make believe she was Diana Ross, get high enough to suck your dick and ask if you wanted to fuck.

When I was 14, and was hanging out with some cool guys from the projects, Phillip Bowser, Alfred Springer, Bobby Haney, Robert Miles and Daryl

Sanders, we used to go to this Episcopalian Church dance socials on Saturday night and a lot of outside the project girls would be there, nice girls from nice homes, mostly light-skinned girls, and a couple of them liked me. One lived in Dorchester and actually came home with me to my project apartment while my mother wasn't home one day, and we had some fun, fooling around and doing some little kid fucking on the couch, the other girl's father was a big time real estate guy, and she liked me a lot, we went out a few times on real dates to a movie.

One night I brought her home and walked her to her big house up the hill, after we kissed outside and all, and were saying sweet nothings to each other, her father came out and told her in an angry voice to go in the house, after she went in, he looked at me and pulled out a gun. He said, *if you ever came back around here again or try to see my daughter again, I will kill you.* He pointed the gun at my head, and went back inside the house. I figured it must have been my process and the doo rag that he didn't like, or the smell of the ghetto and projects on me must have been too much for him to take. But, I got it. I saw the girl a few time afterwards and she always tried to talk to me, and even though she was fly and fine, I didn't think that I wanted my ass shot off for some pussy that probably wasn't that good anyway.

Well this girl was different. She wasn't a home girl or skank and neither was she an up the hill girl. She was 5'9", with a smile and twinkle in her eyes that said, I'm down for some extreme adventure, she kissed me on my lips and said, *I've been watching you and I like you.*

She was wild, this girl, like nothing I'd ever seen before and for the next almost two months, we would be at the motel on Saturday, after the Club let out, after we would dance all wild and shit and drink everything in sight, smoke our Kool cigarettes, and yell and scream and dance to the sounds of some raggedy ass R&B band playing the hits from 1969, and then we'd fall out of the Club at two in the morning running through Sheppard's Air Force Base, with all the other eighteen and nineteen-year-old gonna, wanna, gonna be warriors, for good ol Uncle Sam, just getting paid and all, the United States Air Force Governments best; all fed, drunk and paid, heading for the nearest and quickest motels.

We had our favorite, they knew us and all, and we'd head there with some confiscated alcohol and our Kool Cigarettes, open the door fall on the bed and kiss long and hard, hard and long, long and hard, and roll around, clothes falling off, and liqueur bottle up and cigarettes burning and finger fuck and pump, finger fuck and pump, finger fuck and pump, me finger fuckin her and her pumpin me.

She said she wasn't ready to have no baby and that no rubber was gonna contain that big ol thing, so we'd have to settle for some huggin, kissin, playin and finger fuckin and pumpin all night. Finger Fuckin and pumpin, we comin, we comin. I remember one night, all night, finger fuckin and pumpin to Red River with John Wayne and Montgomery Cliff. I'll never forget when we came all over John Wayne and Grandpa McCoy as they stood arguing with one another, yelling right along with them, and then I'd hear it: her little small town girl laugh, her looking right at me the second after we would come, right in my face looking right at me, right in my fuckin face and her eyes would twinkle and she would throw her head back, all out of breath and laugh like she was dying for some more. Which of course she was! And I almost forgot why I was there at Sheppard in the first place.

For my birthday October 11, 1969, I turned nineteen-years-old, and while we were kissing, finger fucking and pumping, she said that she wanted to give me a birthday present and suck my dick, which was cool with me, until she said that if she did that she wanted me to do it to her. Now, man, I had never eaten no white pussy before in my life and wasn't about to begin now, birthday or no birthday. So we decided on this, she would suck my dick, like she was doing a 69, while I was finger fucking her, looking at her pussy from behind; she loved that shit and we both came together, it was a great birthday and a great night.

Man, I'm telling you, the food was good, the money was good, and the pussy smelled good, what more did a home boy from the ghetto need. Well home boy needed to graduate from Jet Mechanic School and wasn't doing such a good job at doing that. Luckily with all that finger fuckin and pumpin going on with my small town pussy, I had a skank, from Rhode Island and a couple of home girls, one from Chicago and one from Milwaukee, to keep my dick wet.

8

Unluckily, with all that pussy going on in the Motels, it wasn't helping me in the classroom. Four months outside the ghetto and six months outside of High School and it's the same old shit again, I'm fuckin up and need a

Mr. Hector, some Nuns or Staff Sergeant Jenson again. So I try to get some help. In my class there's this homie from Durham, North Carolina, this guy is like country as a motherfucker, but knows his shit better than anyone in the entire class. It's like he's teaching the teacher shit.

I can still see the little motherfucker now, walking around with his tools and shit, been working on cars and engines and machines his whole life, hunched over, peering at and seeing everything clear as a bell, crystal clear. He gets these airilons and flaps and hydraulic oil systems, he gets the main and rear instrument panels, he gets the radar altimeter, the attack indicators, the Missile and Weapons release control panel, the attack indexer and SHOOT light, the ground speed indicator. He gets the right sub panel warning lights, he gets the whole damn aircraft, what it is, what it's for and what it's used for…everything.

I just know that's she's beautiful and I want to ride in her, but slowly and surely that little motherfucker, when I can understand him, is teaching me better than the instructor, what it all means and how this beautiful beast is put together, frame by frame; and how all the components work together to make the F4D Phantom Jet work. And I begin to get it, but it's too late and when the final test comes when we have to walk around the plane and do all the things that a crew chief does and know all the things that a crew chief should know. I ace it, but when it came time to sit in the classroom and write the answers to the millions of questions, I flunk it by eight percent down, because I can see it and do it, but I can't explain what I'm doing, and within two days I learn that I won't be graduating from Sheppard with my class.

I am being sent back, but I fight it, I won't accept it and I state to my instructor that the eight percent of questions that I missed were because I was fucked up and drunk when he was teaching those classes. He laughed and thought that was the funniest shit he'd ever heard, but it was true and he tested me on everything else but that part again and a I passed. So what he did was this, he sent me back but to learn only the parts that I missed on the first test, which meant that instead of being sent back for the whole three months again, I only had to do another month and could make it home on leave for Christmas, instead of Thanksgiving like my class was going to do.

The thing was everybody was leaving, everybody I knew was going home and the barracks was clearing out. I said goodbye to all my homies in the barracks and we all swore to stay in touch. We had all drunk together, rode together and had many adventures together at the Airmen's Club and beyond. One time me and the some of the homies had got a car and rode together on some drunken road trip to Oklahoma City to visit one of the homies, it was Davis, to visit Davis's uncle at Tinker Air Force Base, in Norman, Oklahoma.

It was a wild trip. Davis's uncle was a Staff Sergeant in the United States Air Force and was crisp and shining, had the wide hat and everything. We went to his place and drank and hit all the Black Clubs in Oklahoma City and drank, danced and partied with the home girls all night, we ended up crashing at Davis's uncle's place and drove back the next day.

I loved them guys, but they were all going home and I was like down, you know sad and shit, it was like I had failed, but nobody was saying anything, like it was okay. It was Sweet Daddy Rose', and he was cool so it must be okay to be held back, because if Sweet Daddy Rose' is being held back, then fuck it, it must be alright, Sweet Daddy Rose' can get himself out of anything, he's going to be fine. So, I tried hard to be brave and cool for my homies, let them know it was going to be okay and that I was going to make it, no problem. Hugged them all, said Happy Thanksgiving, exchanged numbers and said that we would write each other. They had their assignments, some were on their way directly to Vietnam and some were on their way to other Bases in Asia and the United States, I wanted to go to Vietnam and was a little envious of those who were going.

And finally it was just me and my roommates. When I was younger, I had learned to deal with ghetto violence like this. Just walk up to a motherfucker and punch him in his face preferably his nose or eye, no talking about it, you only talked if the motherfucker was bigger and older and you had to talk your way out of some shit.

9

It was the same way that I dwelt with White boys who hated Black people, although with them, and some white people in general, I also learned that they needed to be educated. Back in the early eighties when I moved to New York City, I was one of the first three hundred people to live in Battery Park City, the most exclusive and best place to live in the Manhattan, outside of Upper Fifth Avenue in the 60's going up. The cabs had finally learned that there were people living on the Hudson River in BPC, off the

West Side Highway across the street from the old World Trade Center and so the yellow cabs began to line up.

Sometimes, instead of taking a limousine or taking the A-train Uptown, I would want to take a cab and I began to notice that these just arrived motherfuckers from India or Pakistan or somewhere where you had to wear a rag on your head, would pass me by to get to a white person. So, what I did was, when they did that, was to go over and as the white people were settling themselves in the cab, I would open the door and take the man by his elbow first and say gently, *I know that you saw that I was waiting here first* and escort him or him and his bitch out of the cab and get in. I knew that I was educating them and sure enough often when the cabs came around and one made the mistake of passing me by and going for the white persons, they would back off and point the driver to me, as of course I would be walking over to get in the cab.

I was well known because between 1983 and 1997, there were never more than twenty or so Black people who lived at Battery Park City. So, I always considered that I was educating white people. I also began educating the cab drivers, who had been uneducated by some white motherfuckin cab driver or some asshole from the ghetto who had tried to rob them, in either case they needed to be re-educated as to who to pick up and who not to pick up.

I had to educate a lot of white people in my thirties and forties when I was pretty rich, and something to be reckoned with, and not some low life motherfuckin ghetto motherfucker, which in a sense I always was, except I had the money, fame and game not to look like it.

One of the more memorable times was even as late as 2006, when I was at The Venetian Hotel in Las Vegas. I was eating dinner by myself in one of the more exclusive and expensive restaurants in the hotel, sitting at an upper tier table and I heard and saw a white guy at an all-white people table say, loud enough for me to hear him, "look at the nigger sitting up there, thinking he's something", well the next thing I knew was that I had floated down to his table, and was standing beside him, I think it happened so fast that most people at the table including him didn't even know I was there, I was like a ghost.

I reached down with my left hand and pulled him by his collar, my left hand between his tie and shirt collar and his neck, and pulled him close and up towards me, and with my right hand I smashed him real fast, six times, Boom, Boom, Boom, Boom, Boom, Boom, in his nose with my right fist breaking his nose and sending blood all over the place. I then let him loose to fall on the floor and upturned the table and food all over the nice white men and women sitting at it. It all took five seconds. I then looked at each one, to make sure they understood, and walked out of the restaurant, out of the hotel to the valet service, gave my receipt for my car, my car came, and I drove over to the Luxor where I was staying.

I always loved the Luxor Hotel because it was cheap, but the rooms were extra, extra huge. I never liked paying a lot for shit I didn't have to. But, in any case I loved educating white folks and as you may know by now, I never really subscribed to that Martin Luther King, Jr. bullshit of Non-Violence, as you may remember in my list of heroes from my teen years in the sixties as great a man as ML King, Jr. was, he wasn't in my top ten.

You see in educating white people I never believed in all that yelling and screaming and talking and shit, because all they will do is shoot you and say to the police, *this crazy nigger comes to our table and starts yelling and screaming about some crazy shit and we had to kill him, he might have had a gun*, case closed, crazy nigger dead. No, I believed as ol dad would say, *If you gonna shoot a motherfucker shoot him, if you gonna hit a motherfucker hit him, talk about what!*

But, no, this was November 1969 and I hadn't got as finessed as I would later be, although in less than two months in Asia I would find myself having to educate a White Airman in a club for Blacks only. You see, the White guys had been telling the Asian ladies not to deal with the Black soldiers since World War Two and the Korean War had ended. White boys told the Asian bitches that we had tails and live like monkeys in the trees, you know racist shit like that.

I always found that the White boys were always afraid of our dicks and would do everything they could to put fear and loathing about us and our dicks in their White women. They thought that their White women would be scared to death of us. Then I saw that they were doing and saying the same thing to the Asian women. The only thing was that their White women didn't seem to be so afraid of our dicks as the White men were. In fact, though, the White girls wanted to put our dicks in their pussies and mouths a lot just so they could see what it was all about, as did the Asian girls, which was cool with me.

So what was happening all throughout Asia and Southeast Asia was that the clubs were separated between the white and black enlisted men in the cities where the bases were situated, and so were the girls. Asian girls that went for country music, Elvis Presley, and White boys were called T-Shirt Girls and Asian girls who liked soul music, Ebony Magazine and Black boys were called Coco Butter Girls, so in our clubs all the girls only went with Coco Butter Airmen. My nickname with the all the girls was Chop Stickey, because I was so skinny.

Anyway, one night, a White boy came into our club in Japan and walked up to the bar where I was standing there drinking and shit, and said, *What are ya'll boys doing*. Well, this was the sixties and if you were White, you didn't call Black men, boys, and expect it to be okay. Probably, this country White boy didn't know that, the news hadn't reached him yet, or probably he did and had been calling Black men, boys, for so long that it came natural to him. In any case, before he could say another word I hit him with a right hand down on the left side of his face and cracked it, broke his face, he tried to fight back, but it was essentially over at that point, but I loved a good fight, and I carried him all over the club, beating the shit out of him every step of the way, there was blood everywhere, his blood was all over me.

Finally, the brothers pulled me away from him, white boy was on the ground crying and shit, they took his wallet and found out his name and who he was, the MPs came and I was thrown in jail, again, and the First Sergeant, had to come down to the jail and get me, again. He was upset, but that didn't last for long because I was a maverick Crew Chief, top of the Flight Line Dude. I was fast, smart and fearless, the kind of shit the military likes in its warriors, and besides my orders were being cut for Vietnam via Korea, so, I was gone anyway.

The things that always bothered me about that particular fight was that, I might have scarred that Airman for life. Last time I saw him he had a big crack on the left side of his face, with blood coming out of it, and I realized I had done a cruel thing. The brothers told me who he was and where he Barracked, and so I sent word to him in his Barracks that I wanted him to pay for my cleaner's bill, my clothes had his blood all over them and I wanted to him to pay for my cleaner's bill. All the brothers thought that was some crazy, funny shit, but, I was dead serious, this was some projects shit, and I wanted that motherfucker to pay for bleeding all over my clothes.

I sent word that if he didn't pay, I was going to come up there and fuck him up again. White boy sent twenty dollars down for my cleaner's bill by one of the brothers in his Barracks. Some of the brothers didn't like that I had done that shit, and started to ostracize me.

To this day I feel bad about that shit, but I bet he never called a Black man boy again, because he had now been educated. As I said, I didn't have then, the sort of finesse I would later learn to cultivate in life. I mean at that time in Asia, I was like less than a year and two seconds out of the ghetto, and I was still learning how to live, be and act like a human being. It would take a while, but I would get there one day.

And so, I never had any real trouble like that with my racist roommate, once I had straightened him out. In fact, he just stayed out of my way, never said one word to me and so I never got the chance to educate him. But, Waco, well, he at some point, started talking to me, which was good, because he was built like one of those bulls in the rodeo and looked like one of those guys who ride them. He was bowlegged and his arms and fists hung down to his knees, he would have been a little hard to educate if I had thought it necessary.

The day he left for home on leave after graduating, we actually hugged and shook hands, said that we would write each other. He said that he had learned a lot through our talks and friendship; that I was the first Black friend that he had ever had and he would never forget me. I don't remember a lot that we talked about during our time at Sheppard, but I do remember that day. I can still see him walking down the hallway, his duffle bag over his shoulder, a blonde guy, looked like good old boy America, stopped at the exit door, turned around, looked at me and saluted, I saluted back. We stared at each other for five seconds as Peter, Paul and Mary sang "Leaving On a Jet Plane". He turned, opened the door and I never saw what could have been a good friend again.

10

The Barracks was cleared out and I was the only one left, and then she came. She stood outside. She had her WAF's uniform on. I had my fatigues on when I came outside. It was cold, one day before Thanksgiving, and she was leaving for small town, California. She was a California girl, a small town girl, a swimmer, an athlete in High School. She said she loved me and as we kissed I called her Lizbeth, and she said she loved me. I told her I loved her too, we said that we would see each other again and she looked up at me with that Lizbeth twinkle in her eyes and laughed her throaty laugh out loud, like she had just come.

She said she had to go, her plane was leaving at 5:00pm. I held her close and kissed her again, lightly and said goodbye and watched my future walk off. She turned once and waved wildly with all of her crazy self and got on the base bus.

The skank I never saw again, one of the home girls I would see again when I was driving through Chicago on my way from Los Angeles to Boston in the summer of 1976. She had her own pad and we would spend a whole night together fucking. It was good, like it had been back at Sheppard, she told me that she loved me that night and had missed me, and asked me to come back to Chicago and live with her, I said yeah that sounded good, but I left the next morning, got on the road to Boston and never saw her again. Lizbeth, her name was Elizabeth the Great, I would see again, briefly, in a desolate fucked up place 8,557 miles away, and then in three years she would save my life, miscarriage my baby and love me for the next two and a half decades.

I would jump into a class that had less than a month to go, test well, pass, take pictures with the F-4D Phantom Jet with guys I hardly knew, become a fully accredited, certified 'Crew Chief' on F-4D Phantom Jets, and most important get my permanent duty assignment; the 375th Tactical Fighter Squadron-475th Tactical Fighter Wing, Misawa, Air Force Base, Misawa, Japan, and get my 15- day leave.

I was overjoyed, I was happy, I had made it all the way and just like that, five months after I had left my mother, five months after I had left the ghetto, Roxbury and Dorchester, five months after I had left my father and all that shit, five months after leaving the ghetto, six months after High School, I was somebody, Crew Chief, Airman First Class Rose. Five months after leaving the ghetto, I was boarding a plane for my third airplane ride and I said to myself, man, that Lackland and Sheppard shit was a trip! And then I was back home in the ghetto.

THE AUTOBIOGRAPHY OF AN
AMERICAN GHETTO BOY

VOLUME FIVE

THE EARLY AND LATER TEENAGE YEARS

WALPOLE STATE PRISON

MAY–DECEMBER, 1966

1

My father was a true gangster. He loved Frank Sinatra, Dean Martin, Barbara Streisand, Lou Rawls and whenever referring to Johnny Mathis, he was always, *That little fuckin faggot, Johnny Mathis.* He stayed strapped and loose with a 45 and a snub-nosed 32.

By the time I met and got to know my father, he was 37-years-old in 1966, and I was a fifteen-year-old boy. In the eight months I was with him, I learned everything I would need to and want to know about him, and then that was it. In December 1966, two weeks before Christmas, when I had just turned sixteen-years-old, I came down the stairs in the house at the top of Columbia Road near Blue Hill Ave., across the street from Franklin Park in Dorchester, MA, that my father had rented for us two months after I came to stay with him in April of '66 It was the first house I had ever lived in except for my grandmother's house, after I had been beat to death and almost died while protecting the young girls from the Whittier Street Housing Projects gangs who were raping them, and Lou my step-mother was smoking and reading the Record American newspaper I had grown up selling in the projects, and she pushed the newspaper towards me. Ol' dad was on the front page with a paper bag over his head. I knew it was him because I recognized his shirt, and his hands were cuffed behind his back with the shiny things I knew were handcuffs. The newspaper said that my father had broken into the State District Attorney's office to steal some files for the Mafia and had been arrested.

It was two weeks before Christmas, he would do a two to four-year stretch in Walpole State Prison and I would never get to spend a Christmas day with him and everything I got to know about him, that anyone would want to know about him, I knew, during the eight months I lived with him when I was fifteen.

2

BRING THAT ASS OVER TO THE CAR

In those eight months we spent together he saved my life, and taught me everything a poor ghetto project boy should know about the serious con, about the serious pimping, the serious sex with the serious women, the real serious police, he said that unless you were willing and able to shoot and kill a police officer, always show respect and your hands and never say nothing to them, just ask for your attorney. He showed me the difference between the serious crime and doing stupid shit, how to seriously fight, beat and shoot a nigger down, the serious drugs, the serious drinking, I would meet the serious Mafia guys and he told me to never, ever work for the white man, unless you absolutely had to and they were paying you some real serious money. I would remember that advice, and make it work for me my whole life.

One of the more really memorable and great things ol Dad taught me was how to roll the right side window down an holler at a fine thing while driving up and down Blue Hill Avenue in the ghetto. See, he would say, *you roll the window down and roll up on her and say", "hey baby, you lookin good, come on over here and let me talk to you.* The sweet thing knows she's lookin good, smiles and brings that ass on over to the car, of course you have to be lookin good too, and I always was, so she would either jump in the car right then and there and I would get some pussy on the run or at the very least I would get a phone number for later. I can't even begin to tell you how much pussy I got over the years while doing that, and it worked in every ghetto throughout America. You could find girls with real good pussy, money, great jobs, nice apartments, shit, everything a poor ghetto boy could want while coming up in the world. Ol Dad was always looking out for me with shit like that, and saving my life.

He graduated me with my street master's degree from the projects and how to beat the world at its own game. He drove me to Dorchester High from time to time, knew all my friends, we drank together, and collected money from the girls. It was beautiful! After he went back to jail, I returned to the serious streets, and wouldn't see my father until August 1968, and then ol dad would be up to his old tricks and on November 11th, 1968, all hell would break loose and my family would be front page international news, again.

THE AUTOBIOGRAPHY OF AN AMERICAN GHETTO BOY

VOLUME SIX

MURDER - THE HITMAN

AN EXCERPT REPRINTED WITH PERMISSION

"HITMAN THE UNTOLD STORY OF JOHNNY MARTORANO: WHITEY BULGER'S ENFORCER AND THE MOST FEARED GANGSTER IN THE UNDERWORLD" BY HOWIE CARR

The true story of my father, his Mafia friends and the mass murders at The New England Grass Roots Organization (N.E.G.R.O.) November 13, 1968.

.

"CHAPTER 5 - PAGE 136"
BWANA JOHNNY

Lawyer: When you met Hubert Smith and killed him, you got into a car with him, is that right?

Martorano: Yes, I did.

Lawyer: There were two teenagers with him, isn't that right?

Martorano: When I met him in Roxbury, there was three people in the car, and I took it to be three guys. It was the middle of a snowstorm at two in the morning.

Lawyer: How far away were you from Mr. Smith when you shot him?

Martorano: A foot.

Lawyer: And people in the car were right next to him, isn't that right?

Martorano: Was the middle of winter. They were dressed in winter clothes, and I just got in the car and started shooting…He was supposed to be alone. I saw three, what I took, what I believed was three men, and I said to myself I better shoot fast because they may have the same thing on their mind for me as I have for them.

Martorano: I just shot three times. After the first flash, it was just shadows.

When Steve Flemmi got excited, he would stutter. His speech would dissolve into sentence fragments, as if he were too angry to put together a coherent thought. On the morning of January 6, 1968, early in the day for Steve to be up, he was stuttering and spitting out his words.

He was talking on the phone to Johnny Martorano, and he was in a rage.

"Basin Street...down there looking for you...got a beating...that big nigger Smith...motherfucking nigger...your fuckin' place, Johnny ...they held me down...what the fuck..."

At first Johnny couldn't believe such a thing could happen at Basin Street. All through the '60s, the club kept changing hands, going back and forth between the Martoranos and the Lamattinas. In early 1968, it was the Lamattinas' club. But as far as everybody in the city was concerned, Basin Street would always be Johnny Martorano's place. He still hung there, it was where you went first, if you were looking for him. And Johnny still owed Stevie, at least that's the way Johnny figured it, and that was how Stevie saw it, too. Stevie had tipped Johnny that Palladino and Jackson were going to testify against his brother Jimmy. Of course it wasn't true, but Johnny Martorano wouldn't know that for another thirty years.

"Motherfucker held me from behind, Johnny...give me a beating...slapped on the head...Johnny, your place?"

Johnny told Stevie he would take care of it. All day, he could think of nothing else. He didn't really know this Smitty, everybody at Basin Street called him. Lived in Dorchester, about forty-seven years old. Johnny would have to figure out what happened, and there was only one way to do that. He would seek out Smitty and ask him directly. That night, a Friday, Johnny met up with another of his buddies, Steve Brucias, Steve the Greek. The Greek lived on Dudley Street with his two teenaged kids, whom he was raising alone. He owned a piece of a bar out in Hyde Park. Johnny filled him in on what had happened the previous night.

The next day, a detective from the Boston Police Department vice squad would file a report about the scene at Basin Street South a few hours before the murders: "I see Smitty in Basin Street every night. I get there between 1:15 and 1:30am. He was drinking Friday night, which is very unusual. He is usually on the door, but Friday night two young colored kids were on the door, dressed in sport jackets like the band."

The detective saw Johnny Martorano in a 1967 or 1968 black Pontiac two-door H.T hardtop.

Even though snow was forecast for after midnight, Basin Street was hopping. When Johnny arrived, he spotted Smitty sitting by himself at the bar, sipping a drink. Johnny told Bracius he needed to talk to Smitty alone, so Bracias went down to the other end of the bar while Johnny parked himself on the stool next to Smitty and bought him a drink, then another, and another.

I said to him, 'I heard Stevie was in here last night and he got a beating.' And he says, 'Yeah, yeah'. I say, 'What happened?' And he says to him, "This is a friend of mine, Stevie, he comes down here and you give him a beating?"

What Johnny didn't know, what Stevie hadn't told him, was that the reason it wasn't such a big deal to Smith was because he'd just been following orders, from Rocco Lamattina and John Cincotti, the two Mafia soldiers who at the moment ran Basin Street. When he pinned Stevie's arms back, Smitty had just been doing what he was told to do.

What I find out later is, Stevie's been shylocking to Rocco's son. Now, Rocco is a loan shark himself. Stevie shouldn't be doing this. And now he's down in Rocco's own place, which is what Basin Street was at that point, looking for Rocco's kid, over $300 bucks. I didn't know this, but it was actually Stevie who was out of line, not Smith. Smith was a big guy, so he grabbed Stevie's arms while Rocco and Cincotti worked him over. And of course Stevie is humiliated, but he can't do nothing about the two Mafia guys, so he blames it all on the black guy. That's when he calls me.

An FBI informant later recounted the incident in vague terms, perhaps not realizing the connection to the three murders:

Informant stated that recently Stevie Flemmi had been beaten up over $300. Flemmi had tried to collect and met some fast talk. Flemmi later went back to a bar where he was beaten up by a Negro bartender…Informant stated that Stevie Flemmi was in pretty bad shape; however, stated that he would take care of the matter himself…by calling Johnny Martorano again.

At Basin Street that cold Friday night in January, Johnny Martorano continued pumping Smith for information, asking him the same questions over and over again. Smith either didn't think it was that big a deal, or he believed that he shouldn't be talking about the Lamattinas' family business. He was observing the underworld code, and it was about to cost him his life.

"He kept giving me all the wrong answers," Johnny Martorano said. "He didn't give me any respect. All he has to do was say, 'I didn't know he was your friend. I'm sorry.' That's all he needed to say. It would have been a whole different ballgame."

Finally, Johnny drifted away, back to the other end of the bar, where the Greek had been watching them silently, drinking steadily. Over the din of the band and the drunken conversation, Johnny recounted to the Greek what Smitty had told him.

The Greek was drunk, so his instant recommendation was to kill Smith. Johnny agreed. Now he had to figure out a way to get Smith alone so that he could kill him. A new after-hours game had just started in Roxbury, so Johnny went back to Smith and asked him if he was going over there after last call.

Smith nodded, sure. Johnny said he'd never been there, wasn't sure exactly where it was. "Why don't I meet you somewhere," he said to Smith, "and then we can go over there together." Smith agreed, so Johnny told him he'd catch up with him on Normandy Street, but first he had to pick up some money for the game.

Smith was okay with that, so Johnny left. But he wasn't going to pick up some money; he was going out to get a gun.

Johnny and Brucias drove to the Greek's place on Dudley Street. The Greek ran upstairs and returned with an untraceable, 38-caliber snub nose, five or six shots. Then they drove to Normandy Street, where they saw Smith's 1967 Mercury station wagon. By now it snowing heavily; there were already several inches on the ground. It was a little after 3 a.m. in the morning of January 7, 1968.

Smith had the Mercury idling, and Johnny could see the exhaust. At the corner, he told the Greek to circle the block and come back and pick him up. Johnny got out and trudged through the snow toward the Mercury. He immediately noticed that there were three people inside, and he thought to himself, he'd better shoot fast. He had his hand on the gun as he got into the car. The first one he shot was Smith, in the driver's seat. The other two Johnny could barely see because he'd been practically blinded by the flash of the first shot. He later told cops all of the shooting had taken no more than three seconds. He had shot all of them behind the ear.

Lawyer: It's not your testimony that if you saw it was a woman, you would have stopped it, is it?

Martorano: If I knew it was a woman, I wouldn't have done it. But I couldn't stop and leave people behind.

Lawyer: Because is it your testimony that you don't kill woman?

Martorano: Positively not.

The Mercury was full of smoke from the gunshots. There was no sound in the car, no moans. They were all dead. Johnny reached into the front seat, turned off the ignition, grabbed the keys, but left the headlights on. Then he got out of the car and started walking slowly down Normandy Street, toward Blue Hill Avenue, expecting Steve Brucias to pull up any moment. But the Greek never returned.

It was 3:30 in the morning. Johnny's prospects looked bleak. He was white guy in Roxbury, in a snowstorm, covered with blood. He had to get away from the scene, but first he had to get rid of the gun. There was an alley just before Blue Hill Avenue, so he dumped the gun and the shells under a pile of trash and snow. He threw the car keys as far as he could, into the snow, then walked out to the Blue Hill Avenue and got lucky. He hailed down a cab. He told the cabbie, stop at the first pay phone you see, and then wait. Johnny called Stevie at Marion Husey's house and told him he was coming over, and that it was important.

Then he had to get directions to Marion's place because he'd never been there. It was Dorchester. When Johnny finally got there, he paid the cabbie and sent him away. He explained to Stevie what had happened, and Stevie gave him one of his coats, which was a little small on Martorano. Johnny handed his own bloody coat to Stevie, and he never saw it again. Than Johnny told Stevie, let's go back and find the Greek; he's still out there somewhere looking for me.

They drove back to Roxbury, not getting to close to Normandy Street, but they couldn't find the Greek anywhere. As they started making the rounds of the after-hours joints, they could hear sirens in the distance, but that was nothing out of the ordinary in Roxbury. Finally, they spotted the Greek's car outside one of the clubs, so Johnny walked in and saw Brucias sitting there playing cards.

Johnny asked him, what happened to you?

"I got stuck around the corner," the Greek said. "We'll do it tomorrow."

Johnny shook his head. There is no tomorrow, he told Steve the Greek. It's over. Now get outta here and go home.

The three bodies were taken to the Southern Mortuary, where they were identified. The victim in the back seat was Douglas Barrett, age seventeen.

(Note from Tony Rose – *I knew Douglas Barrett real well when I was a young teenager. He lived in the Lenox Street Projects and was real cool. I knew when he was killed, but I never knew until I read this, why he was killed.*)

Nobody at that time knew why, just that he had been shot in a car. Life is a bitch! In his pockets, police found one quarter and a package of Tip-Top cigarette papers. It has never been established what he was doing in the station wagon with Smith.

In the front seat was the body of a teenaged girl who would have turned twenty on February 4, 1968, Elizabeth Frances Dixon, better known as Liz. She was unemployed, a graduate of St. Joseph's, a parochial girls' high school in Roxbury. She had taken up in recent weeks with Smith, despite the age difference. The papers would describe her as a go-go dancer.

"She thought Smith was real nice," a neighbor told police. "Sometimes I ask her where she is going and she would say Basin Street and I would say, 'Do you think that is a nice place to go to? And she said, 'Mother said I will be alright."

Another neighbor told the cops; "She talked about Smitty as if he was a friend. She smoked as much as I do. I think her brand was Kool."

According to the homicide report, Dixon's head was resting against the driver's right knee. There was a cigarette case in her hand. This case fell to the floor of the car when her body was removed."

In addition to his topcoat, Smith was wearing a brown tie and a white shirt when he died. The inventory of his personal effects turned up a black onyx ring on his right finger, two wallets that contained a total of $64 cash, and a slip of paper that said, "Smitty, Tina was in here to see you."

The police also recorded that he was wearing a "Timex watch, still running, indicating correct time."

After leaving the Greek, Steve Flemmi drove Johnny to his girl-friend Barbara's place in Quincy. On the way, neither one of them said much. It was almost dawn. Johnny slept fitfully for a couple of hours, then borrowed Barbara's car to drive back to Boston to have breakfast in a diner on Mass Ave. With Stevie and Frankie Salemme.

By this time, I'd heard on the radio that there was a woman in the car. I was very upset with myself. Then, at the diner, Steve and Frankie asked me, do you want us to kill the Greek for you? I said no. If they clipped him, his two kids, I don't know what would have happened to them. Their mother wasn't around. I told them, just tell him to go to the Cape, go away, I never want to see him again.

The police investigation reached a dead end very quickly. It wasn't until later that night that Johnny learned what had happened at Basin Street the night before he killed three people in the snow on Normandy Street. He never discussed the murders again with Stevie, and certainly not with the two guys from IN Town who had worked over Stevie as the late Hubert Smith pinned Flemmi's arms behind him.

"What could they say? If they indicated to me that they know what happened, then they'll have a problem. What are they gonna say anyway? They're just glad that they weren't there that night, or the same thing might have happened to them.

The newspapers' front pages were full of Joe Barboza stories, each more fantastic than the last. He was hold up on Thatcher's Island in Rockport, and the feds were guarding him, the Sunday Globe reported, "against a possible intrusion by torpedoes, machine guns or aerial bombs."

The Record American reported that a Chicago hitman had gotten himself arrested for public drunkenness, then used his court appearance to scout out the security measures in the Pemberton Square courthouse. His verdict on the odds of successfully killing Barboza there: Mission Impossible.

After the district attorney received death threats, the Boston police assigned their best man to the job of guarding his office, a Medal of Honor recipient from World War II. Barboza was whisked about the Boston area in helicopters and police motorcades. Newspaper readers learned the name of his dog (Zero), as well as his preference in cigarettes (English Ovals, a pack and a half a day). When he was scheduled to appear before a Suffolk

County grand jury, police dogs were reportedly released the night before to roam the darkened corridors of the sixth floor, where the grand jury met, to guard against any possible assassins from La Costra Nostra.

Barboza's first court appearance came in January 1968, when he testified against Jerry Angiulo and the three hoodlums he'd allegedly convinced to murder Rocco DiDeglio, an ex-boxer with whom the other three had been sticking up Mafia-protected card games.

On January 18, 1968, Jerry and his co-defendants were all acquitted. Outside, on the courthouse steps, the Mafia underboss of Boston talked to the press saying, "I was in the Navy during World War II. Now I know what I was fighting for. I want to go home to my poor old mother."

Twelve days later, as Barboza's lawyer, John Fitzgerald was climbing into Barboza's gold Oldsmobile in Everett, he was almost killed by a bomb that had been planted under the hood by Stevie Flemmi and Frankie Salemme.

This time they had gone too far. They could kill one another as much as they pleased, but Fitzgerald had a reputation, however undeserved, as a straight arrow. They'd tried to shoot him two nights earlier, driving around his neighborhood, looking for the James Bond car. They had ended up killing the wrong guy, a civilian who had the misfortune to be driving a similar Olds.

The day his car was bombed, Fitzgerald had left his law office late in the afternoon. He was carrying two guns. Suspecting that his office phone had been tapped by the Mafia. Fitzgerald walked across the street to a drugstore and used the pay phone to make a few calls. His last on was to H. Paul Rico of the FBI. It was a rainy day and Fitzgerald kept the door open and his left leg outside the Olds while he turned the ignition and put his foot to the accelerator. When he did, two sticks of Dynamite exploded.

"The windshield began breaking into a thousand pieces," he wrote later, "as if someone had hit it with a sledgehammer. Fragments were coming at me and there was a grinding effect. It felt like my teeth were tearing my jaw apart."

Windows in houses across the street were blown out. A cop on traffic detail a block away ran to Fitzgerald who was lying on his back in a widening pool of blood. The cop bent over to listen to what might have been the lawyer's last words.

"Call Rico of the FBI," he rasped, before losing consciousness.

Rico and his partner Dennis Condon immediately canceled their plans for the evening, to interview a young prospect for the Bureau, a high-school teacher from South Boston named John J. Connolly. Connolly's father was a longtime friend of U.S. House Speaker John McCormack, who was close to J. Edgar Hoover. Rico and Condon Knew they would have plenty of other chances to get to know young Connolly in the years ahead.

They drove instead to Whidden Hospital, where surgeons operated on Fitzgerald for five hours. He lost his right leg just above the knee. Politicians visited him in the hospital. As Barboza sardonically noted in his autobiography, "They had pretty much ignored the gang war all those years with the excuse it was just punks killing punks and good riddance, but now that a lawyer had been maimed and crippled they rose up in wrath and tried to outdo each other in pious indignation."

It didn't take Johnny long to figure out who had done it, or why.

It was a favor Stevie and Frankie did for the Mafia. But there was more to it than that, at least for Stevie. Fitzgerald was Barboza's Lawyer, so he may have known how much of a role Stevie played in inventing Barboza's lies about the Deegan hit, putting Mafia guys in the car to protect his brother Jimmy. So Stevie had a reason for wanting to get rid of Fitzgerald other than impressing Larry, which was all Frankie cared about at the time. See, once Stevie hit Fitzgerald, how could anyone ever suspect him of being in on the deal to flip Barboza, if he blew up the guy's lawyer.

Barboza's next trial was in federal court in Providence. Patriarca and a couple of his henchmen were charged with conspiracy in the murder of two brothers who'd been running an unauthorized card game on Federal Hill. He Man had been urged to flee to Haiti until a deal could be worked out, but Angiulo's acquittal had emboldened him. He would stay in Rhode Island and fight the charges. At one pretrial hearing in Providence, as Barboza left the courtroom, Patriarca looked him in the eye and silently mouthed two words: "You rat."

Barboza lunged for him, screaming the usual: "You fuck your dead mother in the mouth!" The marshals got to Barboza before he reached Patriarca, but nothing could save Patriarca from the Rhode Island jury. He was convicted, sentenced to five years, and shipped off to Atlanta.

That left the Deegan murder trial. It started in Boston in July 1968. Barboza was on the witness stand for nine days. On cross-examination, the defense lawyers punched one hole after another in his perjureous testimony. At one point Barboza was retelling an inside joke. He said In Town wanted Deegan dead because he'd broken into a Mafia bookie's house and stolen $82,000 in cash, the exact figure Tash Bratsos and Tommy De Prisco supposedly had on them when they were murdered in the North End in 1966.

On July 31, the jury brought back guilty verdicts against all six defendants, four of whom had nothing to do with Deegan's murder. Two ended up on death row at MCI-Walpole. It would be another thirty years before Johnny Martorano would be able to follow through on his offer to testify on behalf of the men whom Joe Barboza and the FBI had framed.

A couple of days after the trial ended, FBI agents Rico and Condon stopped by Wimpy Bennett's old garage in Roxbury, which was now run by Cadillac Frank Salemme. The two G-men were elated, especially Condon. In his testimony to congressional investigators in 2003, Salemme recalled his conversation with FBI agent Condon.

He made the statement, "I wonder how Louie Grieco likes it on death row, and he wasn't even there." I was thinking, *why was he saying that?* I said, "You're a Knight of Columbus, your Holy Name Society."

Condon shrugged. "If you're so smart, why don't you get up on the stand and testify?"

"Dennis, who's going to believe me? But you won't get by St. Peter at the gate, you can't. You broke one of the Ten Commandments, thou shalt not bear false witness, Dennis. You can't get by him, Dennis."

Dennis was irate at such insolence. Frank Salemme wouldn't be on the street much longer.

The old Nite Café on Commercial Street, where Tash Bratsos and Tommy DePrisco were murdered by the Mafia in 1966, had re-opened under new management, sort of, as the 416 Lounge. In October 1968, just outside the 416, police responding to a call of men fighting found a young man bleeding, clutching his stomach.

It was Arthur Pearson, the Everett ex-con who had gone to jail two years earlier rather than testify against Barboza. He had been stabbed seventeen times, and was pronounced dead on arrival at Mass. General Hospital.

Witnesses reported seeing two men in "navy uniforms" running toward the coast guard base farther up Commercial Street, but no arrests were ever made in Pearson's murder.

Zip Connolly still wanted to join the FBI. At age twenty-seven, he was tired of teaching high school in Dorchester. Rico and Condon hadn't been able to meet him the night Fitzgerald's car was bombed, but it didn't hurt Zip's prospects. He still had those Southie connections to John W. McCormack, the speaker of the U.S. House of Representatives. His father was known in South Boston as "Galway John." How much more did the speaker need to know about anyone?

In August 1968, Speaker McCormack, second in line to the U.S. presidency after Vice President Hubert H. Humphrey, wrote a letter to his friend J. Edgar Hoover.

"Dear Edgar," it began. "It has come to my attentions that the son of a lifelong personal friend has applied to become a special agent of the Federal Bureau of Investigation...."

John J. "Zip" Connolly Jr. was appointed to the FBI in October 1968.

Lawyer: Now, Mr. Hicks, Ronald Hicks, who I believe you testified you murdered, was going to be a witness against friends of yours right?

Mortorano: Against people that I hadn't met yet. They weren't friends until after.

Lawyer: Well, at some point they came to you to ask for your help with an attorney for their defense?

Mortorano: Nope. That's....at one point his wife came to me and asked for some help with an attorney for their defense.

Lawyer: And at some point, you went to see Mt. Hicks to dissuade him from testifying against the woman's.....

Mortorano: No, I met with him. I had a couple of drinks with him, socialized a couple of times, and I didn't like the guy, and I decided to take him out…I didn't go looking for Hicks. He came to my restaurant.

Abie Sarkis, Andy Martorano's old business partner in Luigi's, had a club on Columbus Avenue, the 411. It had a long bar, with bookies hanging out near the door, waiting for the daily number to come in the late afternoon, after which they'd start making their collections and payoff. Farther back were the working girls. Johnny Martorano knew the place well and one night a girl from the 411 came to Basin Street looking for Johnny.

Her name was Roberta Campbell, Bert, for short. She needed a favor. She was crying. He told Bert to sit down and the waiter brought her a drink. He asked her what she needed.

"Have you heard of the Campbell brothers?" she began, and Johnny's answer was yes. Alvin and Arnold Campbell weren't exactly household names like Joe Barboza, but they were well known enough in Roxbury. Bert was Alvin's wife. The Campbell's father was from the Islands, but his sons had been brought up in Boston. He'd taught the boys his trade, which was robbing banks. They'd been arrested in 1957 for a bank stickup in Canton. When the Judge sentenced them, Alvin was twenty-three and Arnold twenty-five.

Despite their race, up until the bank robbery in Canton, the brothers had somehow led a charmed existence with the law in Boston. At their sentencing, the judge angrily read their rap sheets aloud in court, describing what he called "fix after fix after fix."

"This is a sordid picture," the Judge said. "Never in my life have I ever seen such records."

They were good guys, the Campbells. Even Whitey Bulger liked them. He told me later he'd been working out one day in the weight room in Leavenworth, and he heard some guys talking behind him. It was pretty obvious from their accents that they were from Boston, and when Whitey turned around he couldn't believe they were black. It was the Campbells. They used to all walk the track together at Leavenworth, around and around and around, just talking about Boston.

Abie Sarkis liked them, too. He was always helping them out whenever they were in a jam. They were just good people.

GUIDO ST. LAURENT AND FREDERICK B. ROSE, THE FOUNDERS OF N.E.G.R.O.

By the time the Campbells were paroled, Roxbury was awash in federal money. The War on Poverty was in full swing. The Campbells were looking to get a foothold in the rackets, but the money from Uncle Sam was just as tempting. Other local hustlers had gotten there first, though, especially another black ex-con named Guido St. Laurent. St. Laurent had lost his eyesight in an accident at Walpole State Prison, but his blindness didn't stop him from quickly figuring out how to prime Uncle Sam's pump. By 1968 he had set up a sardonically named antipoverty agency of his own, N.E.G.R.O., which stood for New England Grass Roots Organization. Its offices were above a sub shop on Blue Hill Avenue.

At N.E.G.R.O., St. Laurent surrounded himself with thugs, mostly ex-cons like himself. Some of them weren't from Boston, which seemed to bother the Campbells. In November 1968, N.E.G.R.O. was on the verge of its biggest score yet, a $1.9-million federal grant to run a "manpower program" that was supposed to train 500 hard-core unemployed Roxbury residents as auto mechanics. Even the Campbells had been promised jobs, in the program management, of course. Like the characters in Ton Wolfe's essay "Mau-Mauing the Flak Catchers," none of the parties involved had any interest in learning a trade that would require them to go to work every morning.

But St. Laurent would not live to enjoy his payday. Early on the morning of November 13, 1968, three men, later identified as the Campbell brothers and their top enforcer, Deke Chandler, burst into N.E.G.R.O. headquarters.

According to newspaper accounts, Alvin Campbell first pistol-whipped the blind ex-con, then shot him. St. Laurent's top muscle, another ex-con, was also shot to death, as was a third man. Two other N.E.G.R.O. members and ex-cons were wounded, Frederick Rose, a pimp/gangster and a founder/director of N.E.G.R.O., and Calvin Hicks a pimp /hustler. The Campbells and Chandler were quickly arrested and were being held without bail at the Charles Street Jail awaiting trial when Alvin's wife showed up at Basin Street to seek Johnny Martorano's assistance.

The Boston police offered protection to the two survivors from N.E.G.R.O. but both turned down the offer. One of them went, Ronald Hicks, a thirty-one year-old armed robber on parole, went on television and said the shooting was a result of a turf struggle between militant groups over the federal funds. It looked bleak for the Campbells.

Bert Campbell was just looking for any kind of help she could get, money, lawyers, talking the other militant black groups in the city into supporting her husband. Johnny liked her. He wasn't thinking about killing anyone, not until he met the min witness against the Campbells, Ronald Hicks. He was a regular at Basin Street, and after Bert's visit, Johnny made a point of getting to know him. Johnny wanted Hicks to relax around him. He was pleased when Hicks started going out with one of the Barmaids, that way he'd be around Basin Street even more often.

What Johnny quickly learned was that Hicks was a drug dealer and a pimp. One night he casually asked Hicks about the Campbell's trial.

"I'm gonna get even with the motherfuckers," Hicks said.

Johnny began thinking about the Campbells, locked up in the Charles Street Jail, awaiting trial and possibly facing the death penalty because of this guy. Even though he'd never even met the Campbells, Johnny made a decision to murder Hicks.

He thought it was the right thing to do.

He had just seen Peter Limone and the other guys from In Town get railroaded onto Death Row because of Joe Barboza. Now it was happening again. It didn't matter to Johnny if they had killed those guys at N.E.G.R.O. Johnny's mind was made up. This Hicks was no damn good, he was a lying piece of shit.

It was personal, too. Now Johnny was thinking, *this could be me; I could be in this exact situation. First Peter Limone, now Alvin Campbell, who would be next?* And if he didn't help, it would be his fault if the Campbells were put to death, because who else could step up for them?

Johnny came to a conclusion. It was the right thing to do to kill Hicks. His conscience was telling him to do it.

On the evening of March 19, 1969, Johnny Martorano and another guy went looking for Ronald Hicks. They checked out the new hot spot in town, the Sugar Shack, where Hicks was a regular. The Boston police already had reports of "Hicks pushing H & C (Heroin and Cocaine) with a big fat

Negro male at the Sugar Shack; Hicks has also been seen in the company of a white blonde.

As always, Johnny knew the car his prey was driving, a 1967 Cadillac Coupe, brown, with a rose colored top. In other words a pimpmobile. Around 1 a.m., the other guy with Martorano decided to call it a night and go home. But Johnny continued searching for Hicks by himself in the South End.

Around 1:50 a.m., Hicks drifted into Slade's, the joint on Tremont Street near the Taylor brothers' old Pioneer Club. At Slade's, Hicks ran into a woman he'd once dated. He seemed pleased to see her. She later told the police, and the two decided to go across the street to Birley's to get a hamburger. Afterward, the BPD report continued, "He drove her home. He told her he had business and would like to come back and see her about getting together again. He said he would be back about 4 a.m…Hicks did not appear to be worried or frightened when he was with her."

After dropping her off at her place, she watch as Hicks made a U-turn in his Cadillac on Huntington Avenue. That was the last she saw of Ronald Hicks.

Johnny spotted him in the Fenway. He honked and waved and Hicks pulled over into Forsythe Park, near the Museum of Fine Arts. Johnny parked and came over and got in the passage side. Hicks seemed glad to see him. He may have been planning to pull over anyway because he had a bag of cocaine that he got out of his pocket as soon as Johnny got in the car. Hicks cut two lines of coke right there on the car seat. Johnny was sitting next to him on the front seat when Hicks leaned over and snorted one of the lines. He still had his head down when he asked Johnny, "You want a line?"

Those were the last words Ronald Hicks ever spoke because at that moment Johnny Martorano shot him in the head. Hi head snapped back against the horn on the steering wheel and it started blaring, just like in a movie. Johnny grabbed the keys but left the headlights on, just as he had at Normandy Street a year earlier. The cops made note of the similarities in the MO, but it wasn't nearly enough evidence to pull anyone in on.

Hearing the horn, a security guard at the Forsythe Dental center ran outside and saw the car, pointed towards Mass Ave. Hicks was declared dead at 3:05 a.m. at Boston City Hospital. The District Attorney, Garrett Byrne, immediately ordered the sole surviving witness of the N.E.G.R.O. massacre, Frederick Rose, picked up and placed in protective custody.

"A very vital witness has been assassinated," said the somber prosecutor. "The witness had refused protection."

But the police had to admit that a lot of people had wanted Hicks dead. They had no suspects, although the police report did mention that Hicks's girlfriend who had been with him at Slade's "stated that she was a waitress at Basin Street South and that John Martorano was there all the time.

Steve Flemmi, meanwhile, was still keeping the FBI up-to-date on both his own brother and Johnny Martorano. "On April 14, 1969, informant advised that Jimmy Flemmi is running with Johnny Martorano and that Johnny Martorano is still 'hustling girls' out of Enrico's. Informant advised Martorano has in the past purchased some stolen merchandise and he suspects that Martorano is dealing in some kind of drugs."

THE AUTOBIOGRAPHY OF AN
AMERICAN GHETTO BOY

VOLUME SEVEN

THE END OF MY TEENAGE YEARS

ME AND GOOD OL DAD

1969-1970

1

What happened was that my father was just being himself, being slick, and he brought in the Campbell brothers who he had jailed with many times while on vacation at the Billerica House of Corrections and Walpole State Prison. He brought them in on the job to essentially rob himself and take all the money. He just didn't know that the Campbells and Deke Chandler had decided to kill everyone, including him. They shot ol dad five times, but as dad always said, "Jesus couldn't kill him", and most certainly the Campbell brothers couldn't kill him either, not that day, and now he was a witness.

We were on our way over to see one of his favorite working girls, some chick in Watertown, Mass., an Italian girl who was making a lot of money for him, when he told me all this. Said the Campbells had fucked up, but the Italians had not killed him, because he was not going to rat against the Campbells; and he didn't during the trial in June 1969, he stated on the stand that he didn't know who had killed Guido St. Laurent and the others at N.E.G.R.O., that he couldn't recognize anybody, and that he would take care of the situation himself, besides he knew Whitey and all the Mafia guys and they knew he was a stand-up-guy. The Campbell brothers and Deke Chandler were acquitted and ol dad died a natural death in 1989. He had to do some jobs for the Italians but that was just the cost of staying alive.

It was August 1970, I was nineteen years old, and I was just home from the War, and while we were riding I told dad that I wanted to do something different, that I was feeling something for the music, so he told me to sing him something. I sang, *I Can't Get No Satisfaction* by the Rolling Stones. Dad gave me the second and last piece of advice he ever gave me, the first was when I had to go back to the projects. He looked at me after I shouted *I Can't Get No Satisfaction* trying to sound like Mick Jagger and he looked at me like he'd never seen me before, and he said, "You know, you should go down to Miami. There's a lot of old woman down there that would pay you for sex. It's a good hustle and you would do well".

When *Stone Killers* by *Prince Charles and the City Beat Band,* produced by me and Prince Charles Alexander came out under my Solid Platinum Records and Productions record deal with Virgin Records in 1983, I came to Boston from New York City where I was living and went up to his Ghetto pad on Thornton Street in an almost condemned building, with my limousine parked outside, and my new all black leather jacket and pants outfit on, and we did some bad motherfuckin coke together, while my album Stone Killers was playing on the turntable in the background. It was always some wild shit with dad, but I loved that old gangster motherfucker, he was always so cool.

I didn't know it, but good ol dad was saving my life again. I wouldn't go to Miami, but three years later I would go to Los Angeles, and the wife of a very famous musician would take a liking to me and my dick, and put me in the door at the Burbank Studios on Barham Boulevard, the home of Warner Brothers and Columbia Pictures in the 1970's; And just like that I would have a career for the rest of my life in show business; and a poor boy like me would find hundreds and hundreds of women in the 1970's and 1980's to make sure that my rise to the top of the music industry would be cushioned by their love, sex and money. Ol dad didn't have much advice and I didn't see or talk to him often, but his saying, "It's a poor rat who only has one hole", certainly worked for me.

I learned early in life, as a real young man, to always have a bottom lady, who cooked good food, kept a clean house, had a car, some good loving, a job, or a good income coming in to support me, and to always keep a few dozen girls of different sizes, shapes and colors on the side for some extra money, but mainly to smoke weed, do drugs, especially cocaine, get high and watch her dance, be all sexy and have some crazy, freaky sex with me. With all the varied colors and shapes of all the black girls I had to choose from, I always felt bad for White boys, because now they couldn't just take a Black girl and rape them like they wanted to and when they wanted to, like in the good, bad old Jim Crow, slavery days. Now they just had to settle for that same color; that white pasty ass, white bitch, all day, every day. Now they had to pay for some Black Pussy. I felt bad for them.

2
AN AMERICAN GHETTO GIRL

I got married for the first time September 17, 1970 to a seventeen-year-old ghetto home girl from Trenton, New Jersey in Somerville Massachusetts. I was nineteen and my father was my best man. I had been the best man when I was fifteen, at his wedding in 1966. Her name was Betty Jayne and her mother was a hard core street prostitute and had been selling Betty Jayne as a prostitute since she was 11-years-old. We made a great pair, we both had bruises from our mothers. The palms of Betty's hands were badly scarred by her mother because she wouldn't suck some guy's dick because her mouth was sore from the three men whose dicks her mother had made her suck the night before. So her mother had held her hands over an open flame on the stove for punishment.

We were made for each other. Both of us started out as drug addicts and alcoholics, but pulled it together when Betty got pregnant. We both had monsters for mothers, although hers might have been just a little bit worse. It was a rocky beginning to what would be two years of success, six months of failure and one baby.

From a room on Seaver Street, to the Stratten Street Projects at Franklin Field, and with the love and support of two great men, Boston's first Black City Councilman, Thomas A. Atkins and my old newspaper partner, Melvin B. Miller, the GI Bill and my Grandmére, I would buy my first home when I was twenty-one-years-old, October 5, 1972.

I would help Tom Atkins when he ran as the first Black candidate for Mayor of Boston in 1971. He would reward me with a Boston city job in 1971 and present Betty Jayne with a five-year scholarship to Northeastern University in 1972. She would graduate from Northeastern U. in 1979. Melvin B. Miller would run for the United States Congress, with my help in 1972, and his real estate knowledge, advice and friendship would serve me well as I succeeded in buying my first home and later as I released my first hit record *In the Streets* in 1979, and as I was building my Solid Platinum Records and Productions record company throughout the 1980' and 1990's.

But, it would be the Northeastern University Scholarship and finishing *The Life* short story for what I hoped would be my second writing award at UMass that would be my undoing. As my wife would find a boyfriend that would do drugs with her during her freshman year at Northeastern University, and I would beat her ass into the hospital and she would leave our just bought home that November and December 1972. She would come back in January and we would live in that house together until April of 1973. When in one quick moment at a Northeastern University party I would see her dancing with that same guy and I would make a scene and beat both their asses, putting her ass back in the hospital and breaking his arm.

And just like that my marriage would be over and I would be back pimping with my father, until a Dorchester Court judge said for me to leave town, and I would leave Boston July 1973 and end up in Los Angeles, where Lizbeth would save my life up in the San Francisco Bay area. But all that's another story and another book.

3

EMMA, BOOKS AND MUSIC

And as the 1960's ended, Emma, a girl I had met earlier in February, the year I went into the service and had brought to my father's *winning the lottery for twelve hundred dollars* and *going away to Bermuda under the Witness Protection Program* party in April 1969, was busy sucking my dick at the bottom of the stairs at ol dad's house. And when I came home on leave from Lackland and Sheppard Air Force Base that Christmas 1969, she was still busy sucking my dick all day and night and night and day in a room on Washington Street, down near Chucks Furniture store, up the street from Egleston Station, while I was straddling the bedpost, my dick going in and out of Emma's mouth, until her lips and nose were bleeding and she was complaining about her neck hurting and I shot come all down her throat.

And as the 1970's began on New Year's Eve, I rocked Rosalind's pussy from behind at my mother's house and we awoke New Year's Day 1970, drenched in our sweat. And in two days as 1969 was ending, I would be on a plane on my way over to Asia and Southeast Asia, where I would get more Asian pussy than I could ever dream of, three square meals a day, all I could eat, with snacks, fight with all the people I could find to fight, and oh, by the way, do my thing in a war personally brought to me courtesy of good ol Uncle Sam and the United States Air Force, and get paid for all that.

It was around that time that I began to realize that I had a great passion for playing and listening to music and writing short stories and poems and lyrics and reading books. But, what I loved most was getting my dick sucked by home girls. I didn't, mostly, like white girls sucking my dick, their lips were too thin and they couldn't make all them smacking noises home girls could do.

4
PUSSY TASTES LIKE COLLARD GREENS AND PEPSI COLA

And so as the 1970's began I was as happy as a just turned nineteen year old home boy could get, and my beautiful African American blood, made up of African, Native American and Cape Verdean blood, and the Portuguese, English and French rapist's blood was in full effect. I was at my full height, '6 3" and a half, and weighed a skinny 170 pounds of pure project hard muscle, with a flat, stomach, slim waist, broad shoulders, and long legs. I was a coco brown, with some carnation milk thrown in boy, with a long neck and a beauty mark on my lower right face cheek, and another beauty mark on my upper left neck. I had soft lips, and big brown eyes, with long full eyelashes, and my eyebrows were long and dark. I looked soft, but I had my father's rangy handsomeness, the hardness and love of adventure from my Cape Verdean whaler grandfather and my mother's chiseled face, with high cheekbones like my mother's father and my Cherokee Indian great-grandfather, and all the girls said that I had a big dick.

I am a schizophrenic and paranoiac young man; crazy and wild, with skin so golden and brown, full of the triumph, power and beauty of my youth; driving hard and fast through life; a Stone Killer, a violent and talented motherfucker, loving girls whose pussy tastes like collard greens and Pepsi Cola; ready for the world, and off to do Uncle Sam's business, in the 1960's. Proud to be an American, an African American, a Native American, a Cape Verdean American Ghetto Boy; just getting warmed up for the 1970's and 1980's. And that was what it was really all about, right?

I fall asleep on an American flag, I wear my diamonds in poverty. I pledged allegiance to my dad, for teaching me everything he knew, and he is bare and in the sky with Girls, Cigars, Cigarettes, Bourbon, Heroin and all, and I am praying for him and my Grandmére.

5
THE HUSTLE

I would for most of my life love to drink alcohol, do drugs and have sex with a lot of women. The question I always asked myself was, could I have been *greater* without all that and the answer was always, yes. And then, I would ask, could I have been *great* without all that, and the answer was always, no. Because of my childhood all three relaxed me, and because I was good looking enough and could pretty much get all the freaky girls I could stand, all three, because of my childhood, stopped me from becoming a rapist and murderer. It was just that simple, just like that to me. I drove women hard, but just so hard that they liked it.

And so the demons from my childhood would always be with me and I would spend decades enmeshed in the joys and pitfalls of women, drugs and alcohol, fights and hard battles, long negotiations, bad women, good women, bad drugs, and great deals. My hustle would be "Hard Core", and along the way there would be gold and platinum albums, millions of dollars made, most of it in increments of $25,000 dollars and up, more awards for my accomplishments than I could ever have dreamed of. My adventures, businesses, and products, would span the world, and I would go on and have this incredible and phenomenal life, becoming famous and internationally known as a record producer and book publisher, all my wildest dreams come true.

I would have the greatest friends, marry a beautiful woman who would become my life's partner, be admired and loved by everybody, except, most of my children, my mother, most if not all of my relatives and all those who didn't love, admire or know me; and become an NAACP Image Award Winner for Literature, everything a home boy straight outa the Whittier Street Housing Projects, straight outa the ghetto, could want to aspire and dream about, all my dreams come true.

But remember, I prayed hard, every day, on my hands and knees, and God sent me some of the greatest people, boys and girls, home girls and sisters, men and women, black and white that a poor boy from the projects and ghetto could ever hope for. They all saved my life. Always taking me to the next step and I always gave back, taking thousands of more people with me. I am without a doubt, absolutely, the epitome of GOD ANSWERS PRAYERS and IT TAKES A GHETTO TO RAISE A CHILD!

This is the first of a trilogy of books. The second volume is *The Autobiography of the Rise of an American Ghetto Man - The 1970's and 1980's*, Volume Two is due Winter 2017. The third volume, *America: The Black Point of View – The Autobiography of an American Ghetto Guy - The 1990's and 2000's*, Volume Three is due Winter 2018.

AN EXCERPT FROM VOLUME TWO

"THE AUTOBIOGRAPHY OF THE RISE
OF AN AMERICAN GHETTO MAN"
THE 1970'S AND 1980'S

THE 1970'S AND 1980'S

BY TONY ROSE

It was early 1975, I had been working in the A & R department at RCA Records in Los Angeles, and PME Management, and had signed an act, Robbie Hill and the Family Affair after producing a few songs on them, to my new management and production company Nova Productions that I had opened up on Hollywood Boulevard with the financial help of one of my main girls, my bottom lady, Brenda Lee. I had just gotten my Artists' Management License, becoming the youngest Licensed Black Artist Manager in the State of California, so I was good to go and found and signed a young comic, Shirley Hemphill, that I worked at comedy clubs like Mitzi Shore's, The Comedy Store on Sunset Blvd.; and after calling Norman Lear's casting agent Joan Murray's office a million times, helped Shirley get signed to the Norman Lear produced television show, *"What's Happening!!"*, in 1976.

RCA's number one R&B singing group, the Main Ingredient whose lead singer was Cuba Gooding (you know his son, the actor Cuba Gooding, Jr. and you know the song *Everybody Plays the Fool*) came out to Los Angeles from New York City to set up offices, record and tour the West Coast. I went to Don Berkheimer, head of A & R at RCA Records, and inquired about signing my group to RCA to do a couple of singles and he said "Yes, but why don't you sign them through Cuba Gooding and Luther Simmons." RCA had just given the Main Ingredient their own production deal. So, I went to Cuba and he said, "Sure, let's hear them."

In the meantime, the Main Ingredient needed a band to accompany them on tour, so Robbie Hill and the Family Affair became the Main Ingredient's band for their West Coast tour and I went on as their tour manager.

Eventually I went on to sign the group with Super Group Productions to be distributed by RCA Records.

I had been living out in Los Angeles since September of 1973, and had started working at The Burbank Studios, (Warner Brothers and Columbia Pictures) on Barham Boulevard, in February 1974. I began in the mailroom delivering mail to successful producers and directors such as Ray Stark and Herbert Ross and then I worked as a production assistant on films such as *Doc Savage* and made some serious entertainment connections; I then started working at Warner/Electra/Atlanta Records (WEA) in June of 1974, where I learned record company accounting, sales and distribution practices.

I then went to work at Warren Lanier Public Relations on Sunset Boulevard in West Hollywood, July 1974, part time or in the evening as Warren Lanier, Sr. needed me. His gossip column was syndicated in over 300 Black newspapers in the country, including Jet Magazine. His clientele included most of the 1970's major Black actors and actresses, as well as major recording artists like Barry White and included major film studios such as Warner Bros. Pictures and 20th Century Pictures and Records.

I apprenticed with Mr. Lanier and he personally taught me Public Relations, Marketing and Publicity as well as paying me $75.00 per week. I was able to learn to be a public relations account executive and worked on films like Uptown Saturday Night with Sidney Poitier and Bill Cosby. I actually met and dated many beautiful, famous Black actresses of that era, while working for Warren Lanier PR.

I then went to RCA Records in December 1974-1976, where I signed acts, worked with the Main Ingredient, learned how to engineer, produce, package, manufacture and distribute records nationwide. I also became friends with some very serious music industry contacts in radio, television, newspapers and magazines like Billboard Magazine and the Hollywood Reporter. I knew most of the people at RCA Records, East and West Coast, and was friends with most of the major label record company's A&R, Marketing and Promotion people in Los Angeles and New York City.

By early 1975, at twenty-four-years old, I was a music industry executive in Los Angeles, making money, drinking hard, getting plenty of pussy and moving fast.

In 1977, during one of my trips back to Roxbury/Boston, I saw a group called the Energetics, and shortly after, met with their manager Roscoe Gorham. I told Roscoe that if he had any tapes I would take them back to Los Angeles with me and would shop them around to see if there were any buyers/deals I could get for the group. So, I took the tapes back to Los Angeles and got the Energetics music tapes a distribution deal with a small label. They paid $8000 for the tapes, and Roscoe paid me 10% of it. It was cool.

While making the deal in Los Angeles, across the hall working in a small studio was the legendary Motown producer/songwriter Brian Holland, so I went over to say, "Hi". He asked me what I was doing there. I told him I was closing a deal for some tapes that I had from a group in Boston called the Energetics. He said he knew the group and had been interested in them. I told him I would let the group's manager Roscoe Gorham know. So I did, and Roscoe and Brian got together. Brian Holland signed the group to an album deal with Atlantic Records. The album came out in 1979 and I would be responsible for getting the first major record deal of my era for a Black recording act from Roxbury/Boston, Massachusetts.

In 1979, I had left Los Angeles, because shit had happened with Cuba Gooding, and I was back in Boston. During a February blizzard I was listening to the radio and heard a song called *Bout Time I Funk You Baby*. The announcer came on and said that the guy who was just on was Maurice Starr and that he would be appearing live at a club called Corteez on Washington Street in Dorchester. At the time, I was twenty-eight-years-old, my Los Angeles years and living were far behind me, and I was living in the ghetto, in Dorchester at 428 Talbot Avenue….so I went to check him out.

When I met Maurice Starr that February night we formed an instant bond. We were both on the verge of finding something…doing something big… and even though we were both living in the ghetto….we felt it. Together we had a special energy…his to me, mine to his. He also knew that I had done that deal for the Energetics and that was giving me big credibility. He introduced me to his set in Roxbury/Dorchester, at all the clubs, we hung out, came over to my place and we talked. We were giving each other that energy we needed to move to the next level. Soon we started going out, doing television shows, radio interviews, promoting the record. Maurice had originally put his record out ('Bout Time I Funk You') on his own Boston International Records label. I did a lot of work to help him, including talking to the people in A&R at RCA Records like Jerome Gasper, Wendell Bates and Ron Mosley. Eventually I got the record deal for him and Maurice Starr signed a 'one single' record deal with RCA Records, and we went out on tour and I had helped the second act I met from Roxbury get a major record deal.

I became like his manager and worked with him touring in Buffalo, New York, Cleveland, places like that. In his band was a young guy named Charles Alexander. While on tour, Charles mentioned that he had a song sketch called *In the Streets* and asked if I would work with him on it. Michael Jonzun (Maurice's brother) also heard the song and mentioned that it might be something that I might want to get involved with. Maurice laid down some killer bass, guitar lines and production, I did some production work on it, Charles laid down his lead vocals, some flute and funky bass lines on this Lyricon instrument that he had and Michael laid down the backbeat. I did some more work on it, took it back in the studio and we mixed it down.

So, I put out the record *In the Streets*, on my Solid Platinum Records and Productions label in October 1979, doing all that with a fifteen thousand dollar loan from one of my girlfriends, Marcia Tappin. I distributed it, promoted it, marketed it, publicized it, got it on the radio and sold it all over America and eventually all over the world. With RCA Records pushing *Bout Time I Funk You Baby* b/w *Baby Come On*, nationally all over the United States with Maurice Starr's name as producer and songwriter and with me pushing *In the Streets* by *Prince Charles and the City Beat Band* on my *Solid Platinum Records and Productions Record Label,* with Prince Charles Alexander as artist/producer/songwriter (who I would manage and co-produce with for the next ten years), Michael Johnson and Maurice Starr as producers/songwriters and me as executive producer/producer/songwriter. It began and gave us the careers we'd all been looking for. I made *In the Streets* a major record that propelled all of us to world-wide fame. It got our names out there. It put us all on an International level. At that time, I had known Maurice and Michael for exactly nine months, and Prince Charles Alexander for four months....and we all became friends for life, to this very day.

And in three years on March 4, 1983, I would sign the fourth Black act and my third act from Roxbury/Boston, Mass., *Prince Charles and the City Beat Band,* to a major international record label with Virgin Records, through my record company, *Solid Platinum Records and Productions.*

Oh yeah, and the third act to sign a major record deal from Roxbury was produced by Maurice Starr and ripped off by, and signed to MCA Records by Jheryl Busby, and the fifth act to sign a major record deal from Roxbury would be Michael Johnson of the *Jonzun Crew* with Tommy Boy/Warner Bros' Records.

So out of the first top five acts signed out of Roxbury/Boston Mass., I would work with all of them and be responsible for signing three of them to major record labels.

In a matter of just a few years in the 1970's and 1980's all of our dreams would come true. Well, not all of them, because in the 1990's and 2000's there would be many, many more successes to come, and many more dreams to fulfilled and come true for all of us.

The 1950's film *A Streetcar Named Desire*, the play written by Tennessee Williams, starring Marlon Brando and Vivien Leigh, the character Blanche Duboise played by Miss Leigh says, *"I have always depended on the kindness of strangers."* In the 1960's the Beatles sang *"I get by with a little help from my friends."*

And as the 1970's ended, I said, *"Thank God for all the sistas, home girls, Black women, girlfriends and babies' mamas who held a brother down. Feeding, fucking and sheltering me, paying the rent, giving me money, some good sex, keys to cars, apartments and houses. Believing in me, feeding me and loving me, you all know who you are. You're my girls, my bottom ladies. Thank you to each and every one of you! Oh, and to you Cali Girl, you're always in my heart forever!!* – Tony Rose

BOOK THREE

PROJECT LIFE

I wrote most of this in 1968. It's about death, mothers, and men in the projects.

1
THE GREAT BIG UGLY GORILLA

Russell's mother was a great big, ugly gorilla, at least that's what Russell's younger brother Spencer thought. Earline thought it was cute, the way Spencer who was only three, would look up at her when she would try to pick him up and say, "Get away from me you great, big, ugly gorilla!" Earline would look at him and say, "O, isn't he cute".

2
EARLINE

Earline had six rooms, one 9x12 front room, one 7x11 kitchen, three bedrooms, and a bathroom; also four boys and three girls. Russell was one of my friends, so I was always over there.

3
BIG AND FLAPPY

Earline was a big nice pleasant woman, whose main attraction were her breast, which were big and flappy. I used to always see them, because she would always be breast feeding someone.

4
IN THE NAVY

I must have been eight the summer that Russell's father came home. He was in the Navy, at least that's what Russell had been telling us for years. He was only home for five days, but, wow, he sure made a lot of little boy's happy. For some of us, it was our first real physical up-closeness of a man. The size of him, his smell, his voice. Another thing I would do, me and

Wilbur, would be to wait for Russell's father to go to the bathroom, so we could see how a real man's looked. I caught him once and I watched closely, he knew I was watching him because he slowly turned around with a grin on his face, he didn't say nothing, just looked at me.

5
WOMEN'S WORLD

We were sad when Russell's father left, you see we lived in a women's world, and they weren't big enough to pick us up and throw us around.

6
TWO BABIES

We all knew that Russell must have had a father, not only did he say he had one, but we all knew that somehow father's and mother's meant babies, and Earline sure had plenty of them, so we knew that there must have been someone there sometime. That's why when Russell's father came home we weren't so surprised, although a few of us were a little skeptical even after seeing him, especially Bupsey, who told me that his mother had told him that Russell's father had been gone for four years and Earline had two babies that were five months and two years old. We didn't know what that meant, but it must have been important since a mother had said it, so it was enough to keep us skeptical.

7
SHUT UP

At first we thought that, that wasn't Russell's father, but just another friend of Earline's, and everybody's mother had lots of friends. But, what made me believe that he was Russell's father, was when he punched Spencer in the mouth for calling Earline a great, big, ugly gorilla and told Russell to shut up for laughing. Soon after Russell's father left, Spencer told her he hated her.

8
FAT AND UGLY

Earline never could control Spencer. As we got older, the more names he could think of to call her. She did get to be fat and ugly, but she always had plenty of friends and uncles for Russell, I guess because she tried harder.

9
FAT BASTARD

Earline was a good mother, at least better than most. She would sometimes try to kill the roaches and she did bathe the kids, although from what I can remember not too much could be said for her own cleanliness. But, she smiled and talked, and she was young and she lived also. She probably had dreams to. The apartment stayed the same though, year after year. One year, about seven years after the first time I had seen him, Russell's father came back, but I guess Earline looked too tired or used or something, 'cause he just fucked her and left. (By this time I knew what friends and others did to women) He didn't even hit Spencer, when Spencer called him a fat bastard.

10
GOING TO KILL HIM

Earline never worked and from what my mother told me, she couldn't get on aid either, because her husband was in the Navy. But, her friends never seemed to mind, they lived with her, Russell and the kids, eating up all the food from them. Russell told me one time that he was going to kill one of them, because he had taken the money that Earline had been saving to buy some food; he had gambled it up and Russell was going to kill him, 'cause his mother was crying, and her friend had knocked her down for swearing at him.

11
PUSSY

Ronald's mother was the top girl in the projects. My mother was always telling me about Cynthia, plus Ronald was my best friend and I was always over his house too. Anyway, Cynthia was the top girl, she must have been about twenty when I was eight, because she knew how to tell the men. She never refused anybody, if they wanted to buy food and clothes and maybe pay the rent good, if they didn't that was fine also, but they weren't getting anymore pussy from her.

12
MAMA

Cynthia was filthy, Ronald was the mother. After Cynthia would come home from the hospital, she would hand the new baby to Ronald and go out. One night one of the babies was just beginning to talk, and he was crying and saying, *ma, ma, ma, ma.* Ronald went to pick him up, and the baby actually thought that Ronald was his mother, because he laughed and said, *mama*, in a gurgling tone. Me and Ronald laughed.

13
A GOOD MOTHER

I used to spend my nights over there, sometimes, in fact, in the summer I would try to spend all my nights over Ronald's. I met Ronald when I was four and we remained friends until I was eleven. He lived in the apartment all his life. Ronald was a good friend and mother.

14
THOUSANDS OF ROACHES

When I was little I used to watch Cynthia breast feed her babies. Cynthia only breast fed because there was never any milk or food in the house, so she gave what she had. Cynthia never cleaned the house, never, Ronald would try, but with four, then five, then six children, it was hard. In the end the apartment went under. Thousands of roaches infested the place. One night while spending the night with Ronald, I woke up to find a nest of roaches crawling in and around my head. Cynthia never minded though, so long as she had her Pepsi and men. Cynthia died in 1966, along with her new son in childbirth.

15
WAKES AND FUNERALS

Earline was close with my mother; they would talk on the phone for hours about everything. Since neither worked they had plenty of time on their hands. One way in which they used their time was to go to wakes and funerals of people they didn't know. Earline would read the obituaries and anybody in Roxbury who had met their death violently was observed at their funeral by Muriel and Earline.

16
INSIDES TORN AND PULLED OUT

They would sit in the front row with the family and talk about the deceased. After the funeral they would talk with the funeral director and the deceased family, then they would come home and discuss the death for days, and of course tell us. One case they actually solved before the police. It seemed that a young girl's body had been found in the Fenway with her insides torn and pulled out. By going to the funeral and talking with the family and friends, they agreed that the girl had been pregnant and gone to an abortionist. The abortion had been a failure and instead of taking the girl to the hospital or letting her go, they killed her by ripping her out, then taking her body to the Fenway and dropping her in the water. They even had the names of the abortionist and her help.

17
BROKE THE CASE

I remember that my mother would be happy that she had this information, because it meant her trips to the wakes and funerals were worthwhile. Two weeks later the police broke the case open, it had happened exactly as Earline and Muriel had said.

18
SQUIRMING AND DYING

One night as I was being held by my arms over the seventh floor roof; while some of the big boys were trying to steal .20 cents from my pocket and all fifty of the Record American Newspapers I sold at night had been kicked off the roof into the dark; and I was wondering how we were going to eat the next day; Spencer called his mother a black tramp. (80% percent of all Black people in this country need mental help) Earline's mind snapped and she raised her now 400-pound frame, ran screaming to the son she loved more than life, and sent him Spencer screaming through the front room window; six floors, to the playground. *Where he lay for an hour,* my mother said, while everyone watched him squirm. The ambulance came; Spencer fought for two days and died. His mother was admitted to Mattapan State Hospital for two years. Russell went to stay with Ronald and an aunt took the rest.

19
A LOT OF FUN

Ronald had a sister named Cissy who was the second oldest, just under Ronald. She was different-looking than the rest of us, because her father had been white. She had long black hair and would have been pretty except she had emphysema and asthma. Cissy will always stay in my mind as the skinny little girl whose dress was always up. That probably was the main reason all of us liked to stay over Ronald's. At night, since all the kids slept together, Cissy would come over to Ronald's side and we would all play games, she was a lot of fun. But, as we got older and Ronald died and she got older, what she did wasn't fun anymore. She had lost her emphysema because one night when I was coming from a show downtown, I saw her lined up with a lot of other girls outside of *Goodtime Charlie's*. I walked by and she said, *hey, hey mister*. I looked at her and she remembered me, she remembered the filth, the hunger, the babies crying, the horror of having to grow up in hell. She turned her head and I walked away, both of us with a lifetime of memories.

THE PROJECTS—1961

I wrote this in 1969. It's about me and my Grandmére.

1

The project was a red fortress filled with screaming children, cold brutal gangs and women. There were five hundred units: 50 three-room apartments; 150 four-room apartments; 125 five-room apartments; 75 six-room apartments; and 100 seven-room apartments; all unfurnished and all painted a dull green and grey. There were five buildings, seven stories high, nine three story buildings with approximately two thousand five hundred poor and hungry people living together. Babies were born and died here. Life went on in an exciting way, for this was life; a dangerous sort of life; not a way to live, for many didn't live; but, for those that survived, they had known life. Welfare prevailed and strange men abounded.

2

The project was built to resemble a square and was surrounded by four streets, Whittier, Ruggles, Tremont and Cabot Street. The housing project area stood in the heart of Roxbury; three blocks from Mass Avenue, where a fantastic array of nice people, lived with pimps, murderers, rapists, thieves, prostitutes, hustlers, con-men, gamblers, addicts, homosexuals and tricks, who preyed on each other every day, minimizing one another's chances of survival. A separate story could be told of my later encounter and life as part of the madness, but for now, I shall concern myself only to what happened one summer in 1961

3

Across from the project on Whittier Street was the Health Unit, we had our teeth pulled there, and played basketball on the court outside. In the summer we played in the wading pool and played baseball on the concrete. On Cabot Street, there were two small grocery stores, Al's and Morris's.

4

Morris was a cheap Jew and would give no credit, Al's let everybody have credit, half of the project owed him money and probably still does.

5

There was nothing on Ruggles Street but death. Ruggles Street was the home of a gang, a vicious and cruel gang that terrorized Roxbury and the projects.

6

Tremont was one of the longest streets in Roxbury. The street started at Egleston Station and went all the way downtown. The only reason it seemed for this streets existence seemed to be for the large number of liquor stores, nightclubs and soul food cafes on it. In the middle of all that stood the project and me.

7

We were lucky though, we escaped the project once a year; one week in the summer. My sister was afraid of the old woman and only went because she was hungry, I went for survival.

8

I loved my Grandmére's porch and back yard. I would sit on the porch in the sun and imagine I was all kinds of heroes, I would lie on the grass and think of nothing.

9

My Grandmére would sometimes take me on the bus to Harvard Square, and then on the underground subway train to downtown Boston. She would go shopping in places my mother never went, Saks Fifth Avenue, Bonwit Teller's, and Gilchrist.

10

Mama's main place was Jordan Marsh Basement or Dudley Street Station area. Mama was poor, hungry looking and on welfare. My sister and I would try to love her, she was crazy, but, she was all we had.

11

I was eleven the summer Ronald was killed. While we were rummaging through Morris' Grocery store, a policeman's bullet hit Ronald in the back of his neck, shattering the vertebrae and snapping the skinny eleven-year-old's head off the shoulders, causing him to die with a licorice stick in one hand and some bread for his mother in the other.

12

Lying in my Grandmére's back yard, I did a lot of thinking that summer. I thought about Ronald's death and I began to plot my escape.

HOW MY FATHER CHANGED MY LIFE AND SAVED ME

SHORT AUTOBIOGRAPHY OF TONY ROSE

My short autobiography from birth to eighteen years old. This biography is very, very graphic. The people are real, the events are real and the language is real. It is the life and language that I lived and used as a child and teenager in the moment and time that I lived it.

Do not read this biography if you are easily offended and sickened by extreme violence, strong language and extreme sexual matters.

THE FIRST TIME

1
BOSTON CITY HOSPITAL

I was born at Boston City Hospital. My mother brought me home to her mother's (Grandma) house, as my father was in jail. When my father came out of jail, I was about one and a half years old and my mother moved to my father's, mother, Grandmére's house in Cambridge. When my father went back to jail, I was about two years old, and my mother was pregnant with my sister. My mother and I moved back to her mother's house.

2
SHINY THINGS

My mother had my sister on June 24, 1953 and we moved to Townsend St. in Roxbury, where one of my earliest memories is of a cat being struck by lightning, and my father getting out of jail. I would next see and recognize my father when I was three and a half years old in a large room, sitting with my mother and seeing my father sitting with other men in white clothes, behind a rail with benches, his hands bound by something shining. I saw my father get up, some men say something, and my father is led off by other men.

3
KINDERGARTEN

The next time I saw my father, we were living in the Whittier St. Housing Projects in Roxbury, we had moved there when I turned four and I was now five and going to kindergarten. He came in the door, we lived in three rooms, a kitchen/front room, two bedrooms and bathroom, on the fifth floor; and he went into the bedroom with my mother and they made a lot of noise, my mother screaming over and over, that yes, she wanted another child. He left and I didn't see him again until I was almost six or seven years old, and this is when my father changed my life for the first time.

4
INVITED HIM UP

What happened is the final version as told by mother when she went in for her operation last year, and what I saw when I was young. I had been told many versions over the years, but I believe this is what happened. It seems my father had been in jail again and had gotten out. He sent a boy up to our apartment with candy. My mother invited him up and he moved in.

5
HAVING SEX WITH A LOT OF WOMEN

My mother was working at Mass General Hospital and had met a wonderful friend named Millie. My sister and I loved Millie, she made our mother laugh; my mother was finally getting herself together, she was on welfare, but, wanted to do better, she was a nurse's aide and wanted to be a nurse. (She started crying here) I was coming home from school, and my sister was staying at grandma's house, and my mother was picking her up on the weekends. My father told my mother that he would stay at home and watch my sister. My mother found out that he was having sex with a lot of the women in our building while she was at work.

6
PATIENT ALMOST DIED

On this fateful day in early October 1956 or 1957, my mother went to work. Sick with thinking about my father and other women, she put a patient in a tub, and went in the back to have a smoke and to talk with Millie about her problems with my father. The patient almost died in the tub and my mother was fired. She came home early, opened the door and yelled for my father. She said she didn't hear anything and went to the bedroom and the door was locked. She started banging on the door and said she could hear my sister in there. She said my father finally opened the door and that my sister seemed to be listless. She started screaming at my father and told him to get out.

7
VAGINA CHECKED OUT

She called her mother and her mother said that my father was in there probably bothering my sister. My mother said she questioned that, but, my grandmother said that he had been, and that she needed to take my sister to the hospital and have her vagina checked out. My mother did. My grandmother called Grandmére and told her that my father had been sexually molesting my sister. My father arrived at my Grandmére's house and she told him. He wrecked her kitchen and pulled a gun and said he was going to kill my mother and grandmother. My Grandmére called my grandmother and told her what my father had done and said. My mother took us from the hospital to my grandmother's house.

8
ON HIS WAY TO KILL EVERYONE

My Grandmére told her what she had done and that my father was on his way from Cambridge to kill everyone. My grandmother thought we would all be safer at my aunt's apartment in the Lenox St. Projects. I remember that long night-walk to my aunt's house very well, as my mother and grandmother were very scared that my father would find us. We arrived at my aunt's house, where my mother and grandmother called the police and told them what had happened and where my father was going. At this point, we were all terrified. The police called and said that they had a man at our apartment and wanted my mother to come and identify him. We walked from the Lenox St. Projects to the Whittier St. Projects.

9
SHINY THINGS AGAIN

There were police everywhere in my building. We went up to the fifth floor and into our apartment where the police and my father were. The shiny things were around his hands and the police asked my mother if this was him. I remember looking at him. I can still see him in that apartment, at the door, surrounded by policemen, screaming at my mother, as she said, *yes,* that was him. I remember the police dragging him out.

10
FINALLY WENT INSANE

I would not see him again until February 1965. I believe that was the night that my mother finally went insane. I'm not sure if I was near six or seven, I'm inclined to think six, because that would make my sister at the right age three not four. My mother says she can't remember and neither can I. But, what I do remember is that I was about seven when we went to visit Uncle Robert, my mother's brother. My mother's brother was doing twenty-five years in Bridge-water State Hospital. He did fifteen or so. In 1949 he had gone on a major crime spree in Boston. And here, I must tell you that all of his feats and my fathers were well recorded in the newspapers and radio during their day. His crime spree ended with a standoff on Mass. Ave and Columbus Ave., with the police and my grandmother begging him to surrender, and my uncle shooting and wounding a police officer, (He later lost his leg) and then turning the gun on himself, shooting himself in the head.

11
BLEW HIS EYES OUT

Instead of blowing his brains out, he blew his eyes out, and was blind for the rest of his life. With all the notoriety, the newspaper and radio coverage, the trial and the sentencing; the Faulks, my mother, my two aunts, my grandmother and grandfather, my uncle, were disgraced and ostracized from the community. They were hated and whatever little standing they might have had in Boston, in Roxbury, in the community, because of my mother's great and phenomenal ability to play classical music; it was lost. Her music career was over, there was no more money for her lessons, for her gowns, for her aspirations, all the money went to that asshole, my uncle for his lawyers, his trial, for his appeal, for his comfort in jail, for his life and for my grandmother's guilt, and that's when I believe my mother began to go insane.

12
USED TO VISITING PEOPLE IN JAIL

They could no longer hold their heads up and sank into despair and everything for them went wrong and that's what we, my sister and I, and my cousins, the next generation, were born into. But, on that day when I was seven years old and visiting my uncle in jail, I didn't know this, in fact, I was very used to visiting people in jail. I had been visiting my father in jail since I had been two years old, and visiting a favorite cousin of my mother's, so my uncle was routine. But on this day when I was seven years old, Hall, my Aunt Phyllis' new boyfriend, drove my aunt, my mother, my grandmother, my sister and me, to visit my uncle.

13
WHICH HAND IS IT IN

I thought it was fun, a fun day. I was a child and wanted to do child things. My aunts, grandmother and mother got out of the car to visit my uncle. Hall stayed up front in the driver's seat, (I can still see him here smoking a cigarette, bored, babysitting me and my sister). Well, us cousins and me and my sister had a game we would play whenever we could, it didn't cost anything, and could be played anywhere. It was called which hand is it in. It could be a pebble, a penny, a button, it didn't matter as long as it could fit in your hand and not be seen.

14
YOU PUT YOUR HAND BEHIND YOUR BACK

You put your hand behind your back, brought it out for your partner to slap your hand and you had to open it. If that hand held the button, then it was their turn to be it. The game was played at breakneck speed. You had to guess which hand held it, slap the hand that you thought held it, when the hand opened and didn't, you put your hand behind your back and switched it or kept it in the same hand, moved your balled hands up in front of your partner and said which hand is it in.

15
HAD I BEEN BOTHERING HER

It was a fun game, a guessing game. Every once in a while Hall would tell us to stop making so much noise. It would be the last time I would ever play that game or any game with my sister again, to this day. It would be the day that my father would begin to change my life. When the adults came back, here's what they saw, my sister and me in the back seat of the car hot and sweaty, clothes askew. What happened later, I can't remember except that my mother when we got home kept asking me had I been bothering my sister and asking my sister had I been bothering her. I had no idea what she was talking about and neither did my sister, but, after my mother kept going on and on and on, and us crying, and her hitting me, my sister said yes, I had been bothering her and my whole life changed.

16
HEROIN

My father was a heroin addict, as well as a pimp, murderer, gangster and button man (Hit Man) for the Mafia. I knew that after I got older, and my mother said she remembered his works and saw him shoot up a few times without him knowing it during their marriage. I always wanted to believe and once I got older and started dealing with drugs, I wanted to believe that probably my father had been shooting up that day when he and my sister were in the bedroom, and he didn't want my mother to know it, and was trying to clean up, or he had just started and wanted to finish getting high. But, what I did know was that I had not bothered my sister and had no idea what that meant, outside of hitting her, which I hadn't; and that day, and all the times I was accused of that, until I reached twelve years old and then all of a sudden it stopped, I never knew why my life had changed.

17
TORTURED AND ABUSED

Why I was being crushed physically, mentally and emotionally by my mother, why I was being tortured and abused by my mother? Because from that day on, I was never held by my mother; never told I love you, by my mother; never told, by my mother, that I'm proud of you. Not being told I love you and not being held by my mother as a child damaged me severely. When I take care of my mother today, I know what a woman must feel who is forced to care of, in some way, an aging father who sexually abused her from the age of six to twelve and then it stopped; and you are told to never tell anyone. Well, it's the same thing to me. I am taking care of my abuser.

18
THE BEATINGS, NAKED AND HUMILIATED

For five or six years this went on. I will not tell you all the things that were done to me. But, I will tell you the beatings, the beatings, the beatings went on forever, naked, with black and blue marks all over my body. The humiliations; it tore my sister and me apart, I was deathly afraid of her, my sister held life and death over me. One wrong word from her. I could be awakened at night, out of sleep, interrogated and beaten like a dog. I lived with no hope, defenseless and nobody ever coming to help me, to save me.

19
NO IDEA WHAT LOVE WAS

At seven, I hated my mother; at eight, I wanted to kill my mother; at nine, I was planning on how I would kill her; at ten, I had no soul left; at eleven, I had no idea what love was; at twelve, I was dead to anything; and then she stopped. Because an old boyfriend named Randy got out of jail after serving fifteen years for murder, called my grandmother, came over and moved in with us.

20
THE MONSTER

He was a 100% mentally disabled World War Two veteran and she got distracted for the next fifteen years in trying to get his disability check which was controlled by his step-mother. I won't go year by year and tell you what happened to me, it would take too long, suffice it to say that I was damaged in every way possible you could damage a child. What I am is a child who grew up without love, without being held, who lived in a house with a monster, a child who lived in fear, a child who gave up hope of anyone ever saving me. And then one day it just stopped, as if nothing had ever happened. I was told over and over and over by my mother to never tell anyone what she was doing to me and then it just stopped, her attention went somewhere else. It seemed.

21
BACK END OF THE IRON CHORD

In 1965, after it had stopped for a while, Randy went back to the hospital. He did drugs and medication drugs and smoked all day, and would go crazy. People would come get him from the VA, take him to the mental ward. She started up again, and accused me of something, it could have been anything. She told me to take off my clothes and brought the iron chord in, the back end, and proceeded to hurt me again, badly. I realized while she was doing this, that I was almost as big as her, and I wrestled the iron chord from her and threw it out the window, and then I tried to throw her out. She never hit me again.

22
FIND ALCOHOL AND ALL MY TROUBLES OVER

Soon after, at fourteen, I would find alcohol and all my troubles would be over. Soon after, that same year, when I reached puberty, I realized what my mother had been talking about all those years. She had been accusing me of sexually molesting my sister since I had been six or seven years old. When she told my sister and me the story of my father last year, we asked her why she had listened to her mother about me sexually abusing my sister. She said she had and she hadn't, mainly she was mad at my father and that this had been her way of getting back at him, by hurting his son.

23
BLAMED MY GRANDMOTHER

All these years I had blamed my grandmother for putting those ideas in my mother's head. I was right though, my grandmother had accused my grandfather of molesting one of my aunts in the 1930's, she had accused one of her sister's husbands of molesting their daughter in the 40's, she had accused me of sexually molesting my sister in the 50's, my mother believed her and took it to the next level, and on and on and in the eighties she accused my cousin's first husband of molesting his daughter and broke up their marriage.

24
NO GOD FOR MY MOTHER

What I found out in 1992 when I wrote a letter to everyone about what had happened to me as a child, was that my grandmother had been sexually abused as a child by her father and a step-father. The collaborative evidence was that one of my second cousins could remember Daddy Herbert my grandmother's father, sexually molesting her in the 1960's when he was living with her parents. So you see when I was growing up we were poor, but, there was no God for my mother, no church for my mother, no love from my mother, no nothing, just pure bleakness, no joy, no hope.

25
PROSTITUTES, ALCOHOLICS AND DRUG ADDICTS

I found my joy outside the home, outside the family. All I am is from those times. I tried to stay out of the apartment as much as I could. I started a paper route in the projects so I could eat. I ran errands for people in the projects so I could eat. I was being starved by my mother. She would not feed me. So I started credit at Al's, a local grocery store, and brought Al our welfare check, so that we could eat. It wasn't just that we were poor. I think my mother had a cruel streak and she was insane. I found other outlets and strangers to feed me, to look after me, to shelter me. I lived in a world of prostitutes, alcoholics, drug addicts, you name it I lived in it and knew it. But, these were the people who looked after me. I lived in complete horror inside and outside my little project apartment, but, I learned how to survive.

THE SECOND TIME

26
JAIL TIME

The second time my father changed my life and saved me, was when I was fifteen in 1966. Back during that incident in 1956 or 1957 he had done some jail time for being on parole and carrying a gun and from what I saw in his papers after he had died, he had been in jail again in 1959-61 and again in 1962-65. He had just gotten out of jail when I met him again in 1966. I met him because I had discovered alcohol and weed in 1965 and I was in gangs and I wasn't going to school and I was violent.

27
I LOVED HIM

I loved him and I felt sorry for him. I could remember the last time I had seen him. But, something would happen in April 1966 that would change me, not right away, but, I would know something else about me.

28
RAPING LITTLE GIRLS

That April, when I was fifteen, I went up against 18, 19, 20-year-old gang members in the project I grew up in. They were raping 11,12, 13 year old girls, had been doing it for years, little girls would be pregnant all the time. One of the girls raped was my sister, I saved her once, but I couldn't be there all the time. I was beat to death and lived, the police finally came to the projects, there was an investigation, and the rapes stopped.

29
WORKED FOR THE MAFIA

My father had just been released from prison and I hadn't seen him for eight or so years. When I was released from the hospital I couldn't live in the projects for a while and I went to live with my father for about eight months, until he went back to prison. He taught me a lot during that time. My father was a pimp, a drug dealer and drug user, a real gangster and a murderer, an out an out criminal. He was no joke, the real thing. Everyone in Roxbury, Dorchester, hell in Boston, Cambridge, Medford, Summerville, Malden, Lynn, Revere, New England, Rhode Island, everyone, everywhere, feared him and knew him. He worked for the Mafia and was proud of that.

30
FINGER FUCK THEM

His crimes and jail time were recorded in the newspapers and television and he was proud of that. He fucked everything in sight and was proud of that. He was beautiful and he was proud of that. I loved him. We would go pick up money from the girls, sometimes he'd have to beat them and sometimes they would give me blow jobs and let me finger fuck them. My father got a kick out of that, he would laugh and the girls would laugh, and I thought I was cool. Sometimes he'd have to get out the hanger and show me how to beat them bitches, but, I never really got into that.

31
A POOR RAT WHO ONLY GOT ONE HOLE

He would say it's a poor rat who only got one hole. He believed in multiple women and girlfriends. He taught me how to have a bottom lady, one who's taking care of you and running the other bitches. How to handle thirty, forty bitches at a time. How to make women make money for you, how to sex them and keep them giving you money. He told me everything a poor boy like me would need to know, to be successful with women, to get their money and hearts. I became very, very good at it and learned to appreciate the knowledge he gave me.

32
FIGHT MY WAY BACK IN

He never paid me or gave me any money, not ever. During the time I was with him, I worked with and for him, and he never gave me one dime. He fed me though and gave me a bed. And, he told me this, before he went back to prison. That I would have to go back to the projects, back to my mother's apartment and that I would have to gain entrance back into the projects, that I would have to fight my way back in.

33
CARRIED A BAT

Well I knew that. I was ready to fight. He said no, that I would have to hurt someone, one of the guys that hurt me. That I would have to hurt them bad, that they would have to know it came from me, but, be afraid to retaliate, and he told me what I had to do. Well, I had always carried a bat to protect myself, when I was growing up selling newspapers, kept it in my newspaper bag.

34
THROWING PEOPLE OFF THE ROOF

One of the guy's I went up against was known as Cliff. Cliff was especially cruel and was known for throwing people off the roof, as well as raping little girls. Two days before my father went up, I snuck into the project at night, went to Cliff's building on Ruggles St. Cliff was sitting on the benches with his boys, I knocked the lights out in the hallway and two floors up and down from Cliffs apartment, and waited in the dark inside the hallway near his apartment. I had known Cliff all my life, I knew what he smelled like and how he walked.

35
HE WAS DRUNK AND HE SMELLED

When he came I hit him hard on the side of his head, twice, and threw the bat down. When he came out the hospital, he made funny noises with his mouth and he walked with his head bent over and to the side. He was never right again, and the kids and people used to make fun of him. I never made fun of him. He went back and forth to jail a few times and the last time I saw him in Boston, back in the eighties, he was a raging queen, a faggot. He was drunk and he smelled.

36
I WAS BEAUTIFUL AND WOMEN LOVED ME

I'm sure I'll have to pay and answer for that, but, I hope whoever is taking names, that they'll remember, that maybe I saved a few little girls. I never had any trouble, anymore, in the projects. What I learned from all that was, that I had great courage, could stand up for the underdog, and that I was beautiful, and women loved me.

THE THIRD TIME

37
SHOT FIVE TIMES AND LIVED

The third time my father changed my life and saved me, was on November 11, 1968. My father was shot five times and four other men were killed in a storefront office called N.E.G.R.O (New England Grass Roots Organization) on lower Blue Hill Ave. The newspapers and television stations reported that he had been shot three times and three were killed, but, they found two more bullets later in the hospital and one of the other men died later. My sister and I would live through the same thing my mother's family had lived through twenty years before. A horrific violent crime broadcast throughout the state and nationally, because they were touted as civil rights leaders.

38
ONE HUNDRED THOUSAND DOLLARS

What they were was ex-cons who had found a way to con the state and government out of some money. I always believed that Guido St. Laurent, the Director, was real and had the best intentions for the organization. I knew my father and knew there was a scam behind it, and when he told me a few years later how he had set up the hit because he thought that Guido had one hundred thousand (government given) dollars in a hidden safe and how he had recruited the Campbell brothers to break in and rob the place, and that the Campbell brothers had turned on him and tried to kill him, well, I knew that was the truth. I wrote about it in a short story I called, "The Life", and won a short story award at U. Mass.

39
BODIES WERE BEING FOUND

But, on November 11, 1968, my father was being touted as a community leader who had been shot and the "dead" others were being eulogized as community heroes. The violence was extraordinary and for months and years afterwards bodies were being found, related to the N.E.G.R.O. shooting. Finally, that June 1969, the Campbell brothers were acquitted because my father wouldn't identify them, saying he would take care of them himself. His true colors and criminal record surfaced for all to see and he and all of us were ostracized and scorned once again.

40
DRINK AND GET HIGH

But, my father was changing my life, and my life would be saved. On November 11, 1968 when I was one month from seventeen years old and now eighteen years old, I had no idea what grade I was in. I hadn't been to school since 1966, except to fuck around with the girls, get high, fight, and make fun of the teachers. I was lost, all I did was drink and get high.

41
GIVE US ALL BLOW JOBS

I belonged to a gang in Grove Hall, a fighting gang, a gang that believed in getting high; by drinking, bombers, heroin, pills, glue, anything that got you high. We had two white girls named Dottie and Anne who would come from Malden on the weekends to hang with us and give us all blow jobs. Since 1966 when I joined the gang I did nothing but, get high and write poetry, I'm sure I had some lucid moments but I can't really remember any.

42
I HATED MY MOTHER

I hated my mother and my family, except for my cousins and I still had nothing really to do with my sister.

43
SUCKED MY DICK LIKE A DOG

In January of 1968, when I was seventeen, I met a twenty-three-year-old woman named Rosa. She had her own apartment and all the scotch, rum, and liquor I could drink and she sucked my dick like a dog. She had everything I needed, so I was never home. I never had to see my mother or sister or Randy, and I never had to go to school.

44
UP FRONT AND PERSONAL VIOLENCE

My best friends in the gang were The Mighty Hawk, a raging alcoholic; CP, a stone psychopath; The Hunter; and Petey, a heroin addict and our leader. I was

TC, Freddie the Lover or Freddie. We were a gang of about thirty who traveled to parties in tens, started fights over other gangs' bitches. We were pretty boys, who could and liked to fight. I carried and had carried since I was fourteen, two switchblade knives and knew how to use them well. I would buy knives and carry knives for many years. I loved up front and personal violence.

45
ROCKED WITH THE LATEST JAMS AND GET HIGH SMOKE

We would rob some places, only businesses, not people. We would do crime and fuck with the police. But, I know our main thing was getting high. I had been living like this for years. I had no other life. I loved my life. I was free and could get high anytime I wanted to. I had lots of girlfriends, but, Rosa was my bottom lady, kept me rocked with the latest jams, get high smoke and all the liquor I could drink.

46
ISN'T THAT YOUR FATHER

This is how I was living on November 11, 1968. And then my life changed. When my father was shot, I got noticed, people started to notice me. The kids were first. They said, *isn't that your father?* The people in the street; the prostitutes, pimps, drug people, said, *isn't that your father?* When I went to school the teachers and the good kids said, *isn't that your father?* I was a mess, I probably smelled, I was a ragamuffin, unloved and unwashed. But, I looked totally opposite of what I was. I looked soft, I fooled many people over the years, until I would bite.

47
FOUR LAPS AT THE BOYS CLUB

So, when I went to Dorchester High at the beginning of December 1968, I was just there to get high and walk the hallways with my knives, and fool around with the good girls who were giving me some attention because of my father being shot. And this white guy, who I remembered was the headmaster, came up to me, and said, I know what happened and that Fred Rose is your father. He said, "If you can swim four laps at the Boys Club, I'm going to graduate you."

48
SEXUALLY MOLESTED AS A CHILD

I almost spit on him; but, I looked down on him and said, "I can swim four laps." One of the things I did as a child to get away from my mother was to join the Boys Club and the YMCA where I became a champion swimmer and where I became the only person in my family, outside of my grandmother, to be sexually molested as a child. I was eleven years old and probably the staff man at the YMCA saw me, always there alone, no parents, nobody interested in me.

49
GET SOME MORE MONEY

He invited me down the basement steps one day and played with my pee pee and gave me a bunch of quarters, when I asked him what he had done, he said one day I would know. I ran home to the projects and my mother was sitting on a bench, I showed her the money and said the guy at the YMCA had given it to me. She took the money from me and put it in her bag. I went back to the Y the next day looking for the man so I could get some more money, but they said he had quit. I looked for him all the time for a while, wanting the money. (I understand completely why and how kids get picked up and killed.)

50
SWAM THE FOUR LAPS

Anyway Mr. Harrison, who has risen to sainthood in my mind today, kept his word. I swam the four laps and graduated from Dorchester High School, with kids I hardly knew, with a ninth grade education. I swam the four laps that December and never went back to Dorchester High again, never took a test, never did nothing, but walk up there and get a diploma. Without Mr. Harrison, I would have been a High School dropout and would never have been the person I am. I would have died a long time ago like Petey, in jail, with a heroin needle in my arm. Without Mr. Harrison, there would be no me and no you. I pray for his forgiveness at how I treated him and thank him always, for noticing me, for seeing me.

51
MY PAIL, MY MOP, MY BROOM

In May 1969, my mother moved from the projects to 77 Jacob St., but, it was too late for me. I was gone. I was lost, but, I did have that High School degree. My mother told me either I get a real job or get out. I saw a job in the paper at a nursing home on Townsend St. and went down to apply for the job. The man let me in and showed me my pail, my mop, my broom, how to lift the old ladies up and wipe their pee and shit down, how to put the rubber mats underneath them, how to wash the floors. He showed me my life, he showed me what my life could look like. He walked me to the door and said, "I'll see you Monday". And then GOD took my hand and walked me down to Washington St., then to Egleston Station.

52
BECOME A GOOD CATHOLIC AND GO TO MASS

I knew GOD, I had put myself in St. Francis De Sales Parochial School. When I was eight years old in the fourth grade. When I was seven and eight I used to go up to the rectory and get food for my sister and me. There were two Priests. One was Monsignor. Kerr, the other, was Caribbean-American, his name was Father Paul Francis. He asked me one day if I would like to come to the school, I said yes, he came and talked to my mother and said that he would have the Diocese pay for my tuition from the fourth to the eighth grade, if I would become a good Catholic and go to Mass.

53
BEEN A RAPIST OR MURDERER

Father Paul Francis kept his promise and to this day I have kept mine. While my mother was killing me, the Priest and Nuns were trying to save my life, and they did. Without those wonderful saints, I know that I would have turned out much worse. Without having that little knowledge about GOD and goodness that they gave me, I would have been a rapist or murderer of women, which is what happens to most boys who are severely abused by their mothers.

54
I KNEW GOD

So on that June day I knew GOD, and GOD took my hand and put me on the bus to downtown Boston. I had no idea where I was going. To this day, I have no idea of where I was going. I got off the bus at Tremont St. and walked up the street and I saw a sign that said "Uncle Sam Wants You". I remember to this day thinking, "Somebody wants me". I walked in there, and the white guy said, and this is verbatim "Oh you made it, good. Where do you want to go?"

55
LEAVE RIGHT NOW

Now, I don't know where there's anywhere to go, since I've never been anywhere. Nobody in my family had ever taken me anywhere. No trips, no nothing. So the only place I know to go that this guy with a uniform is asking me to go to, is Vietnam, I had seen that place on TV, with other people in uniforms. So that must be where you go. I told him Vietnam. He said no problem we can get you there. He asked me to sit down and asked some questions. I asked if I could leave right now. He said no, that I would have to wait a month.

56
I COULD GET OUT

I signed all the papers and left knowing that in a month anything could happen to me. But, I left knowing that GOD and me had found out that I didn't have to be in the ghetto anymore. I had a diploma, I could leave, I could get out.

57
SHE WAS INSANE

I went to Rosa's but I left after a few days, we were just getting high all the time and I was tired of that. I went back to my mother's, but, she was insane. I went to a friend of mine in the projects and crashed there and then I went to CP's house where we began to go on a crime spree.

58
A DRUNKEN DOG

I then stayed with my uncle's girlfriend on Blue Hill Ave. and partied with her for a week while my uncle was in the hospital in some more therapy. She was a drunken dog, but we had fun at all the bars, hanging out, go back to her place and do everything to her. My uncle and her had adjacent apartments, so I'm in there one morning in the bed with her and he comes in, but, he can't see. So she takes him in another room and starts fuckin him. I get my clothes, go out to the ledge and climb down.

59
DOING CRIME WITH A GUN

CP, The Hawk, Petey and me start doing crime with a gun and robbed this stadium at the end of June. Petey is so high on heroin that he just stands there with the gun going AuUUUUU. I take the gun from him and leap over the counter and tell the guy to give up the money. I take the money, give it to CP and race up to the street in my flip flops. There is a bus at the top of the hill and I get on it. The bus driver sees me get on and shortly the police come and ask the driver if they had seen anybody running through. I'm sitting there holding my breath, looking out the window, being cool. The white bus driver waits a beat, looks at them and then says no. The police get off and he rides down the hill with me on it.

60
PAPER BAG SANDWICH

I go back to Rosa's for a few days and then to my mother's house. My mail is there and they want me to come to the Army base in South Boston on July 11, 1969. I make it till then, and leave from my mother's house, with a paper bag sandwich, and no goodbyes. I was eighteen years old and I never came back to live in her house again.

61
A DRUG ADDICTED, ALCOHOLIC,
GANG MEMBER WHO WROTE POETRY

On July 11, 1969, I walked out of the real ghetto, alone, a drug addicted, alcoholic, gang member. A criminal; a physically, mentally, emotionally and sexually abused child, who wrote poetry. I took that walk to the United States Air Force and I've never stopped walking, never stopped learning, never stopped trying, never stopped.

THE BEGINNING

62
EIGHTEEN-YEAR-OLD POOR GHETTO BOY

That eighteen-year-old poor ghetto boy, could have never imagined the places he'd go, the things he'd see. I did get to Southeast Asia, just like the recruiter said, become a Crew Chief for F-4D Phantom Jets, and came back an Honorably Discharged—Disabled American Military Veteran.

63
STRANGERS

Since I was sixteen I have been on my own and handled my life, every day. I've made hundreds of mistakes, and had hundreds of successes, hurt hundreds of people, been hurt by hundreds of people, helped hundreds and been helped by hundreds. I took that walk, with no one to talk to, no one to give me advice and help except strangers, and everyday I've tried to better myself and drag as many as I can with me, with honor.

64
HOW FAR I'VE COME FROM WHENCE I CAME

When I received an *Official Resolution* from Boston City Councilor Charles C. Yancey and the City of Boston on January 14th, 2009 for my achievements in the Music and Book industries, and spoke in the Boston City Hall, City Council Chamber, it was one of the proudest moments of my life. When I received *Gold and Platinum Albums and Golden Reel Awards* for my work in the music business, when I received *the NAACP Image Award for Outstanding Literature* in 2013, all I could think of was, "how far I've come, from whence I've come from". On my own will and initiative, I crawled out from under the squalor I was born in and came from, and made something of myself.

65
THE AIR FORCE TRAINED ME

The Air Force trained me, to, *as I look out for myself to look out for others.* The road was hard and rough, but, I never whined, felt sorry for myself, or blamed others about the cards I'd been given. What I did do was try hard to become the best man I could and to restore my family's name. And I have done that. In this country and other countries and especially in my home town, Boston, when they hear my name, they think of success, not some criminal, and when you meet people who know me, you can hold your head up with pride.

66
NO REAL FAMILY

I have worked hard to be what I never knew how to be, a father and a parent. I had no idea what being a father or parent was. I had no uncles, no brothers, no family of any consequence. Nothing. They taught me nothing and never, ever, gave me anything. I had no idea what a father did, what a mother did.

67
FORGIVE HER AND TRY TO UNDERSTAND HER PAIN

I first heard my mother say she was proud of me in 2005. I brought her to live near me, when she needed me, not because I loved her, but, because I am a good son. Over time I have learned to try to love her, and to truly, with the help and love of God, forgive her and try to understand her pain, then and now.

68
TRY TO RESPECT MY MOTHER AND FATHER

I have always, even at their worst, somehow, try to respect my mother and father. When my father needed money in 1986 to pay the taxes on my Grandmére's house I paid $16,000 in back taxes. When he needed money for a cancer problem in 1988, I left a $15,000 check for him with my attorney, and he picked it up. He died a few months or so later, but, I know that he used that money for his pain and that the medication and money gave him some comfort before he died. When my mother needed a home I bought her one.

69
MAYBE A CARD FOR MY BIRTHDAY

I have helped my family hundreds of times over the years. My sister I gave fifteen thousand dollars to, so that she could buy her first condo, and she used that money to move on up. I've spent thousands of dollars in putting my mother in a home near me and have spent thousands more to keep her there and made her life free and easy. I have helped and tried to be there for all of you with money, love, advice, my time, my energy, my passion and love for all of you and never asked for anything but your love back, and maybe a card for my birthday.

70
HAVE A BABY, GO BACK TO SCHOOL

And the rest of my early life, well, I would get married and have a baby, go back to school and go to college on the GI Bill, get a great job with the City of Boston, buy my first home on the GI Bill at twenty-one years old and have great success in the music and book worlds.

71
SHIT HAPPENS

And, as it happens with most ghetto kids, shit happens, and by twenty-two years old, I would lose my wife, child, home and job and it would get worse, a whole lot worse, before it would get better, and then even worse, and then better, and then one day better, and one day, even more better, but, that's another story, that's another book or two, and I can honestly say, "I've done well, from whence I've come. And so that's "How My Father Changed My Life and Saved Me".

POEMS FROM THE SIXTIES

BY TONY ROSE

Fade out in a dream and mixed conversations

NOVEMBER 27, 1968

"If you don't know what I mean, then you can't have a meaning for what you don't know, understand"—Fredro

I woke up to standing room only, after I had been washed ashore by them waves, but it was a little too late to go into that song and dance routine, after all, everybody and nobody had seen that. So I proceeded to stand there and glare, I might have exposed myself, if I hadn't decided that I might repulse them as they repulsed me and thus lose my identity of being the only one to feel this sense of nausea, which is actually very pleasing to those of us who must face this sort of thing all the time. It does get kind of depreciating to have to be bombarded with all this and more; still though, I seem to feel that my relationship with the throngs might somehow be of some good.

You know I was just thinking the other day; how good it was to have attained this high position in life. After I thought it I had to burst out laughing from the sheer actuality of having thought that. I could have gone into shock, might have too, but then that knock came on the door, and I was pulled under by Channel #5, Jean Nate bath oil and Norform Douche Tablets. After all of that I decided to skip the day and retain my sense of depression by just farting through it. Which is something I seem to do very well, you know I farted through one day a total of 293 times, I might have a world's record or something, I don't know. You know all this black awareness is getting to me, all the time having to be aware.

And talk about everyday nothings! Unconsciously I awoke to a screaming thought that maybe it was I who had dreamt this nothing of life, but so would others, I'm not alone here! There are millions who dream, nothing happens, but still life goes on. It's made to happen that way. I know it doesn't seem as though all this could possibly be happening, I hope not because if all this tranquility is real, then what are we being so desperate about? I know, it must be the scene we're in today, act 1, act 2, act 3, etc., and all that, yet we try to play it through, because it's fun having to live. And you know that to be true! it really is, if it wasn't you would be dead and not really existing in your mind and ways.

No! It's not so, not if you want to believe you're really dead, extremes and all them hardship cases of pure soul. Ha, it's hell now? Wait until you can count the screaming few, who'll really be existing for a cause, if there are any left to speak of. And while you're waiting for whatever it is your waiting for, try not to think how long you've been waiting for it, you might actually die before it comes, but, there must be lots of things to do in this mind of ours, that's what it is you know, yeah, it's just a mind and you're trapped right in yourself, engraved forever with you, ha, ha, poor soul, that's too bad. But, I've got mine too, forever! Rewards sometimes come too late!

You know! It must have surprised a lot of people when you started with them long steeples.

And how did you feel when they weren't surprised anymore 'cause, you were strung out and dead.

And whatever for and what for, did we do that for, I mean, it wasn't even cool, not really, but! But, you know all those un-together times, doing it, doing you, to me and dyyyyyyyyying to boot and then not wanting to return, to an unrealistic realism, and you thought that you had won, and you wasn't even yourself, because you wasn't cool, at the time.

Prelude to Conversations – March 1967

Not too loud, brothers and sisters
least the man hear you, (like he usually does)
You're bad, keep cool, don't be no fool,
just because you didn't go to school
I mean, like, you have to have, some intelligence (to drop out)
Wow, you're a real super cool, your sister pimps your mother
and you tried your dog, girls, in parks, elevators, alleys, hallways,
and my bathtub.
Issac's a cool alcoholic, found with a transistor radio around his neck
and a bottle of T Bird wine in left back pocket
Wow, like a good fuck, is to lay and lay and lay it on her
Wow, great, but can you do it to her real good?
Thighs, mound, legs, breast, hair, face,
her body actions and make-believe love, with sweat
Wow! Over, you want to sleep, she wants to talk about her mother
Filled her body with mines and now she wants to talk about
her mother

CONVERSATIONS – APRIL 1967

Tired heart, tired people, tired longings, with overdue payments, on living expenses, on someone else's time.

Gregory

Jackson

Ty

Gerald

Amil

Deggie

Issac

Shelia

And many, many others, have all died in 1967. This is one night out of their lives, they, could not survive.

Setting - any steps, everyone is high or trying to get high. It is about 10:30 pm and it is a summer night. They will have between them .39 cents. It is nothing and tonight they will realize that.

Scene - Steps - 10:30pm

Jackson - Jesus is coming. He's going to...

Gerald - You ain't nothing Ty, you ain't no good, you ain't even going to do what you said, you ain't nothing Ty.

Ty - (Laughing) Are you taking my name in vain. Ty yi, Ty yi.

Jackson - I do believe that he's the one, my man! You know I used to....

More Conversations
Act 1

Amel - (He has on a long flowing multi-colored dashiki, with pink silk underwear on underneath, while sipping wine) this wine tastes bad, you know they even selling bad wine to us. Black people ought to.........

Gerald - (High Already) Kill them motherfuckers. (nods again)

Ty - (Singing to himself and humming and looking around, looks at Deggie, who's talking with Issac.)

Deggie - "Ha, ha, you was cool, when you wasn't high, ha, ha, look at you now, you look out there."

Issac - (Scratching his thigh, eyes rolling down) "Your mother was out there too last night, she was highhhhhh.

Ty - "Ti yi!" (still looking at Deggie) "Hey piss, pass me some wine!"

Deggie - (Taking another sip of wine, some of it dribbles down his chin) "Fuck you!"

Shelia - (While scratching her stomach) "You must have forgot I was here."

Gerald - "You want some dizope man? Or is you high already on Jesus?"

Amel - "That white Jesus."

Deggie - "In drag". "Ha".

Jackson - (Slowly smiling and looking exalted) 'Bump you, you clowns, that's why all of you are nothing, nothing! Because you can't be something and always be thinking of nothing, there must be something you think about." "You! You, Ty, what do you think about".

Ty - Another note (What he thought about all the time, is of course as American as apple pie, but due to environmental control, we choose to censure it).

(All in Chorus)

Amel - "Shut up!" (violent all of a sudden, he doesn't even realize why) "Shut up, you stupid motherfuckers. Jackson's right, what do we think about! Dope! How high we can get? (tone rising) Yeah, that's all, this is it, all of it. We're nothing but shadowless prints, implanted and embedded right here on these steps, we've always been here and we'll always be here, until someone guesses how really useless we are and removes us".

Gregory - "And how high are you, brother." (Gregory had been sitting, just sitting, not moving or speaking, Gregory has been thinking thoughts into this conversation, for he knows its talkers are as useless to themselves, as society is useless to them)

Amel - (Amel turns and looks upward towards the back and top of the steps where Gregory's voice came from. As he turns, he's puzzled by the seemingly unemotional, but angry sound in Gregory's voice and wonders what prompted him to speak as such)

Shelia - (Throughout this short and endless nothing, Shelia has become sick. Nobody pays attention to her as she throws up over the side of the steps)

Issac - "You alright, Shelia>" (Issac out of his nod, notices Shelia's plight, and realizes he might cop some.)

Shelia - "Yeah, help me to the back Issac."

Issac - "Sure baby". (Shelia and Issac move to the back to shoot up. Junkies make love to dope, not each other.)

Gregory - "Everybody here is going nowhere, why don't we just kill each other, it's quicker than just sinking away".

Ty - "We are killing each other, but you first".

Hunter - "Let's go in the back and get Shelia, I saw her go in the back with Issac". ((Ty, Petey, Hunter and Deggie go towards the shadows.)

Amel - "Ain't you going back there too Greg".

Gregory - "Naw, I spent two months going back and forth to the clinic because of her".

Amel - "Ha, ha, and they all gone back there, to her". (Amel and Gregory laugh together)

Act 2

(There isn't nothing in existence)

We're a joke, a great big complex joke, not allowed to laugh. We can't be real, not now, not again, not here. We should have been extinct decades ago, yet we still flourish, we're still abundant, still producing. Still wanting. Still hoping. Still hoping to get some when there is nothing for us to get, it's already been used, it's came and begot. There ain't nothing left for us. Why haven't we realized it yet? Because we don't want to, we have nowhere else to go, so we've decided to die here, without a struggle. We've also decided to help society along, if we have to die, and we must, we've decided to die cool, high. Society labored us, so we allow you to wallow in us. You won't crumble, you're too strong, but you'll remember us with your decadence. Society adapt yourself to us, not we to you, it's too late. We know there is nowhere for us to go, and I guess the majority of us have resigned ourselves to a slow nothing in death or a quick recovery in surviving. It really all depends on how many of us are still strong enough to withstand all the drawbacks.

Act 3

Jackson - (looking at Greg and Amel, watching them laugh. Thinking of why they were still here and what drew him back each night, why was it he was laughed at all the time and looked down upon, just for his belief in some-thing? Was it because they were scared to believe in anything else, as their earlier beliefs had gone into nothing. Nobody had anything to contribute. To have any hope or belief in their eyes meant leaving them behind, thus you have to be hated and scorned. No, he thought, they already consider themselves dead. Maybe they are right. Maybe we as a people are.

All in Chorus.

Hold up the tradition, onward with action, before, it's too late and we haven't lived a day.

(November 27, 1966, 104 murders in Boston, I knew some.)

Peace and love.

The Projects and Jail - September 18, 1968

Red walled and useless to the eye and all that musky smell tearing and touching all through your imprisoned glob of flesh. Standing up only, room only signs, and you, for the first time in what you know won't be the last time, make believe that you're not where you are; singing birds, green grass, lakes and girls and girls, and more shy then clouds can cover, forgetting you, and staring up and forgetting what you remembered; remembering where you are, clang, clang, doors clang tightly shut against you, protecting you from whatever they are protected from, and it smells so bad in here, and it's cold and dark, and it's un-touching your touched eyes, from this perverted and distorted magnet that clings to your very body, fungus from the countless hollers and screams that have come in this very place where you now lay.

The walls close and so do your lids. Wail sirens wail and bells ring and boots stomp and men scratch, moans are heard, toilets flush and doors clang. Castle keepers are heard to shout, walls are creaking, orders are passed, men move about, you're watched by all that moves and what doesn't watches too. You crunch and munch your scenery and you fill your glass of air as you look up the ceiling reaches you in one fast blinding motion, you remember, colors and shapes and sizes and smells and, and you remember it all.

This place has no time and existence only has a color scheme; it's hell to pay for existing, the walls might gather your screams, and passing time is an endless adventure of endless corridors and thoughts which are recorded in a moment of time, by these very walls which record all that you look, it measures your face and scans your movements and remembers your thoughts and laughs at your array of distortions; the floor falls back from you and you wait for whatever it is you're waiting for; you hear laughter and you feel as helpless as when you squat, forgiven already is tomorrow, for sure, you can't hate if there is nothing there to hate.

Stomp, boots stomp and you wonder if that was you or your echo. Clang, doors clang shut, you lay and all the torments are piled on you. The walls laugh as they reach inward and pull out the gray depressors, ah, how large they look, how somber they are, as they look at you, look at them, waiting for you.

Scurry, rats scurry, all over, and you wage a fierce good battle for your very existence in sanity; you dare not get up for fear of having company when you return.

The sun shines bright on my home and illuminates my cage. I'm you, I am you, I say to the walls. I have known you and you have covered me and your stink in my breath, I am cold and no amount of hell can warm me. It is gray and images are less than shadows.

Turmoil and utter confusion reign behind those walls, hate is king, and lust is queen. Suspicion is essential behind those walls, inside it is dark, it is a wasteful bondage to those who inhale it, unreality has no real greatness for the men and their prison, if you listen hard enough with your eyes, you can see that the wall really does talk, sometimes you add in another voice that's insizzored in your brain for life.

Bree, whistles bree, lights glare all over the walls, blinding you, back and forth, covering all, missing no spot. The walls whisper, whisper, doors will shut, men will riot; the walls are alive now; it as not some electric source that aroused this condemned fortress; the walls echo with shouts, from deep down they are coming, from deep down they start, until the roar crashes against the walls, until the noise is so deafening, as to make you realize the horror you are living; and you lie, and you weep, and you remember; pretty, soft, music, slowly dancing, whispering creeping lakes, tranquility; and you hear shouts, walls, ceilings, bars, doors clang, and you scream and you hide behind the noise, and you rush, rush on.

Head, noise, walls, and you; masses, arms firing, and you scream, blood, red walled and useless to the eye and all that musky smell tearing touching all through your imprisoned glob of flesh, standing up only signs, and you for the last time make believe you're not where you are, and you then remember.

GOD SAVE THE DOPE - MARCH 21, 1969

Hey! Black people
what you doin your own race in for
I mean we love life too
O, you talk of love and love one another
Unity in one cause for Hicks
Man you dead, dead, dead
Rose love yourself, don't die
can't die, can't live either
in this world, kill him, before he kills you/yourself
Run cowards of night, curse your deeds
You motherfuckers of hells hopelessness
all cursed by your mother's deeds of shame
Live on, live on Rose
Give your name Rose
He loves to live, to give
Save us O race, save us O race, save us O race
A man died last night, why
Tears don't be shed for naught, and shame
Be torn, least you cry a bitch before you shit
Man who wants to live a life of shit and
Ahhhhhhhhhhhhhhhhhhhhhhhhhhhhhhhhhh
God save the dope!

MURDER REDUX

*The following is an excerpt reprinted with permission from "Gangsters of Boston"
by George Hassett.*

New England Grass Roots Organization (N.E.G.R.O.)
Guido St. Laurent and Frederick Rose

NOVEMBER 13, 1968

THE N.E.G.R.O. OFFICE - 370 BLUE HILL AVENUE ROXBURY, MASSACHUSETTS

It was 3:45 a.m. but the small Civil Rights office was full, with five men speaking of plans for the future. The next day, the first installment in an almost two-million-dollar government contract was expected to arrive. But Guido St. Laurent, the blind man who led the activist storefront from obscurity to Civil Rights prominence, could feel uncertainty in the voices of the men in his office.

The tension could have been due to the three men expected to arrive; a crew of infamous gangsters looking for a piece of the $1.9 million grant. Tonight, the Campbell Brothers, the crime bosses of Roxbury, would try to muscle in on the Civil Rights movement. St. Laurent, Fred Rose and the other men in the basement were no strangers to crime, though—except for Ronald King, an anti-poverty worker from Cleveland, each man there had a criminal record.

In particular, St. Laurent and his longtime friend Carnell Eaton had risen to black power prominence after stints in prison. In 1956 the two men robbed the office of a Mission Hill housing project, entering with handkerchiefs covering the lower half of their faces. They tied up six people and St. Laurent hit one in the back of the head before they emptied a vault of $1,085. St. Laurent was sentenced to 18 to 20 years in prison and Eaton 10 to 12 years.

Official prison reports say St. Laurent was blinded when a barbell slipped from his grip and hit him on the head, irreparably damaging his eyes. Other reports indicated rival inmates may have been involved.

St. Laurent later counted his blinding as a positive event—a turning point.

"It wasn't until I was blinded that I began to see,"

He said, explaining that he would have probably spent the rest of his life in and out of prisons if the blinding had not made him think about ways to use his skills constructively.

In 1963 St. Laurent was released from prison. Two years later, he opened the small storefront office on Blue Hill Avenue and named it N.E.G.R.O. for New England Grass Roots Organization. He described it as a public relations office for Boston's black neighborhoods "to let the world know about the people in the black community doing the little things that never get attention from the press because they aren't sensational."

Equipped only with a few telephones, St. Laurent set up contacts with the press and publicized small, positive activities such as a group of teens building their own recreation lounge and mothers campaigning for a stoplight. He held job forums to publicize the "10-mile gap" between employers and Boston's black neighborhoods and the lack of transportation that contributed to urban unemployment. He kept the office open 24 hours a day and quickly built a reputation as a local leader to watch.

His old crime partner, Carnell Eaton, was also pivotal in St. Laurent's development as a Civil Rights figure. Sarah Ann Shaw, a Civil Rights activist who would go on to become the first black woman to work as a television news reporter in Boston, says it was probably Eaton who first brought St. Laurent into the movement.

After his release from prison, Eaton was a reliable member of Boston's grass-roots activism community. In one campaign, Eaton worked with the Boston Action Group to demand that Wonder bread and Hood Milk hire local black drivers. After marches and calls to boycott, Eaton was hired at Hood.

"Carnell was very outspoken," Shaw says. "He said what he wanted to say when he wanted to say it. He was very pro-black, very much for the community."

THE RIOT THAT WASN'T

The high point of N.E.G.R.O.'s leadership came in April 1968 when St. Laurent, Rose and Eaton helped keep Boston streets safe after Dr. Martin Luther King Jr.'s assassination. St. Laurent had operated citizen band radios as a hobby after his blinding—experience that would come in handy as Boston threatened to burn.

The morning after King's death, Washington Street and Blue Hill Avenue—the black community's two principal thoroughfares—were pocked with smashed windows and burned-out stores. A leaflet distributed by the Black United Front said flatly,

"Non-violence is dead. The Black Community Faces Disaster."

As tensions rose, N.E.G.R.O. and St. Laurent counseled caution. He set up a radio communications network for a team of volunteers, mostly young black men and women, who had formed their own Roxbury Youth Patrol. The volunteers reported fires, kept track of crowd disturbances, transported Roxbury citizens to their homes, carried the injured to hospitals and phoned for legal help for those arrested. They also passed out leaflets that afternoon saying,

"Cool it. The riot squad has M-16 rifles-Mace-a machine so high pitched it will make you deaf."

They urged young people to stay home that night and watch James Brown perform live at the Boston Garden on local television. "Don't go downtown brothers," the patrol said. "Stay home. Put on the TV and watch cool James do his thing."

N.E.G.R.O. was the central communications office for all the action. St. Laurent relayed calls from volunteers in the street to the fire and police departments. Partly as a result of his efforts, Boston began to cool off. Within days, peace had been restored with relatively mild damage to the community—21 injured, 30 arrested, barely $50,000 in damage. This was small compared with what happened in many of the 197 other towns and cities where riots broke out in the aftermath of King's assassination.

Just a few years earlier St. Laurent was an anonymous, blind prison inmate. Now, on the night of King's assassination, he was credited by the Boston Police Department with preventing serious outbreaks of violence in the city. However, St. Laurent would always be distrusted: by other Civil Rights figures who questioned his motives; by Boston cops who resented St. Laurent's security patrol that observed police actions in Roxbury; and by the FBI who stepped up their surveillance of him after he stopped the riot.

On Blue Hill Avenue, even St. Laurent's neighbors looked at N.E.G.R.O. with suspicion. The office was located on a strip of the avenue so dotted with community action groups it was known as Agency Row. By the time St. Laurent showed up in mid-1966, many of the agencies had been established in the community for a decade or more. When he was awarded a huge federal grant within two years, "The community was very suspicious about how Guido had hooked up these federal funds and we were all watching to see how this was going to work out," said Shaw, an activist on Agency Row before her television career. "We never knew if Guido was out for the community or just out for Guido. He was very power hungry and could be very cutting in his remarks. I felt he was a bully."

The FBI was also suspicious. As COINTELPRO, their campaign of dirty tricks against Civil Rights leaders, intensified, the feds were monitoring St. Laurent too. At least five informants were sharing information with the FBI about St. Laurent's daily activities and meetings. "Subject [St. Laurent] described by one source as vicious and has talked in terms of mass destruction where white men are concerned," said a confidential FBI report. One FBI informant claimed St. Laurent was collecting guns, hand grenades, nitroglycerin and holding classes to make fire bombs.

On June 8, 1968, Boston Police stopped St. Laurent's station wagon with the vanity plate N.E.G.R.O. They found a .38 caliber revolver in the tire wheel, a bayonet under the dashboard and two machetes in the back seat. St. Laurent told police he had written permission from Mayor Kevin White to carry the weapons. The police checked with City Hall and handed the weapons back. St. Laurent went on his way.

Although Eaton and St. Laurent had grown from convicted armed robbers to well-known Civil Rights figures in the community, some tension remained. "There was always a rivalry between Cornell and Guido for who would be the one in control," Shaw said.

On this morning, in the basement office on Blue Hill Avenue, they were unified though; if only as a defense against a more serious threat.

The men they were expecting were the notorious Campbell brothers, the crime bosses of Roxbury, and their top enforcer Dennis (Deke) Chandler.

THE CAMPBELL BROTHERS: BOSTON'S BLACK GODFATHERS

Before they ruled the Roxbury underworld, the Campbell Brothers had both been standout students at Boston Technical High School, with older brother Alvin earning a scholarship offer from Princeton University. However, he turned it down in favor of the family business of robbery—the Campbells' father was allegedly a skilled bank robber.

"The Campbells had a reputation. They were known to carry guns," **Shaw says. "They were scary guys. If you knew them they could be nice** **guys; but they were scary guys."**

In 1957, the Campbells robbed a bank in Canton of $32,000. Sentenced to 25 year terms in Leavenworth Federal Prison, the brothers formed an unlikely bond with infamous gangster and notorious racist Whitey Bulger.

In Howie Carr's *Hitman*, John Martorano relates what Whitey told him about his friendship with the Campbells. "[Whitey] told me later he'd been working out one day in the weight room in Leavenworth, and he heard some guys talking behind him. It was pretty obvious from their accents that they were from Boston, and when Whitey turned around he couldn't believe they were black. It was the Campbells. They used to all walk the track together at Leavenworth, around and around and around, just talking about Boston."

A successful appeal freed the brothers after just four years. They were released to a different world: the new ideas and reforms of the 1960s were in full swing and older brother Arnold got a job with Action for Boston Community Development. "I came from their ranks," he said of the hardcore unemployed men he worked with, "so I could relate to them."

When the Campbells continued carrying guns and extorting cocaine dealers their sincerity to the movement was questioned. "They were the same gangsters they always had been," says Rodney Draffen, a drug dealer from that time. After Draffen and his brother started a small but lucrative operation they heard the Campbells were coming for a cut.

"They had back up too—that was their whole thing." They'd say, 'If **you don't believe me I'll get the mob to come after you and kill your** **family.' And every time you turned around, someone they messed with** **was getting shot and killed."**

The Campbells must have noticed Roxbury had more federal money coming in than cocaine profits. The problem was St. Laurent and N.E.G.R.O. had already gained control of the $1.9 million grant. Carnell Eaton offered the Campbells jobs, in middle management. When the Campbells heard about a quick trip St. Laurent, Rose, and Eaton made to New York with Ronald Hicks, and out of town activist Ronald King, they started to think they were missing a big payday.

Now, the Campbells were on their way to 370 Blue Hill Avenue to see St. Laurent, Eaton and the others about how to divvy up the federal money. One party not in the room but integral to the rising confrontation was federal subcontractor Woolman Systems, a mysterious defense firm that fit the term 'poverty pimp' better than St. Laurent, Rose or the Campbells did.

POVERTY PIMPING THE FEDERAL GOVERNMENT

The Campbells' sudden political awakening was not unusual for gangsters in the 1960s. Gang leaders in major cities across the U.S. were turning street credibility into federal funding during the last, liberal days of the war on poverty. It was the era captured in Tom Wolfe's essay "Mau-Mauing the Flak Catchers" when known gangsters were given preference for government funding based on their criminal convictions.

"Corporations, politicians, well-meaning white liberals were all bending over backwards to show that they were not prejudiced, they weren't racist…"

In stepped Dr. Myron Woolman—an educator looking to profit from the war on poverty. The time was right: the government was suddenly pouring millions into urban revitalization projects and profitable corporations such as oil and gas firms were competing for millions.

In May 1966 Dr. Woolman was terminated from Lincoln Jobs Corp Center for charging excessive fees for educational work not being done. Woolman was quickly retained by Northern Natural Gas, also chasing anti-poverty money.

With the hiring of Woolman and connections in the Department of Labor and other federal agencies, Northern Gas was poised to implement a program in Roxbury to net them millions. That is, until Guido St. Laurent and NEGRO got in the way.

According to FBI reports, "NEGRO set out to stir up the community against an outsider like Northern coming into Roxbury and called instead for a local group like NEGRO to run the program."

Dr. Woolman saw a solution, however. He left Northern and approached St. Laurent with a deal to operate jointly, FBI documents reveal. Woolman formed Woolman Systems and won a $1.9 million grant from the Department of Labor.

From the beginning, Woolman and St. Laurent plundered it. St. Laurent and Fred Rose formed a for-profit venture that hoped to obtain $147,000 from the grant. On Nov. 12, Woolman hosted St. Laurent, Eaton, Rose, Ronald Hicks and King in New York City. They discussed how to divide the money and, in the case of King who was from Cleveland, how to expand their program to other cities.

Woolman had fought for the grant, even betrayed his original partner to team up with St. Laurent. Now, the multimillion dollar reward was near. It was Woolman, with some help from the Department of Labor, who put into motion these events. But he would not be in the Roxbury basement the next morning when it all came to a fatal tipping point.

MURDER SCENE

On that Nov. 13 morning the only regulators taking a close look at the grant money was the Campbell Brothers gang. According to Fred Rose, who survived the attack, the Campbells and Deke Chandler entered the headquarters and after pushing a gun into the face of Eaton made their way into the back office.

Rose later testified in court: "At one point one of the Campbell brothers, I think it was Arnold, pushed me into a chair. After I was in the chair I saw everyone had a gun in his hand. Carnell was standing in the middle of the floor saying 'What's this? What's this?'"

"Alvin then slugged Guido St. Laurent and the gun discharged. Arnold Campbell was standing over on the other side of the room and he slugged Ron Hicks. I hear Guido saying, 'Don't do that. I have a plate in my head.' Next I heard someone say: 'You won't feel it long baby.' Then Guido was shot in the chest."

Unluckiest of all may have been Ronald King, the only one in the basement without a criminal conviction. "Hey what's going on?" he asked the killers as they rushed him. "I just got here from Cleveland."

"Sorry, cuz, you should have stayed in Cleveland," one of the killers replied and shot him in the head.

Fred Rose and Ronald Hicks were shot but managed to survive. St. Laurent, Eaton and King each died. "No one was supposed to be left alive, that's for sure," said a Boston Police detective investigating the incident.

"This wasn't a case of an emotional outburst. It was simply a cold-blooded killing."

The triple murder was a shock to local activists and St. Laurent supporters mourned the loss of his leadership. "He was a man in the process of becoming," said one friend. "Tomorrow was his permanent address."

The murders also brought scrutiny to the manpower program. Little had been done; five months after the money was released only twelve men were enrolled. Woolman had announced each graduate would receive a job from local companies who pledged their support. In reality, the companies were only compelled to hire 40 of the 500 graduates.

In 1969 the $1.9 million grant to train 500 hardcore unemployed men was canceled.

AUTHOR BIOGRAPHY

Tony Rose, Publisher/CEO, Amber Communications Group, Inc.
NAACP Image Award Winner for Outstanding Literature
African American Publisher of the Year

Tony Rose is the Publisher/CEO of Amber Communications Group, Inc., the nation's largest African-American Publisher of Self-Help Books and Music Biographies; *The 2013 44th Annual NAACP Image Award Winner for Outstanding Literature; The Los Angeles Leimert Park Book Fair / Jessie Redmon Fauset Book Awards, "2014 African American Book Publisher of the Year"; and The Harlem Book Fair / Phillis Wheatley Book Awards "2013 African American Book Publisher of the Year".*

ACGI's imprints include: The NAACP Image Award-winning Amber Books Publishing; Amber Classics Books - Self-Help Reference Books;

Colossus Books - Music Biographies; Amber/Wiley Books - Self Help and Financial Books Co-Published with John Wiley & Sons Inc.; Joyner/Amber Books - Co-Publishing with the Tom Joyner Foundation and Desmoon Books - Fiction.

Tony Rose led the movement towards modern Independent Book Publishing for the African American Self-Publisher and Independent Book Publisher as we know it today.

In 2001 he responded to the needs of the growing market of self-publishers and founded Quality Press, the nation's largest "African American Book Packager For Self-Publishers", in order to accommodate authors who wished to self-publish their books, and placed the Quality Press Self-Publishers Book Division under the direction of Yvonne Rose who is also an Associate Publisher for Amber Communications Group, Inc. and the Director of Quality Press. Over the last fourteen years Quality Press has been responsible for turning many, many thousands of African American writers into Published Authors and Book Publishers.

In 2004 Tony Rose co-founded and became the Executive Director of The African American Pavilion at BookExpo America bringing together as exhibitors and attendees a community of thousands of African American book publishers and book publishing industry professionals, a feat that had been unprecedented in the over 100-year history of BookExpo America. In 2005 Rose founded the Katrina Literary Collective, which has been responsible for collecting and donating over 90,000 books for the Hurricane Katrina Survivors. He also serves as a founding Director of the Harlem Book Fair National and The Harlem Book Fair/Roxbury, Mass.

He is noted as the first African American Independent Publisher to ink a multi-book, multi-year, Co-Publishing/Imprint deal with a major book publisher (John Wiley & Sons, Inc.), and the first book publisher to have titles licensed by Black Expressions Book Club with thirty-five titles signed to date. In addition, Rose has acquired/licensed paperback rights from: Simon and Schuster, Harper Collins and Hyperion Books for publishing and distribution by ACGI.

He has also, successfully negotiated numerous world-wide partnerships, licensing and eBook licensing deals for ACGI in the United States, South Africa, Canada, Europe and Asia, setting the pace, signing a seven book exclusive eBook international licensing rights deal with K-tel International for Colossus Books.

On February 1, 2013, Amber Books, the award winning imprint of Phoenix, AZ based, Amber Communications Group, Inc., was announced as an *NAACP Image Award winner for "Outstanding Literary Work - (Youth/ Teens)"* - for its title, *"Obama Talks Back: Global Lessons - A Dialogue With America's Young Leaders"* by Gregory J. Reed, Esq. (Amber Books), and has earned an NAACP Image Award for Literature at the 44th Annual NAACP Image Awards Show, Shrine Auditorium, Los Angeles, CA.

On July 19, 2013, Tony Rose, Publisher/CEO, Amber Communications Group, Inc., was announced as the Harlem Book Fair / Phillis Wheatley Book Awards *"2013 African American Book Publisher of the Year"* at the 15th Anniversary of the Harlem Book Fair, in the Langston Hughes Auditorium, Schomberg Center for Research in Black Culture, New York City, NY.

Tony Rose was born in Roxbury (Boston) Massachusetts, raised in the Whittier Street Housing Projects, was honorably discharged from the U.S. Air Force after serving in the Vietnam War, and attended the University of Massachusetts, the University of California in Los Angeles and the New England Conservatory of Music, Boston, MA. He was employed as a production assistant at the Burbank Studios (Warner Brothers and Columbia Pictures), in the accounting and sales division at Warner/Electra/Atlantic Records (WEA), an accounts representative at Warren Lanier Public Relations and as an A & R representative at RCA Records, Los Angeles, California.

Rose returned to Boston and along with record producer Maurice Starr became the primary architect of that, which in the late 70's and 80's would be called "The Boston Black Music Scene" a movement that ultimately led to the discovery of the international blockbusters Prince Charles and the City Beat Band, The Jonzun Crew, New Edition and New Kids on the Block. In 1979 he formed Solid Platinum Records and Productions and in 1982 he was named one of the "Top Ten Record Producers in the World". Rose in the 80's held recording / production deals with Virgin Records, Atlantic Records and Pavilion / CBS/Sony Records.

Rose was a successful Executive Producer, Record Producer, Record Company Owner, Personal Manager, Music Publisher, Recording Studio Owner, Recording Engineer, Song Writer and Composer for more than fifteen years.

His Solid Platinum Records and Productions was the first African American production company to have a production deal with Virgin Records.

In 1983, albums produced by Rose *"Gang War"* and *"Stone Killers"* by Prince Charles and the City Beat Band reached Gold Album status and shared the charts with Michael Jackson's Thriller for six consecutive months in the number one, two and three positions throughout the world and his legendary "Prince Charles and the City Beat Band" albums *"Gang War"*, *"Stone Killers"*, *"Combat Zone"* and singles, have accounted for more than Four Million sold worldwide. Rose's many music awards include "Gold" and "Platinum" Albums and "Ampex Golden Reel" Awards for recording and engineering New Kids on the Block. Rose, has also penned *Before the Legend – The Rise of New Kids on the Block and …A Guy Named Maurice Starr – The Early Years,* published August 2008**.**

Rose is the recipient of several publishing awards including: *The 2013 44th Annual* **NAACP Image Award Winner for Outstanding Literature** - Best Literary Work (Youth / Teens), *Obama Talks Back: Global Lessons - A Dialogue With America's Young Leaders (*Amber Books*)*; *The 2015 First Read Expo Lifetime Achievement Awardee for Outstanding Literary Work and Leadership; The Los Angeles Leimert Park Book Fair / Jessie Redmon Faust Book Awards, "2014 African American Book Publisher of the Year";* The 2014 Blacks In Government-Greater Orange County CA Chapter Award for *"Outstanding Contributions and Service to the African American Publishing Community";* The Harlem Book Fair / Phillis Wheatley Book Awards *"2013 African American Book Publisher of the Year";* The City of Phoenix, Arizona - Office of the Mayor *"Official Resolution for Fifteen Years of Successful Book Publishing & the* 2013 *NAACP Image Award for Outstanding Literature",* The City of Boston and the Boston City Council *"Official Resolution for Success in the Music/Recording Industry and the Book Publishing Industry";* The 2008 Harlem Book Fair / Phillis Wheatley Book Awards *"For Literary Work That Transcends Culture, Boundary and Perception";* The Chicago Black Book Fair and Conference *"Independent Publisher/Press Award";* The BlackBoard Bestseller's *"African-American Publisher of the Year Award";* The American Library Association *"Reluctant Reader"* Award; The 1st YOUnity Book Reviewers, Disilgold Soul Magazine *"Publisher of the Millennium" Award";* The Diamond Literary Festival *"Certificate of Appreciation Award";* The Harlem Book Fair, Boston/Roxbury *"Charles C. Yancey" Literary Award*; The Commonwealth of Massachusetts, House of Representatives,

"In Recognition of Promoting the African American Experience Through the Literary World" Award"; The City of Boston *"Continuous Promotion of African American Authors"* Resolution; The Black Caucus of The American Library Association (BCALA) *"Appreciation Award";* The BookExpo America *"Founders Award";* The Haki R. Madhubuti *"Independent Publisher of Note* Award"; The City of Los Angeles, State of California, Leimert Park Village Book Fair, *Certificate of Appreciation, For Extraordinary Contributions to the African American Literacy Legacy Award";* The Los Angeles Black BookExpo, Certificate of Appreciation *"Outstanding Contributions in Promoting Black Literature Award"* and The Cape Verdean News *"Millennium Award for Book Publishing Excellence".*

He also has served as a Literary Sub-Committee Member in the Category of Non-Fiction Literature and Instructional Literature for the 2007 (38th), 2008 (39th), 2009 (40th), 2011 (42nd) and 2012 (43rd) NAACP Image Awards (Show); the Co-Founder and Executive Director of the African American Pavilion at BookExpo America, the Nation's Largest Book Publishing Trade Show from 2004-2010 and the Founder of Amber Communications Group, Inc.'s African American Pavilion Booth at BookExpo America, 2011, 2012, 2013.

Tony Rose, NAACP Image Award Winner was selected to be a part of the 46th Annual NAACP Image Awards Nomination Committee, responsible for voting on the submissions received for the NAACP Image Awards, which cover Television, Motion Pictures and Recording.

Among ACGI's most notable and diverse titles are: *An Investigation and Study of the White People of America and Western Europe; The Autobiography of an American Ghetto Boy; The Investigation and Study of the White People of America and Western Europe & the Autobiography of an American Ghetto Boy – From the Projects to NAACP Image Award Winner; Yoga Meditation and Spiritual Growth for the African American Community-If You Can Breathe, You Can Do Yoga and Find Inner and Outer Peace-The Ultimate Yoga Book for Beginners and the Young at Heart; Lady Gaga: Born to Be Free; Beyonce'-Before the Legend: The Rise of Beyonce' and Destiny's Child, The Early Years; Kanye West-Before the Legend: The Rise of Kanye West and the Chicago Rap & R&B Scene, The Early Years; Obama Talks Back: Global Lessons - A Dialogue with America's Young Leaders; The African American Criminal Justice Guide-Staying Alive and Out of Jail; The African American Scholarship*

Guide-Thousands of Scholarships and Grants for African American Students; The African American Employment Guide-Finding and keeping a Job; Ageless Beauty: The Ultimate Skincare and Makeup Book for Women and Teens of Color; The Revised Second Edition-Is Modeling For You? The Handbook and Guide for the Young Aspiring African American Model; Tom Joyner Presents: How To Prepare For College; African Americans and the Future of New Orleans; Beautiful Black Hair - Real Solutions To Real Problems; The African American Family's Guide to Tracing Our Roots; The Afro-Centric Bride - A Style Guide; African American History In The United States of America, An Anthology-From Africa To President Barack Obama, Volume One; Born Beautiful: The African American Teenagers Complete Beauty Guide; The African American Guide to Real Estate Investing; Lil Wayne: An Unauthorized Biography; Jay Z and The Roc-A-Fella Records Dynasty; How To Get Rich When You Ain't Got Nothing: The African American Guide To Obtaining and Building Wealth; Pay Yourself First: The African American Guide to Financial Success and Security; Aaliyah – An R & B Princess in Words & Pictures; Destiny's Child: The Complete Story; God Made Dirt: The Life and Times of Ol' Dirty Bastard; Memoirs of a Super Freak – The Confessions of Rick James; and Before the Legend: The Rise of New Kids On The Block and....A Guy Named Maurice Starr, The Early Years; Eminem and the Detroit Rap Scene: White Kid in a Black Music World; Amy Winehouse: Too Young To Die...Too Old To Live and Nicki Minaj: The Woman Who Stole the World.

Rose is the editor of numerous books and the co-writer of the national bestseller, ***Is Modeling for You? The Handbook and Guide for the Young Aspiring Black Model,*** written with Yvonne Rose, and has penned the critically acclaimed, international best-seller, ***Before the Legend: The Rise of New Kids On The Block and A Guy Named Maurice Starr, The Early Years***.

He has written, compiled, edited and published, the award winning, international best-seller, ***African American History In The United States of America—An Anthology—From Africa To President Barack Obama, Volume One***, a Top Ten Best African American Book and has recently written the critically acclaimed, international best-seller, non-fiction book of the year and a Top Ten Best Black Book of 2015, ***America the Black Point of View—An Investigation and Study of the White People of America and Western Europe & The Autobiography of an American Ghetto Boy—The 1950's and 1960's—From the Projects to NAACP Image Award Winner, Volume One***.

And has recently re-vised into a separate book An Investigation and Study of the White People of America and Western Europe and also re-vised into a separate book The Autobiography of an American Ghetto Boy.

For Further Information, Go To

WWW.AMBERBOOKS.COM / WWW.QUALITYPRESS.INFO /

WWW.AFRICANAMERICANPAVILION.COM OR

WWW.GOOGLE.COM and Google Search -
Tony Rose and Amber Communications Group, Inc. / Tony Rose and The African American Pavilion at BookExpo America / Tony Rose and Before the Legend: The Rise of New Kids On The Block and A Guy Named Maurice Starr, The Early Years / Tony Rose and Prince Charles and The City Beat Band / Tony Rose and Solid Platinum Records and Productions

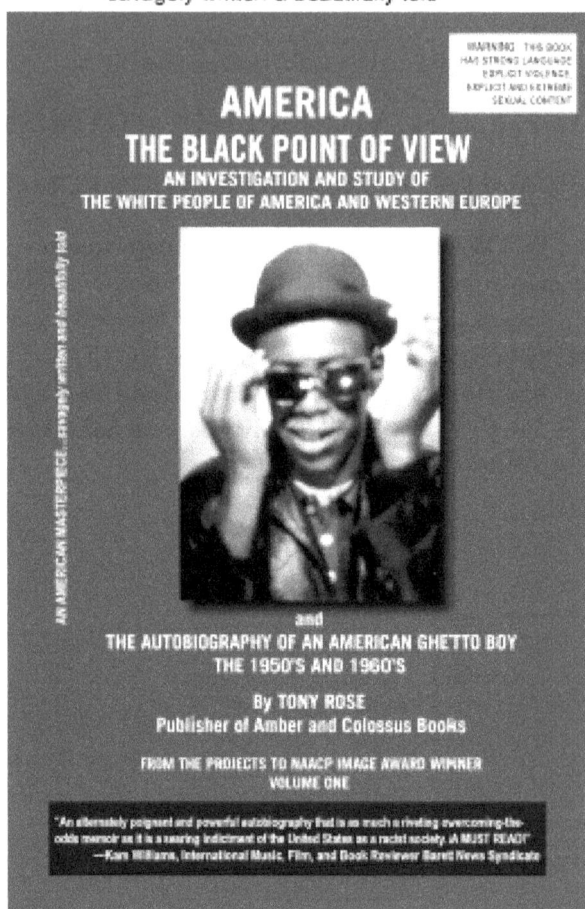

A TOP TEN BEST AFRICAN AMERICAN BOOK

- Kam Williams, International Music, Book and Film Reviewer

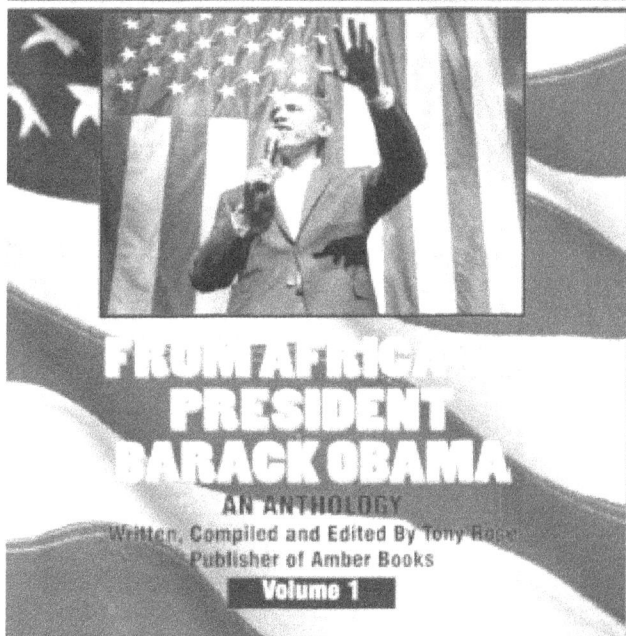

AFRICAN AMERICAN HISTORY

IN THE
UNITED STATES OF AMERICA

FROM AFRICAN
PRESIDENT
BARACK OBAMA

AN ANTHOLOGY

Written, Compiled and Edited By Tony Rose
Publisher of Amber Books

Volume 1

AMBER BOOKS

Paperback ISBN #: 978-0-9824922-0-8 - 432 PAGES / $17.95
eBook ISBN #: 978-1-937269-17-3 // $5.00

The history of Africans and African Americans and Europeans and European
Americans (Black and White people) in the United States of America

Books are available everywhere and at all on-line and digital sources,
including Amazon and BarnesandNoble.com
Contact: amberbk@aol.com for information

WWW.AMBERBOOKS.COM

SLAVERY, SEGREGATION
INSTITUTIONAL RACISM
Savagely written

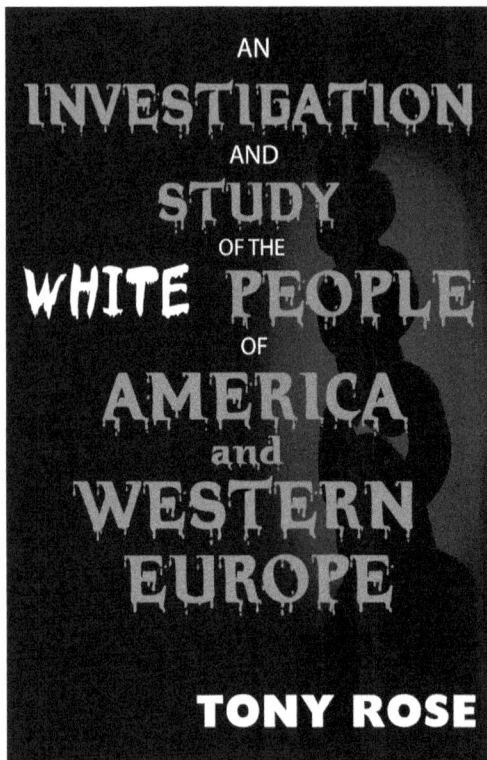

A CHILDRENS' STORY

Tens of millions of Black children locked away
in the segregated, redlined ghettos
and housing projects of America.

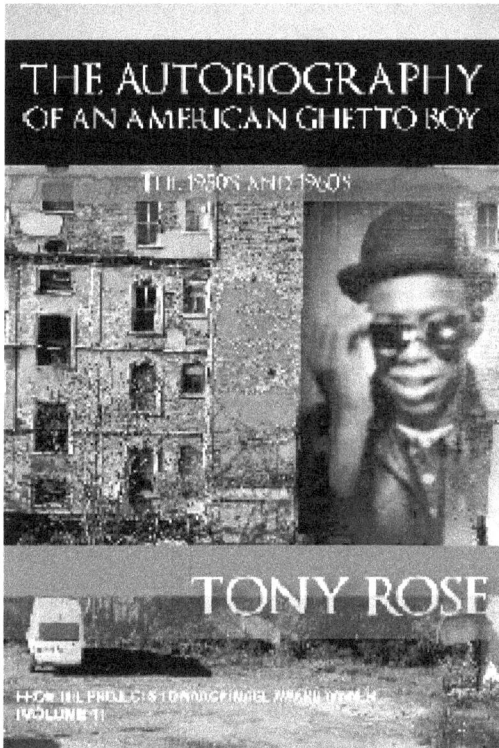

AMBER BOOKS
Paperback ISBN # 978-1-937269-52-4 / 412 PAGES / $19.95
eBook ISBN #: 978-1-937269-53-1 @ $6.00

"A poignant and powerful autobiography, a riveting overcoming-the-odds memoir. "
- Kam Williams, International Book Reviewer

"A lasting impression of the chaos, deprivation, and psychic ravages of the ghetto."
- David Rapp, Kirkus Book Review

Books are available everywhere and at all on-line and digital sources,
including Amazon and BarnesandNoble.com
Contact: amberbk@aol.com for information

WWW.AMBERBOOKS.COM / WWW.THEGHETTOBOY.COM

BOOKS BY TONY ROSE

- *An Investigation and Study of the White People of Western Europe and America (ISBN # 978-1-937269-48-7)*
- *The Autobiography of an American Ghetto Boy (ISBN # 978-1-937269-52-4)*
- *An Investigation and Study of the White People of Western Europe and America & The Autobiography of an American Ghetto Boy – The 1950's and 1960's -From the Projects to NAACP Image Award Winner, Volume One* (ISBN # 978-1-937269-50-0)
- *African American History In The United States of America - An Anthology - From Africa To President Barack Obama, Volume One* (ISBN # 978-0-9824922-0-8)
- *The Rise of New Kids On The Block and....A Guy Named Maurice Starr, The Early Years (*ISBN # 978-0-9790976-7-6)
- *Is Modeling For You? The Handbook and Guide for the Young Aspiring Black Model* (ISBN # 978-0-9790976-9-0)

ORDER FORM

**Mail Checks/Money Orders to: Amber Communications Group, Inc.
1334 East Chandler Boulevard – Suite 5-D67, Phoenix, AZ 85048**

Please send _____ copy(ies) of *The Autobiography of an American Ghetto Boy* by Tony Rose ($19.95)

Please send _____ copy(ies) of *An Investigation and Study of the White People of America and Western Europe* by Tony Rose ($15.95)

Please send _____ copy(ies) of *America The Black Point of View - An Investigation and Study of the White People of America and Western Europe and The Autobiography of an American Ghetto Boy, The 1950s and 1960s* by Tony Rose ($21.95)

Please send _____ copy(ies) of *African American History in the United States of America from Africa to President Barack Obama* by Tony Rose ($17.95)

Please send _____ copy(ies) of *Obama Talks Back: Global Lessons...A Dialogue for America's Young Leaders* by Gregory J. Reed, Esq. ($19.95)

Please send _____ copy(ies) of *The African American Family's Guide to Tracing Our Roots* by Roland Barksdale Hall ($14.95)

Please send _____ copy(ies) of *African Americans and the Future of New Orleans* by Philip Hart, Ph.D. ($16.95)

Name: _____

Address: _____City: St: Zip: _____

Phone:(_____) _____Email:_____

I have enclosed $_____, plus $5.00 shipping per book for a total of $_____.

For Bulk or Wholesale Rates, Call: 602-743-7211
Or email: Amberbk@aol.com
Please visit: WWW.AMBERBOOKS.COM

The Whittier Street Housing Projects where Tony Rose grew up from 3 to 18 years old.

THE HOUSING PROJECTS AND GHETTOS OF
AMERICA CHILDREN AT RISK FOUNDATION
1334 East Chandler Boulevard – Suite 5-D67, Phoenix, AZ 85048
Phone: 602-743-7211 / Email: amberbk@aol.com
WWW.THEBLACKPOINTOFVIEW.COM
WWW.AMBERBOOKS.COM

Mission: To give a HOUSING PROJECT AT RISK CHILD, exposure to another life, beyond the one that they are currently living in.

Dear Friend:

My name is Tony Rose. I am an abused child, who grew up in a bad environment, with bad parents, in a violent and poor housing project and I am the Founder/CEO of The Housing Projects and Ghettos of America Children at Risk Foundation.

I am an *NAACP Image Award Winner for Outstanding Literature* and the award winning Publisher/CEO of Phoenix, Arizona based, Amber Communications Group, Inc., the nation's largest African-American Publisher of Self-Help Books and Music Biographies.

I was born in Roxbury (Boston) Massachusetts, raised in the Whittier Street Housing Projects, honorably discharged from the United States Air Force, a disabled American Veteran; and attended the University of Massachusetts, the University of California in Los Angeles, and the New England Conservatory of Music. I later became a world-renowned, Gold and Platinum album selling record producer, music publisher and record company owner with music production deals on Virgin Records, Atlantic Records., Pavilion/ CBS/Sony Records and numerous record licensing deals with major labels internationally.

I grew up as a child understanding that one has to be innovative and come up with a new way to survive, a new way to live, a new idea or thought process that can move you from one place to another, a new way of doing things. Whether it was getting credit as a child at the local grocery store, or becoming a paperboy selling newspapers, or shining shoes with my home-made shoe shine box, or fighting older and more violent boys to keep my two project buildings with customers that I could rely on to run errands for, to run their numbers, to get their groceries, drugs or alcohol, to get anything they needed, so that my sister and I could eat. Innovation was a survival tactic for me and in my new book, ***America The Black Point of View: An Investigation and Study of The White People of America and Western Europe and The Autobiography of an American Ghetto Boy - The 1950's and 1960's - From the Projects to NAACP Image Award Winner, Volume One*** (Amber Books) by Tony Rose, I talk about these situations and much, much, more in great depth. www.theblackpointofview.com

I slowly, as a child and then teenager, began to find and become exposed to some amazing people who would begin to change my life and save me. You see, I come from another America, the America nobody wants to talk about; it is not middle class and does not pay taxes; it is below the ground poor and embellished in violence and poverty. There are a few things that can save a child born into this condition, in this America; one of them is exposure to the outer world, the other America.

The children we want for our foundation are like I once was – children whose parents don't pay taxes, can't pay taxes and don't even think about paying taxes. These children will usually come from inter- generational poverty. They are poor and living on the fringes of society – usually on welfare, some type of government assistance or illegally gotten income. They come from the people that America doesn't want to think about. They are from the underbelly of America, usually abused and ready to be thrown away by mainstream America, until they surface as rapists, killers, crack or heroin addicts; and become a part of the two million African American men, women and children imprisoned in America's penal institutions.

Yes, I am from that other America; and yes, I too was once a Housing Project Child at Risk, and like most real ghetto people, a victim. But, I was one of the lucky ones. I had a grandmother who cared; I found nuns and priests who cared; I found a newspaper publisher who cared; I found a Boy Scout leader who cared; I found a politician who cared; I found and joined the military and they cared; I found a public relations man who cared. I had God's good fortune and found some amazing people in my life, who cared and exposed me to their lives. My intention is to utilize my life – my having survived those conditions. My intention is to utilize my NAACP Image Award as an instrument to better help those children as victims, who come from that bad environment – bad schools, bad parents – with no one who cares for them. I feel that by exposing them to people like you and giving them an opportunity, these children, between the ages of five and ten – and hopefully that isn't too late – that by exposing the children to people like you, who are doing relevant and positive work, inside and outside of your communities, that this may help change the lives of these children; and thus I am asking for your help to be a recruiter or a partner with The Housing Projects and Ghettos of America Children At Risk Foundation.

There are a lot of leaders out there, including: Reverend Al Sharpton, National Action Network; Reverend Jesse Jackson, Operation Push; Ben Jealous, former NAACP, President/CEO; Senator Corey Booker; and even Barack Obama, the President of the United States. There are many leaders who have attempted to help the poor and at risk children of this country through their words and example. The problem is that 99.9% of these leaders don't come from where these children come from…they haven't lived their lives, and aren't able to truly understand the dangers that are all around them.

These leaders haven't lived day after day, night after night, year after year as children with violence, poverty, degradation, drugs, child abuse, and the horrors of prostitution, drug dealing, drug addiction, alcohol addiction, depravity and no hope all around them.   Poverty in itself, is an evil. The reason we don't have leaders coming from such a horrific place is that the majority of the people who come from this bad environment – bad parents, bad schools – living with no hope, living in a no-hope condition are mentally, physically and emotionally unable to perform as leaders; or they're in jail, or they're on drugs, or they're on alcohol, or they're still living on the fringes of society in a bad condition in a bad way…in poverty. Maybe you or someone you know shares my story. Now is the time to remember how you dared to dream and found your future. It's a matter of who will win the battle for the hearts and minds of the Housing Project and Ghettos of America At Risk Children.

There are three ways you can participate:

1. Become a Recruiter – Pinpoint at risk children who live in the housing projects in a community near you. Allocate the best Community Organizations that serve these children and identify the best children for the program.

2. Become a Business Partner – If you are the owner of a business, an officer of a corporation, the director of a radio or television station, the editor of a newspaper or magazine, an attorney, a doctor, a restaurant owner, etc. we need you to participate as a business partner (role model).

3. Become a Corporate Partner – Donate Sponsorship Funding to be used for operating expenses, as well as: transportation to the venues, lunch, T-shirts, school supplies, etc. for The Housing Projects and Ghettos of America Children At Risk Foundation.

Here's how the Children Qualify:

These Children who need some kind of help in gaining exposure to the world beyond their housing projects and communities should be between five and ten years old.

All the Children must live in a housing project.

All the Children must have either one or both parents in jail or on drugs.

All the Children must live in households that have some type of pu lic assistance, such as welfare or food stamps.

To be considered for The Housing Projects and Ghettos of America Children At Risk Foundation, all children must have a public assistant coordinator or a court officer appointee and belong to at least one community organization.

The Housing Projects and Ghettos of America Children At Risk Foundation will operate on a specific day of the month and time (to be determined) when the children are invited to various places of employment. They will spend one hour at the location – a half-hour watching the employees work and a half-hour asking them questions.

Some of our book publisher friends can donate books in a bag, note pads, pencils and school supplies, as well as lunch.

Can I count you in to participate in The Housing Projects and Ghettos of America Children At Risk Foundation? I implore you to join my team – to become a foot soldier in the battle against poverty and neglect…and to free one child at a time from the perils of inter-generational poverty, of being and living poor in a bad environment, with bad parents and bad schools, living with violence and poverty forever, by having exposure to people like you.

Thank you.
All the very best,
Tony Rose, Founder/CEO
The Housing Projects and Ghettos of America Children At Risk Foundation

www.ingramcontent.com/pod-product-compliance
Lightning Source LLC
Chambersburg PA
CBHW062151270326
41930CB00009B/1497